How Organizations Act Together

How Organizations Act Together

Interorganizational Coordination in Theory and Practice

Ernest R. Alexander

University of Wisconsin–Milwaukee

Gordon and Breach Publishers

Australia Austria China France Germany India Japan
Luxembourg Malaysia Netherlands Russia Singapore
Switzerland Thailand United Kingdom United States

3 Boulevard Royal
L-2449 Luxembourg

British Library Cataloguing in Publication Data

Alexander, Ernest R.
    How Organizations Act Together:
    Interorganizational Coordination in
    Theory and Practice
    I. Title
    302.4

    ISBN 2-88449-173-2 (hardcover)
            2-88449-174-0 (softcover)

CONTENTS

List of Figures and Tables viii

Preface... ix

I   Knowledge: Definitions, Theories and Research

Chapter 1   What and Why: Definitions and Premises........... 3
  1.1   What Is Coordination?.............................. 3
  1.2   Premises: Why Does IOC Occur?..................... 7
  1.3   Preconditions: Enabling or Limiting IOC............... 15
  Summary 21
  Notes.. 22

Chapter 2   Where and How: Contexts, Relationships and Tools... 25
  2.1   Networks and Fields 26
  2.2   Interdependence 31
  2.3   Coordination Strategies 36
  2.4   Tools.. 40
  Summary 43
  Notes.. 45

Chapter 3   The Mechanics of Coordination: IOC Structures 47
  3.1   The Concept of IOC Structures 47
  3.2   Coordination Structures: From Solidarity
        to Hierarchy.. 52
  3.3   A Structuration Theory of IOC....................... 66
  Notes.. 75

**II   Practice: Interorganizational Coordination
   Structures — Design, Operation and Performance**

Chapter 4   Coordination Without Hierarchy: Informal
            Coordination Links and Networks 81
  4.1   Associative Links: Kinship and Community............. 86
  4.2   Solidarity Links.................................... 87
  4.3   Informal Links and Networks 91
  Notes.. 111

Chapter 5   Formal Coordination: Micro-Structures in Action   117

   5.1   The Liaison and Boundary-Spanner   118

   5.2   The Interorganizational Group.   121

   5.3   The Coordinator   142

   Notes.   151

Chapter 6   Coordinating Organizations: Organizations
            as IOC Structures   153

   6.1   The Coordinating Unit.   153

   6.2   The Lead Organization   177

   6.3   The Single Organization   183

   Notes.   195

Chapter 7   Mutual Organizations: IOC in Interorganizational
            Networks   199

   7.1   Types of Interorganizational Networks   199

   7.2   Cooperative Networks: Consortium to Cartel.   201

   7.3   Networks for Processing and Production   214

   Notes.   225

Chapter 8   From Markets to Hierarchies: Meso-Structures
            for IOC   227

   8.1   New and Artificial Markets   227

   8.2   Mandated Frameworks   235

   8.3   IOC Systems.   253

   Notes.   264

III Synthesis: Theory and Practice

Chapter 9   Integrating What We Know   269

   9.1   What Is IOC and How Does It Happen?   269

   9.2   Thinking About IOC.   274

   9.3   Effective Coordination: IOC Structures
         and Their Fit   280

   Notes.   294

Chapter 10 The Architecture of Institutional Design:
            IOC Structures, Contexts and Fit.   297

   10.1 IOC Meta-Structures.   297

   10.2 The Interorganizational Network
         and Its Environment.   304

   10.3 Interorganizational Network Factors   309

   10.4 The IOC Task   318

   Notes.   328

CONTENTS

Appendix: Interorganizational Networks or Sets 329
References 335
Index 353

FIGURES and TABLES

Figures

1. Interorganizational Coordination Structures   55
2. Interorganizational Informal Links in the Bay
   Area Public Transit System 1978–80   100
3. Organizational Structure of the Lafayette Court
   Family Development Center.   193
4. The Farnham County CMI Community
   Support Network   216
5. The Japanese *Keiretsu*   222
6. Conceptual Framework for IOC.   276

Tables

1. Facilitators (and Inhibitors) of Interorganizational
   Coordination (IOC)   15
2. A Typology of Interorganizational Networks   202

PREFACE

It was late afternoon at Waterloo. The battle had been raging since the morning. The Duke of Wellington, whose Anglo-Dutch army was challenging Napoleon's advance on Brussels, was growing despondent. After throwing back repeated French attacks, but losing its defended bastion in the hamlet of La Haye Sainte, the British center was threatening to crumble under a renewed onslaught by Marshall Ney's cavalry. Sitting on his chestnut horse Copenhagen, under the elm at the Mont St. Jean crossroads which was his command post, Wellington kept looking at his watch. Someone heard him mutter: "Night or the Prussians must come" (Longford, 1969: 473).

The next two hours were the crisis. Still standing fast in their squares, the British troops mowed down Napoleon's Household Guards cavalry as they charged their positions and tried to overrun them. The Highlanders even advanced in a counterattack on the dazed Guards' flank; the French army for the moment was blocked. But Wellington's forces were exhausted; after the day's casualties his army was down to only about thirty-five thousand men. Just then, surveying the battlefield through their telescopes in the last glimmering of daylight, Wellington and his staff saw the extreme right of Napoleon's army begin to break up and flee, as it came under crossfire from Von Bulow's Prussian Corps.

> An aide-de-camp from the Duke himself came spurring down from the Highlanders' rear: 'The day is our own! The Prussians have arrived!' This was the decisive moment. 'Oh damn it!' (the Duke) exclaimed. 'In for a penny, in for a pound' and taking his hat off, he waved it three times toward the French. In a flash his signal was understood, as the foremost regiments swooped on to the plain. (Longford, 1969: 479)

Arguments continue about who won the Battle of Waterloo.[1] But the fact is that the victory was the result of successful joint action by the Anglo-Dutch army, under Wellington, and Marshall Blucher's Prussian army. As allies in the war against Napoleon, the two commanders concerted their strategy, and resolved to confront Napoleon together, while Napoleon's movements aimed to prevent the junction of their forces. Blucher's help almost arrived too late, but, as Wellington himself said in his dispatch after the battle:

I should not do justice ... to Marshall Blucher and the Prussian Army if
I did not attribute the successful result of this arduous day to the cordial
and timely assistance I received from them. (Longford, 1969: 487)

In the event, the British army's steadfastness in the face of Napoleon's
attack, combined with the Prussian advance on the French right,
routed the French forces,[2] ensuring Napoleon's ultimate defeat and
surrender.

*   *   *

As astronaut Neil Armstrong stepped onto the surface of the moon he
said, for the benefit of millions of watchers and listeners back on Earth:
"That's one small step for (a) man, one giant leap for mankind."[3] Armstrong's step was the completion of a mission that had lasted almost
ten years: the Apollo program which had been launched on May 25,
1961, when President Kennedy told a joint session of Congress:

I believe that this nation should commit itself to achieving the goal,
before this decade is out, of landing a man on the moon and returning
him safely to the earth. (Brooks, Grimwood and Swenson, 1979: 29)

The Apollo program was run by the National Aeronautics and
Space Administration (NASA), an agency created only ten years
before in reaction to Soviet Russia's launch of *Sputnik*, the first satellite in space. NASA itself originally consisted of four almost autonomous centers. Later the Apollo program involved concerting operations among NASA's relatively independent Manned Spacecraft
Center at Houston, Texas (Flight Operations Division), Marshall
Space Flight Center at Huntsville, Alabama (rocket propulsion systems), Kennedy Space Center at Cape Canaveral, Florida (launch
operations), and NASA headquarters at Langley, Virginia.

Landing a man on the moon was such a vast undertaking that
many doubted whether it could be done in the decade Kennedy had
set. The concepts and necessary theoretical physics were already
available, and NASA was a functioning and growing agency with
some experience.[4] But to meet this goal NASA had to initiate major
technological innovations, design and procure engineering systems
of unprecedented sophistication and complexity, and develop an
enormous and often novel organizational infrastructure.[5] Besides
concerting the operations of NASA's four Centers, the Apollo program involved supervising the work of five prime contractors and
thousands of subcontractors.[6]

In fact, the Apollo program was a coordination nightmare that
only surfaced when things went seriously wrong. For example, the

probable cause of the spacecraft fire that killed astronauts Chaffee, Grissom, and White was a spark from a cable in the Environmental Control Unit. The cable's location was not consistent with the original plans, after several repositionings in the course of thousands of design changes, and it had become exposed as a result of abrasion by the metal edge of the door to the lithium oxide storage compartment. A microscopic leak in a length of aluminium tubing that carried glycol cooling fluid fueled the spark, which the oxygen-atmosphere in the spacecraft turned into a fatal inferno (Murray and Cox, 1989: 190–191).

Another coordination failure caused the oxygen tank explosions that aborted the Apollo 13 mission. Astronauts Lovell, Swigert, and Hage only survived safely thanks to the improvised use of the Lunar Landing Module as a "lifeboat" for their return voyage to Earth. The explosions were due to a monitoring breakdown and a communications gap. The tanks were damaged during a loading test, when a tank temperature gauge, built only to register temperatures up to the safety limit of 85°F, did not show dangerous internal temperatures because of a defective safety switch. The safety switch's failure was the result of a communications lapse eight years earlier, when a subcontractor neglected to inform the supplier of the safety switches that the power specifications had been changed from 28 to 65 volts. As a result, during the test, when the temperature in the tanks rose to the level that was supposed to trigger the switch, the switch was instantly fused shut by the 65-volt current that exceeded its design limits.

The successful moon landing was the culmination of the Apollo program: a complex coordinated effort involving NASA and thousands of other organizations. Unquestionably, the insights of theoretical science; the innovations of advanced technology; and the contributions of individual leadership, courage, ingenuity, and perseverance were instrumental in this achievement. But the effective completion of the Apollo program would not have been possible without successfully organizing the operations of NASA itself, its diverse and often contentious Centers, and its far-flung network of consultants, contractors, and subcontractors.

*   *   *

The "OPEC revolution" possibly represents the most massive transfer of resources in human history. If this "revolution is to be pinpointed to a single date, the day is February 14, 1971" (Rustow and Mugno, 1976: 28). This was the day on which the international oil industry capitulated to OPEC — the Organization of Petroleum Producing Countries — and signed the Teheran agreement. The oil majors did not surrender easily, but only after OPEC's threat of unilateral action, and tough talk in an earlier meeting in Paris from Iran's Finance Minister Jamshid Amouzegar.[7]

The Teheran agreement, in which OPEC raised world oil prices by 24 percent, and its members' revenues by nearly 40 percent, is not significant so much for these steep increases; some later ones were far greater. Rather, it marked the culmination of a long process in which the oil-producing states took control of their own resources. In Teheran and afterwards, OPEC succeeded in imposing its will both on the major oil extracting corporations and on the petroleum consumers of the world.

"Since 1973, OPEC has probably influenced the material well-being of more people worldwide than any other international organization" (Danielson, 1982: iii). How did OPEC come to exert such power? Essentially, OPEC is a successful cartel. Its charter, drawn up at the first meeting of its founding members[8] in Baghdad in September 1960, defines OPEC's purpose as: "the coordination and unification of the petroleum policies of Member Countries".[9]

Whether we welcome its effects or deplore them, OPEC has largely accomplished its goal: to raise world oil prices as high as possible, consistent with the interests of its member states, desirable stability, and the (relatively loose) constraints of the world oil market. Though its achievements and survival as a cartel are also attributable to favorable circumstances,[10] OPEC is an outstanding example of effective coordination.

*   *   *

What do the Allies' victory over Napoleon at Waterloo, the Apollo program's moon landing, and the "OPEC revolution" have in common? They were all achieved by organizations acting together. No single organization could have carried out all the tasks involved in bringing these undertakings to their successful conclusion. Interorganizational coordination (IOC) was a critical element in each of these cases: if coordination had failed, the outcomes would have been very different.

In the campaign that finally defeated Napoleon, Britain and Prussia formed an alliance to concert their strategies, and coordinated the deployment of their armies through an old military device: the liaison officer.[11] NASA was the lead organization managing the Apollo program and coordinating the host of subcontractors. The oil-exporting countries formed OPEC as a cartel to set oil prices and increase their revenues. The alliance, the liaison, the lead organization, and the cartel are some of the ways in which organizations have concerted their decisions and actions.

Coordination and Implementation

Coordination is one of the golden words of our time. Offhand, I can think of no way the word is used that implies disapproval. But what does it mean? (Wildavsky, 1979: 131)

Typically, Wildavsky answered his own question. In a detailed analysis of federal development and employment programs in Oakland, California, he shows how often we aspire to coordination and how difficult it is to achieve. The subtitle of the book on this subject is "How It Is a Wonder that Federal Programs Are Ever Accomplished at All" (Pressman and Wildavsky, 1973).

This view of how programs and projects are implemented, based on the Oakland study, has gained wide acceptance. The rhetorical question about the success of complex program implementation has come to be called the "Pressman–Wildavsky Paradox." It expresses the sense that successful coordination is exceptional, and that the failure of complex undertakings is to be expected (Bowen, 1982: 1–2).

But surely this surprise at the accomplishment of complex tasks involving several agencies or many organizations is exaggerated. No one is surprised to receive an airmail letter from abroad, even though this is the result of an elaborate set of interactions between the postal services of several countries, air carriers, and several other agencies. On the contrary, I may only be annoyed at the occasional failure of this service, when a letter I am expecting is delayed or one that I sent is misdirected and lost.

Nor am I surprised at the completion of my international telephone call, the result of an equally complex task. Rather, I will be irate if my call to Bangkok ends up in Bucaramanga instead. I am not astonished at the marvel that is any urban transportation system, again the result of the concerted action of a vast multitude of organizations, from governments and engineers planning and executing the infrastructure — the roads, tracks, and freeways — to the agencies maintaining and operating the systems: local traffic departments, transit operators, and so on. Instead, I will fume if my car is held up in two miles of solid steel on the Santa Monica Freeway, and sense that something has gone wrong.

Perhaps, someone might say, what all these examples have in common are highly developed technologies; what about "low tech" manpower intensive programs? Why, then, is the welfare mother more likely to be indignant at the delay of her AFDC check than to be surprised at its timely arrival? Even though the AFDC program is just the kind of complex federal undertaking that the experts have called impossible — involving coordination between federal, state, and local governments and a multitude of agencies — the regular delivery of its service is regarded as routine.

How can we account for this contradiction between the evidence of our daily experience in the post-industrial societies in which we live, and the cases suggesting that the implementation of complex programs is difficult to the point of being impossible? There are two answers to this question.

One answer comes from looking at the relatively abstract level of general models of the implementation process and finding what it is that distinguishes the successful experiences from the failures. The "Pressman–Wildavsky Paradox" is based on a model that sees the process of carrying out policies as a sequential chain linking a set of independent actors. Even if the probability of the participating institutions agreeing and concerting their actions at each linking node is quite high, by simple multiplication we find that the chance of the policy's final implementation is low.

Several suggestions have been presented for modifying such complex tasks to enhance the chances of successful outcomes. These include simplifying programs, reducing the length of the "chain" of interdependent actions, and trying to "package" otherwise only loosely related approvals (Bowen, 1982).

But a more radical response is that the instances of failure that provide the concrete evidence for the "Pressman–Wildavsky Paradox" are actually a special case. They usually involve a kind of linkage between decision points where the participants are totally independent of one another. This is not necessarily so: organizations involved in a joint task are often bonded by common values, mutual interests, reciprocal obligations over time, or coordination structures that have been mandated or agreed upon.

And the kinds of programs that provide the evidence for the "Pressman–Wildavsky Paradox" occur in situations that are also by no means universal, for example: the launching of a new, controversial program or service in a conflict- and turbulence-ridden environment. Many other undertakings, no less complex, can succeed because their implementation models are not structured in the same way, and because they are carried out in more stable or more supportive circumstances (Alexander, 1991).

There is another response to the question of why our intuition contradicts the pessimistic conclusions of implementation analyses. It is to recognize what all the projects and programs that are the subjects of this enquiry have in common. They involve complex and ambitious tasks in highly developed and interconnected societies. Due to their complexity and scope, they must engage more than one organization. Indeed, they usually demand the concerted effort of many agencies and organizations. Such undertakings, then, mean organizations acting together to accomplish mutually agreed-upon goals.

Concerted action among organizations does not happen by chance.[12] It is the result of interorganizational coordination (IOC). One of the ways to explore the differences between complex enterprises that succeed and ones that fail, then, is to better understand how IOC takes place in each of these cases.

Interorganizational Coordination: When, Where, and Why?

Interorganizational coordination is important because it is almost ubiquitous in modern society. True, there are many tasks and areas of effort which only involve a single societal unit or organization acting alone or interacting independently with its relevant environment. These are undoubtedly important.

A single household's lifestyle, its consumption and location decisions, for example, can be understood quite well in isolation. Combined with multitudes of other such decisions, it may have profound effects on whole societies. These include regional population shifts (like the growth of the Sunbelt in the United States), demographic changes (such as the drop in the rate of population increase in Western countries), and economic cycles. The simple firm's production, pricing, and marketing decisions can also wreak changes affecting society at large: economic prosperity or depression, for instance, are mainly the systemic result of the decisions of single organizations.

But large and critical areas of activity demand the involvement of many organizations acting together. This is especially true in modern society, when complexity and the lengthening of chains of interdependent actions make coordination among organizations necessary (Kaufmann, 1986: 217–218). IOC has become increasingly widespread as the scale of undertakings has grown, limiting the potential of independent action by any single organization (Lustick, 1980).

"Interdependent delivery systems" develop when complex problems or policies become "too big for one organization to handle"
(Hage, 1975: 211; Van de Ven, Emmett and Koenig, 1975: 26–27). Such
problems are pervasive in the public and private sectors alike. In the
public sector, one symptom is the growth of "third party government" in the United States and in other Western countries (Palumbo,
1987: 97–99), in which the government agency mandated to carry out
a task delegates its responsibility to a network of other agencies that
may include other (lower) levels of government and private organizations.

Government agencies' capability to act on their own has been
reduced by the "interconnectedness" of today's policy environment.
Interconnectedness means the interdependence of actors and outcomes, so that the actions of one agency both constrain and impact
the actions of others. As a result, most policy development and
implementation demands multilateral cooperation, blurs or elimi-
nates traditional boundaries and jurisdictions, and needs the deployment of many actors (Luke, 1991: 26, 32–35).

In the public arena, it is almost impossible to think of a sector that
is not characterized by interconnectedness and complexity. Public
policy issues that demand attention, such as poverty or industrial
policy, and functional areas such as transportation, housing, or environmental protection, cannot be addressed without deploying multiple agencies and a host of other organizations and institutions.

Today, the development and implementation of public policies
usually involves a "policy issue network" (Kirst, Meister and
Rowley, 1984). At various stages of the process this network may
change, but it may include legislators, interest group organizations,
various executive agencies, implementing organizations (governmental units, other public agencies, and private firms or corporations), and affected parties.

Take an issue which seems relatively simple on its face: installing
safety belts in school buses to avoid accident injuries to children.
Developing legislation including appropriate standards involved
legislative committees, and consulting with lobbyists and organizations representing bus manufacturers and operators, bus drivers,
school teachers, and child-welfare organizations. Implementation issues included not only the cost of alternative types of installations,
but also the feasibility and effort of enforcing the seat belts' use. An
effective seat belt system demanded a high order of coordination
between bus manufacturers or retro-fitters, and the bus operators,

teachers and drivers charged with instructing the children in the seat belts' use and ensuring their utilization.[13]

Programs for special populations or client groups: children, the elderly, the handicapped, ethnic minorities, neighborhood communities and others, all involve complex delivery systems which are far beyond the capability of any single organization to develop or implement on its own. Area-based programs or projects, ranging from relatively simple facility and infrastructure construction, to comprehensive projects such as neighborhood revitalization, enterprise zones, or regional development, demand the concerted efforts of many agencies and organizations.

In the private sector the picture is no different. Complex manufacturing and production are rarely undertaken by a single organization, and even when they are, the corporation has to develop appropriate organizational structures and coordination mechanisms for the task (Galbraith and Kazanjian, 1986). Often, however, a large project may be a joint enterprise involving several complementary partners, or, as in automobile manufacturing and aerospace, it may be spread over a host of subcontractors. Designing and producing a Boeing 747 airplane, for example, is not limited to the Boeing Corporation alone, but involves thousands of other firms. Organizing and monitoring these is a massive task all on its own.

Construction is also a complex job involving many actors. Besides the client (who may or may not be the ultimate user), participants include the architects, engineers, heating and environmental control systems designers and suppliers, the main construction contractor and specialist subcontractors for work such as electricity, plumbing, air conditioning, flooring, windows, roofs, external landscaping and roads. In many ways their relationship does not seem problematic, since for standard projects it has become quite routinized. But for large projects it is still sufficiently complex to demand the services of construction managers who have acquired the expertise to coordinate all these participants so as to ensure timely and on-budget completion.

Many other aspects of private enterprise commonly involve multiple organizations or organizational units, and require a high order of coordination. Research and development, finance, marketing, and public relations demand the concerted deployment of a large variety of different kinds of firms and specialized consultants. The largest corporations have often internalized some of the relevant tasks in their own special organizational units, but even they have to coordinate their projects with some outside organizations.

In its product research and development, Abbot (pharmaceutical) Laboratories has to interact with academic research laboratories, the U.S. Bureau of Patents and patent law consultants, not to mention exhaustive coordination with regulatory agencies. When KLM needs capital to finance the purchase of new airplanes, whether through issuing shares or by borrowing, it has to go through a complex process managed by its Finance Department, involving the coordinated action of corporate counsel and other legal consultants, banks, and share or bond underwriters. Remington's marketing campaign for its electric razor involves consumer research specialists, advertizing agencies, interaction with media markets and agents, producers for the relevant media, packaging designers and producers, product designers and the firm's own engineering and manufacturing units. None of them can "go it alone."

Another growing area of complexity is the interface between the public and private sectors. If the boundary between them was ever clear, today it has been virtually obliterated. National defense, for example, is considered the public good *par excellence*. But arms procurement and production is no longer simply a matter of the government manufacturing its cannon and ammunition in its national armories (as Britain, France, and the United States used to do).

Rather, defense procurement has become the concern of an elaborate interacting network of organizations embracing the public and private sectors alike. Even when the development and production of weapons systems is ostensibly competitively purchased by contract (as is the case in the United States), in fact the "military-industrial complex" has become a public-private partnership with a stable set of mutual expectations and obligations among its members. These range from the Pentagon and the military services, Congressional committees, and major defense contractors, to the dependent businesses and local governments of areas with major defense installations or corporate plants. As a result, the development and implementation of effective defense procurement policy faces coordination problems that are almost insoluble.

The burgeoning arena of public-private partnerships adds an extra dimension of complexity to a world which is already complicated enough. We can see this happening in a wide variety of fields. One area where public-private interaction has always been strong is infrastructure development and construction. Here, procurement and funding come from the public sector: a government agency, a special service district or public utility. The programming, specification, and engineering design may be carried out under a variety of arrangements, involving public agencies interacting with private consult-ants. Finally, construction is contracted to private firms, but again the concentration of expertise may lead to a blending of public and private supervision.

Municipal services are another area where the public-private spheres increasingly blend. Complex relationships between the pub-lic "consumer" and the private supplier ensue with privatization of services such as waste collection and disposal, public safety, and transit (Savas, 1982; Donahue, 1989; Kamerman and Kahn, 1989). In education various novel kinds of public-private interactions have appeared. These range from the joint academic-corporate research enterprise to corporate sponsorship of high school enrichments.

In development, too, private investments have been combined with government funding and commitments in public-private part-nerships for projects ranging from downtown shopping malls to suburban industrial parks (Frieden and Sagalynn, 1989). All these organizational innovations may well provide an important gain in effectiveness, or offer the opportunity to undertake projects which would otherwise be infeasible. But they also make service delivery and project implementation more complex, so that without due at-tention to coordinating the efforts of all the involved units, there is a higher risk of failure.

It is clear, then, that broad and important areas of activity in today's world are beyond the scope of any single agency or organiza-tion. These activities — policies, programs, projects — are under-taken by groups of organizations. The relevant group of organiza-tions may be defined around a focal organization: its "organization set" (Evan, 1966). In this way we can think of the development of a new line of computer hardware and software involving an "organi-zation set" with IBM as its focal organization, and including micro-processor developers and manufacturers, software partners such as Microsoft, subcontractor hardware manufacturers, major potential users, and so on.

Other ways of thinking about networks of organizations are the "action set" or "implementation set," where the relevant organiza-tions are identified based on their common undertaking or the imple-mentation of a particular project or program (Aldrich and Whetten, 1981; Hjern and Porter, 1981). So the actors and agencies involved in the Cuban missile crisis can be described as an action set, or the organizations carrying out the European community's 1992 unifica-tion program are an implementation set.

Finally, we can envisage an interorganizational field: a system of organizations where our focus is on the types of relationships between the organizations and the field is defined by their interdependence (Lehman, 1975). In this fashion, we can talk about the national interorganizational field in which trade associations are formed, for example, the U.S. tobacco industry, or a local interorganizational field such as health services in San Francisco in which hospital consortiums emerge.

In interorganizational networks, action sets, or interorganizational fields — just as in the single organization — many factors can be responsible for the success or failure of complex undertakings. Such factors can range from the micro- to the macro-scale. Sometimes the success of an enterprise can be clearly attributed to one individual's personal qualities: his initiative, her leadership or charisma, his willingness to take risks, her prudent appraisal of constraints and opportunities. A good deal of research and attention has been devoted to this aspect of organizational performance.[14]

Other cases present examples of factors at work at the macro-scale. Failure due to changes in an organization's ecological niche; for example, a corporation's delay in adopting technological innovations in its industry. Or success in taking advantage of cyclical opportunities, like Levitt's exploitation of the post World War II returning veterans' market for his suburban housing developments.

Contextual factors, such as social or economic conditions, can also be critical: how many firms, whole sectors, and industries were affected by the Great Depression? How many public policy initiatives were successfully implemented, and how many new agencies were launched, and survived, due to the same crisis in the United States and the resulting "New Deal"?

But complex projects or programs undertaken by organization sets or action sets of organizations include a factor that is unique: interorganizational coordination (IOC). Undoubtedly, effective or ineffective IOC can be, and often is, a contributing factor in their success or failure. It is enough to review some of the many evaluations of such programs that include analyses of their coordination, to be convinced of that fact.[15]

The importance of coordination for the success or failure of the complex single organization is recognized, as shown by an extensive literature (Mintzberg, 1979). Sometimes IOC is dismissed, however, as little more than an expression of wishful thinking, or an exercise of political power to achieve preferred values (Wildavsky, 1979). Based on pessimism about achieving effective coordination, and apparently justified by the lack of well-founded knowledge about IOC, this dismissal is unwarranted.

How This Book Is Organized

We have seen how important IOC is in the increasingly interdependent and complex world of today. It is clear, also, that effective IOC can be critical for the successful outcomes of large undertakings involving the participation of many organizations. Finally, a considerable body of knowledge about IOC has accumulated. Some of this is the result of over twenty years' study and research into the behavior of organizations and their interactions. Some is the fruit of experience, and of observing the successes and failures of IOC efforts in practice.

The chapters that follow review this body of knowledge. The first three present the results of study and research, in the form of theories about IOC, and the concepts that have been developed for analyzing interorganizational relations in general and IOC in particular. Chapters 4 through 8 use one of these analytical concepts, IOC structures, to array some of the experience of IOC in practice that has become available. The book closes with two chapters synthesizing theory and practice. Chapter 9 integrates the diverse IOC concepts which have emerged over time. Chapter 10 offers some directions for institutional design, based on the "fit" between IOC structures and their settings.

In this book I address several pertinent questions about IOC. When and why is IOC necessary? The answer involves exploring definitions and objectives of IOC, and considering what the alternatives to IOC might be under various circumstances. What forms does IOC take? Some of the concepts reviewed later answer this question, and the IOC structures that are presented provide a framework for describing and analyzing the formal "mechanics" of IOC.

How can IOC be more successful? Much of IOC theory and many of its concepts are descriptive: they enable us to analyze and explain the behavior of organizations and their interactions. But they provide few answers to this question. Here, however, theory and concepts are augmented by a pragmatic orientation which asks: what does this mean to someone attempting to effect IOC in the real world?

What can current knowledge about IOC tell the manager looking for the best way to coordinate her far-flung network of subsidiaries? What can it tell the policy analyst evaluating alternative program designs for a state energy-subsidy to the poor? What can it tell the director of a regional agency about the most effective way to interact with all the other stakeholders in his development project? The results of research and study, therefore, are complemented with an evaluation of IOC experience. Together, they offer some lessons for the design of IOC structures and future IOC practice.

NOTES

1. Some even suggest that no one won the battle, but that Napoleon lost it by a combination of omissions and errors of judgement.
2. Wellington's Anglo-Dutch troops were too mauled by the French attacks to have any energy left to pursue Napoleon's fleeing army. That had to be done by the Prussians under their commander-in-chief Gneisenau, whose army prevented Napoleon's regrouping and entered Paris (Longford, 1969: 481–482).
3. Armstrong claims that he said "a man," but as recorded and transmitted the "a" was omitted (Murray and Cox, 1989: 356).
4. When the Apollo program was launched, NASA had already put astronauts into Earth orbit in Project Mercury.
5. Just one example is the development of Mission Control (MOCR: Mission Operations Control Room) from the modest monitoring facility that served the Gemini program. MOCR in Houston incorporated thirteen specialized monitoring, guidance, control, and communications functions (Murray and Cox, 1989: 270–307).
6. See pp. 180–183 for a detailed presentation of the Apollo program.
7. See pp. 207–213 below for a more detailed analysis of OPEC.
8. Iran, Iraq, Kuwait, Saudi Arabia, and Venezuela.
9. Declaratory Statement of Petroleum Policy in Member Countries, Resolution XVI.90 adopted at 16th OPEC Conference, June 24–25, 1968 (Rustow and Mugno, 1976: 167).
10. It is to changes in some of these circumstances, together with divergence in political interests between groups of OPEC members, that the relative oil glut of the 1980s and the drop in oil prices are attributable.
11. Unlike later, more complex campaigns that demanded a joint command structure, for example, the Allies' European advance in World War II, in which General Eisenhower was the supreme commander over U.S., British, French, and other troops.
12. In some cases of IOC it can look as if the outcomes occurred by chance: this has been called: "partisan mutual adjustment"; it will be addressed later.

13. This issue came up in Wisconsin after a serious school-bus accident, but the complexities could not be overcome, and the proposed legislation never passed.

14. See, for example, the literature on leadership, reviewed by Yukl (1989).

15. Some of these are presented in chapters 4 through 8.

I.
KNOWLEDGE

Definitions, Theories and Research

CHAPTER 1

What and Why?

Definitions and Premises

═══

1.1. What is Coordination?

If we do not know what coordination is (as Wildavsky suggested), it is not because there are no definitions. On the contrary, if there is a reason for ignorance, it is because there are too many different definitions, and too little agreement. Rogers and Whetten and their associates reviewed much of the research on IOC in 1982.[1] In this review, IOC is defined as

> the process whereby two or more organizations create and/or use existing decision rules that have been established to deal collectively with their task environment. (Mulford and Rogers, 1982: 12)

The problem with this definition is that it leaves several issues unresolved. Does IOC happen between organizations, to produce outcomes that are different from what they might have been if no IOC had occurred? Or is IOC a structure of relationships between organizations? Or perhaps, like light in physics, which can be at the same time a particle or a wave, IOC can be a process and a structure, depending on the point of view and the situation.

Is coordination a property of decisions, relations, or actions? And do we call decisions or actions "coordinated" if they simply reflect one actor's taking into account the decisions and behavior of another? Or should we limit the use of this term, perhaps arbitrarily, to decisions,

3

relationships, or outcomes that involve some degree of deliberate control?

How one answers these questions often depends on one's underlying ideas about coordination. Mulford and Roger's definition, for example, includes a reference to "existing decision rules". This lets them extend their review of IOC to cover mutual adjustment strategies, i.e., IOC that comes about just by taking other organization's actions into account. Other approaches to IOC do not see mutual adjustment as a form of coordination.

Probably the first person to take an analytic view of coordination was Charles Lindblom. His definition of coordination saw IOC as no more than a systematic relationship between *decisions*. Coordinated decisions, according to this view, are ones where either mutual adjustment between actors or a more deliberate interaction produced positive outcomes to the participants and avoided negative consequences (Lindblom, 1965: 23, 154).

What distinguishes this approach to coordination is its inclusiveness. Any decision that takes the organization's environment into account can, by this definition, be called coordinated, because the organization acting upon the decision is adjusting its behavior to the other organizations and actors around it. This inclusiveness has its advantages and its drawbacks.

The advantage of this definition is in recognizing mutual adjustment as a coordination strategy.[2] More limited definitions of IOC which focus on the controlling aspects of coordination make it easy to forget the potential of mutual adjustment. Yet there are coordination mechanisms which rely entirely on mutual adjustment between rational and self-interested actors which are of major importance. These are markets.

A market, in the sense of a systemic relationship of resource exchange between independent participants, can take a variety of forms. We are most accustomed to thinking about economic markets, where individual firms, organizations and households exchange material resources as producers and consumers of goods and services. Here mutual adjustment takes place on the basis of information on supply, demand, prices and other relevant factors in the economic environment, and the medium of exchange is money.

However, in much the same way we can think of coordination through mutual adjustment and exchange in a political market. Here transactions take place in legislatures, committees, regulatory and executive agencies, and informally between organizations (Buchanan and Tullock, 1967: 17–39; Wildavsky, 1979: 121–124; Lindblom, 1988:

239–244). The resources exchanged, while including goods, services and funds, may include votes, information, authority, political support, or power (Ilchman and Uphoff, 1969).

A program providing some specific service to an identified beneficiary group, such as a child-care supplement for working mothers, or a loan guarantee program for selected exporters, is often the product of such a political market. It may be less the result of a rationally coordinated process of interaction between the relevant actors and interests than we would like to believe, and more the result of self-interested bargaining and mutual adjustment in a political market. Market-like relationships also provide the arenas for coordinated interaction between individuals and organizations in a variety of settings.

Common resource pool associations are a case in point. Examples range from cooperative fishing villages in Japan to farmers' water resource associations in California (Ostrom, 1991). Other examples are quasi-markets in regulated sectors, such as "Transferable Development Rights" (Roddewig and Ingraham, 1987) which provide for exchange of the right to develop urban land, and "Tradeable Emission Rights" which enable industries that are sources of air pollution to trade pollution permissions among themselves (Yandle, 1989: 77–83).

What all these have in common is a framework of rules and mutual obligations which creates a market-like interaction between the participants to ensure mutually beneficial coordinated actions. We will return to such markets and market-like frameworks when discussing the design of coordination structures later.

The drawback of a definition of coordination which includes all mutual adjustment is that it dilutes the concept to the point of making it almost meaningless. What decision that is not completely trivial is not coordinated in this sense? How can we distinguish between decisions that are coordinated, and ones that are not? Is it (per Lindblom's definition) by looking at the outcomes: those producing actions that prove to be beneficial and which avoided undesired consequences are judged to be coordinated, and those with negative outcomes are not?

But this is simply to equate coordination with success, and the lack of it with failure.[3] Some approaches to coordination in fact do this. One is when coordination is identified as a goal for an organization's or an interorganizational system's performance (Alter and Hage, 1993: 82–86).[4] This is not uncommon; for example, lack of coordination is identified as the major problem that the U.S. social welfare system has to address (Jennings and Zank, 1993: 3–5).

Viewing coordination as: "the linking together of resources and processes to achieve desired outcomes" (Jennings, 1994: 53) has the same flaw. The only defining characteristic here is the desirability of coordinated action. From this perspective, coordination is also associated with cooperation and an absence of conflict (Alter and Hage, 1993: 86–87). Sometimes, too, coordination is identified with collaborative behavior. But, though coordination and collaboration are related, they are quite distinct. Collaboration is an interactive process, which, if successful, may produce coordinated action as a result (Gray, 1989: 14–16).[5]

These definitions, then, provide little for us to identify coordination by some intrinsic characteristics, as distinct from the success or failure of its results. If we are looking for a definition of coordination which will be helpful in understanding what it is, this is a major defect.

After Lindblom's association of coordination with decisions, others defined IOC as a relationship between *organizations*. Hall and his associates saw coordination as "the extent to which organizations attempt to ensure that their activities take into account those of other organizations" (Hall et al., 1977: 459).[6] Finally, coordination can be related to *actions*: "Coordination happens insofar as different actions of various actors become linked to constitute chains of actions" (Kaufmann, Majone and Ostrom, 1986: 790). This definition highlights another important aspect of IOC: interdependence.

Views of IOC focused on mutual adjustment or premised on voluntary exchange of resources contrast with approaches stressing the aspect of control (Hage, 1974). In these:

> coordination is a means of directing the operation of units so that their joint behavior attains a specific goal with higher probability and at lower costs (and with) a common expectation of reward. (Kochen and Deutsch, 1980: 126)

Coordination becomes a deliberate intervention which makes participants recognize their interdependence, and which puts in place arrangements to concert their decisions (Tuite, 1972: 12–13). Here is a much more active approach than seeing coordination as little more than mutual adjustment and voluntary resource exchange: "Coordination means getting what you do not have" through influencing or compelling participants to act in the way desired (Dunsire, 1978: 16–17).

These definitions show how wide the range of attitudes to IOC can be. At one extreme, coordination is implied in any decision involving an organization's voluntary strategic adjustment to its environment.

In the middle of the range, IOC means a recog
ence and ways of coping with it. At the of
institutionalized arrangements, power, and (
count for these differences, and can we reso

To explain these diverging perspectives on IO
the thinking behind them. What are the theories descri
tional behavior and explaining interactions between organiza
which these people brought to their definitions of IOC? How does
each of these theories account for IOC? A review of the premises
underlying the various definitions of IOC may be enlightening.

1.2. Premises: Why Does IOC Occur?

The study of organizations and organizational behavior has generated
a substantial body of theory. Some of the major theories of organization also explain why coordination occurs between organizations. In
this way, different organization theories are the premises behind
different definitions of IOC, accounting, in part, for the various definitions of IOC which we have observed.

There are three major schools of organization theory which are
relevant for our exploration of IOC. The oldest is exchange theory.
More recently, organizational ecology and contingency theory have
developed to account for certain aspects of organizational behavior.
Transaction cost theory is a relative newcomer in the area of organization theory, though in economics transaction cost theory has quite
a long tradition.[7]

Exchange Theory

Exchange theory sees resource exchange as the main factor that explains organizational relations and behavior (Benson, 1975). The assumption behind exchange theory is that the primary incentive for all
organizations is survival. Since organizations usually exist in an environment where resources are limited, they are dependent in varying
degrees on other organizations for resources which are critical for their
continued functioning (Grandori, 1987: 58–60).

This is true of private and public sector organizations alike. The
corporation manufacturing and selling a product, whether it is
Nabisco's breakfast cereal, Toyota's automobiles, or Bayer's aspirin,
is dependent on resources from numerous other sources for its survival. It needs loan financing from banks, equity participation through
institutional investors and the stock exchanges, raw materials from

uppliers, machinery and plant from other producers, marketing expertise from advertising agencies. The list goes on, and applies in similar fashion to any firm in the private sector, whether it is a manufacturer, or produces services. These organizations, then, have to exchange resources with all the other organizations with which they have relationships of mutual interdependence.

The public agency is no less dependent on resource exchange than the private firm (White, Levine and Vlasak, 1975). Only the relevant resources and network of participating organizations are different. The social service agency, for example, is linked to other government bureaus for essential funds in what may be a politically mandated relationship. But the political funding decision may be made in a legislative body, and the exchange between the agency and the politicians considering its refunding may be in the form of satisfied voters (the result of a positive decision) or the threat of demonstrations by disgruntled constituents (in case of a negative one). The agency will often be dependent on other organizations for the clients that are its service population: other government agencies determining eligibility, or referral organizations. Resource exchange, then, in the public and private sectors, offers a basic reason for what organizations do and why they do it.

Exchange theory proposes resource exchange as the main incentive for IOC as well (Pfeffer and Salancik, 1978; Benson, 1982: 142–145; Mulford and Rogers, 1982: 15–16; Mulford, 1984: 78–88). This has been the dominant perspective in IOC theory in general (Skelcher et al., 1983: 420), and among American scholars in particular. When IOC is premised on exchange theory, the focus tends to be on voluntary coordination and mutual adjustment. This is because exchange theory tends to imply symmetry; unequal relations involving asymmetries of power are of less concern (Zeitz, 1989: 80–81).

Hall and his associates (1977) tested how much exchange forms the basis for IOC on a sample of agencies dealing with problem youth, which were clustered around eight core organizations in 12 cities. They found that most of the interorganizational interactions they observed (74%) were indeed voluntary resource exchanges, and confirmed their hypothesis that domain consensus in such cases was an important precondition for successful IOC. But more formal types of coordination, such as mandated interactions between public agencies, are less well accounted for in this fashion (Hall et al., 1977: 469–470).

However, the exchange and resource dependence approach has been elaborated to cover these as well, and Raelin (1980) has suggested that three types of resource exchange are the basis for interorganizational relations. These are voluntary exchanges, exchanges resulting from power dependencies, and interactions which are the result of legal-political mandates — themselves the products of prior exchanges of one or the other kind (Raelin, 1982: 243–244).

The observation of interorganizational relationships offers numerous cases of fairly literal applications of exchange theory. One example is an analysis of the "water resources network" in Kansas, which showed how exchange determined the participants' roles and interactions (Keller, 1984). Another example is a study of industrial location decisions in Great Britain (Dunkerly, Spybey and Thrasher, 1981), which concluded that organizations' strategic choice becomes a matter of power and control over the network.

Provan, Breyer and Kruytenbosch's (1980) analysis of social service agencies linked to the United Way is based on exchange theory. Their study concluded that the degree of resource dependency explains each organization's power within the network, but that this can be modified by links to the network's environment. So, for instance, an agency with additional external funding sources would be more powerful in its interactions with the United Way and other organizations in the network than its resource dependency would lead one to expect.

A longitudinal analysis also provides empirical evidence confirming exchange as a basis for IOC. Van de Ven and Walker's (1984) study of interactions over time among Texan child care and health organizations found that resource dependence and mutual communications were the major factors responsible for the emergence of relations between pairs of organizations.

Exchange theory is widely accepted today as a major source for understanding interorganizational relations. Perhaps this is not surprising. After all, it is simply common sense to realize that an organization can induce other organizations to bias their actions in a direction it desires if it can offer them incentives in the form of resources, especially if the relevant resource is essential for the other organization's survival.

Without much deep pondering, this has been the basis for governments' intervention in the form of categorical grant programs. In the absence of constitutional or legislated regulatory powers, government agencies could still induce other units of government, agencies, or private firms and households to act in a desired way, in concerted pursuit of common legislated objectives. The way this is done is through resource exchange: the categorical grant program provides a valued resource: funding, in exchange for actions meeting program criteria and goals.

Resource exchange, then, is recognized to be an important incentive for IOC. But it is in the nature of exchange theory to focus our attention on voluntary transactions, even when it is expanded to encompass mandated frameworks for IOC. Other theories have been proposed to supplement exchange theory and to provide more complete accounts of organizational behavior.

Contingency Theory and Organizational Ecology

Contingency theory and organizational ecology are another two schools of thought about organizations. Here they are presented under one heading, because they have an important theme in common: both address organizational adaptation. In contingency theory, however, the focus is the single organization's adaptation to its environment. Organizational ecology, on the other hand, looks at populations of organizations, and examines their "fit" with their relevant "ecological niche" (Grandori, 1987: 21, 121–122).

The survival and success of organizations, contingency theory suggests, depends on how well they adapt to their environments. Organizational structure, and strategies of organizational behavior, are the symptoms of the organization's responses, for better or for worse, to changes in its environment. Contingency theory received its name from its conclusion that there is no one best organizational form or strategy, but that these are contingent on the situation in which the organization finds itself (Lawrence and Lorsch, 1967).

For example, contingency theory explains changes in the structure of large corporations by the degree to which they have had to adjust their operations in moving from an exclusively domestic to an international market. From a functionally divisionalized structure (production, finance, marketing etc.) of the domestic corporation, the global enterprise has had to adapt to its new environment and change its structure to a matrix form of organization in which functional and geographic (area or country) lines of control intersect (Galbraith and Kazanjian, 1986).

Contingency theory suggests organizational adaptation as a reason for IOC as well. This obviously applies to the voluntary adjustment of an organization to the other organizations which make up its environment. But it can also account for more formal and institutionalized IOC. Just as contingency theory proposes that the reason for different structures in the single organization is the organization's adaptation to its environment, it can account in the same way for the emergence of interorganizational structures.

For example, an industry's need to respond to an increasingly regulated environment will produce an interorganizational cooperative structure such as a trade association or federation. The phenomenon of hospital chains and consortia can be similarly explained by the changing environment of health services delivery, where increasing cost sensitivity is combined with growing competition (Fennell, 1980).

Contingency theory addresses many of the same issues as exchange theory, but suggests a different basic motivation for organizational behavior. An attempt to integrate resource dependency with the contingency approach suggests that each of these models may be a better explanation at a different stage in the organization's life cycle. Resource dependency, in this view, is strong in the organization's infancy, while as the organization matures, it will be more motivated by the need to adapt to its changing environment (Burns and Manet, 1984).

As its name implies, organizational ecology developed through the transfer of the ecological paradigm to organization theory. Just as the subject of ecology is biological populations and their environments, organizational ecology looks at "populations" of organizations and explains the success, failure, and survival of organizations by their environmental "fit" (Hannan and Freeman, 1989; Aldrich, 1979).

Organizational ecology offers some concepts describing interorganizational relations, which are useful to analyze IOC. Borrowed from biological ecology, these include symbiotic and commensal relations between organizations. Both these terms describe forms of interaction between organizations in relation to each other and their resource environments.

In symbiosis organizations in the same ecological niche interact for their mutual benefit, analogous to the relation between organisms in biological symbiosis, for example the shark and the pilot fish, or the rhinoceros and the tick-bird. Commensality describes several organizations drawing from a common resource base (implying some cooperative relations of sharing or rationing), just like herds of different species of antelope grazing on the same range have evolved habits to avoid overgrazing that would exhaust their common crop. Essentially these are specific types of interdependencies; they and other kinds of organizational interdependence will be discussed more fully later.

According to organizational ecology, IOC is the response of organizations to factors in their environments that create interdependence between the members of an organizational population. So we can translate the explanation for hospital consortia into organizational ecology terms, and describe them as the response of an area's population of hospitals to pressures of competition and cost control.

As we can see, this is very similar to the contingency theory explanation for IOC, but here the focus is the "population" or group of organizations existing in and adapting to a common environment, rather than the isolated organization interacting with others in response to changes in its individual circumstances. Which approach, contingency theory or organizational ecology, is more useful depends on the frame of reference one chooses.

Contingency theory and organizational ecology imply definitions of coordination which tend to embrace more deliberate forms of IOC. They put less emphasis on mutual adjustment and voluntary coordination than exchange theory does, and pay more attention to the emergence of formal coordination structures as organizations' responses to the demands of their environments. Another theory, however, has institutionalization at its core; this is transaction cost theory.

Transaction Cost Theory [8]

Transaction cost theory originated in economics. It attempts to explain what classical economics, assuming a perfect market, ignored or took as a given: the presence of different forms of organization. In classic economics markets are made up of a multitude of independent small firms. But in the real world organizations vary enormously, from the mom-and-pop store to the multinational conglomerate.

To account for this phenomenon, transaction cost theory questions some basic economic assumptions. Instead of the perfect rationality and complete information of the classic market, transaction cost theory sees bounded rationality, costly information, and opportunism. Where classic economic theory assumes that assets — capital, plant, labor, etc. — can be exchanged and substituted at will, transaction cost theory asks about the costs of their redeployment.

Transaction cost theory explains the emergence of hierarchical organizations in the economic market by the desire of firms to minimize their transaction costs. In the classic transaction between the buyer and seller of goods or services, which, at its most complex, is formalized by contract, these costs are low. But many transactions involve additional costs: the acquisition of information needed to undertake the transaction and monitor its performance, and the investment costs of assets which are specific to that transaction. These may include capital such as special tools or plant, and human resources such as trained personnel or specialized experts.

Even if nonexistent in the classic economic market, such transactions are pervasive in the real world. Specialized plant or facilities making a product which is a component for another manufacturer is one case: this is basically a technological linkage creating interdependencies between actors in a common production process. Production of a highly differentiated product for a single buyer is another: the sole-source defense contractor is a perfect example. The links between a client and consultant providing a service involving expertise specific to that type of transaction is another instance of transaction-specific investments, for example the relation between a specific corporation and its bond counsel.

Depending on how high these types of costs are in a transaction, and the degree to which transactions are recurrent and uncertain, they will modify "classic" contractual market relationships. Such modifications include bilateral government (e.g., the framework of corporate law controlling investor-management relations) and relational contracting, such as industry-wide bargaining setting the framework for corporate-labor contracts.

Finally, if transaction costs are high and recurring over time, they may produce unified governance, in which internalization and hierarchical organization substitute for market exchange. Vertical and horizontal integration are cases of this process at work. For example, a corporation like Dole controls its entire production process, from the plantation where its pineapples grow to the plant where they are canned. The 19th. century development of transcontinental railroads in North America is an example of horizontal integration, when long-haul contracts with their economies of scale increased and coordination of separately owned and run end-to-end lines became an insurmountable problem.

Transaction cost theory explains the emergence of different forms of corporate structures in the private sector. It can be extended to public sector organizations, and from the single organization to embrace interorganizational systems, as well. Although originally developed by economists, it is natural to apply the transaction cost approach with its focus on institutionalization to the study of organizations.[9]

Many of the kinds of transactions that are the central focus of transaction cost theory need coordinated action by several interdependent parties. Coordination costs, then, may be a critical transaction cost. In transaction cost theory terms, more complex and hierarchical forms of organization are a form of coordination that develops to lower transaction costs if these are too high when isolated firms or agencies interact through mutual adjustment alone. Similarly, when the cost of coordinating actions in complex organizational hierarchies becomes too high, they are disaggregated and more "market-like" forms of coordination are substituted.

By extension, transaction cost theory also offers an alternative account for the emergence of interorganizational systems and IOC. While it has not been the premise for much work in IOC so far, the transaction cost approach offers significant potential for explaining variations in IOC structures (Kaufmann, Majone and Ostrom, 1986: 799–800).

One of the few applications of transaction cost theory to the study of IOC is an analysis of the organization of the European aerospace sector (Koenig and Thietart, 1988). This study looked at the different ways in which the joint British-French (Concorde) and European (Airbus) aerospace efforts were organized over time, and used transaction costs to explain the relative success and failure of the various types of coordination structures. Another is De Hoog's (1990) analysis of IOC strategies in municipal service contracting, which showed how transaction costs affect which strategy to adopt: competition, negotiation or cooperation. A third is Bryson and Ring's (1990) exploration of policy intervention in higher education, using specific cases in Minnesota. Identifying different types of transaction costs, they showed how these relate to variations in policy response.

Transaction cost theory implies an even more structured definition of coordination than do exchange theory, contingency theory or organizational ecology. Coordination becomes a way of structuring the relations and interactions between units of an organization or between organizations so that their respective transaction costs are minimized. Such coordination structures include the hierarchical organization itself and interorganizational systems in different forms.

At the same time, the transaction cost approach allows us to recognize mutual adjustment as a form of coordination as well, if we pay attention to the institutionalized norms within which mutual adjustment takes place. Coordination structures, then, are developed to reduce the transaction costs of unconcerted actions. IOC can take place through systemic frameworks of norms in markets or rules in market-like settings in which coordination is limited to mutual adjustment, or through more hierarchical forms of organizations, organizational units, or interorganizational systems. This is the view that will be adopted here, when we examine IOC structures later.

1.3. Preconditions: Enabling or Limiting IOC

What makes IOC easier? And what constrains coordination between organizations? We know something about the preconditions which tend to facilitate or limit coordination between organizations which may initially be or perceive themselves as relatively independent. Table 1 below summarizes some enabling and limiting factors.[10] Often, the one is the mirror image or the negative of the other.

Table 1. Facilitators (and Inhibitors) of
Interorganizational Coordination (IOC)

Interpretive	Contextual
Perceived relation of needs, benefits, and rewards to (threat, costs, or risk of loss)	Relation of actual needs, benefits, and rewards to (threats, costs, or losses)
Positive (negative) attitudes	Decentralization (centralization)
Administrative/staff consensus	Professionalism (professionalization)
Maintenance (loss) of organizational/paradigm integrity	Standardization (specialization)
Maintenance or enhancement (reduction or loss) of organizational leadership/staff prestige/power/domains	Informal contacts/exchange of information/resources (bureaucratization)
	Broad range of tasks/services
Perceived interdependence	Presence (absence) of boundary-spanning/permeability roles
(In)ability to serve new clientele	Structural similarities (differences)
Higher (lower) service effectiveness	Similarities (differences) in resources, needs, services, goals, operations, or tasks
Positive (negative) evaluations of other organizations/staff	(In)frequent/(in)adequate external communications
Rewards (costs) of environmental outreach	
Cosmopolitan ethos	Scarce resources
Accessibility (barriers; e.g., socialization, leadership approaches, staff training) to other organizations	Organizational/environmental norms of innovation, coordination
	Occupational diversity
Good (poor) historical relations with other organizations	Differential outputs
	Geographic proximity
Common commitment	Voluntary association membership
Existence of (lack of) common language	Volatility (fragmentation) in political/economic system
(Vested interests)	
Agreement (disagreement) on domains/value of coordination	(Turnover of policy personnel)
	(Inadequately trained governmental personnel)
(Client alienation)	(Governmental intrusion and disruption)
(Perceived sanctions by network members)	

Source: Adapted with permission from *Interorganizational Coordination: Theory, Research, and Implementation* by D.L. Rogers and D.A. Whetten, ©1982 by Iowa State University Press.

Here the factors are shown under two broad headings: interpretive and contextual. Interpretive factors are perceptual and subjective. They relate to the image which members of one organization have of another. The contextual factors are ones which actually exist in an organization or its environment, which affect the potential relation between it and other organizations which could be partners in IOC. For the purpose of discussion these factors can be grouped under three headings: the organization, coordination costs, and interaction potential.

The Organization

Some organizational characteristics seem to predispose organizations towards IOC. Others inhibit them from joint action with other organizations or responding to others' initiatives. Outward looking organizations are likely to be more ready to undertake coordinated efforts with other organizations.

In terms of organizational culture, this means a cosmopolitan and pluralist world-view, rather than a narrow one focused on local concerns and the particularity of the organization and its mission. The norms of the organization and its relevant environment would stress innovation and encourage cooperative interaction with other organizations to achieve that end. And there would be a high level of consensus among the organization's administrators and staff.

Looking at the organization's interaction with its environment, the presence of well-defined and supported boundary-spanning roles suggests its openness to cooperative interaction. The absence of such roles might mean that they would have to be institutionalized as part of a successful IOC effort. Frequent external communications indicate an open organization too.

The organization's accessibility to other organizations in its environment will make communications easier and is also associated with a favorable attitude to IOC. Such accessibility is related to the socialization of organization members, leadership attitudes, and staff training. However, just as these can promote openness to interaction with other organizations, they can create barriers to IOC if they foster the image of a self-centered and narrowly focused organization. Membership in voluntary associations, whether institutional membership by the agency or organization, or support of participation by the organization's staff, is also a symptom of positive IOC potential.

Another ingredient for the emergence of some kinds of coordination is a culture of trust. This can be based on cultural norms. For example, mutual cooperation is valued in Japanese traditional culture, while it is discouraged by American individualism and competition (Alter and Hage, 1993: 264–266). Trust may be the result of shared values, a history of positive interactions, or common associations of kinship, professional or educational background.

Some structural characteristics make the initiation of IOC easier or more difficult. The more an organization is centralized, the less open it is likely to be to coordinated efforts with others. Conversely, a decentralized organization, perhaps due to its own positive experience in coordinating its internal units, will be more receptive to joint undertakings with other organizations. Some task standardization makes IOC easier, but a high degree of specialization will make it more difficult. An organization with complex tasks (Alter and Hage, 1993: 266) and a broad range of products or services will be more receptive to IOC than one with a narrowly focused mission.

A diversity of tasks may also be reflected in the variety of occupations among the organization's personnel, another factor facilitating IOC. Task complexity is also associated with professionalism in an organization, in the sense of expert competence of its staff. This enables IOC as well, possibly because it enhances the organization's self-confidence and opens it to interactions which might otherwise seem threatening. Well trained personnel, by the same token, are more receptive to IOC than poorly trained staff.

By contrast, professionalization, meaning membership and affiliation of an organization's staff with a formal profession and its professional body, and the use of professional credentials in recruitment and promotion, may inhibit IOC across professional boundaries. This is an important factor in evaluating IOC potential in health care and education, for example.

Some "slack" resources will also predispose an organization more towards IOC than if it is operating under severe resource constraints. Such resources include human capital: expertise, energy, and enthusiasm for potential solutions that IOC may make possible, and the institutional infrastructure of available funds and effective routines (Weiss, 1989: 110–112).

Informal contacts within the organization and across its subunits, with free exchange of information and resources, are another indicator that the organization will be receptive to IOC. Coordinating very bureaucratic agencies, on the other hand, where roles are highly formalized and procedures rigidly prescribed, is likely to be difficult.

Several qualitative factors will effect an organization's IOC potential. If it can expand or adapt its tasks, or change its services in response to new or changed client needs, and if it is generally effective in performing its mission or delivering its programs, an organization will be a positive candidate for IOC. To the extent that this is not the case, and the organization suffers from an alienated client population, coordination initiatives will be threatening. Finally, coordination will be inhibited by rapid turnover of policy personnel, which may also be symptomatic of other problems.

Coordination Costs

Consistent with transaction cost theory, the potential costs of coordination are an important factor in predisposing an organization to accept or reject IOC. In relation to the organization's expected rewards from participation in the coordinated effort, these costs may be perceived as the risk of losing or spending scarce resources or a threat to the organization's critical values. The anticipated benefits of IOC must outweigh the perceived risks for an organization to be a positive prospect for IOC.

Of course, this effect is not due only to the organization's subjective sense of its relative costs and benefits from IOC, as it considers a mutual undertaking or joining an interorganizational network. The objective balance of IOC costs and benefits is relevant as well, although perception may be indistinguishable from reality until the decision has been taken and its consequences can be evaluated.

The perceived costs of coordination may include the threat of dissolving the organization's fundamental integrity or undermining its basic paradigm. An organization which senses such risks is obviously going to be a poor prospect for IOC. On the other hand, among the perceived rewards of participation in a coordinated network or joint enterprise may be solving a shared problem (Weiss, 1987: 103–104, 110), maintaining the organization's integrity or enhancing its basic values; or the potential for collaborative learning of new skills and technologies (Alter and Hage, 1993: 268–269). In this case the prospects for IOC are good.

IOC costs and rewards are also relevant as perceived by salient groups within the organization. If IOC is seen as threatening the vested interests of a ranking manager, important administrators, or of a critical unit in the firm or agency, the organization is unlikely to agree to participate voluntarily. In this fashion, for example, cooperative agreements between agencies to develop a common data base have been sabotaged by middle-level officials or managers who saw such developments as a threat to their control of valuable information.

Interaction Potential

Here are included all the attitudes and relations of one organization to another or to the other organizations making up its relevant environment. In summary, if these are positive, an organization is likely to be favorably disposed to IOC, if they are negative, it will not.

Several factors may combine to produce these attitudes and interactions. One of the most important is the organization's perceived interdependence with other organizations in its environment. A high sense of interdependence will also usually be accompanied by commitment to common values and goals, and a common "language" of task-related discourse. A history of good relations with other organizations also promotes interaction between them. Where these are weak or absent, the prospects for IOC are relatively poor.

Interdependence may not only be perceived; it may be real. One objective source of interdependence is similar resource sources and needs. Above, we called this "commensality", based on the ecological concept of biological populations "dining at the same table". In the same terms, symbiosis is another type of interdependence. Both these may elicit IOC in a variety of collective action strategies (Carney, 1987: 344–349).

In mandated networks, resource incentives are important in facilitating IOC; witness the effectiveness of some categorical grant programs. On the other hand, such programs have failed when inadequate or no funding was provided, suggesting that "tack-on" mandates are unlikely to stimulate much positive interaction (O'Toole and Mountjoy, 1984).

Symmetries or asymmetries of network interdependence can also stimulate IOC. Examples of this are status inequalities between organizations implementing human service programs, and between hospitals in health services networks (Chase, 1979; Tennell, 1980; Milner, 1980). Technological linkages, or production interdependence, are of course a prime motivator for IOC, as suggested by transaction cost theory (Williamson, 1971, 1985). Common goals and compatible values will tend to promote organizations' engagement in joint decision making (Walton, 1972; Howe, 1981). Tasks, operations and services which are similar or complementary are other reasons for interdependence which will enhance the prospects for IOC between organizations.

Structural similarities between organizations will increase the chances for IOC between them; significant differences will be a constraint. Such similarities include technological consistency and comparable technostructures, as confirmed in a large sample of California business and government organizations (Gillespie and Mileti, 1977).

Another important factor affecting organizations' attitudes to IOC is domain consensus. An organization's domain is the area on which its mission is focused: its agreed upon or mandated arena of activity. Agreement between organizations on their respective domains is a necessary precondition for them to cooperate. Disagreement on domains means that one organization perceives another to be invading its reserved field of action. This is a frequent source of conflict between organizations, and sometimes mandated resolutions have to be imposed for effective IOC to occur (Aldrich, 1976: 423–424; Nuehring, 1978: 440; Howe, 1981: 66).

Significant differences between organizations' outputs will reduce the potential for domain disagreements between them, and increase their chances of mutual involvement in IOC. Obviously, in situations where conflict between organizations over their mutual domains is latent or open, the prospects for IOC are low.

Problem or issue characteristics are another factor which can affect the potential for IOC and its success. Reviewing prior research and cases, Paulson (1977) relates the type of initial problem with the strategies adopted and the types of outcomes. Problem types include service delivery problems, resource processing problems, moral involvement issues (i.e., value conflicts arising out of resource allocations) and domain consensus problems.

Other problem characteristics affect the adoption of IOC and its outcomes. A study of three IOC efforts in Germany revealed that time and complexity can severely constrain coordination. The report recommended avoiding IOC in issue areas that are overcomplex and extensive, and where a temporary coordination effort cannot master the problems in its limited time of operation.

As we shall see from other cases later, time is often a critical aspect of IOC efforts. We often underestimate how long it takes to develop an IOC structure and even begin to implement the coordinated undertaking. Conversely, when an issue enjoys political priority in response to some crisis, time pressures for a solution may enhance the readiness to undertake IOC and increase its chances of success (Bars, Baum and Fiedler, 1976).

Organizations' geographic proximity seems to favor IOC; this is the basis for the IOC tool of colocation. Colocation means encouraging joint action among organizations by providing shared facilities for programs or services with the same clientele, for example welfare referral, social services caseworkers, and basic health and diagnostic services in a central city community center.

Contextual factors can also enhance or constrain IOC. Volatility of the organizational environment, and fragmentation of the political and economic system, will tend to encourage IOC. This is probably because organizations' sense of mutual interdependence is sharpened in such circumstances, and they look for more certainty and more predictable interactions with one another in a more turbulent and uncertain environment.

A politically mandated coordination structure may create IOC where there was none. This is only likely, however, if the mandated IOC structure is overlaid on a network of organizations with traits and relationships inclining them to favor IOC, according to the factors reviewed above. On the other hand, heavy handed governmental intrusion may disrupt a delicately balanced local interorganizational network, and hinder IOC rather than foster it.

Summary

What is coordination? Definitions vary on a continuum ranging from voluntary adjustment to systematic control. At one pole is the most inclusive definition, which sees as coordinated any action that takes other organizations' behavior into account; that is, organizations' spontaneous mutual adjustment to their environments. At the other extreme is the most limited view, which defines IOC as controlling organizations' decisions so as to concert their actions and achieve mutually beneficial outcomes.

These various views of IOC can be explained by differences in their underlying theoretical premises. Exchange theory, which accounts for organizational behavior by resource dependence and exchange, focuses on mutual adjustment and voluntary coordination. Contingency theory and organizational ecology see IOC as a way in which organizations adapt to their environments. With these approaches as underlying assumptions, IOC definitions pay more attention to deliberate coordination.

Transaction cost theory directly addresses the issue of how organizations evolve and change their forms. In these terms, IOC is defined as the structure of relationships adopted by organizations to minimize their transaction costs. These relationships can range from market or market-like mutual adjustment within a system of rules or norms which is the framework for individual actors' decisions, to more hierarchical IOC structures and organizations. This is the premise for our exploration of IOC structures later.

What makes IOC easier or more difficult? Knowledge based on previous research and cases identifies many factors, both perceptual and objective. These fall into three related groups. The first covers characteristics of the organization itself. To be a good candidate for IOC, the organization must be open to its environment: in its organizational culture, structure and behavior.

The second addresses the relation between IOC costs and benefits, both perceived and actual. For an organization to agree to participate in a coordinated effort, the prospective rewards of IOC must be greater than its costs, risks or threat to the organization or relevant vested interests within it. The third group includes factors describing the relation between organizations. Overall, these must be positive for IOC to have a chance.

Positive attitudes and relations between organizations are the results of perceived and real interdependencies which can take several forms and may result from similar needs, resource dependencies, and complementary services or technologies. Other sources of good relations between organizations may be commonalities of structure, tasks, and language, and a history of positive interaction.

Its context also affects the prospects of IOC. Relevant factors include issue types, problem traits such as time and complexity, and environmental characteristics. Finally, domain consensus is a necessary prerequisite for successful IOC. Only organizations which are not in conflict, latent or open, about their respective domains, will be open to cooperation.

NOTES

1. This review serves as our point of departure, and the focus here will be on later work.

2. Mutual adjustment as described by Lindblom (1965: 32–34) ranges from "adaptive" adjustment (where organization X seeks no response from organization Y in its environment) to "manipulated" adjustment which includes negotiation and bargaining, partisan discussion, and authoritative prescription. This is a very broad definition of mutual adjustment, and covers too much to be useful. Here, mutual adjustment will be limited to adaptive mutual adjustment and informal reciprocal interactions such as bargaining, negotiation and discussion. Formal transactions (ranging from compensation to authoritative pre-

scription and prior decision by third parties) do not come under this term as I use it.

3. This is the basis for Wildavsky's trenchant criticism of the concept of coordination (1979: 131–132) which is well warranted.

4. In an effort to operationalize this goal, Alter and Hage (1993: 83–85) distinguish between the comprehensiveness, accessibility, and mutual compatibility of the interorganizatinal system's elements. But this is essentially a format for program evaluation, and its relationship to coordination is tenuous.

5. Gray (1989: 15) calls collaboration as an "emergent process", while defining coordination as a structure of formal institutionalized relations among organizations. Thus, collaborative interaction between interdependent organizations addressing mutual problems may produce IOC structures as part of the agreed upon solution, for example an advisory group to address problems of neighborhood disinvestment, and public-private partnerships to combat school dropping-out and to stimulate inner city redevelopment (Gray, 1989: 95–103, 185–190).

6. In terms of including strategic adjustment, this definition is not much less inclusive than Lindblom's, but their discussion suggests more of a focus on structured relationships — based on resource exchange or mandated frameworks — than their definition implies (Hall et al., 1977: 465–470).

7. For an excellent and concise review of these, see Grandori (1987: 1–79, 103–124) where exchange theory is called the "resource dependence" perspective, contingency theory is "structural contingency theory", and transaction cost theory is described under "markets and hierarchies".

8. For a fuller account, see Alexander (1992), which is the source of much of this section.

9. Robins questions this, contending that transaction cost theory is ahistorical. Experience, he says, does not confirm the assumption he attributes to transaction cost theory, that "markets are the natural forms of organizational exchange" (1987: 77). This misreads the transaction cost approach, which simply takes the "classic" market and contractual relationships as an "ideal type" to explain other forms of organization. Indeed, transaction costs can just as well account for the dismantling of hierarchies and their "marketization", as demonstrated in corporate decentralization and creation of "profit centers", or the privatization of public services.

10. This is based on Halpert's (1982) review of previous research on conditions facilitating or inhibiting IOC, which he calls "antecedents" and "consequences" of coordination. Gray's (1985) review structures many of the same factors a bit differently, grouping them under three phases of collaboration: problem-setting, direction-setting, and structuring.

CHAPTER 2

Where and How?

Contexts, Relationships and Tools

Where does coordination between organizations emerge and how does it play itself out? There are different ways of describing the IOC context. First, we can focus on the meaning of *between*: how do we define and describe the relational network of organizations which is the locus of IOC. There are some models which are independent of the existence or nature of IOC. Others, which come under the heading of "interorganizational fields", do relate to IOC's presence or absence, and its type.

Next, addressing *between* in another sense, we can explore the kinds of links that may exist between pairs or among sets of organizations. Each form of interdependence elicits a different type of IOC, leading us into second part of the question: the *how* of IOC. One concept developed to describe this is IOC strategies: processes which encourage coordination and which are employed to initiate IOC and carry it out.

Finally, the *how* involves a particular kit of tools to implement IOC. These are the basic elements of the IOC process, and include informal and formal tools. For example, at the most informal end of the range, information exchange over coffee at the downtown diner between officials of two agencies is one IOC tool. At the range's most formal pole, joint strategic planning by a set of interdependent organizations is another.

2.1. Networks and Fields

One way of looking at organizations is from the point of view of one particular organization. In this sense, the array of organizations in which we are interested makes up the relevant environment of the focal organization. This has been called an *organization set* (Evan, 1966).

The organization set is a useful basis for analyzing interorganizational relations and behavior. It is important to realize that, while the focal organization is one point defining the set, the relevant relationship or interaction is another. Thus, the same organization may be the focus of different organization sets, depending on the purpose of the analysis.

For example, if we wanted to identify an organization set focused on IBM, and the concern of our analysis were research and innovation, we might include organizations such as universities and research institutes and labs, other firms specializing in hardware component (e.g., semiconductor) and software product development, and competitors doing R&D in the same areas. On the other hand, if we were looking at strategic planning and adaptation to the organizational and market environment, the set would be the firms making up the segments of the computer industry in which IBM is involved, and those constituting its relevant market.

It is possible, of course, to identify an organization set defined solely by the focal organization. Such a set would be the sum of all the sets that could be identified for any specific relationships; i.e., all the organizations that are relevant to or interact with the focal organization in any way. For a large complex organization (like IBM, or the U.S. Dept.of Health and Human Services) such a set might be so large as to be almost indeterminate; for a smaller one (like, say, a local computer sales and service firm, or a County Welfare Department) it might be quite manageable.

Organization sets have some intrinsic dimensions which may provide a useful way of analyzing them. Whetten and Aldrich (1979), for example, focused on size and diversity in their study of several employment agencies' organization sets and how these affected their relative success. They found that a large and diverse organization set, typified by a great number of organizations in the set, with a wider range of specializations and a broader range of services represented, indeed characterized the more effective organizations.

Another way of defining an interrelated system of organizations is to identify its participants by their common object or arena of involvement. In this way the organizations interacting in pursuit of a common goal or interacting in the context of some joint activity can also be called an *action set* (Aldrich, 1979: 280–281; Aldrich and Whetten, 1981). Examples of action sets could be firms and agencies involved in grain export, or organizations delivering support and services to the handicapped.

There are more specialized "subspecies" of action sets. One is the *policy issue network* (Kirst, Meister and Rowley, 1984) or *policy system* (Wamsley, 1985). Using the policy issue as a way to identify a network of related organizations can be an effective tool for analysis. It will expose the interdependencies linking often very diverse organizations around an issue such as welfare support and the family, national industrial development, intermodal transportation subsidies, or controlled burning in national forests. Focusing on the policy development stage, Sabatier (1988) suggests a subset identifying organizations belonging to an *advocacy coalition*; examples cover policy areas ranging from air pollution control to oil export subsidies.

The *implementation set* (Hjern and Porter, 1981) is another type of action set. What links the organizations in the implementation set is their involvement in a common program or project. This is a pragmatic and intuitively appealing form of delimitation which is often useful. In project or program evaluation, and for analysis of program-related IOC, identifying the implementation set is essential. Every project and program, ranging from the new parking lot behind the town hall to the regional development of the Upper Volta, and from "meals-on-wheels" for the homebound elderly in Dane County, Wisconsin to the General Improvement Areas neighborhood revitalization program in Britain, has its implementation set of organizations.

In contrast to the organization set, the action and implementation sets and policy issue network have in common a latent IOC potential, if not IOC actively in progress. This is because all the last three types of interorganizational system are linked by some relational interdependence: joint action, or a common policy issue, project, or program. The organization set, on the other hand, is defined only by situational interdependence, i.e., the links between the organizations in the set and the focal organization.

The *interorganizational field* (Aldrich and Whetten, 1981) is similar
to the organization set in that respect. It is also neutral with regard to
actual or potential IOC. Still, without a focal organization or a specific
base for its organizations' interdependence, the interorganizational
field (even though it is an open system) has to be defined or bounded
somehow. This may again be by some common orientation: "the
semiconductor industry", "high-energy nuclear research", "executive
outplacement agencies", or "tertiary hospital services". Or the interorganizational system or field may be bounded using a geographic-ju-
risdictional or areal unit as a surrogate for its sociocultural and
economic context: the interorganizational system of community organizations in Oakland, California (Warren, Rose and Bergunder,
1973), or the interorganizational field of Swedish universities (March
and Olsen, 1976).

While the basic interorganizational field is indifferent to IOC,
Lehman (1975) in his study of coordination in the health care area,
described several different kinds of interorganizational fields which
vary in their levels of IOC. In the *feudal field* each organization is like
an independent baron, and the prevailing form of IOC is spontaneous
mutual adjustment. It is worth emphasizing Lehman's analogy, however, to note that the feudal field is not identical with a market (which
is usually assumed as the context for mutual adjustment) but differs
in some important ways.

The "perfect market" is limited by the "small numbers" condition;
i.e., the units must be small, and they must be numerous, so that no
firm can influence the market on its own to any significant degree
(Grandori, 1987: 31, 35). The feudal field is not such a market: given
the study's subject of health care organizations, the feudal field is seen
as including several large, but independent, organizations. A number
of separate hospitals in an area, for example, might make up such a
feudal field.

Thus, unlike in the market, organizations in the feudal field which
limit their interaction to spontaneous mutual adjustment do so as a
result of organizational culture or strategic choice. At the same time,
because of their relatively small numbers, these organizations' actions
tend to affect each other. Thus, the independence which defines this
field can rarely be sustained over time.

The feudal field, therefore, is intrinsically unstable, and the potential is there for its evolution to an *interorganizational network*: a loosely
coupled system with some more stable subsystems; e.g., an interlinked set of community organizations with a power elite as its subset
(Aldrich, 1979: 281–284, 323–327). Such a network will contain or be

organized in one of the other types of fields with more formal IOC, and can be described by some intrinsic characteristics.[1]

In his analysis of intercollegiate athletics, for example, Stern (1979) looked at this interorganizational network's administrative structure, the types and number of ties between organizations, and the flow of resources in the network. Other network dimensions that can be the focus of analysis are organizations' resource dependency, mutual awareness and consensus, and the frequency and formalization of communication (Van de Ven, Walker and Liston, 1979).

The *mediated field* consists of organizations which are conscious of their interdependence. Their interactions can involve mutual adjustment and voluntary coordination. In the health services field, for example, a mediated field might be made up of a group of hospitals linked through overlapping board memberships, and perhaps also through some voluntary task forces addressing issues of mutual concern. Or the hospitals might be formally linked through a mediating agency which facilitates their collaboration: funneling resources, channelling communication and information, and coordinating services. But coordination remains on a somewhat ad-hoc basis, and the participating organizations retain control of their operating goals.

In the *guided field* formal IOC prevails. The hospitals would be linked in an association or through a set of formal joint undertakings. Agreements between sets of hospitals in areas such as recruitment of medical interns, division of labor in areas of specialization, joint purchasing, etc. would be executed through joint planning, budgeting, and monitoring by individuals with assigned coordinating tasks or boundary-spanning personnel. At an even more comprehensive level, coordination between all the hospitals might be formalized by their incorporation into a federation to which the participating hospitals would delegate some of their strategic functions and decisions, such as assigning service areas or fields of functional expertise, and allocating selected resources.

Finally, with hierarchical internalization IOC may even turn into interunit coordination in a single organization. Health service organizations linked to a leading institution as subsidiaries (in what Lehman calls an "empire"), and hospitals operating in a corporate framework as members of a chain or divisions of a holding company occupy this pole of the guided field.

Though Lehman did not define them in quite these terms, it is clear that the characteristic distinguishing his interorganizational fields from one another is their respective degree of hierarchical organization. Another observer explicitly used this trait to define three types of interorganizational fields (Hegner, 1986).

Solidarity fields are made up of organizations linked mainly through communalistic reciprocal transactions. Traditional societies would be made up largely of such fields, and they might be found today in ideological arenas linking issues such as women's rights or the environment. *Hierarchy* describes interorganizational fields linked by hierarchical forms of IOC; these will be our focus when discussing IOC structures later. In *market exchange* organizations interact solely through mutual adjustment.

What we are looking at, then, are classifications of interorganizational contexts at the highest — most extensive and abstract — level: a level we can call the macro-scale. These contexts are interorganizational fields. Hegner's scheme is a division of the interorganizational universe between community, hierarchy, and market. In Lehman's classification interorganizational fields are arrayed on a scale of relative hierarchical organization, from the "perfect" market at one end, with the feudal field close to it, and ranging to the unitary field at the other pole.[2]

At a somewhat lower level of abstraction, we can find a wide variety of interorganizational networks or *interorganizational collectivities*. The interorganizational collectivity is defined as two or more interdependent organizations with common goal-directed activities. Decisions in such collectivities are the result of role-occupants' interactions which commit the participating organizations (Van de Ven, Emmett and Koenig, 1975: 25–27).

Such networks or collectivities include alliances, federations, and corporate networks (conglomerates and holding companies). Other variations are the consortium, joint venture, and corporate system (Evans and Klemm, 1980). The *mutual organization* has been defined as a type of network which takes its place somewhere in the intermediate range between hierarchy and market (Koenig and Thietart, 1988); many of the interorganizational networks mentioned here fit into this category. Another kind of network fitting between hierarchy and market is the *associational network*: a trades union federation is an example of this type.

The difference between interorganizational fields and these networks is their respective level of abstraction. They have in common the attribute of more or less hierarchy. Later we will see how the degree of hierarchical organization can be used to relate interorganizational fields and networks to other aspects of IOC: coordination strategies, structures and tools.

2.2. Interdependence

Interdependence between organizations is critical in relation to IOC. As mentioned above, the perception of interdependence is an essential precondition for IOC. In addition, the type of interdependence linking a pair or network of organizations will have a significant effect on the form of IOC they adopt.

Some types of interorganizational interdependence are identical to, and simply an extension of forms of interdependence between distinct units of one organization. In a single complex organization its sub-units may be differentiated by technological division of labor (e.g., machine parts production, body parts production, assembly, etc), functional specialization (e.g., R&D, engineering, finance, sales; or planning and programming, program services, legal etc.), or geographical area. But these can also be separate organizations in an industry, market, or interorganizational field.

Thompson (1967) identified some types of interdependence, based on input/output relationships or transfer interactions between organizational units. *Serial interdependence* exists when one unit's product or output is the input for another. Between organizational units this is a simple transaction which can be programmed and administered by relatively standardized procedures.

Serial interdependence between separate organizations has been called *sequential interdependence* (O'Toole and Mountjoy, 1984: 493–495). It may be just as simple, or it may be much more complicated, depending on the circumstances. Transaction cost theory gives us some tools to analyze these and to come to some conclusions on the types of IOC that might evolve. If the object of the transfer is relatively standard and widely available in a market consisting of multiple buyers and sellers, the serial interdependence is easily mediated by procuring the product or service through purchase or contract. The relevant coordination process in this case is spontaneous mutual adjustment through which the parties adapt their behavior to available information on supply, demand, and prices.

But if the serial interdependence involves an interorganizational exchange that demands transaction specific investments or resources, we have seen that mutual adjustment may not be sufficient. Depending on the criticality, frequency and uncertainty of the transaction, the parties may have to invoke other coordination mechanisms. These may range from informal interactions to concert the relevant transaction process, through various levels of formal coordination.[3] At the most basic level of contract enforcement a coordinator may be needed in conditions of ambiguity: an arbitrator or referee. When these are more widespread (e.g., in an entire sector or industry) coordination may be imposed through a voluntary or mandated framework.

Such types of IOC are what Williamson (1975) called "relational contracting" and "bilateral governance". An example of such a voluntary framework is the real estate industry's self-regulation of seller-realtor-purchaser transactions. Examples of socially mandated frameworks are the body of corporate law addressing investor-management relations, and the regulatory framework (including a coordinating unit, the National Labor Relations Board) controlling industry-wide bargaining and management-labor relations.

Even simple sequential interdependence, on the face of it, if involving idiosyncratic transactions (ones with heavy transaction-specific investments in human or capital resources) that are frequently repeated over time and uncertain, will elicit increasingly formal coordination and control. Ultimately, the result may well be fully hierarchical coordination in the form of merger into a single organization: vertical or horizontal integration.

Vertical integration results in the corporation which controls a process from its raw-material inputs to marketing its product, or the bureaucracy which administers a cluster of goal-related programs from the originally legislated funding to the "street-level" services. The classic example of serial technological linkages producing vertical integration is the petrochemical refining industry.

As a case of horizontal integration resulting from idiosyncratic sequential interdependence Williamson (1981) cites the 19th. century integration of North American transcontinental railroads. The sequential interdependence linking their end-to-end predecessor firms was the transfer of freight from one line to the other. Though this looks like a simple problem, the growing demand for long-haul traffic turned it into a coordination nightmare. As incentives to capture high volume freight traffic increased, and the resulting economies of scale grew, market contracts with shippers were no longer effective, and merger proved to be the ultimate solution.

More complex than serial interdependence is *reciprocal interdependence* (Thompson, 1967) which links organizations where one unit's output is an input for the other's activities, and at the same time that unit's product is the other unit's input. An example of this type of interdependence is the interaction between a research institute and a pharmaceutical corporation. The institute's research discoveries are the input for development of new products, but the corporation's product development needs may also orient the institute's research program. At the same time, the corporation's own R&D Division supplies the Institute's researchers with data for their testing design, and the corporation's Marketing Division provides the human subjects for the Institute's experiments.

Regulating the transactions involved in reciprocal interdependence is obviously more demanding than coordinating sequentially interdependent organizations. This is true, without considering the transaction characteristics which may also be a complicating factor. Continuous needs for detailed information prescribe complex coordination mechanisms. Again, there will be a tendency to adopt increasingly hierarchical coordination structures to the degree that the interdependencies are critical, and to the extent that the transactions are idiosyncratic. At the extreme, it may become obvious that organizational autonomy is dysfunctional, and the interdependent units may merge. These cases suggest that for IOC, unlike what Thompson suggested for coordination within the single organization, the simplicity or complexity of interunit interdependence is not what determines the form of coordination. Rather, it is a combination of interdependence type and transaction characteristics.

The third type of interdependence is *pooled interdependence*. Here, unlike sequential and reciprocal interdependence, which involve linear processes, the interdependence between organizations is the result of some mutual commonality. It may be *competitive*, when the respective organizations' efforts are focused on a common target (Pfeffer and Salancik, 1978: 124–126). This describes the relationship between firms in the same industry or sector, for example, which are linked not so much by their use of similar or identical technologies (though that may also be the case) as by their competition in the same market. In the public sector we find pooled interdependence as well, when a number of agencies are servicing the same client population. This was the case, for example, among the agencies serving the inner city's poor population, which were embraced in the Model Cities program (O'Toole and Mountjoy, 1984: 493–494).

Other types of pooled interdependence are symbiotic and commensal interdependence. These terms are borrowed from ecology, where they describe relations between biological populations; here the same type of relationship is transferred to groups of organizations. *Symbiotic interdependence* in an economic sector, for instance, may be the result of technological heterogeneity (Pfeffer and Salancik, 1978: 123–124; Carney, 1987: 346–347). We can see this as an apt description of the interdependence between hardware and software manufacturers in the computer industry, for example.

Commensal interdependence describes the relationship between organizations dependent on the same source of resources, analogous to herds of different species grazing on the same pasture or drinking at the same water-hole. This can describe the market-interdependence of firms in a mature industry (Carney, 1987: 346–347), or a group of agencies funded from the same program.

The distinction between symbiotic and commensual interdependencies is revealed in an analysis of Swedish joint programs and ventures (Erdstrom, Hogberg and Nordback, 1984), though the authors do not use these terms. They describe variations of "resource dependency" among organizations, identifying organizations that seek partners with complementary resources (potential symbiotic interdependence) vs. organizations which are dependent on resources from their environments (commensal interdependence). In the former a strategic approach leads to joint ventures, while the latter is preceded by transactional (i.e., buyer-seller) relationships.

In a study of four telecommunication projects Carney (1987) looked at the results of symbiotic and commensal interdependence, and found that they generated several types of coordination structures. The two cases of symbiotic interdependence produced consortia of various degrees of integration, while the two cases of commensal interdependence ended in a joint venture and a trade association.

All these types of pooled interdependence have been classified as "outcome interdependence", when results are the product of interdependent efforts. This distinguishes them from "behavior interdependence" in which the participants' activities themselves are interdependent in the same way that players in the same game are linked by a common set of rules (Pfeffer and Salancik, 1978: 41–46).

Several observers of interorganizational relations have linked different types of interdependencies with various outcomes in terms of resulting IOC strategies and structures. Some see various degrees of integration, ranging from joint ventures to merger (i.e., the single organization coordination structure described later) as frequent responses to competitive interdependence. Technological interdependence, on the other hand, may lead to diversification as an avoidance strategy (Pfeffer and Salancik, 1978; Pfeffer, 1982).

O'Toole and Mountjoy (1984) proposed another way in which to view interdependence, identifying several different combinations of sequential, reciprocal, and pooled interdependence. This classification distinguishes between two stages in IOC behavior. The first is the formative stage, reflecting the kinds of interdependence involved in setting up the mutual undertaking that demands IOC. The second is the operating stage, describing the interdependence between organizations with an established structure of IOC interaction.

The Model Cities program shows the institutionalization of pooled operating interdependence.[4] Block grants, such as the U.S. General Revenue Sharing program that existed up to the late 80s, produced some spontaneous mutual adjustment in response to resource incentives, while reciprocal formative interdependencies led to bargaining among the relevant organizations. O'Toole and Mountjoy's analysis found that pooled interdependence usually resulted in low levels of IOC and failed to generate very well integrated coordination structures. Sequential interdependence produced some satisfactory examples of interorganizational integration, but many were delayed and uneven in quality. Their study concluded that resources play a key role in interorganizational implementation.[5]

Scharpf (1978: 352–358) suggested yet another set of dimensions for describing interdependencies. Basing his analysis on exchange theory, he identifies four kinds of dependence, depending on the suitabilty and the importance of the source of resources, ranging from complete independence when both are low, to high dependence when both are high. And, depending on the symmetry of exchange relations, he distinguishes between "mutual" interdependence and "unilateral" dependence.

Reviewing the indirect linkages between organizations, Scharpf shows us three kinds of IOC associated with different types of interdependencies. "External" coordination (which may often be hierarchical) may occur laterally between a set of agencies each linked to a common superordinate organization. "Indirect" coordination may connect several organizations in a feedback relationship through a mutual organizational link, while "coordination from below" involves organizations which are "the servants of several masters" concerting the decisions of their superiors in their own mutual interests. Using examples from German central-local government relations, Scharpf shows that the latter may be more the rule than the exception (1978: 359–362).

It is clear that these types and dimensions of interdependence are a very useful tool for analyzing interorganizational relations and IOC. But there has been too little convergence in applying this repertoire of concepts to the empirical analysis of IOC cases.[6] As a result, the discovery of a clear association between types of interdependence and the resulting emergence (or lack of) IOC remains an unfulfilled potential. One reason for this may be the absence of any integrating framework to describe IOC at the level between fields and strategies, and coordination tools. Below we will see whether coordination structures can fill this role.

2.3. Coordination Strategies

A whole range of behaviors and relationships, from relatively general and abstract (e.g., cooperation) to quite concrete and specific (e.g., contracting) have been called IOC strategies. Coordination strategies may differ if only two organizations are involved, or if the issue is multilateral IOC. Strategies can all be subsumed under two basic approaches: cooperation or control (Mulford and Rogers, 1982: 17–31; Mulford, 1984: 49–52).

The time dimension is also an important aspect of coordination strategies: they can be anticipative, or they can be adaptive. Anticipative coordination is coordination by plan,[7] adaptive coordination takes place in real time, and is based on monitoring, feedback and control (March and Simon, 1958: 158–169). Coordinative planning can include any of the strategies which follow, but the planning stage is particularly important for the structural approaches. After all, coordination by routinization of tasks or restructuring interorganizational links can hardly be effective once the relevant activities are already in progress.

Another dimension distinguishing between different groups of coordination strategies is their "medium",[8] or how the strategy achieves the desired interorganizational integration (Metcalfe, 1976). "Cultural" strategies depend on compatibility between the goals of the focal organization and its organization set, or consistency in the relevant action set's values. Securing support for an IOC undertaking by enlisting professional values is an example of such a strategy. "Normative" strategies are based on conformity of expectations and norms among members of the relevant interorganizational network. Creating a mandated hierarchical framework based on organizations' recognition of legitimate authority, for instance, is such a strategy.

"Communicative" strategies depend on mutual awareness of interdependence and common interests. Negotiation, making manifest and resolving conflicting demands of members of an action set, is such a strategy. Indeed, many information-based and persuasive strategies would often fall under this heading. However, depending on the content of the information or substance of the argument these strategies could come under some of the other headings as well. For example, if it is value-based a persuasive strategy might really be "cultural", or if the argument is premised on interests and potential incentives or sanctions it could in fact be "functional" (see below). This example illustrates how the same strategy, depending on the nature of its "medium", could be described by one or more of these terms.

"Functional" strategies are based on reciprocal exchange or power relations between members of the interorganizational system. An example of such a strategy is coalition-forming between more power-ful and less powerful organizations to advance their interest in coor-dinating the system. Or a focal organization could try to exclude some potentially powerful rivals from the prospective action set so as to make the common undertaking more manageable.

Cooperative strategies are ones involving voluntary interaction. They include collaboration (Beder, 1987), which can be elicited in a variety of ways: "financial" strategies (Sharpe, 1985) involving bargaining and resource exchange (Brager and Holloway, 1978), co-sponsorship and cooptation (Sharpe, 1985). Cooptation is a popular coordinative strategy: it can use patronage (e.g., mutual purchasing agreements of goods or services) and membership on formal consult-ative bodies to help to generate a supportive frame of mind. An example of the latter are the interlocking memberships on corporate boards which are a widespread coordination tool in the private sector (Pfeffer and Salancik, 1978: 145–146) and the public sector (Milner, 1980; Alexander, 1983) alike.[9]

Informational strategies include persuasion and consensus-build-ing. Persuasion can invoke common values based on shared ideology, or partisanship and party loyalty (Sharpe, 1985). However, in the context of broad scope problems such strategies may founder on the issues' complexity, and they may involve transaction costs in delaying decisions and action. In the German intergovernmental context of which he writes, Franz (1985) also sees conflict avoidance as a prevail-ing coordinative strategy.

Control strategies aim to coordinate organizations' behavior by biasing their decisions to produce action which they might otherwise not have taken. Of course, there is a grey area between cooperative and control strategies, which is occupied by strategies (e.g., some forms of persuasion) which suggest potential, but not actual, threats or incentives. Control strategies may invoke sanctions based on the exercise of power or the threat to withhold critically needed resources. The latter falls under what Sharpe (1985) called "financial" strategies. Scharpf et al. (1978) labelled them "allocation quotas", and suggested that this strategy is used to address maintenance and structural prob-lems.

These include the reverse of resource sanctions as well: the incentive to cooperate by promising needed resources. Resource incentives (e.g., funding, or access to service populations) are also sometimes combined with structural strategies (see below) to generate IOC. Many central government efforts to create local-level horizontal coordination in a particular sector work this way.

For example, Hage (1975) recommended the allocation of funding to local agencies as an incentive for them to participate in "coalitions" of human services delivery organizations which would be governed by a managing committee. In the U.S., local coordination in the health sector and among agencies funded for servicing the elderly was promoted in this fashion (Alexander, 1983). Resource allocation is also often the arena of other coordination strategies: bargaining and exchange, as in Brager and Holloway's (1978) case of formally coordinated local human services delivery agreements.

Resources are also the basis for the coordination strategy of "competition". Here the market is used or market-like frameworks are created to coordinate relevant organizations' actions, as in De Hoogh's (1990) example of municipal services' delivery. Contracting in the market is an element of this strategy, but we will address contracts later under coordination tools. The categorical grant program, in which local agencies compete for federal funds in a political "market", is another example of this competitive strategy.[10]

If it is not based on resource allocation, power usually rests on authority, which can also be deployed in an appropriate mandated framework. Authority can influence organizational behavior to coordinate actions in a desired direction, as shown by affirmative action in the U.S. (Pfeffer and Salancik, 1978: 57–60), and numerous other examples of legislated and mandated programs.

Finally, control strategies include a repertoire of ways to induce organizational change or the restructuring of interorganizational relationships. These restructuring strategies may be responses to maintenance or structural problems (Scharpf et al., 1978). But their adoption is often constrained by high political costs (Alexander, 1980) and the resistance of self-interested organizations to reorganization which assaults their vested interests (Scharpf et al., 1978).

One structural coordination strategy is "structural positioning". This may involve redefining the legitimacy of a group's assigned organizational function, or changing an organization's domain, to fit new demands, or creating a new unit or structure of relationships. In the context of their cases, local human services delivery organizations in the U.S., Brager and Holloway (1978: 174–175) found that the question of using an existing entity vs. creating a new unit was critical, as was the group's specific composition in each case. A new ad-hoc unit has the advantage of bringing a fresh perspective to old problems, and lacks the burden of conformity to old norms, existing routines and procedures. But it may also lack the network of existing patterns of coordinative relationships that a standing unit which already exists may have.

Another structural strategy is to reorganize and shift the level of control. This was done, for example, in British local government reorganization which moved power from the regional or District level to the center (Sharpe, 1985). Finally, merger is a recognized strategy to accomplish coordination of previously discrete organizations. This is the case in the private sector, where merger is used for horizontal or vertical integration of firms engaged in complementary or competitive activities (Williamson, 1975; Pfeffer, 1972), and in the public sector, where agencies may be merged to take advantage of complementarities and to eliminate redundant duplication (Hult, 1987).[11]

Among structural strategies are also negotiation and cooperation. In this context negotiation means negotiating a modified market framework of relational contracting. In her example of municipal service contracting De Hoog (1985: 325–329) describes this as a limited solicitation of selected suppliers, and bargaining agreements without the strict formalities of a priori bidding.

Cooperation is essentially creating some form of partnership between the local government agency and the service supplier, as has been done in the municipal services, human services, and R&D sectors (De Hoogh, 1985: 329–334). Another example of structural cooperation is the public-private partnerships that have emerged in the area of downtown and industrial development in the U.S.A. (Frieden and Sagalynn, 1989).

The main practical purpose that is served by knowing about these coordination strategies is consciousness-raising. At most, the coordination strategies reviewed here can provide a kind of repertoire for possible action. Almost all the research and case studies which are the sources for these coordination strategies are descriptive or analytic; at most, the adoption of one strategy or another is related to some problem characteristic or contextual variable. None of these studies has an evaluative component offering a cause-effect explanation that links strategies to outcomes. As a result, the conditions to develop any normative theory, even a contingent one, are absent.

There are several reasons for this. Summarizing the consequences of various coordination strategies in terms of their effects on different interest groups, Mulford and Rogers (1982) remark: "little is known about the impact of coordination", and comment on the problematic aspect of evaluating IOC from different stakeholder perspectives. Another reason is the lack of convergence among much of this work. Without any agreed-upon integrating framework of concepts and terms, cumulative research is difficult, and each study "reinvents the wheel" (Alexander, 1993).

A striking exception is Alter and Hage's (1993) analysis of IOC strategies (they call them: coordination methods) that were adopted in fifteen local networks of human services organizations. They did evaluate the networks' effectiveness, relating it to the use of various methods of administrative coordination and task integration. Administrative coordination could be effected by impersonal methods: rules and standard operating procedures, personal monitoring and communication, or group interaction. Similarly, coordination strategies for operational task integration included sequential or reciprocal linkage between actors (presumably related to kinds of interdependence — see above) or forming a team.

Based on this analysis, they suggest that effective coordination is a matter of the relationship between the method chosen, and the kind of interorganizational network involved. While these conclusions are quite valuable for these specific types of networks, their scope is rather limited.[12] Consequently, though the idea of relating coordination strategies to types of interorganizational networks is suggestive, we still await a more general theory that could tell us in what conditions which coordination strategy might be most effective.

2.4. Tools

These are the basic elements employed to effect IOC. Elmore (1987) calls them "policy instruments" (and of course they can serve purposes other than coordination too) and groups them under their alternative uses: inducements, capacity building, and system change. Listing such tools, Rosenthal (1984) calls them: "independent management devices" which are deployed to insure loose-coupling of interorganizational systems instead of the totally independent action or noncompliance that would exist in their absence.

A source of confusion is the interchangeable terms: strategies and tools, which are used for some of these by many authors (Mulford and Rogers, 1982: 17–19), or grouping together of some strategies and tools under other neutral headings, e.g., "coordination mechanisms" (Eckstrom, Hegberg and Nordback, 1984: 148; Jennings, 1994: 55). Joint planning, overlapping board memberships, and contracts are among what we are here calling coordination tools which have been referenced in this way.[13]

The basic logic behind the distinction between strategies and tools used here, is their relative level of abstraction and process character. The more general and abstract processes are strategies, the more concrete and specific activities or types of linkages are tools. Consistent with this definition, tools can be "nested" in, or used in the framework of strategies, but not the reverse. Thus bidding and contracts would be coordination tools used in the context of a competitive strategy, or overlapping board memberships could be part of a cooptation strategy. Joint planning and budget signoff might be employed as tools in a cooperative strategy, or be built into organizations' or organizational units' prescribed relationships in a structural strategy of reorganization.

Coordination tools comprise formal and informal processes and linkages. "Informal coordinative mechanisms" include interpersonal contacts and informal channels of communication (Chisholm, 1989: 64–85), which may be effected through ad-hoc meetings, telephone contacts, or correspondence (e.g., distribution of informational material to a wider mailing list than the people formally linked to the source).

Informal communication may be the most commonly used coordinative tool there is, and it often complements more formal coordination mechanisms. In some situations it may be very effective, as in the case Chisholm (1989) describes of proactive and reactive communication between traffic managers of San Francisco Bay Area transit agencies to resolve issues of mutual concern. In other situations, where there is too much reliance on informal communication to relieve the bureaucratic blockages resulting from overcentralized control, this tool may be inadequate. This was true in the case of German highway planning described by Garlichs and Hull (1978).

A common coordination tool, interlocking memberships in corporate boards (Burt, 1982; Mizruchi and Stearns, 1988) and on public agency governing commissions (Alexander, 1983) is in the grey area between formal and informal tools. On the one hand, such an appointment constitutes a formal role, which gives the incumbent access to the information and participation in the decision making responsibilities which are the essence of her coordinative functions. On the other hand, the board member's representative capacity as an official of another organization, which is the reason why he was appointed, is often only informally acknowledged.[14]

Formal coordination tools can be grouped under various headings. One set of formal coordination tools are structural coordination devices which include formalization and standardization of tasks. This can be done through standard operating procedures and routines, schedules, and blueprints (Hage, Aiken and Marrett, 1971).

Another type of coordination tool are linkage devices, such as interorganizational agreements and contracts which assign responsibilities or regulate resource exchanges (Gottfredson and White, 1981). Linkages in the area of anticipatory coordination can be achieved by joint planning (Scharpf et al. 1978) and joint budgeting (Honadle and Cooper, 1989). Other kinds of linkage devices are enacted to coordinate programs or services by creating programmatic interconnections. These include staff exchanges, collocation, joint or combined services delivery, "outstationing" of personnel, and mutual consultation (Tucker, 1980).

Program management devices (Rosenthal, 1984: 470–471) are another form of coordination tool, which can work in different ways. One way (which is essentially structural) is defining the scope and mission of the undertaking, and identifying the participating units' or organizations' relevant domains. This can be done through legislation, budget allocations, formal regulations including mandates and prohibitions, and interpreting regulations and participants' responses (for example, in reviewing program grantee's or grant applicants' assurances and plans).

Some of these tools effect coordination by manipulating what is "at the core of every network[:] ... a fiscal spine which flows from the ... treasury". They include grant allocation formulas, categorical grants, loan guarantees, insurance, subsidies, and tax incentives or deferments (Milward and Wamsley, 1985: 113). Essentially, these tools produce coordinated action as a result of resource exchange.

Another set of program management devices address the coordination of service delivery or project execution. These include procurement tools such as bid solicitations and requests for proposals, funding and reimbursement procedures, and technical assistance for or training of personnel involved in these activities.

They also include program control tools such as plan review and approval, licensing, contract terms, interpretation of regulations and discretionary waivers, audits, monitoring and evaluation. Program control also involves the threat or invocation of sanctions such as stopping funding, withholding future funding, or closing programs or facilities. Specification or participation to influence the selection of key personnel is another way of exercising program control (Rosenthal, 1984; Honadle and Cooper, 1989).

Some coordination tools can be described as information sharing devices or communication approaches (Jennings, 1994: 55). They can work in two ways. One way is in enhancing actors' appreciation of their mutual problems and interdependencies. The other is influencing their decisions and actions. Information sharing tools include some structural tools such as creating liaison roles, forming committees or task forces (in effect, forming coordination structures, as described later), and colocating activities or facilities. Others are processes such as organizing meetings, conferences and seminars.

Finally, coordination tools can involve joint action so as to influence participating organizations' behavior. Some joint action is in the area of anticipatory coordination linkages referred to above: joint planning or budgeting. Other tools are deployed in coordinating current activities: personnel loans or exchanges, joint training, and joint supervision (Honadle and Cooper, 1989: 1535–1536).

Summary

The question: IOC, where and how? can be answered from several perspectives. "Where" implies coordination *between* organizations; one way of defining "between" is to identify the relevant interorganizational network. This can be an "organization set" defined by the organizations' relation to a focal organization, or a functionally related network: an "action set" or one of its subtypes, a policy issue network, an advocacy coalition, or an "implementation set".

At the highest level of abstraction organizations are located in interorganizational fields. These have been characterized by their prevailing relationships: from laterally linked "feudal" fields where interaction between organizations is limited to mutual adjustment, to the "guided" field involving hierarchically structured relations between organizations.

Another classification divides interorganizational fields into "solidarity" (communalistic traditional or value-ideologically linked), market exchange, and hierarchy. Between the poles of hierarchy and market are various types of "collective-" or "mutual" organization, including joint ventures, consortia, alliances, associations, and federations. At the hierarchical pole is the single organization formed by merger or integration, and the corporate system. Another aspect of "between" is how organizations in a network are linked: what is the nature of their interdependence? Outcome interdependence is when results are the product of interdependent efforts; behavior interdependence is when activities themselves are interdependent (analogous to a game). Sequential and reciprocal interdependence are two forms of behavior interdependence. Outcome interdependence includes various kinds of "pooled" interdependence: competitive, symbiotic and commensual interdependence.

The symmetry of organizations' relationships produces "mutual" or "unilateral" dependency, each of which is associated with different kinds of IOC. Interdependencies may be distinguished on a time dimension too: "formative" interdependence exists before IOC or in the process of its development, "operating" interdependence occurs when IOC is in progress.

The "how" of IOC involves, among other things, IOC strategies and tools. A whole range of behaviors and relationships, from general and abstract (e.g., cooperation) to concrete and specific (e.g., contracting) have been called IOC strategies. Here we distinguish between strategies, as more general and abstract processes or relationships, and tools, defined as concrete and specific linkages and activities which can be "nested" in or used as part of one IOC strategy or another.

Coordination strategies may be dyadic or multilateral, and include proactive and reactive responses. Anticipatory coordination is coordination by plan; adaptive coordination involves monitoring, feedback, and control. Strategies may be cooperative or competitive. Cooperative strategies involve voluntary interaction which can be induced by bargaining and resource exchange or cooptation, for example. Informational strategies include influence and persuasion. Control strategies aim to bias organizations' decisions in a desired direction; they include financial incentives or sanctions, authoritative mandates, and structural approaches such as reorganization.

IOC tools are among policy instruments which can be put to various uses: inducements, capacity building, and system change. Informal coordinative mechanisms include interpersonal contacts and informal communication affected through meetings, telephone, and correspondence. Formal coordination tools may be structural (e.g., task standardization), linkage types or instruments such as colocation or contracts, or for program management.

Program management tools address structural management (e.g., by legislative mandate), fiscal control (e.g., budget allocations, grant formulas), and implementation (e.g., monitoring and evaluation, plan review and approval). Information sharing tools include meetings and workshops, while other tools involve joint action, such as staff exchange or joint planning.

NOTES

1. Interorganizational networks and their relevant characteristics are discussed extensively later; see Chapters 4 and 7, and the Appendix.

2. Compare with Grandori's (1987: 166–167) "Continuum of Organizational Forms", which uses an identical scale of relative hierarchy.

3. These are also discussed below under "IOC structures"; see pp. 47–75.

4. See pp. 258–263 below for a more detailed description of IOC in the Model Cities program.

5. It included 191 cases of IOC, based on General Accounting Office reports.

6. Alter and Hage's (1993) analysis of local social services networks, in which they implicitly associated types of interdependence with coordination strategies (see below) is an exception.

7. This is one of the reasons for the association between coordination and planning (Alexander, 1993: 328–329).

8. My term; Metcalfe's original article calls this: "dimensions of social integration".

9. The case of interlocking board memberships illustrates the complementarity and duality between strategy and process, on the one hand, and structure, on the other, which pervades the discussion of IOC. Gidden's (1979, 1984) Social Structuration Theory gives a well argued explanation of the relationship between structure and process-action. Here, we see interlocking board memberships as a manifestation both of process — the coordination strategy of cooperation through cooptation — and of structure: the coordination structure of informal linkages (see pp. 91–111 below). As a basic building block of strategy and structure, we are calling this a coordination tool (see pp. 40–43 below).

10. Competition as a coordination strategy offers more examples of process-structure interaction. Its structural aspects are the market or intentional market-like frameworks and the non-administered program as coordination structures (see pp. 227–235 and 249–252 below).

11. The structural counterpart of the merger strategy is the "single organization" coordination structure; see pp. 183–195 below.

12. See pp. 200–203 below for the kinds of interorganizational networks they defined. Their findings are stimulating and useful for these kinds of networks, and the extension of their normative recommendations to interorganizational networks in general (Alter and Hage, 1993: 259–297) is interesting, but unsupported by the empirical analysis.

13. The integrative framework presented below sorts out these ambiguities; see pp. 274–280.

14. When membership is formally considered a personal, not an organizational role attribute, the board member retains his position even when she resigns from or changes her organizational affiliation. This is often the case with corporate directorships and membership on public commissions.

CHAPTER 3

The Mechanics of Coordination:

IOC Structures

3.1. The Concept of Coordination Structures

Over twenty five years ago Littwak and Meyer (1966: 39–42) referred to "mechanisms of coordination" in a study of community social service organizations. Brickman, analyzing the coordination of national research and development policy, called them "coordination formats" (1979: 73–77). Grandori, in her overview of organization theory and organizational structures, identifies "coordination-systems" or "-schemes" (1987: 26–27). But, in the observation and analysis of IOC over the period covered here, these references have been few and far between.

Indeed, as the review in the previous chapter confirms, research and study of IOC have neglected what we might call the "mechanics" of coordination. Instead, attention has tended to focus either on the relatively abstract and general, or on the very concrete and particular. So, at the abstract end of the spectrum, scholars have invoked broad organization theories to explain IOC as an observed phenomenon, sociologists developed taxonomies of interorganizational fields, and theorists analyzing interorganizational behavior discussed general strategies of IOC.

At the other, concrete, pole of the continuum, we find lists of coordination tools as detailed, specific and realistic as contracting or budget signoff. Here is also the place of the extensive array of IOC cases which has been produced over the last two decades. These studies offer an invaluable source from which to learn from direct experience, but the richness and detail of the observed episode are limited to the single case or at most a narrow range of instances.

There is an explanation for this split focus. The study of IOC has evolved in two branches, recruited from separate disciplines, motivated by different concerns, and often speaking past each other in distinct languages. One branch is organization theory, where IOC received attention as a subset of interest in interorganizational relations and behavior. This branch is well represented by Rogers and Whetten (1982) and in Mulford's (1984) review.

The other branch is less systematically developed, and draws from the policy science, planning, public administration and implementation literatures. Other unwitting sources, especially for cases of IOC, are researchers and practitioners in the various applied sectors and professions: education for cases of IOC in reorganizing school districts, social work for analyses of coordinated case management, public health for studies of IOC in hospital consortia, or city management for cases of intermunicipal service delivery arrangements.

IOC theory in the first branch is descriptive and explanatory: it develops and verifies models of interorganizational behavior, classifies interorganizational fields and networks, and explains the emergence of IOC in general and the use of IOC strategies in particular.

Sometimes, organization theorists have drawn prescriptive implications from their work. Whetten and Bozeman (1991: 89–95) summarize some of these into four "Guidelines". But, like much prescriptive theory at this level of abstraction, their "Guidelines" offer little more direction than healthy common sense: "Identify internal needs for policy coordination", "identify a wide array of policy partners and seek linkage with (the) ... most compatible", "provide adequate support for ... coordination systems", "Anticipate and reduce ... negative side effects" and: "Recognize limits and set reasonable goals".

The second branch of IOC literature is more concerned with practice and action. It focuses on the concrete, specific, and particular, seeing

the task of interorganizational policy studies to identify: the objective need for specific types of IOC with reference to the requirements of a particular type of policy within the constraints of a particular decision structure; as well as the empirical factors facilitating or impeding necessary IOC in actual policy processes (Scharpf, 1978: 350).

This orientation sees IOC as something to be achieved, not just a phenomenon to be studied and analyzed. By implication, in this view, IOC becomes a matter of "the design of implementation systems and the linkage of policy goals to policy instruments" (Linder and Peters, 1987: 459). As McCann (1983: 178–181)) suggests in his analysis of IOC among Minnesota corrections agencies, the "structuring" of interactions between organizations is critical. Or, as Weiss concludes from her review of human service program coordination: "organizational arrangements ... is what coordination boils down to" (1981: 43).

This historical divergence has produced a gap at the intermediate level of analysis. At the abstract level, dealing with the interorganizational system as a whole, organization theory has provided us with a useful array of concepts and models. At the most concrete level of the basic unit of interaction, the individual in an organizational role, or the organizational unit, strategies, tools and cases offer the components of IOC. But no systematic attention has been devoted to the mechanics of coordination: how we describe the structures which transform the interaction of an interorganizational system so that coordinated decisions and actions ensue?

As a result of this gap "we lack a clear formulation of the range of possible (coordination) formats ... the development of criteria of evaluation in choosing one format over another, and an identification of the factors which condition the objectives, procedures and results of policy coordination in different settings" (Brickman, 1979: 73–74). Here, such a "range of possible coordination formats" is proposed; they will be called: coordination structures.

"A great variety of coordination structures ... are conceivable and do exist", Schleicher (1985: 512) noted in his study of institutional frameworks for water pollution abatement. His definition suggests that "A *coordination structure* ... is a structure where the decision centers are linked by one or several coordinating mechanisms."[1] For our purposes, a coordination structure is the form of the coordinating mechanism linking the decision centers in an organization or of the relevant organizations in an interorganizational system.

Coordination structures exist at various levels. They can be found within the organization: the interdepartmental liaison, the project coordinator, or the task force. These are what Mintzberg (1979: 161–175) called "liaison devices" in his review of coordination within organizations. At a higher level, but still within the single organization, alternative ways of structuring the organization itself are essentially coordination structures: the hierarchy of traditional management and control, the matrix form of organization, the divisionalized organization, or the holding corporation (Galbraith, 1977: 112–172).

Since the focus here is on coordination *between* organizations, not coordination *within* organizations, we will not pursue the discussion of these intraorganizational coordination structures.[2] As we proceed, however, you will notice some overlap between intraorganizational and interorganizational coordination structures. This is due to the fuzziness of the concept of organization itself.

In fact, the boundary defining the organization is quite subjective. For small, simple organizations their formal components are easily defined: there are few doubts about what is or is not part of a household, a city agency, or a small firm. But as organizations grow in size and complexity, their identity becomes more a matter of analytical convenience than empirical reality.

In a multidivisional conglomerate such as Philips or General Dynamics the relevant organization, depending on the frame of reference, can be the organization as a whole, or its functional units and subunits interacting as an interorganizational system. Looking at a complex, multilevel government bureaucracy, for example the U.S. Department of Defence, we can define the organization as the total agency (as represented in pronouncements such as "The Pentagon responded negatively to"), or decompose it in more detailed models of its component elements, right down to viewing its competing units and bureaus as virtually separate organizations and the agency as essentially an interorganizational system.[3]

Defining organizational affiliation or membership also becomes more arbitrary with organizations of greater scope and complexity. The family- or owner-managed firm presents few problems, but are the shareholders in a giant corporation, its franchise holders, or its customers part of the organization? To what extent is a Congressional oversight committee or a beneficiaries' lobby organization an integral part of a public agency? For example, are the Senate Veterans' Affairs Committee and the "Veterans of Foreign Wars" "stakeholders"[4] in the Federal Veterans' Administration, or do these together make up an interorganizational system?

None of these questions has a correct answer; the answer depends on the point of view that is most useful for addressing the problem at hand. This is why we will find some coordination structures (for example, the hierarchical organization, or the holding corporation) which are at the same time intraorganizational, and IOC structures, depending on the frame of reference. Here, however, they will be discussed in their interorganizational aspect only.

Coordination structures, as a concept, can serve two purposes. One is as an integrating framework for research and analysis of IOC. The use of coordination structures, for example, to cluster case analyses and evaluations of IOC in practice, can show the results of using different coordination structures in various settings. To the extent that such research provides data on the relative success of these efforts, this framework could also yield some contingent conclusions about the relative effectiveness of these coordination structures in different contexts.[5]

The other purpose of coordination structures is to offer a repertoire of possible formats for the structural aspect of implementing policies, programs and plans: institutional design (Brandl, 1988; Bolan, 1991; Alexander, 1993). Organizational design, which is institutional design in its intraorganizational aspect in the private sector, is already a recognized field of research, and a well developed area of management and executive training (Galbraith, 1977; Rummler, 1990: 169–186; Mintzberg and Quinn, 1991: 330–350). The place of institutional design in effecting IOC is less well appreciated.

Coordination among organizations demands institutional design under a variety of circumstances (though it is rarely described in these terms). In organizations and interorganizational systems seeking to adapt themselves to changes in their environments, one of the most frequent adaptations is structural change. Deliberate structural change in an organization or an interorganizational system demands institutional design.

It is easy to cite cases of institutional design involved in such structural adaptations. The emergence of hospital chains and consortia in the U.S., and, in extreme cases, hospital mergers in response to level or declining demand and increased competition (Arnold, 1991), is one example. The creation of trade associations (e.g., the Tobacco Institute) to represent an economic sector in an increasingly regulated environment is another. The design of regional institutions as a vehicle for transnational coordination in the face of increasing globalization of economic activity — the EC, NAFTA, and others on the drawing boards, is one more.

Some institutional design involves structural change, not to adapt to a changing environment, but to change the environment itself. The deliberate break up of AT&T ("Ma Bell") and the design of its successor corporations, in order to stimulate competition in telecommunications, is a case in point. The creation of artificial markets is another. One example of this is the legislation of "pollution points" in the context of U.S. environmental regulation. Another is the proposal for "managed competition" which is part of the health care system reforms presented by the Clinton administration.

Institutional design is also part of the planning and implementation of every new undertaking of any complexity. When a new project or program is launched in an existing organization or planned to be carried out by an interorganizational system or "implementation set", the policy or program plan will include an element of institutional design. The plan must identify the appropriate existing organizations, organizational units, and individual roles that will be involved in the undertaking, and specify how the new enterprise will restructure their interactions and relationships. Often, such restructuring will include defining new roles and functions, or creating new organizations or organizational units. All these are aspects of institutional design.

IOC is even more dependent on institutional design than coordination within organizations, because preexisting interorganizational coordinating structures are rare. While the existence of an organization in itself provides some internal coordinating structure, in many projects which involve multiple organizations and demand IOC this is not the case: there are no formal channels to manage the interdependencies involved in their mutual interaction. In these situations institutional design: the specification of the coordination structure necessary for the project's implementation, coincides with the planning of the undertaking itself.

The set of coordination structures presented below can serve as a menu of "ideal types" from which to select, or to combine appropriate features of several structures, in planning or modifying the interorganizational structure of policies, programs or projects involving several or many organizations. These coordination structures, then, are like the orders of an architecture of institutional design.

3.2. Coordination Structures: From Solidarity to Hierarchy

Coordination structures exist in organizations and in interorganizational systems. In the interorganizational area, on which our discussion is focused, coordination structures can also be identified at several levels. At the highest level, which embraces the interorganizational field as a whole, are what I call "meta-structures". These structures define the basic characteristics of interorganizational interaction in their fields, from the market characterized by spontaneous mutual adjustment to the organization with its hierarchical central control.

The next level, covering a particular interorganizational system, "action set" or "implementation set" of organizations, is where the "meso-structures" are. Meso-coordination structures are essentially the various forms in which interorganizational systems are linked for IOC. They cover a wide range, from the informal network in the market context, through various types of "action sets" and mutual associations such as joint ventures and federations, to more formally linked "implementation sets" of organizations in mandated frameworks, and single organizations of various forms, from the loosely linked conglomerate to the unitary organization.[6]

The lowest level includes "micro-structures" that are devices for linking intra- or interorganizational decision centers. These exist within and in conjunction with higher level coordination structures. They include informal links, the interorganizational group, the bilateral liaison or boundary spanning role, the multiunit coordinator and the coordinating unit.

Though necessarily displayed as a three-part scale on the vertical axis of Figure 1 below, this dimension showing levels of organizational inclusiveness and abstraction is of course a continuum. In reality, the various coordination structures are not necessarily as neatly arrayed on this continuum as they are shown.[7] The essential aspect of the different positions of coordination structures on this dimension is that lower-level structures can be part of, or "nested" in higher-level structures, but not the reverse.

In this way, a joint venture might be a form of "action set" in a market framework, expressed in an agreement between the participating organizations, and it might be managed by a jointly appointed coordinator,[8] or by a member of each firm's staff acting as liaison with the other corporation.

Another form an "action set" might take could be a federation, governed by a board: an interorganizational group made up of representatives of the member organizations. The coordination and implementation of a non-administered program might be entrusted to a lead organization, which itself could make use of interorganizational groups (e.g., interagency committees or task forces) and coordinating units.[9] Another important characteristic distinguishing between coordination structures is their degree of hierarchy. The dimension of hierarchy informs much of the discussion of coordination in organizations and interorganizational systems. It is a major concern of transaction cost theory, which was touched upon above as one of the ways of accounting for IOC, and to which we will return.

In the first systematic analysis of coordination, Lindblom arrayed coordination processes on a continuum of increasing hierarchy, from the one pole of mutual adjustment in the classic market through "mixed systems" to the other extreme of central coordination in an organized hierarchy (1965: 25–28). Mintzberg does the same in his review of coordination in organizations, presenting a set of horizontal coordination mechanisms ranging from mutual adjustment to direct supervision and control (1979: 197–198). A set of organizational coordination models, displayed on the dimension of their relative hierarchy, is presented by Grandori (1987: 145–177) in her synthesis of organization theory.

This simple continuum of increasing hierarchy, however, between the pure market and the formal unitary organization, is not enough to array the real diversity of organizational and interorganizational structures. Markets are distinguished from hierarchies by the difference in their medium of interaction and form of control: market transactions are exchanges based on price; relations in hierarchies are structured by authority and based on command and control.

But the assumption that these are all-embracing and mutually exclusive has been questioned, and it is recognized today that there are forms of organization that exist along with markets and hierarchies. In fact, there are three control mechanisms that govern transactions, and real-life organizations and interorganizational systems usually combine them in various ways. Simply put, these mechanisms are: price, authority and trust.

Transaction cost theory accounts for substitution between price and authority as transaction controls, and explains the transformation of organizations between hierarchies and markets. But there are also situations in which the social context of transactions provides an alternative form of control. When norms of mutual obligation and cooperation limit opportunism, mutual trust can be just as or more effective than price or authority. Such norms exist in settings with ongoing reciprocal relations, based on association (such as kinship, shared ethnicity, culture, educational or professional background) or solidarity: common ideologies, values, or goals (Bradach and Eccles, 1992).

The markets and hierarchies we know can be supplemented with numerous cases of interactions based on trust. These range from the Japanese blending of social and cultural norms with business relations, through the kinship links in family businesses and political dynasties, to the trust-based interpersonal links in networks such as small construction contractors and subcontractors.

IOC structures, organizations, and interorganizational systems, then, can be identified as being hierarchical (command based on authority), market (exchange based on price) or solidarity-association

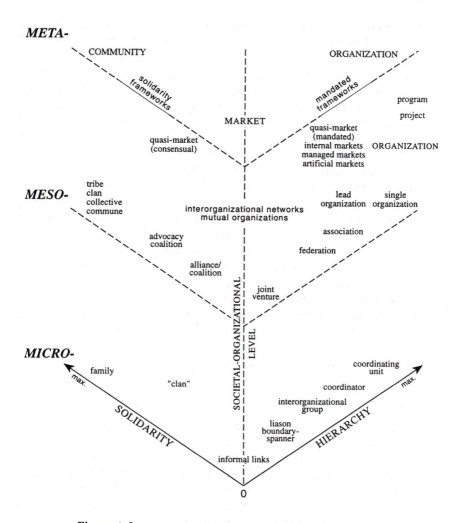

Figure 1. Interorganizational coordination structures.

(consensus/agreement based on trust). In this fashion, describing institutional arrangements for IOC, Hegner (1985: 415–423) classifies them into market exchange, solidarity, and hierarchical systems. A similar terminology, describing coordinating structures as markets, hierarchies, or clans, is the basis for Durant's (1992) analysis of the Bureau of Land management's implementation of national resource management policy.

In Figure 1 the horizontal position of each coordination structure expresses its relative degree of hierarchy or solidarity. The "perfect" market, which is non-hierarchical and non-solidarity by definition, and is controlled purely by price, is at the zero-point of each range. We can envisage a continuum, then, with the centralized unitary organization at the extreme of hierarchy, and the organic community at the pole of maximum solidarity, and with the perfect market in its center.

This diagram is a simplification of reality, of course. But its form is useful for discussing IOC structures, because IOC structures do not occur in the market, which is an IOC structure in itself. If our focus were organizations, we might have to show this as a three-dimensional space, with hierarchy, solidarity-association, and market as separate axes, to reflect how organizations can base their transactions on various mixtures of price, authority, and trust.

Not reflected in the figure is the fact that lower-level coordination structures can be, and are, associated with some of the higher-level structures (as the examples above suggest). The relative horizontal location of a coordination structure does not necessarily express any closer link to the structures directly above or below it, but only the fact that they share a similar degree of hierarchy or solidarity relative to the other coordination structures.

Meta-Coordination Structures

At the "meta"-level, we find coordination structures varying in their character as we move up the scale of relative hierarchy. At the non-hierarchical end of the scale, the basis for interorganizational links is totally voluntary. Even though their interaction may be the result of some interdependence which leaves the actors with few other options, it is the result of free decisions by the organizations themselves, and not imposed by any external agency.

At this pole are located markets, where coordination is purely through mutual adjustment, and the principal, if not exclusive, medium of interaction is resource exchange.[10] In the opposite direction from the hierarchy dimension are the "solidarity" frameworks which lack any hierarchy as well: essentially various forms of community. These include the family, the tribe, and the "clan" (Hegner, 1985: 415–423). In these, concerted decisions and actions are not the result of resource exchange; rather, they are the expression of shared values.

As we move up on the scale of increasing hierarchy, the basis for interaction changes. "Mutual associations" may still be formed on the basis of shared interests and resource exchange. But once they exist they may themselves impose an agreed upon framework of decision rules which are the fruit of past organizational interactions or institutional design, and which have an authority of their own.

Finally, mandated frameworks for interaction occupy the hierarchical end of the scale. Such frameworks, including existing hierarchical organizations, may be the residue of past history. Or they may be created by some external agency as a way of coordinating diverse organizations to achieve some common purpose. Here, authority becomes an important stimulus for action and interaction,[11] though, as we shall see, it usually needs to be supplemented by other media as well: resources, and shared goals and values.

The "Perfect" Market

As described by classic economists, the "perfect" economic market, links producers and sellers of goods and services, consisting of small factories, firms and businesses, with intermediate buyers and ultimate consumers made up of individuals and households, through the media of supply, demand, and price. Each societal unit here is an independent self-interested actor.

The "perfect" political market, too, links independent self-interested actors, made up of organizations, interest groups, legislators, government agencies, political parties and individual voters. In this "market" policy emerges by a process of bargaining and exchange of political resources, analogous to the adjustments of supply, demand, and price in the economic market (Braybrooke and Lindblom, 1963; Ilchman and Uphoff, 1969).

In both these arenas, the market is the perfect coordinating structure.[12] Unlike all the other coordinating structures, this one needs no formal links between its member organizations: coordinated decisions are the systemic result of partisan mutual adjustment of each unit in the market to its perceived environment (Lindblom, 1965).

"Solidarity" Frameworks

Markets have been considered the "classic" coordinating meta-structure in modern society, but there is a growing realization that market coordination is by no means universal. The "solidarity" frameworks which complemented the hierarchies of traditional societies are a coordinating structure which is still widespread and important.

In the solidarity framework, coordination is the result of a sense of mutual obligation among its participating units (Hegner, 1985: 411–423). This may be the product of any or all of several factors: shared beliefs or values, common affiliation, and long-term reciprocal interaction. The family, clan, and tribe are the traditional forms of societal organization which are examples of solidarity-based coordination, but the family is still universal, and clans and tribes remain common in some societies today.

Solidarity frameworks are not limited to these, however. *"Clans"* are found in modern organizations: work groups linked by common professional values and ongoing creative participation in shared tasks (Ouchi, 1980). Some have suggested that such "clans" are the most effective, and perhaps the only way of coordinating highly complex technical undertakings, for example: research and development in computer hardware and software.

Another form of "clan"-like coordination based on common affiliation, and shared values that are the product of often intense socialization is the role of *professionals* in organizations. This is also a frequent basis for intra- and interorganizational coordination in complex organizations and interorganizational systems (Hage and Aiken, 1970), sometimes playing a critical part in professionalized fields such as health care, education, and human services.

Solidarity based coordination can also take the form of a *"collegium"*: a peer-group sharing disciplinary or professional values. Examples are academic governance, law courts, professional and scientific peer review, and professional organizations (Majone, 1985). In the collegium, decisions are not concerted by mutual adjustment as in markets, or by authoritarian fiat, as in hierarchies. Rather, consensus is the result of shared values, and debate (e.g., disagreements between scientific experts) or conflict takes place within a mutually accepted framework of discourse.

Finally, solidarity is often the basis for *"advocacy coalitions"* in many current societies. In spite of prevailing cynicism which attributes most political alliances to self-interested exchange in the political market, common ideology and shared values are the motivating forces behind some of the most prominent coalitions today.

The "Greens" in Europe, based on shared concern for ecology and the environment, and the "Pro-Life" and "Pro-Choice" movements in the U.S.A., mobilized around opposing values on the question of abortion, are examples. Another form of solidarity, combining shared values and common affiliation (almost a larger kind of "family"), has generated movements such as the anti-AIDS coalition in the U.S., associations of homosexual and lesbian organizations, and the feminist movement.

"Market-Like" Frameworks

The "perfect" market exists (even if only as an "ideal type"). Where it does not, or where it has been modified in response to the absence of one or more of its prerequisites, market-like frameworks can be deliberately created. In other words, a set of rules and norms of behavior can be agreed upon or prescribed which will provide incentives or constraints that coordinate organizations' decisions and actions through market-like exchange.

Ostrom (1990) has specified one basis for such market-like arrangements, describing the commonality to which they can be applied as a "common resource pool": a group of households, producers, firms or organizations with a mutual interest in finding a rational way to allocate a common resource. Such "common resource pools" are one basis for developing a consensual framework (see below), i.e., a mutually agreed upon set of decision and action rules. These rules may set up a *quasi-market*, when they ration the relevant resource through a process of market-like exchange. Examples of institutional design of such market-like frameworks include the "auctioning" of fishing areas in Philippine fishing villages, and the allocation of water rights in Southern Californian Water Districts.

Such quasi-markets as coordinating structures are created in mandated frameworks (see below) too, where they are becoming increasingly widespread. Examples include Transferable Development Rights in the area of land development control (as a substitute for rigid regulation by zoning), and the system of exchangeable Pollution Points in the arena of environmental regulation.

Mandated Frameworks

Unlike the voluntary basis for coordination on which markets and quasi-market frameworks are premised, mandated frameworks require coordination on the basis of some externally imposed authority. This may be the historical result of previous voluntary agreement: essentially a consensual framework expressed in a set of decision and action rules that is now binding on the participants. Or it may be an existing or new framework created through some external process reflecting a societal consensus or goal: legislation, regulation, or reorganization.

Mandated frameworks may themselves include *market-like coordination*, as in some of the examples above, where the option of exchanges in a market of notional resources is made available within the mandated frameworks of land development control and environmental regulation. Other forms of mandated frameworks are responses to mixed transaction types which demand modifications in market type interactions (Williamson, 1971, 1975).

One type is *bilateral government*: legal or regulatory structures controlling the interactions of two types of interested parties. Examples are labor law, landlord-tenant law, and corporate law. Another type is *relational contracting*, where contractual frameworks are set up for classes of parties, instead of for pairs of individual actors as in the "perfect" market. Industry-wide bargaining between management and labor is an example. Finally, transaction costs, but also externalities and other market flaws are the incentives for societally mandated frameworks of *comprehensive regulation* covering broad areas, such as land use regulation and development control, environmental regulation, and health and sanitary regulations.

All these mandated frameworks produce coordinated action primarily by providing a legitimized set of rules or norms to govern specific types of resource exchange. Resource allocation is the incentive for coordinated action in another type of mandated framework: the categorical grant program, which is a type of non-administered program.

In the *non-administered program* the decisions of the units making up the relevant action set are concerted indirectly, rather than by direct planning, monitoring and control. This is done by invoking an appropriate set of stimuli: incentives or sanctions (Levine, 1972). The U.S. Bureau of Inland Revenue's collection of the income tax with its self-administered tax assessment is a successful example, building on the incentive of conforming to prevailing social norms, backed up by legal sanctions for noncompliance. In categorical grant programs the prospect of funding is the incentive that biases the decisions of prospective participating organizations.

However, the "pure" non-administered program is rare. It has to be supplemented by other administrative apparatus and other coordination structures to ensure its effective execution (Williams, 1975: 541–542). Program implementation requires regulations and some monitoring of compliance (Rabinowitz, Pressman and Rein, 1976). Without effective authority and the willingness to use it, or adequate resources as incentives, success is unlikely, as demonstrated by the failure of several federal programs of this kind (Williams, 1980).

More direct coordination is involved in the *program* or *project*, a mandated framework which is often the molar unit of coordinating the implementation of public policy (Wildavsky, 1979; Milward, 1991: 65–68). Throughout its evolution and implementation the program is the common integrating framework for an interorganizational network. In anticipation the program generates a "policy-issue network" (Kirst, Meister, and Rowley, 1984) or a "policy advocacy coalition" (Sabatier, 1988); in its existence the program is the basis for coordinating the organizations making up its "implementation set" (Hjern and Porter, 1981).

In an example of the way in which coordination structures defy neat classification, the program or project is also found as an integrating coordination structure at a much lower level: within single organizations. In private sector organizations, for instance, the program or project may be the framework for alternative lines of information flow and control, supplementing the functional organizational hierarchy in a "matrix" form of organization (Galbraith and Kazanjian, 1986).

Finally, we can regard the hierarchical *organization* itself as the ultimate "meta"-structure.[13] In terms of coordinating the actions of its subunits, transaction cost theory explains the rationale for the organization by juxtaposing its hierarchy to the market. In terms of IOC it may be paradoxical, however, to call a single organization a coordination structure.

But this only seems anomalous if we forget that we are dealing with dynamic, not static systems. Thus, single organizations may be created to, in effect, ensure IOC by eliminating the gap between organizations. In the arena of regional coordination Derthick (1974: 195–206) recognized this, as did Pfeffer (1976) in his account of corporate mergers. Single organizations may be formed to coordinate the actions of similar units, or to internalize the interdependence of previously separate complementary agencies (Hult, 1987).

"Meso"-Coordination Structures

The "action set" is any group of organizations which is interacting to accomplish some common purpose or to acquire some mutually beneficial rewards (Aldrich, 1979). At the lowest level of hierarchy the coordination structure of such an action set would be an *informal network*.

Informal interorganizational networks may be one channel for effecting mutual adjustment in economic and political markets: interlocking board memberships are one manifestation. In the private sector they are well documented (Burt, 1982; Mizruchi and Stearns, 1988). In the public sector there has been less research, but they are an important coordination link nevertheless, as shown in various social services (Warren, Bergunder and Rose, 1974; Hall et al., 1977; Alexander, 1983).

The informal network often supplements other coordination structures, in the ubiquitous meshing of informal and formal organizational networks (Katz and Kahn, 1966: 80–81). As the sole channel for concerting decisions between organizations, informal networks appear to be limited to the lowest level of interaction. Higher interdependence and more acute awareness of mutual interests and concerns should elicit more formal and hierarchical coordinative structures.[14]

With the formalizing of interorganizational links more hierarchical coordination structures appear. These can all be subsumed under the *"mutual organization"*, a coordination structure intermediate between hierarchy and market (Koenig and Thietart, 1988). They include *joint ventures, cartels, associations and federations* (Pfeffer and Salancik, 1978), and as variations on these the *consortium* and *corporate system* or "empire" (Evans and Klemm, 1980; Lehman, 1975).

Another blanket term that has been used for these coordination structures is interorganizational *networks*. Alter and Hage define them as "clusters of organizations that ... are non-hierarchical collectives of legally separate units" (1993: 46). This is true of some kinds of networks; other networks do have more hierarchical linkages through other coordination structures.[15]

Among the former are *policy networks* (Marin and Maynz, 1992), which describe systems of agencies and organizations interacting in a given policy domain. For example, around the issue of strip mining reclamation, there is a policy network which consists of coal producers, the Environmental Protection Agency, congressional committees, environmental advocacy organizations, local governments in coal producing areas etc. All these organizations interact in informal and formal arenas such as congressional hearings on pending legislation, comments on proposed regulations, and regulatory implementation and enforcement. Such a policy network can be a more or less structured mixture of bureaucracy, market, solidarity associations or corporate organizations, combining formal and informal linkages (Kenis and Schneider, 1992).

To describe interorganizational networks Alter and Hage (1993: 44–80) identify several relevant dimensions. One kind of network may consist of organizations competing in the same sector ("competitive cooperation"), for example a trade association or a research and development consortium. Another may be based on symbiotic linkages between organizations with complementary functions or technologies, such as joint ventures or client referral networks of social service agencies.

Their typology also distinguishes between networks by the extent of their cooperation, from limited (information and resource exchange, or interpersonal relations) through moderate cooperation aimed at technical, economic, or political objectives, to broad, which includes joint manufacturing ventures and marketing cartels. Networks are also divided between ones with promotional linkages, involving the pursuit of common interests or objectives, and those with productional linkages.

Finally, networks can be differentiated by their extent, between small ones linking two or at most three organizations, and larger multiorganizational networks. In this fashion a purchasing and procurement network can be described as promotional competitive cooperation, involving limited cooperation, while a research consortium or trade association would also be promotional competitive cooperation, but with moderate cooperation. An interagency client referral network, the interlocking directorates of many U.S. corporations, and the even more closely linked Japanese *zaibatsu* and *kairetsu* are all obligational symbiotic networks with limited cooperation.

Under mandated frameworks we find the "meso"-coordination structure which I have called the *lead organization* (Alexander, 1991: 218–219). This term (adapted from the American expression "lead agency" used in the public sector) refers to the arrangement in which one organization is charged with, or assumes the responsibility of coordinating the other organizations in the network. The lead organization's special status may be the result of the problem or issue being more in its domain than in the others', or of its superior power, or both. Besides its coordination tasks, the lead organization has functional responsibilities as well, otherwise it would be a coordinating unit (see below).

In the private sector this arrangement is common.[16] In construction, for example, or in various types of production such as aerospace and shipbuilding the principal contractor is, in effect, the lead organization. As such, Crane Construction will be responsible for casting a building's foundations and erecting its frame, and at the same time coordinate the activities of its subcontractors for electrical, plumbing, heating and environmental controls, wall cladding, roofing etc. Similarly Litton Industries coordinates the construction of U.S. navy destroyers in its shipyards, and Boeing organizes the production of its 747s.

In the public sector, too, this coordination structure is often used, and examples are numerous. Public policies and programs coordinated by lead organizations are found in almost every sector, from infrastructure (e.g., freeway planning and construction), housing and neighborhood revitalization (for example, the U.S. Model Cities Program), to civil defense and human services. In many cases, both in the public and private sectors, this meso-structure is used in combination with a variety of micro-structures (see below).

"Micro" Coordination Structures

We can regard *informal linkages* as the micro-level manifestation of the informal network at the macro- or meso-level. Various kinds of interactions can sustain an informal network, from interpersonal contacts through meetings, telephone calls, or correspondence, information sharing (circulating data, sharing mailing lists), overlapping board memberships, to ad-hoc issue related meetings between representatives of affected organizations. Such meetings, if routinized over time, may span the gap between this coordination structure and another, more formal one: the interorganizational group (see below).

The first expression of any formalization of linkages, usually dyadic ones, is the assigned role of *liaison* or *boundary spanner* to concert decisions and actions between a pair of interacting units or organizations (Aldrich and Herker, 1977; Tushman, 1977; Friedman and Podolny, 1992). The distinctive attribute of the liaison or boundary-spanner is that she is at home in one unit or organization, and is entrusted with the task of affecting the decisions of another. It is in this respect that this coordination structure differs from the coordinator (see below) who is more independent of the multilateral network of units or organizations he coordinates.

A little higher on the scale of hierarchy is the *interorganizational group*. The interorganizational group may come into existence through the routinization of informal contacts such as ad-hoc meetings, or it may be the product of deliberate institutional design responding to a perceived common problem or interdependence. Such a group may be called a board, commission, coordinating committee, steering committee, or task force. Interorganizational groups undertake the whole gamut of coordination tasks, at all levels of organization and in every sector of society.

The "pure" interorganizational group consists of people who are totally identified with their organizational affiliations, and is low on autonomy and persistence. It has no identifiable "place" or budget, and no staff: it is serviced by one or more of its member organizations. Few interorganizational groups are this ideal type: most occupy intermediate points on the continuum of autonomy (Lehman, 1975: 83–95) where the higher part of the spectrum merges into the coordinating unit (see below).

Interorganizational groups can be powerful, like Britain's Public Expenditure Survey Committee (Heclo and Wildavsky, 1974), or limited, like the U.S. Interagency Federal Regional Councils (Derthick, 1974: 197–202), depending on their authority and resources. In the planning arena they are common in all sectors. In physical planning and development control they are legion, from Israel's National Planning Council and the Netherlands' interagency steering committees at the national level, through the U.S.Regional Planning Commissions, the Regional Strategy Teams in the U.K. and Israel's District Planning Commissions at the regional level, to the local Planning Commissions which are almost everywhere. U.S. health planning involved interorganizational groups in rate-setting at the State level, and IOC at the regional level. Interagency planning task forces are common in almost every sector of national bureaucracies.

Higher on the hierarchy scale is the *coordinator*: an individual whose formal function is to coordinate the activities of organizational units or an interorganizational system with respect to a given task, issue, objective, program or project. In the complex private sector organizations he reviews, Mintzberg calls this an "integrating manager" (1979: 165–168); in construction, aerospace, and similar industries this role is called a project manager.

This structure is often used in conjunction with other coordination structures. An example is the federal member of interstate regional commissions in the U.S., whose special task was to coordinate between the region and the federal bureaucracy (Derthick, 1974: 65–72). The independent coordinator acting alone, unattached to any coordinating unit, and unsupported by any other coordination structure, is rare. Examples are the Coordinator of Government Activities in the Galilee in Israel, and the coordinator of some of the General Improvement Area projects in the U.K. (Alexander, 1990). Human services programs frequently use coordinators, for example for case assignment among agencies in a network, or for integrated case management (Polivka et al., 1981).

When the individual role of the coordinator is expanded into an organizational subunit or a whole organization, we have another coordination structure: the *coordinating unit*. Trist (1983) calls this a "referent organization" in his description of the N.E. Energy Corporation, a coordinating unit set up to address energy supply and allocation problems.

The coordinating unit is distinguished from the interorganizational group by its greater autonomy: it will have its own budget and staff. But, in contrast to the lead organization, the coordinating unit does not have any "line" functions, and in contrast to the single organization, it does not implement any of the tasks it is charged with coordinating.

Its restriction to coordinating functions does not mean that this unit is powerless. An example of a powerful coordinating unit is the U.S. Office of Management and Budget (OMB). Coordinating units exist in many organizations and interorganizational systems, though they are not always labelled as such. A common example in the private sector is the "project office" in the construction or manufacturing sectors, e.g., aerospace (Wren, 1967).

In the public sector coordination is often effected through fiscal policy and planning, and coordinating units are found in this area. Organizations like the OMB at the U.S. federal level are found in most countries, and at all levels of government. Planning-type coordinating units are widespread as "staff" agencies linked to a government's or agency's chief executive, or as local or regional government planning agencies, in fields ranging from transportation, through land use, environmental regulation, to human services.

Milward (1982) calls this coordination structure a "federative organization", while Schleicher (1985) calls it a "coordination structure" in his review of water pollution abatement agencies. While more autonomous, by definition, than the interorganizational group, coordinating units themselves vary on a continuum of autonomy, and research and experience suggest that a balance of authority and resources are essential for a coordinating unit's success (Lehman, 1975; Alexander, 1992).

3.3. A Structuration Theory of IOC

Now that coordination structures have been described, we can address some related questions: What purpose do IOC structures serve? Why are IOC structures formed, and how do they come into existence? The answer to the first question may seem obvious: the purpose of

IOC structures is to coordinate. But why, in fact, is IOC necessary at all, and why are IOC structures needed?

IOC is the process of concerting the decisions and actions of several — sometimes many — organizations, for a purpose or undertaking that could not be accomplished by any one organization acting alone. This also explains the need for IOC, which arises in situations demanding concerted action for the mutual purposes of the organizations involved.

While this definition has a hint of deliberateness, intentionality is not intrinsic to IOC. However, it may seem as if organizations' mutual adjustment in "perfect" markets is not included under IOC as defined here. This apparent contradiction (based on the absence of any evident common purpose for the separate organizations in the market) is resolved if we view the market as an interorganizational system. Then the mutual purpose of the actors in the market becomes clear: the exchange of goods and services, which, indeed, is impossible for any of them by itself.

The term "mutual purpose" is deliberately used to cover two different types of situations. One is the existence of a common purpose: a task, a goal, or a set of objectives which the organizations in the interorganizational system or "action set" agree that they want to accomplish together or which is mandated by an external authority.

An example of such a situation is a joint enterprise for marketing between a specialty paper manufacturer and a firm which has developed a color printing technology particularly matched to that paper. Another would be the coordination through a trade association of lobbying efforts of chemical corporations manufacturing pesticides, for the common purpose of relaxing the regulative environment. A group of local social service agencies coordinating their programs through membership on the advisory board of their common funding agency is a case of a mutual purpose mandated by external authority: the federal funding agency's demand to coordinate for more effective service delivery.

The other situation is when the participating organizations agree that some of the particular goals of each is more effectively accomplished by interacting in the relevant interorganizational system. The investor buys shares, for example, to serve his particular purpose of making a profit. But he uses this market (and, in doing so, participates in the process of mutual adjustment and market coordination that makes up the Stock Exchange) rather than buying real estate or stashing gold bullion away in his safe deposit box, because this is the best way he knows of making a profit. Similarly, the petroleum producing countries formed OPEC to coordinate their production levels and marketing, first and foremost so that each could maximize its income, not for an agreed common goal.[17]

IOC, then, is needed when several organizations have to interact to accomplish their mutual purposes. As we have seen, this interaction turns them from isolated and independent units into an interorganizational system, an "action set" or "implementation set" of organizations. But why, in fact, do these organizations have to interact? What is the basis for the interorganizational system which is addressing the organizations' mutual purposes?

The answer to this question is: interdependence. The fact that none of the participating organizations can accomplish its relevant objectives without the others is the result of interdependence between these organizations. Interdependence, perceived and real, is the basis for every case of IOC.

The Stock Exchange is the result of interdependence between investors: the prospective buyer of shares cannot buy without interaction with potential sellers. The trade association is the result of interdependence between the firms in the industry. Even while they are competitors in the same market, each of them needs the others to mount an effective lobbying effort in Congress and the regulatory agencies. The joint marketing venture is the result of interdependence between the producers, each bringing complementary resources (one, the specialty paper, the other, the printing technology) to the enterprise.

A public-private partnership to develop a downtown shopping mall is the result of interdependence between the partners: the city wants to stimulate development to revitalize its downtown, and to enhance its declining tax base, but needs the resources of the private corporate partners to do so. The corporate partners' mutual goals are to reverse the decline in value of their downtown real estate, but they need the city's legal authority and access to public borrowing.

The social services agencies participating in the coordinating committee are doing so because they need each others' referrals for clients, and their cases require the other programs' complementary services. They could ignore this, but at their own risk, because their interdependence has been asserted by the federal agency that is their common source of funds. The countries in OPEC had to cooperate to manage world petroleum prices in their common interest: without creating this cartel which agreed on production quotas to limit total output, no single producer could charge the price that would maximize his revenue.

In §2.2 above we reviewed the various types of interdependence that exist. They range from sequential interdependence, through reciprocal interdependence (the producers in the joint venture are an example), to various kinds of pooled interdependence. Among these, the relationship between the city and corporate partners in the downtown development public-private partnership is a case of symbiotic interdependence, while the local social service agencies are linked by reciprocal interdependence (client referral and program services) and commensal interdependence (their common funding source). The Stock Exchange, OPEC and the trade association are all cases of "mutual interdependence", where no organization in the interorganizational system can accomplish its purposes without the coordinated action of the entire "action set".

Why does IOC need coordination structures, and how do they come into being? To answer these questions, it is useful to regard IOC structures as a particular form of social structure, and to explain coordination structures through a theory that accounts for social structures in general. This is Anthony Giddens' (1984) "Structuration Theory".

A social structure is an organized set of rules and resources or transformation relations that is a property of the social system of which it is a part (1984: 25). The social structure is "recursively organized", meaning that it has to be formed and continually reconstituted through the period of its existence. Social structures enable and (or) constrain behavior, action and interaction. Social structures are not concrete or material: no one can see or feel them, but they are "virtual" entities that persist over time: everyone knows they are there, and can agree on what they are.

Such social structures, of course, exist everywhere, and at all levels of society: the family, the tribe, the firm, organizations, governments, nations, and transnational associations. Even the weekly poker game is a social structure: its rules (who belongs and who does not, meeting every Thursday night at Flaherty's Bar, one dollar "chip" and a $50 limit) and resources (everyone contributes the price of a round of beer) enable and constrain action and interaction. They enable the members to play poker together, and constrain them from playing anything else (no basketball, or even bridge or canasta) or staying home and watching TV.

Just as families, organizations, or governments are different forms of social structures, IOC structures are another kind of social structure. Like all social structures, they consist of a system of enabling or constraining rules and resources which are recognizable over a period of time. The "perfect" market is defined by its rules (e.g., large numbers, free entry, perfect information etc.) and enables the exchange of goods and services, while managed or quasi-markets, such as the Stock Exchange, have formal regulations defining roles, limiting participation and setting the terms of interaction.

The other coordination structures also essentially consist of rules and resources. The interorganizational group, for example, has its general definitional rules, such as: members are representatives of participating organizations. Specific cases (e.g., a local Planning Commission, or an interagency task force) have their specific rules: the ordinance prescribing how the members of the Planning Commission are appointed, for example, or the Secretary's memo appointing the members of the task force. They may also have resources, for example: the City Planning Department officials staffing the Planning Commission, or the program budget that is the subject of the task force's decisions.

Or, to take another case, the "mutual organization" has its rules and resources. By definition, its member organizations participate by mutual agreement, based on common solidarity or resource interdependence. Particular interorganizational networks have their own rules, for example: a joint venture is constituted differently and for different purposes than a cartel or a federation.

Finally, specific cases have their rules and resources, constraining and enabling action in the actual context of each case. Thus, the paper-color print joint venture set up its rules in the partners' contract, enabling their common marketing effort and constraining each participant from acting alone during the period covered by their agreement, and each partner contributed his respective marketing and technological resources. Or OPEC has its rules which prescribe membership, representation and interaction to make binding decisions, e.g., a unanimous vote of all the countries' attending representatives. Its rules include the set production quotas and price ceilings that commit its member countries, who contribute its direct resources (its small budget and staff) and its indirect assets: the member states' petroleum production which OPEC controls.

To understand how social structures (including coordination structures) come into existence and persist, with some continuity and some change, we need to appreciate the relation between structure and action. When we think of action, we cannot divorce the act from the actor or agent: nothing happens without someone — a person as an individual, or acting in a social role, or a homogenous collectivity of people in a social unit viewed as if they were one individual — doing it. Acts also take place in time, and are located in space. But action is more than simply a connected series of discrete acts; rather, it is "a continuous flow of conduct" which intervenes in "the ongoing process of events-in-the-world" and is the cause of intended and unintended consequences (Giddens, 1979: 55–56).

Social structure, then, is part of our history: it is one of the consequences of preceding action. People create social structures when they create formal systems of rules or when their practices are, even unconsciously, influenced by informal norms. At the same time, actions reproduce or transform existing social structures, which themselves enable or constrain those actions. Social structures, or "the structural properties of social systems[,] are both the medium and the outcome of the practices that constitute those systems" (Giddens, 1979: 69).[18]

The analogy of language structure (such as grammar) is helpful in understanding this process. The knowledgeable person, saying a grammatical English sentence in casual conversation, is contributing to the reproduction of the English language as a whole. She speaks English without having formally learned it or knowing the rules of grammar as, say, an 8 year old native language speaker knows her mother tongue. Structure, here the rules of grammar, is enabling and constraining her communication, at the same time as she is reinforcing those rules through her use. On the other hand, she may be also be transforming the structure, if, for example, she introduces a colloquialism which, through frequent repetition over time, becomes part of the accepted language.

This example illustrates how action reproduces or transforms structure, and how structure is involved in the production of action. The duality of structure and action, and their reciprocal interaction, are based on what competent actors know, formally and intuitively, about the society in which they live and its practices. It is in the actors' knowledge of their social setting that social structure becomes manifest to enable or constrain their action, which in itself again reproduces or transforms the social structure.

Structuration theory offers a conceptual framework to integrate alternative explanations for IOC and the emergence of IOC structures.[19] One antecedent for IOC (which exchange theory stresses) is organizations' interdependence on resources. Now we can understand how that works to produce IOC structures. It is the people in the relevant organizations: the responsible decision makers or actors in the appropriate roles, whose knowledge of their organizations and environment makes them aware of their organizations' dependence on other organizations' resources. Their actions (and through them, their organizations' behavior) respond by creating, and reproducing (as long as their perception of the interorganizational system's interdependence persists) the IOC structures that will facilitate their organizations' coordinated interaction.

IOC motivated by perceived resource interdependence is most frequently observed in market or quasi-market contexts, where voluntary exchange is the medium of interaction. The ensuing coordination structures range from joint ventures and partnerships, through various "mutual organizations", to coordinating units and lead-organizations.

Another explanation for IOC is transaction cost theory, which suggests that interorganizational systems structure themselves to minimize the participating organizations' transaction costs. In this view, perceived or actual transaction costs account for shifts between market- and hierarchical structures. Now we can understand how this works too.

Indeed, the temporal aspect of structuration theory fits the transaction cost model very well. At the most abstract level of structuration: agents' actions occur within the constraining and (or) enabling framework of social structure, at the same time reproducing or transforming structure. At the more concrete level of transaction cost theory, they may be actors in a centralized, hierarchical organization or interorganizational system (for example, a governmental mega-bureaucracy) who come to understand their setting, and perceive that this structure is imposing transaction costs (resources devoted to monitoring and control, information overload) which could be reduced or eliminated.

They act to change the structure to a more decentralized and less hierarchical one, perhaps proposing more autonomous regional branches, or more independent functional bureaus. Their actions may be enabled by existing structure, e.g., top-down initiated reforms which can invoke hierarchical channels of authority. They may also be constrained by structure: the scope of changes may be limited by statute or existing regulations, or by other powerful interests that are negatively affected, such as a client lobby which sees itself as more effective at the federal than the State or local levels.

If these agents' knowledge of their setting were different, they might act differently. If they perceived no dysfunctions in the current structure, their actions would reinforce and perpetuate the existing bureaucratic hierarchy, until, perhaps, they were enlightened by a crisis they could not ignore. In this fashion, we see, actors' knowledge (their perceived transaction costs) within a hierarchical structure may produce action that reproduces it or transforms it into a more decentralized and market-like one.

In the same way, small organizations interacting in markets may turn into large, complex hierarchical organizations. Again, human agents: people, enact their knowledge of their social setting. Here, the actors may be the directors of a firm in the market, realizing the transaction costs involved in their relation with a particular supplier. These costs might include acquiring information to monitor contract fulfillment, or potential problems of his taking opportunistic advantage of their transaction-specific investments. These perceptions result in the firm's acquisition of the supplier, and the supplier's integration into what may evolve into a large hierarchical corporation.

Action based on agents' knowledge may create consensual and mandated IOC structures too. Structured markets are one example, for instance: the Stock Exchange, as a result of the perceived transaction costs of unregulated exchanges, such as insider-trading fluctuations and attempts to "corner" markets.

Resource exchange and transaction costs alone, however, may not be the only explanations for IOC structuration. Campbell and Lindberg's (1991: 327–333) account of the evolution of governance regimes in economic sectors (e.g., oligarchy in the U.S. automobile industry, the hierarchies created by 19th. century railroad mergers, and today's state-sponsored and regulated competition in U.S. telecommunications) parallels our discussion of IOC structures in many respects: the governance regimes are actually made up of coordination structures.

They describe a transformation process of governance regimes which is a sequence of institutional changes over time. These occur in cycles which are the result of pressures for change, brought about by perceived anomalies or exogenous factors which disrupt existing production or exchange transactions. At the beginning of each such cycle, these pressures stimulate the relevant actors to try out other forms of governance, and explore alternative IOC linkages and structures, in a search process which finally stabilizes into a new governance regime that fits prevailing conditions better than the old one did.

One factor affecting the evolution of governance regimes is economic efficiency. This subsumes transaction costs and economies of scale, for example in cases of vertical integration or devolution, as in railroads, meatpacking and telecommunications. Another is technological development; examples are how mass production created the hierarchical oligarchies of the automobile industry, and how recent developments in manufacturing and control technologies are creating looser interorganizational networks in the same sector.

Power and control is another factor: actors try to increase their power and reduce the uncertainty of their environment through mergers or vertical integration. This factor also reflects resource dependency, but critics of this explanation question the identification of control with hierarchy, and doubt the implication that interorganizational power distribution is a zero-sum game. Nevertheless, there is clear evidence that in many cases, the respective power of the actors affected the final outcome.

Culture can also affect the governance regime that emerges. One example is how the "corpsgeist" linking steel industry executives facilitated the U.S. steel cartel. Another case is the influence of midwestern immigrant dairy farmers' collectivist ideas, originating in 19th. century Europe, on the formation of the dairy producers' cooperatives. Many argue that culture played a critical role in the emergence of interorganizational networks in Japanese industry.

The mutual trust which is the necessary foundation for successful obligational networks that are an alternative to hierarchies is often based on culture. Common technical roots and know-how underlie the regional small-industry networks that formed in Italy and Switzerland (Crevoisier, 1993; Camagni, 1991). Professional culture enables "collegiums" and formal and informal interorganizational networks based on common skills, norms and rules (Majone, 1986).

Finally, the state may be a powerful factor outside the sector or interorganizational system, which may intervene in the evolution of governance and affect the form that IOC structures take. State policy can be the origin of pressures for change, as illustrated in the role of antitrust legislation in the U.S. dairy, steel, meatpacking and telecommunications sectors, or the role of Japan's Ministry of Trade and Industry in encouraging sectorwide interorganizational networks (Johnson, 1982; Okimoto, 1990).

The state may facilitate the selection of one new regime over another. One example is the immunity of the dairy cooperatives from anti-trust legislation. Right-to-work laws in many southern states of the U.S., which encouraged low-cost auto parts suppliers and enabled just-in-time subcontracting by automobile manufacturers attempting to reduce their vertical integration, is another. The state has even created markets that would not otherwise have existed, as in the case of the U.S. nuclear power industry in the 1960s, and telecommunications today (Campbell and Lindberg, 1991: 319–326, 333–349).

IOC is too complex for a simple explanation of the evolution and transformation of coordination structures. But some or a combination of these factors undoubtedly accounts for the emergence of coordination structures in the past, and of the ones we see around us today.

A "structuration" theory of IOC, then, offers concrete answers to the questions posed above. It suggests that IOC is the result of interdependence between organizations, perceived as part of the relevant actors' knowledge of their social settings. This knowledge is enacted in ways that reproduce existing structures of organization and interorganizational systems, or that change and transform them to create new coordination structures.

This view of IOC has some important implications for practice. It reveals that the actor's knowledge of his social context is the way in which social structure enables and constrains action, and the way action reproduces or transforms structure. The "structuration" theory of IOC therefore suggests that influencing the relevant actors' knowledge: their perceptions of their organizations in their interorganizational settings, is critical to effect IOC and to create or change interorganizational coordination structures.

It also explains the common failure of externally mandated IOC efforts, or coordination structures which have been imposed through authoritative fiat.[20] Enlightening the potential participants in an interorganizational system: making them aware of their interdependence, and revealing to them the mutual objectives they could achieve through IOC, is more likely to generate the common knowledge needed to stimulate effective IOC and to initiate the development of an appropriate IOC structure.

The critical role of agents' knowledge of their social settings makes it clear that institutional design of fitting coordination models is not enough to effect IOC. IOC has to be accomplished by transforming the relevant actors' perception of their setting, and mobilizing them to design, install and implement the IOC structures they believe will suit their mutual purposes.

NOTES

1. Schleicher does not go on to identify or describe coordination structures. This is probably because of flaws in his definition, which he elaborates to add: "to solve one particular policy problem", and to assert that: "A coordination structure in action is called an organization". Both these statements are incorrect. Many coordination structures, for example, exist to address ongoing organizational tasks and interorganizational activities, and not just as ad-hoc responses to a

particular issue. And, as we shall see, there are many coordination structures which are not "an organization".

2. Coordination within organizations is covered in an extensive literature; see Mintzberg (1973, 1989).

3. Models I, II, and III in Allison's (1971) analysis of the Cuban missile crisis illustrate these different perspectives.

4. The term "stakeholders" was invented to identify and include in an organization those who are materially affected by its actions (Freeman, 1984: 24–35).

5. This is essentially the aim of Chapters 4–8. However, this ambitious objective must be qualified by the problems of organizational evaluation: assessing success or failure; this is addressed below (see pp. 82–83).

6. You may recognize some differences in their relative levels of abstraction among the meso-structures too. For example, the mutual organization is a more abstract and general description than, say, a joint venture or a federation, both of which are in fact types of mutual organizations. These differences are reflected in the structures' respective position in Figure 1, but they do not warrant elaboration of the three-level definitional scheme.

7. No interval implication (i.e., how much more abstract one structure is than another) should be inferred from any structure's location in Figure 1 relative to any other's.

8. An example of this combination of coordination structures is the European Airbus consortium; see pp. 218–220 below.

9. This, in fact, is how the U.S. Model Cities program was organized and coordinated; see pp. 258–263 below.

10. This fits the resource dependency model of interorganizational interaction and behavior, as expressed in exchange theory.

11. Authority can also be regarded as a medium of exchange, in a view that integrates mandated frameworks into exchange theory (Raelin, 1980; 1982).

12. This is on condition, of course, that all the assumptions for the "perfect" market are met (Grandori, 1987: 29–31).

13. Again, like the program, this coordination structure cannot be simply confined to the "meta"-level, since in combination with other coordination structures it may appear at other levels as well.

14. Chisholm (1989) disputes this, in his description of "coordination without hierarchy"; see this case of coordination between transit agencies in the San Francisco Bay Area (pp. 95–101 below).

15. Some interorganizational networks are entirely informal and nonhierarchical, for example, the interpersonal network of child protection agency caseworkers described later (pp. 91–92). But in fact most net-

works are made up of informal and formal linkages, and many of them are hierarchically linked through other (micro) coordination structures. Another of their examples, the U.S. interstate Special Needs Adoption Network (Alter and Hage, 1993: 58) is a case in point. In this network the participating agencies support a small central office and staff (a coordinating unit) and the agency CEOs make up a board (an interorganizational group) which governs the Network. While membership in the Network is voluntary and based on the agencies' need for the Network's services, its participants interact through formal and hierarchical links.

16. Putting the private sector lead organization under mandated frameworks may seem paradoxical, but it is not if we realize that this arrangement is a quasi-hierarchy enacting legal contracts. Thus, while the process of bidding which precedes finalization of the structure is voluntary and takes place in the market, once contracts are finalized the structure is mandatory on all the participants.

17. This example also shows that mutual purpose and common purpose may not be identical; indeed, they may sometimes conflict. OPEC's glory days dimmed when the goal of maximizing revenue came to be at odds with OPEC's common purpose of maximizing oil prices, for some producing countries whose output was limited by OPEC's quotas.

18. This is an extremely simplified version of "structuration theory", focusing on its essentials which are relevant to IOC. Much of what is presented here is subject to a good deal of qualification and elaboration. To take only one example: "rules" in the definition of social structure are not limited to formulated rules (e.g., laws, bureaucratic regulations, or the rules of chess), but can range from habits or routines (e.g., middle-class Americans have dinner around six; Spaniards dine around ten), through commonly understood generalizable procedures (e.g., how to speak correct English), to the codified interpretations of rules that we usually think of as rules (1984: 17–25). Another important elaboration is the link between knowledge and action, which Giddens develops in a "stratification model" focusing on the "reflexive monitoring of activity" through which the agent's knowledge, conscious and intuitive, of his social context, informs his actions and their intended and unintended consequences (1984: 5–14; 281–282). See Gidden's (1984) *The Constitution of Society* for the full account of "structuration theory" and its broader implications.

19. These are reviewed in 1.2 above, see pp. 3–7.

20. This is not to imply, of course, that all such mandated IOC structures are failures. It does suggest that the ones that succeed, are effective because the relevant actors know, i.e., understand and have internalized into their routine behavior, the rules constituting this coordination structure; a good example is one case of a non-administered program:

the U.S. Income Tax. Examples of failures, because the participants did not know, i.e., did not perceive the rules to be in their interests, or the prospect of resources as attractive enough to offset the perceived costs of coordinated action, are two other programs: New Communities Development in the U.S. (Alexander, 1980), and the STOP program in Germany (see pp. 250–252 below).

II.
PRACTICE

Interorganizational Coordination Structures:
Design, Operation and Performance

CHAPTER 4

Coordination Without Hierarchy:

Informal Coordination
Links and Networks

Introduction

What we know about IOC is not limited to theory or systematic research. IOC structures have existed perhaps as long as organized society itself. Prehistoric clans cooperated in the hunt, as we can see from the practices of stone-age societies surviving today, and tribes formed alliances and federations in war. Hierarchical coordination embraced vast empires in bronze age and classical times, from the master planning of cities in the Indus valley, to the ramified bureaucracies of Egypt and Babylon.

The runner of Marathon was a liaison officer linking the armies of the Athenian alliance, and the Roman tax "farmers" despised by Jesus' contemporaries were subcontractors in a quasi-market. Merchants have mounted joint ventures since before the Arabian Nights' Sinbad the Sailor, and producers' cartels have fixed prices from the Roman grain importers to the medieval guilds. There is a rich fund of experience, then, in IOC, but learning from this experience has been limited to anecdotal wisdom.

The systematic identification of IOC structures provides a framework to organize this pragmatic knowledge. Structuring this experience in coordinating organizations by looking at IOC structures in action may be a way of extracting some of the lessons of past practice: both the successes and the failures. To do this we need to look at cases, analyze them, and evaluate their outcomes.

Cases can be found almost anywhere, from histories, biography and autobiography, to accounts of administrative, organizational and applied practice. These case sources are often in the professional literature of many sectors, which can range from aerospace manufacture, corporate management, or education, through environmental management, human services programs, or infrastructure planning and construction, to technology research and development, urban and regional planning, or zero-based budgeting.

But to be usable, the source of a case has to provide more than a bare account of events. At least, it must allow the identification of the relevant coordination structure, or of the set of IOC structures deployed to concert the decisions of the various organizational actors.[1]

The account must also cover the entire span of the relevant course of events, from the stimulus and initiation of the interorganizational system's common undertaking, through its development and implementation, to its consequences and impacts.[2] And a good case description should enable some appreciation of its relevant contextual dimensions.

Characteristics of participating actors' organizational context include its turbulence: is its interorganizational field a placid market-like array of small organizations in a relatively stable environment, or, at the other extreme, is it an intensively interacting set of a few large organizations subject to discontinuous shocks and rapid change (Terreberry, 1968)? How much are its actors subject to perceived uncertainty (Duncan, 1972), and what are the kinds of interdependencies that stimulated their interaction in the first place?

Other contextual dimensions concern the issue or problem with which the participating organizations are engaged: is it an allocational or redistributional issue, for example (Barrett and Fudge, 1981)? Is it a structural, "chronic" or long-term problem, or a response to an urgent crisis? Any or all of these differences in issue traits and contextual characteristics may have profound effects on the choice of IOC structures, their operation, and their consequences.[3]

Finally, the case must tell us enough about the results of the coordination effort to allow us to make some assessment of its success or failure. Unquestionably, evaluation is a problem. Not only, as Rogers and Mulford commented in their review, is "little ... known about the impact of coordination" (1982: 93), but evaluating organizational effectiveness is always a challenge, given the absence of any universal criteria of success (Cameron and Whetten, 1983).

This is a challenge, however, which cannot be avoided. To extract any useful prescriptions for future policymakers or analysts, program designers and planners, or managers and administrators faced with the same problems that their predecessors confronted, descriptive case analysis is not enough. After all, if we want to learn anything from the experience these cases offer, we have to know whether we are to emulate the ingredients of success, or avoid the pitfalls of failure.

For any multiorganizational undertaking the question of whose values to select as the basis for assessing outcomes is even more problematic than the choice of one stakeholder's perspective over another's in evaluating one organization (Rogers and Mulford, 1982). In some cases this difficulty can be overcome by adopting a system approach (Zammuto, 1982) as a complement to evaluating goal-achievement from a multi-stakeholder perspective.

In effect this means looking at coordination structures as part of an interorganizational system. Its aims are both to ensure its own survival and adaptation to environmental exigencies, and to transform its resources and inputs into the outputs and results that are the ostensible reason for its existence. This suggests some necessary and sufficient conditions for a positive evaluation, on which a case's source has to provide the needed information.

At a minimum, the coordination structures have to continue to function through their projected life-span, serving the interorganizational system of which they are part. Radical transformation or total dissolution must be considered evidence of failure. Usually, it is not difficult to assess the effectiveness of coordination models on the basis of the information the cases provide, including functional indicators (for example, the time needed to make critical decisions, or to accomplish some necessary action) and the perceptions of relevant participants and stakeholders.

To be considered at least a partial success, the mutual undertaking must produce at least some of the planned outputs or some concrete results.[4] Beyond these necessary conditions some of the cases offer evidence which allows more complete evaluation. This may consist of formal assessment of outcomes, including evaluations of project or program impacts. Or there may be a clearly articulated consensus among all the affected interests on the project's success or failure.

The cases reviewed here are not any kind of scientific sample; their selection is essentially heuristic. They have been chosen because they represent the design, operation and performance of the IOC structures I have described, and because they were available. Another reason for their inclusion is that their sources provided the information necessary for the analysis and evaluation which accompanies each case that follows.[5]

*   *   *

There are three kinds of coordination linkages: solidarity-association, market exchange, and hierarchical command and control. These distinguish between various coordination structures and interorganizational networks and systems. According to the degree to which any of these linkages is present, and the way in which they are mixed, we can locate an organization, an IOC structure or an interorganizational system on a continuum between one extreme pole of solidarity-association (for example, the family) and another extreme of hierarchical control (e.g., an army, or a bureaucracy).

As illustrated above (see Figure 1, p. 55) this continuum has the "perfect" market at its center, where both solidarity-association and hierarchical linkages decline from their respective extremes to zero. In other words, in the market (economic or political) there is no form of linkage at all, but IOC simply occurs through spontaneous and partisan mutual adjustment, to the relevant available information, of the units (organizations, firms, agencies, households) making up the market.[6]

In the review of IOC cases that follows, more attention will be paid to IOC structures occupying the hierarchical part of this continuum, while non-hierarchical linkages are covered in less detail. There are several reasons for this, but the relative coverage given here should not be read to mean that either of these kinds of structures — hierarchical or informal and non-hierarchical, is more common in reality than the other.

Unquestionably, non-hierarchical linkages and IOC structures are no less frequent out there, and no less important in our life-worlds, than more hierarchical ones are. Indeed, in view of some developments in contemporary society, and changes yet to come, perhaps they are more so.[7] Far from having disappeared with traditional societies, clans have emerged as a critical ingredient of the success of Silicon Valley (Ouchi, 1980), and informal associations are credited with Japanese dominance of world markets (Murakami, 1982).

One reason why this review focuses more on hierarchical than on non-hierarchical IOC structures is its practical and normative orientation. An important area in which to apply the lessons of experience is institutional design (Weimer, 1992: 133–134; Alexander, 1994). It is rather likely that more hierarchical frameworks will be the contexts for systematic institutional design. More hierarchical IOC structures are also more amenable design subjects than less hierarchical ones. It is more difficult to artificially invoke an associative-solidarity linked structure into existence than a more hierarchical one: imagine transforming a joint venture into a "family" to address problems of uncooperative partners.[8] And though artificial markets can be and have been created (see, e.g., Campbell and Lindberg, 1991: 349–350), the frameworks in which they function are by no means non-hierarchical.[9]

The example of artificial markets suggests the other reason for concentrating on more hierarchical linkages and IOC structures. It is the fact that, as we shall see, many apparently informal and non-hierarchical networks and IOC structures actually depend on more hierarchical IOC structures to ensure their members' coordinated interaction.

Such hierarchical coordination structures may be meso-structures, as in the case of the mandated or consensual frameworks that enable and constrain interaction in artificial markets: for example, the body of corporate law, market regulation, and the Securities and Exchange Commission which in effect form the U.S. stock exchange. Or they may be IOC micro-structures nested in the apparently non-hierarchical interorganizational network.

One example of such a supposedly non-hierarchical network[10] is the Fulton/Farnham County MD hospice care network. Its organizations (a hospital, private Family Social Services agency, Visiting Nurses Association, Voluntary Action Center, National Cancer Society local chapter, and churches) are actually linked through another private organization, Hospice Care, which acts as a coordinating unit for joint hospice care planning, and houses the interagency team (an interorganizational group) that coordinates service delivery (Alter and Hage, 1993: 141–144).

The pure non-hierarchical network (in the sense of an interorganizational system without any formal authority links) may be more rare than some observers (e.g., Powell, 1990; Alter and Hage, 1993) think. By definition, it must be limited to agencies, firms or organizations which are linked by no more than interpersonal contacts or informal information exchange.

Such networks do exist; an example is the child protection case-workers' network (Alter and Hage, 1993: 52) which is presented below. Other such networks are advocacy coalitions (Sabatier, 1986) and policy issue networks (Kirst, Meister and Rowley, 1984). One such network is the housing-home finance coalition, which has powerfully influenced federal housing policy and the regulation of financial institutions in the U.S. since the mid 1930s.

This network is made up of the U.S League of Savings Institutions (representing the smaller "thrifts"), the National Council of Savings Institutions (an association of the larger savings & loans), the National Association of Homebuilders, and the National Association of Real-tors. These are all formally organized trade associations, but their political alliance is not institutionalized: it consists of informal links between their Washington lobbyists (MacDonald, 1992). These examples, however, again confirm how non-hierarchical structures cannot really be the elements of institutional design.

By definition, coordination that is not hierarchical implies links that are not based on authoritative command and control. Such links may be of various other kinds. Solidarity-associative links are one such kind. These can be very strong, and they are the basis for many kinds of organizations and interorganizational systems.

4.1. Associative Links: Kinship and Community

The associative link of family, in the narrowest sense, or in its wider meaning, the link of kinship, can invoke strong bonds which sometimes override all others in their effects on behavior. These range from the personal bond between parents, children and siblings in a family, which can summon up the ultimate in individual commitment and sacrifice, to the obligational bonds of mutual support between kinfolk in traditional, transitional and often even in modern societies.

Organizations based entirely or primarily on these links — the family, the clan, and the tribe — still exist today in every society. In spite of the fact that we tend to think of them in the context of traditional communities based more on ascriptive ("who you are") than achievement ("what you are", have done, or know) status, the family, clan and tribe still summon up a fund of powerful commitment to motivate peoples' actions today.

Evidence for this is unlimited. The persistence of tribal wars and communal conflict demonstrate that tribal and clan loyalties are as strong as ever. The pervasiveness of nepotism, racism and xenophobia, even in modern societies where they are proscribed by law and regulation, shows that family, tribal and clan-like bonds have not been significantly weakened by progressive norms of equal or achieve-ment-related opportunity.

Associative bonds of family, clan, communal or even ethnic affili-ation are powerful non-hierarchical coordination links in organiza-tions and between them (Ben Porath, 1980). The family firm is wide-spread in many sectors, ranging from small businesses and traditional professions such as law and architecture, to family-based or -linked interorganizational networks such as the Rothschild banks, the Onas-sis-Niarchos shipping dynasties, and the Hunts' financial empire.

Kinship is a potent basis for coordination in the administrative and political arenas as well. It is especially important in unstable transi-tional societies where alternative links are weak; examples are Sad-dam Hussein's family- and hometown of Takrit-based regime in Iraq, Hafez Assad's clan and Alawi core of support in Syria, and the Papandreous of Greece.[11] But more stable and modern societies do not lack their own political dynasties, from England's Churchills to the Daleys of Chicago.

Family ties broaden into ethnic affiliation, merging with cultural norms to create the non-hierarchical links of reciprocity and trust which characterize some sectors. The once (but now less so) Irish police forces in New York and Boston, the largely Jewish diamond exchanges from Antwerp to Tel-Aviv, the Parsee merchant enclaves in India, and the watch industry in the French-speaking Swiss Jura around Neufchatel are some examples.

4.2. Solidarity Links

Ideology and Values

Another basis for non-hierarchical links is shared values. These, too, are the glue bonding many kinds of organizations and linking organi-zations with common ideologies or similar valued goals. Some ide-ologies are themselves an expression of association or affiliation. The feminist movement links women in organizations with widely differ-ent functions and objectives, from the National Organization of Wo-men through Planned Parenthood to university Departments of Wo-men's Studies. Homosexuals find common cause in gay and lesbian rights associations and mobilize organizations to support sufferers from AIDS and lobby for AIDS research and prevention funding.

Black African-Americans have created an interorganizational net-work, from the NAACP and the Black Congressional Caucus at the national level, to community organizations and neighborhood development corporations at the local level. Ramified networks of Jewish organizations exist in many countries, made up of organizations at the national level and local congregations and community groups, and internationally linked in support of Israel. Other ethnic-cultural groups, sometimes associated with nationalities, like the Armenians, Irish, and Ukrainians, have similar interorganizational networks.

Shared values and common ideologies also link groups without a common affiliation. The environmental movement is an example, in which a shared concern for the environment and a common ecological consciousness links a global network of organizations, including the international Greenpeace organization, national interest organizations such as the U.S. Sierra Club, and the political Green parties in several European countries.

Political ideologies are another common solidarity link. National political movements, interparty alliances, and political parties are too common to enumerate. There are also international formal and less formal interorganizational networks based on common ideologies, ranging from the Socialist International to the Neo-Nazi network. Social ideology may blend with cultural and lifestyle orientation to link people in organizations and interorganizational networks, too. Examples of such organizations are communal societies such as communes and the Israeli kibbutz; these are often linked at the national level into interorganizational networks.

Finally, there is the strong solidarity link of religion. Shared religious faith and values can be the basis for reciprocity and trust in informal relationships and interactions. And organized religious denominations and communities form a vast pool of organizations and interorganizational networks. The Roman Catholic Church is one example: a global interorganizational system embracing organizations including parishes, religious communities and orders, and an international hierarchy[12] ranging from the humble parish priest to the Pope in the Vatican. Other religions, such as Islam, are more loosely linked, but can still mobilize their adherents through a widespread network of mosques, religious foundations, schools, universities and courts.[13]

Work-Culture — Education, Professions and "Clans"

Shared education, professional socialization, or common work experience are other solidarity links. Like the associative-solidarity links discussed above, these can also become strong bonds between people in organizations, and, when they fill critical organizational roles, provide a non-hierarchical link between organizations.

These links are expressed in both informal and formal associations. The "Oxbridge" "old boys'" network which, by some accounts, pervaded the British establishment, the clique of graduates of the *Hautes Ecoles* which is rumored to run the French bureaucracy, and the "Ivy League" classmen who seem to make up the upper levels of moderate Republican governments (like the Bush administration) are some examples of the former.

In the grey area between informal networks and formal ones are the officer cohorts in some military organizations, such as the Guatemalan army and the U.S. Navy. Formally, these graduating classes of army or navy officers do no more than hold annual reunions; informally, they are very influential as mutual resource exchange and promotional networks.

Professionalization is another form of non-hierarchical linkage within and between organizations. Professionals are widespread in organizations and society. Today, they are not limited to the "classic" professions of medicine and law, but include newer professions or quasi-professions such as accountants, arbitrators, architects, engineers, family counselors, geologists, land surveyors, psychologists, public administrators, social workers, therapists, and urban planners. Members of the same profession have a common educational background, speak the same technical or disciplinary language, share work experiences and career histories, and conform to a set of common norms of professional behavior (Gargan, 1993). Not coincidentally, they are also linked by mutual economic interests (Freidson, 1986: 63).

Common professional norms and expertise are a frequent basis for informal links between organizations. The exchange of information, advice, and mutual support among professionals can be one of the incentives for informal interorganizational networks like some that developed among human service agencies (Hage and Aiken, 1970), and others illustrated in the cases below.

There are also more formal arenas of interorganizational coordination that are non-hierarchical, to the extent that their decisions are arrived at by consensus premised on common professional or disciplinary language and norms. Majone (1986) calls this type of networking organization a *collegium*. Examples include peer review committees allocating funds for scientific research, the peer review system which selects and edits articles for professional and scholarly journals, and the faculty committees responsible for academic administration in many universities.

Professional links are formally expressed, too, as professional, scientific and disciplinary organizations. These are usually themselves part of interorganizational networks: advocacy coalitions, policy issue networks, and promotional networks that emerge around topics of mutual concern. In this fashion, the American Planning Association joins the Federation of Homebuilders, the International City Management Association, and the National Association of Housing and Redevelopment Officials to lobby the U.S. administration and congress for increased federal funding of housing programs. Or the Royal College of Physicians, and the British Society for Biostatistics interact with laboratories in Kings College and Warwick University and a R&D consortium for medical equipment and instrumentation, in the testing and licensing of a new diagnostic system to detect the hepatitis B virus.

A common work-culture, shared work environments and experience can also forge interpersonal links which, though informal, may form an association almost like a family. This type of non-hierarchical work organization has been called a *"clan"* (Ouchi, 1980). "Clans" form in occupations that link people in intense work-related creative interaction. Technological research and development is one such area, and the success of California's Silicon Valley has been attributed to "clans" in its firms. Other examples are in biogenetic research and development, computer hardware innovation, and the development of new information-processing systems and software. The "clan", however, is more intra- than interorganizational; so it is of less interest to us than other types of non-hierarchical coordination.

*   *   *

Any of these associative-solidarity bonds can be the basis for informal linkages and networks. But, before going on to discuss informal linkages, it is worth noting that these bonds become institutionalized as often as they remain informal. When this happens, more hierarchical linkages and formal organizations emerge, and solidarity-associative links can become the basis for quite hierarchical organizations and interorganizational networks.

We can see the results of this process everywhere. Kinship links the corporation that is family-controlled through preferred shares, as much as it determines the transfer of government in political dynasties. The attributive bond between women has generated the feminist movement and its many constituent organizations. Highly hierarchical organizations and interorganizational networks are based on common values and ideologies, from the Communist party to the Catholic Church. Professional links are transformed into formal organization and hierarchical control, from the American Medical Association to the Zambian Bar.

Informal production networks, too, recently hailed as hotbeds of innovation, are more structured than they appear, and often unstable. The informal regional industrial network in the Swiss Jura, for example, that evolved around watchmaking, became much more hierarchically organized in its successor industries: quartz watch manufacture and electronic precision toolmaking (Crevoisier, 1993).

In Italy, localized industrial districts, such as the informal networks of machine toolmaking workshops in Aemilia Romagna, have been closely studied as incubators of economic development. But they, too, are not as informal as they seem. For example, there are institutionalized coordinators, called *impannatore*, who function as brokers between manufacturing firms and potential customers, and are responsible for assembling the subcontracting network for each project. These regional or areawide craft industries may also be vanishing as informal networks: some of them are already being hierarchically integrated by outside industrial conglomerates (Harrison, 1994). The purely informal network, then, linking people or organizations solely through their solidarity-associational bonds, may be more the exception than the rule.

4.3. Informal Links and Networks

Informal linkages, of course, are universal: spontaneous contact between individuals creating informal channels of interaction. These channels can form between different units in one organization, and between different organizations when individuals interact informally in their organizational roles.[14] Such contacts can take many forms: telephone calls, ad-hoc meetings, faxed notes, exchanges of letters and shared distribution or mailing lists.

Some interorganizational networks may be based entirely on informal linkages. They are probably quite rare in reality, and they are certainly seldom documented. Alter and Hage describe such a case.

Child Protective Services Caseworkers' Networks

During the 1980s caseworkers in child welfare service agencies experienced massive increases in their workloads:

Caseloads averaged 85 to 100 per worker, turnover became 50% per year, and child protection agencies found it increasingly difficult to hire adequately prepared workers. In spite of these conditions, a core of veteran line staff stayed in child protection. They have been able to do so because of their personal networks — workers from private and public agencies who provide each other with emotional support, as well as information and referrals as needed by their clients. (Alter and Hage, 1993: 53)

These are unorganized and non-hierarchical local networks in which professional bonds connect staff in various organizations in an area through informal linkages. The networks rarely interact as a whole, but small groups of caseworkers meet at intervals for breakfast or lunch, and at more formal professional meetings. Members of each network also interact through intensive and frequent telephone communication.

Apparently, shared problems and a need for supportive interaction in a turbulent environment stimulated the spontaneous formation of these networks, which sustain themselves through informal links. The caseworkers' networks have been effective in serving their members' mutual purposes, and have also (incidentally) benefitted the participants' agencies and organizations by keeping up their staff's morale in difficult circumstances and thus avoiding the loss of critical personnel.

It is unclear what support (if any) the "member" organizations gave to these networks. Obviously it would have been in the agencies' interest to give them every encouragement and even formal support (for example, providing facilities for meetings, funding for refreshments or lunches, etc.). On the other hand, these networks seem to perform their task of mutual support and information exchange quite well, based on their informal links alone. One can only guess whether they would have worked even better with some resources and more formal links, or whether the marginal gain in effectiveness would not have warranted the organizational costs.

*   *   *

This informal network was multi-organizational, but it linked quite a small set of local organizations. Multi-organizational networks are often larger, and usually more complex, and then more formal and hierarchical IOC structures tend to link them, as we shall see.

Relatively informal linkages, however, can still be the basis for simple interorganizational systems. These are systems that are limited to dyads, i.e., pairs of interacting organizations, or where dyadic links are the way in which most of the members can resolve their interdependencies. The next case shows the first type of informal network; the case that follows it is an example of the second.

Network Dyads in Apparel, Computers and Telecommunications

Andrea Larson (1992) looked at four small informal networks, to examine how control over decisions and action is effected in nonhierarchical interorganizational systems. Each of her subject networks consisted of a focal entrepreneurial firm, which had close dyadic links to another or a few other businesses in the same industry.

A telephone equipment distributor was the entrepreneur in one of the networks, closely linked to a major telephone manufacturer. Another network was made up of a clothing company, with dyadic links to its main supplier, a clothing manufacturer, and to the apparel catalog firm that was a major source of sales. The third network had a high-technology computer company as its focal entrepreneurial organization, linked to a high-technology assembly plant, and to a manufacturer of technologically advanced computer boards. The last network focused on a manufacturer of electronic support products, linked on one hand to its supplier of circuit breakers, and on the other hand to a number of small independent service contractors and component suppliers that essentially made up its sales force.

These informal networks lasted between five and seven years of stable and cooperative relations, and contributed significantly to the focal entrepreneurial firm's growth and success. Each of these networks interacted entirely through informal dyadic links between its member organizations. While the economic advantage was a powerful incentive, Larson found that social control was the crucial element in these interactions.

Some important preconditions made it possible for these networks to come into existence. One was the personal reputations for integrity and trustworthiness in their respective industries, of the chief executives of the entrepreneurial firms and the other participating businesses. Their firms' mutual history of good relations prior to the network's emergence was also critical.

Another precondition was a "philosophy of partnership" in the focal firm: a sense of the importance of social relations and mutual trust. The CEO of Support Products, one of the focal entrepreneurial businesses, illustrates this. A few years after he founded the firm, a fire destroyed his plant, exposing him to major losses. A group of friends and associates in the same sector gave him technical assistance and financing that enabled him to stay in business. This experience gave him a strong belief in the power of interpersonal relationships built on mutual trust, of social and personal commitment going beyond economic incentives. This "philosophy of partnership" became his basis for running the firm and its relations with its environment, and was adopted by the firm's staff and his son who was his successor.

In the formative stage of the networks, the participants came to perceive their mutual economic advantage in the relationship. However, though that was of course a strong incentive, it was not enough. This stage also involved a trial period of more tentative interaction, which developed the trust that was necessary for the closer network linkages. Finally, one firm in each pair (usually the entrepreneur) had to take the initiator role, and explicitly show its willingness to engage in the cooperative relationship with the other. This could take any of a number of forms, even to the apparently trivial action of one staffer regularly calling her counterpart in the other firm to ask how things were going, and was there anything she could do to make the interaction more effective.

Once they were fully operational, the dyads' integration and control took several forms. Operational integration was assured by a dense network of multiple linkages between them; often their interactions were not like those between separate firms, but as if they were departments of the same organization. Some developed common or linked information systems, others gave their counterparts on-line access to their computer systems. There was a high level of interaction and coordination at all levels of each firm, and communication between them was constant and regular.

There was strategic integration, too. For example, two companies coordinated their shipping, warehousing and inventory systems to facilitate their operations, and even developed a common computerized bar code to enable boxes to move between firms unopened. The circuit breaker manufacturer initiated common projects with his entrepreneurial partner, Support Products, and undertook joint technical development and R&D, so that his design engineers would be current with the latest emerging technologies. Systematic information exchange between pairs of firms produced innovation and improvements in product quality.

These networks were very effective. They were economically successful, without incurring the costs of hierarchical integration. Essentially, the opportunism that some hold to be why these kinds of idiosyncratic transaction relationships end as integrated hierarchical organizations, was eliminated by a mutual sense of reciprocity, moral obligation, and trust.

But this case leaves some unanswered questions. How common are the preconditions that Larson identifies as essential for such networks to form? How often can interdependencies be managed in dyadic interactions? To what extent were the interactions between cooperating firms informal throughout the duration of the networks? It is possible, and even likely, that the kinds of operational and strategic integration described were handled by some of the formal coordinative roles or IOC structures we have discussed: designated staff in boundary-spanning roles, coordinators assigned to joint projects, or interorganizational groups: interfirm planning groups or joint project teams.

*   *   *

More often than they are the sole basis for interorganizational networks, informal links supplement more formal forms of coordination. Informal channels of communication, and ad-hoc interaction between pairs or groups of individuals in interdependent organizational roles can reinforce formal interactions, or sometimes replace the formal coordination channels to expedite decisions and action. Chisholm (1989) has discussed informal links in these roles,[15] illustrating them with a detailed review of coordination between transit agencies in the San Francisco Bay Area. His analysis produces some provocative conclusions on shortcomings of formal coordination structures and the relative effectiveness of informal ones.

The San Francisco Bay Area Public Transit System

The San Francisco Bay transit service area contains six operating agencies: the Alameda-Contra Costa County Transit District (AC), the Bay Area Rapid Transit District (BART), Golden Gate covering Marin, Sonoma and San Francisco Counties, the San Francisco Municipal Railway System (Muni), Samtrans covering San Mateo County, and the Santa Clara County Transportation Agency. With adjacent and in parts overlapping territories, these organizations are interdependent in three areas.

One is operations; a case of operational interdependence is the use of some San Francisco streets by three operators at the same time. This creates the potential of traffic congestion, as shown by San Francisco Muni's attempt (in 1958) to exclude its competitors by initiating an amendment to the San Francisco Police Code. Another aspect of operational interdependence is the joint use of facilities, such as the Transbay Terminal and BART stations.

A second area is service-related interdependence. Travellers on two or more operators average over 35,000 transfers on an average weekday. As a result, one agency's route changes affect others' passenger demand, and unilateral adjustments in fares in this compact market affect many operators' ridership. Service breakdowns, too, impact operators not directly involved.

The third kind of interdependence is planning-related, involving the Metropolitan Transportation Commission's planning jurisdiction, and operators' competition for resources from the same pool: passengers in a common service area, and subsidies and funds from the same sources. However, while important in relation to the interorganizational system as a whole, planning interdependence is less relevant to this case's focus on informal coordination.

Some of these interdependencies have resulted in formal agreements or contractual arrangements between operators. One example is the agreement through which AC's bus service supplements BART's rail transit to areas BART does not serve, or links BART stations to outlying areas. Another is the "mutual assistance" agreements in case of service breakdowns between AC and BART, and BART and Muni.

Chisholm also identifies three types of interdependence (1989: 58–59). "Natural" interdependence occurs when organizations are linked by external forces or circumstances beyond their control; for example, a common pool of passengers. "Voluntary" interdependence is the result of a freely entered link between organizations to secure mutual benefits; for example contractual agreements to coordinate services and realize some economies of scale. "Artificial" interdependence is the result of externally mandated links, such as the planning requirements for obtaining capital or operating subsidies.

If we focus on the Bay Area transit system's natural and voluntary interdependencies, we find a loosely coupled system consisting mostly of bilateral links between pairs of overlapping operators. These interdependencies are frequently managed through informal channels, especially when formal organizational links break down. Informal contacts, based on interpersonal relations and mutual trust, often form more effective bonds than formal channels, avoiding, as they do, time consuming formal constraints and ambiguities about assignment of responsibility.

One example is the execution of the express bus contract between BART and AC. Formally, this is a two-stage procedure in which BART determines the broad parameters in the first stage, and AC works out the details in the second, taking some three months. In practice, however, the process is much more interactive, involving a pair of AC and BART senior staff who have a longstanding relationship that bypasses official channels. To establish a new route, the AC staffer called up his BART counterpart, who immediately set up a joint test run of the proposed route to check out available stops, potential traffic problems, and the bus' compatibility with road configurations: grades, curves, etc. Deciding the route was feasible, both met with the local Public Works Director on the same day and finalized the route. The AC staffer then presented the request to the director of scheduling together with its necessary technical support; service on the new route was operational in less than five weeks.

In the same way, formal procedures are supplemented or bypassed in the grant application and review process. This is also facilitated by operators' use of informal "grant managers" — individuals who develop special knowledge and networks of informal relationships that dramatically speed up grant processing.

Informal links can also replace formal channels, when these are blocked because of organizational politics, decision-avoidance or simple neglect. This was the case when Golden Gate wanted to rent some special buses from AC to run on weekends. The buses were standard length buses which AC had successfully shortened for use on hilly, lightly used or winding routes. After a Golden Gate manager received no response to his formal request for some weeks, he called an informal contact in AC to find out what was holding things up. A check of the files revealed that the responsible official in AC had mistakenly sidetracked the letter and forgotten it. The AC contact then took the Golden Gate proposal to his General Manager, who agreed to the request on the spot, since AC did not use these buses on weekends.

Finally, informal links come into their own when formal channels or procedures simply do not exist. For example, no formal procedures had been devised for BART and AC to coordinate special services for the California vs. Stanford football game. Transit planners in AC and BART met informally and worked out the extra rolling-stock that would be needed, and which AC routes should receive additional buses.

Another example of informal links in action is the AC-BART bus-bridge emergency agreement. On his arrival at BART, the new scheduling director discovered that arrangements for handling emergencies, such as an unexpected rail shutdown, were inadequate. As an ex-AC staffer, he had the benefit of an intimate knowledge of AC's inside workings, and an excellent network of informal relations with AC personnel. Drawing on these resources, he called one of his contacts, the AC operations director, and together they worked out an informal "mutual assistance" agreement, providing for AC emergency bus service in the event of a BART failure.

The agreement was intentionally kept oral and informal, so that interaction would not be constrained by legal formalities. The way it works is that if BART personnel expect any longer than momentary break in service, BART central calls the AC dispatcher who redirects buses or provides additional ones to set up shuttle service around the affected length of the BART system. Once the closed part of the BART line is reopened, AC recalls its buses. This arrangement was activated, for example, when a fallen tree closed the Richmond-Fremont BART line near El Cerrito, closing the line north of Berkeley. AC provided relief service to the three affected stations for several hours until the line was cleared. AC bills BART for this service by computing the marginal costs of labor, fuel, maintenance and overheads, which BART has always paid without question.

The effectiveness of informal links was again demonstrated in the 1979 fire that closed the BART transbay tube for several months. Within an hour of the first fire report, BART Central requested an AC busbridge across the Bay Bridge between Oakland and San Francisco. Luckily, the call came just between shifts and after the evening peak, giving AC enough free buses to meet the extra demand. Later, the additional buses AC could provide were too few, and BART's scheduling director was ordered to do everything possible to get more buses for the next morning from private operators. Lacking direct informal links, he started looking through the Yellow Pages at midnight; somehow he managed to contact some private operators and charter more buses for the morning.

The informal links and relationship of trust that existed between BART and AC personnel led to AC becoming BART's de facto agent for chartering private buses and approving private operators' bills as the transbay tube's closure continued. Eventually, AC shuttle drivers even accepted tickets for the shuttles that passengers bought at BART stations, and complex but still informal billing, accounting and auditing procedures were put into place for the costs that ran into millions of dollars.

Operational interdependence, such as signing, bus stops and routing has been informally handled by agreements between pairs of operators, such as Muni and Golden Gate, to ensure smooth operations on jointly used streets. Sometimes, reaching consensus was not easy, for example when Samtrans and Muni came into conflict over use of buspads at the Daly City BART station. Here, BART acted as informal mediator to produce a mutually satisfactory agreement.

Over the period 1978–80 Chisholm discovered an extensive system of interpersonal informal links among the San Francisco Bay transit organizations. This was not a network, because it essentially consisted of 162 dyadic relationships between pairs of personnel in the various operating organizations (see Figure 2 below). Three more intensively interacting specialized subsets of people were also identified, though again their mutual interaction was too limited to make up an overall network.

One subset was made up of operations-maintenance staff, who primarily exchanged expert advice and factual information, and included operations personnel negotiating and implementing operating agreements. The second was planning, which included some exchange of expertise but mainly the implementation of formal coordination arrangements. The third was management, made up of fewer individuals than the two others, interacting mainly in high-level policy discussions.

This case focuses on informal links and expands on their benefits, though many of the examples show that these links often supplement more formal and hierarchical (e.g., contractual) arrangements. The informal links between the Bay Area transit operators were facilitated by several factors, which go beyond the mutual consciousness of interdependence.

They include prevailing norms of reciprocity, premised on continuous and stable interpersonal interactions which reward informal exchanges. Another factor is the opportunities for informal contacts provided by formal arenas and interactions. Examples of such arenas are the Regional Transit Association (RTA), Metro-Transportation Commission (MTC) sponsored meetings, and interorganizational groups addressing specific transportation issues, such as the San Francisco Northwest Corridor Study and the Transbay Terminal Advisory Committee. Common professional recruitment, and personnel movement between organizations are also powerful facilitators of informal contacts.

Although Chisholm highlights this case as an example of successful informal coordination, the weaknesses of informal organization are not ignored. The personal nature of informal links can be a problem in several ways. One is the potential for inequality and discriminatory relationships. Another is the possibility of subversion for private ends

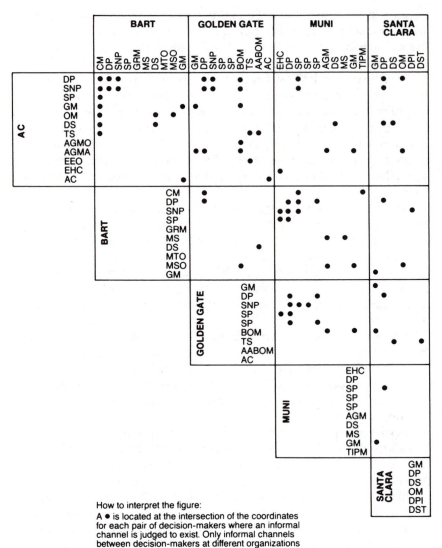

How to interpret the figure:
A ● is located at the intersection of the coordinates
for each pair of decision-makers where an informal
channel is judged to exist. Only informal channels
between decision-makers at different organizations
are represented in this figure.

Figure 2. Interorganizational informal links in the Bay Area Public
Transit System 1978–80 (Chisholm, 1989: 74–75).

or goal-displacement. Some examples occurred in this case. One was
a high level manager's use of his personal network to defeat a new
chief executive's attempt to curtail his power through performance

audits. Another was a planner's attempt to invoke his informal contacts to end-run a manager's decision on buses' color schemes.

System properties can both enable and inhibit interpersonal links. Unquestionably, the decomposability of what superficially looks like a very complex multiorganizational network into much simpler dyadic relationships is a major factor to account for the extent and success of the informal links observed here. Informal coordination was relatively easy, too, among organizations with similar technologies, common professional backgrounds, and compatible goals.

It is likely to be much more difficult, and probably less successful, in a more complex and less decomposable multiorganizational system made up of organizations deploying different technologies, with different professional membership, different disciplinary languages, and dissimilar goals. As Chisholm asks rhetorically (1989: 193):

> Can sanitation districts interdependent with highway departments reach informal accommodations as effectively as interdependent transit agencies? Can police departments informally cooperate with recreation agencies as well as BART and Muni work together?

He thinks they can, in similar situations of organizational interdependence and common interests. But in the absence of these facilitating factors, informal linkages are likely to be fewer, less intensive and less effective.

Finally, enforceability and accountability of informal arrangements may be a problem. This was less the case here than it might have been, because of the reciprocal relationships involved in what was, after all, quite a stable organizational environment. But in different circumstances, such as more turbulent environments with more uncertainty and change, long-term dependence on informal links can be much more problematic.[16]

*   *   *

The complete absence in the Bay Area transit system of another form of informal[17] interorganizational linkage — multiple board memberships — is striking. Overlapping membership of governing boards by officials of interdependent organizations is a very common informal way of coordinating their decisions, in the private and public sector alike.

Boards of corporate directors frequently include officials informally representing other organizations or firms on which the corporation is dependent for important resources (Burt, 1982; Mizruchi and Stearns, 1988). In this way, the board of an automobile manufacturer might include members representing financial institutions and investors, and directors who are officials of raw materials suppliers such as steel or aluminum corporations. Or among a pharmaceuticals corporation's directors there could be a major biochemical research figure, or a corporate lawyer with links to the Washington regulatory arena.

Interlocking board memberships are the informal links connecting sometimes extensive interorganizational networks of interdependent businesses or public and nonprofit agencies. The governing body — Commission or Board of Directors — is the arena for various coordinating activities between interdependent organizations. At the very least, board members exchange relevant information, to which their own organizations can later respond with action that may look like no more than spontaneous mutual adjustment. They can enter informal discussions that lead to more formal interorganizational links, and undertake interpersonal exchanges that facilitate activities based on existing formal agreements. Finally, commissioners and directors, in their governing roles, can introduce interdependence considerations into the corporation's or agency's decisions, and in this way coordinate its actions with those of the other organizations in the network.

Though less well documented than in the private sector, public sector governing boards are also an important arena for informal coordination. They are one of the ways in which areawide networks of "community decision organizations" interact (Warren, Bergunder and Rose, 1973). Interlocking membership on governing boards and commissions is also a way of creating an informal network of nonprofit organizations, government agencies and political units interacting around a particular problem, issue or task. Human services offer many examples (Hall et al., 1977).

Services for the Elderly in Metro-Milwaukee

In the early 1980s an extensive array of diverse services for the frail and dependent elderly had emerged in the Milwaukee metropolitan area. These ranged from medical outpatient treatment and discharge counselling after hospitalization, through home help, "meals-on-wheels", "dial-a-ride" and visiting nurse services, to occupational, physio- and psychotherapy, social and recreational activities, legal and financial counselling and referral, and assistance in nursing home placement.

Over eighty agencies, nonprofit organizations, and firms delivered these services to the elderly population of the metropolitan area.

These organizations included area hospitals and clinics, local senior centers, the Visiting Nurses Association, the Milwaukee County Department of Social Services, the Community Relations-Social Development Commission, voluntary organizations, and private firms and contractors.

Though there was apparent redundancy of services, some duplication was attributable to geographic factors: separate organizations delivering similar services in different service areas. There was some informal coordination at the operational level, for example among agencies that delivered complementary services to clients accessed through a common referral point. More formal operational coordination existed too. Some hospitals provided integrated case management as part of their discharge counselors' roles. Collocation of some programs in several neighborhood facilities (e.g., the Robert Wood Johnson clinic on the North Side) also enabled integrated case management and service coordination.

But on the whole, and certainly on an areawide basis, there was little evidence of any formal coordination in the planning of services or their delivery. Several organizations were involved, separately, in the planning and funding of services for the frail and dependent elderly, who were not generally recognized as a distinct client group.

The closest to such recognition was the creation of the Commission on Aging, a Countywide interorganizational planning group with broad representation on its board, that had some jurisdiction over federally funded (through DHHS) aging programs and sign-off on Agency for Aging (Title 22) grants. But the Commission on Aging had no formal planning or coordinating role where other programs for the elderly were concerned.

Health-related programs and services were funded and planned separately through several public and voluntary bodies. Public funding and programming for mental health was coordinated through the Milwaukee Mental Health Planning Council, a County-sponsored interorganizational group. Other public funded human and social services for the frail and dependent elderly were either directly provided through the County Social Services Department (which had an Advisory Committee), or planned and coordinated by the Milwaukee Social Development Commission, the designated local community action agency.

On its face, the case for some central unit to plan and coordinate the entire array of services for the frail and dependent elderly on an areawide basis, would seem compelling. Surely, without such formal coordination, the area's elderly were suffering from service shortfalls, redundancies and duplication, or ineffective service delivery.

Perhaps surprisingly, this impression was not supported by the responses of service provider organization officials or executives of several planning agencies who were interviewed, or by the perceptions of a limited informal survey of elderly clients.[18] To the extent that this could be ascertained without a formal evaluation, services to Milwaukee's frail and dependent elderly seemed to be quite satisfactory.

What explains the apparently spontaneous coordination of such a complex service delivery system? The answer is that this interorganizational network was coordinated through a system of informal links: interlocking memberships of a relatively small group of individuals on the governing boards and commissions, and advisory committees of the various organizations planning, funding, and organizing services for the frail and dependent elderly.

This group was made up of some social and planning agency executives, and some community and client representatives including elected and voluntary organization officials. They had the frail and dependent elderly as their common concern, usually, but not always, in connection with their current organizational roles.

For example, one of them had been Associate Director for Planning of the Social Development Commission (SDC), where he had been responsible for planning and developing grant proposals for social programs for the elderly. In this role, he was appointed to the Commission on Aging, and was also a member of several other boards, including the County Social Services Department's Advisory Committee and the County Mental Health Planning Council. Later, he left the SDC for a position in a local hospital complex as administrator of gerontology, afterwards becoming a private consultant in health services administration. But his membership in this coordinating network continued, with his becoming chair of the Commission on Aging after he had left SDC.

The informal links between this group were through their memberships in the boards and commissions which coordinated the planning and procurement of services for the elderly. These were primarily governance or advisory bodies for the organizations that controlled the major streams of grant and program funding for the array of services, among them the Commission on Aging, the Mental Health Planning Council, the County Department of Social Services, the SDC and the United Way (Alexander, 1983).

In its way this was a far more complex interorganizational system than Chisholm's Bay Area transit network. Embracing much more diverse services, its service providers did not have the common professional background and orientation that his transit operators did. They ranged from physicians in outpatient clinics, transit contractors operating "dial-a-ride" minivans, and social workers providing referrals, counselling and integrated case management, to retired corporate executives running volunteer home-visit services, ex-housewives catering "meals-on-wheels" contracts, and registered nurses staffing the visiting nurses units.

It is also more complex in its systemic properties. Interdependencies were usually multi-organizational. If they could be decomposed, it was on geographic, service area-related lines, rather than sectoral-functional ones; reciprocal and complementary interdependence is the rule. Consequently, the simple dyadic interdependencies that Chisholm found in San Francisco Bay area transit did not exist among Milwaukee's services for the elderly.

These factors make informal links at the operating level of the kind Chisholm describes unlikely.[19] However, informal interaction at the policy, planning and management level, based on interlocking governance of several formal planning and coordinating organizations,[20] seems to have given the Milwaukee elderly services interorganizational network the coordination it needed.

Systemic, cultural, and environmental factors may account for this. This network of related service providers depended on funding from a few sources: federal programs and voluntary donors. Though not formally interconnected among themselves, each of these resource "streams" sponsored a coordination arena to plan and manage the programs and services it funded. These sectoral coordination arenas facilitated the emergence of the informal links which enabled more general areawide coordination.

There were also solidarity ties that helped to form the informal network. Though they worked in very different organizations in diverse roles, the actors had many common traits. They shared goals of social justice and progressive values. Generally coming from a similar policymaking or management level of their respective organizations, they shared an administrative culture, in spite of quite different disciplinary or professional backgrounds.

The relevant environment of this interorganizational network also supported its informal links. The interorganizational field in Milwaukee of the early eighties was relatively placid, in-and out-migration has been rare and personnel turnover is infrequent. The conservative

Midwest is an ideal setting for longlasting informal relationships based on stable expectations of reciprocity. At the same time, the Midwest's libertarian and populist based advocacy of "home rule" rejects centralized, formal and hierarchical coordination.

*   *   *

Another frequent type of informal network is the advocacy coalition, or policy issue network. These networks are made up of governmental bodies, agencies, and organizations and firms interacting around an issue of common concern. Though they are often transitory, existing only for the duration of their mutual interest, some informal policy networks are quite durable.

Such interorganizational networks form what Laumann and Knoke (1987) have called a "policy domain": they link a set of organizational actors who share mutual ongoing concerns in a particular substantive area, such as energy policy, defense procurement, civil rights, housing, environmental pollution, or mass transit. An organization's participation in this network, or its membership in a given "policy domain", is based on its capacity to affect outcomes, i.e., on its influence on the policies that finally emerge from the interactive process. This criterion is a collective social construct: the actor in a policy domain knows one when he sees one.

The participants in a policy issue network can vary quite considerably between specific issues and events, but a policy domain has a core network that is relatively constant. This is because there is significant historical interdependence between events, so that the same core participants with formal roles in this area or with basic interests will be seen interacting over long periods of time. In U.S. health or energy policy, for example, Laumann and Knoke traced core networks over twenty years and more.

Policy domains are defined by the interactions between their members, but they are linked by a mutual concern, not necessarily by common interests. Indeed, most policy domains include subsets of participating organizations with opposed interests, which may form networks — coalitions or alliances — of their own. For example, in the arena of health policy, suppliers of health services and the organizations representing them oppose cost containment policies or programs, while public agencies (representing government which is, in fact, the largest consumer of health services), third party payers (the major health insurance corporations) and other consumer interests support them.

Though policy domains are non-hierarchical, they include some formal processes and interactions. For example, the process of publication of draft regulations, objections and administrative review is one formal channel of communication between actors. Congressional oversight committees in an area are a focus for policy related communication and interaction, and committee hearings are a formal arena for interaction and debate between members of the policy domain. Coordination among sub-networks in the policy domain also occurs through common membership on boards and commissions, confederations or alliances of organizations, or ad-hoc coalitions.

The core participants in the policy domain form an intensely interacting interorganizational network with constant communication through multiple channels. Though it is no more than an informal social construct, this network compares in the density and frequency of its communications and interactions with more homogenous or functionally interdependent sets of organizations. The most central members in these core networks are usually the governmental actors: the White House, OMB and the relevant cabinet departments, and general trade associations, professional societies, and major corporations. The most peripheral members are more specialized associations with more particular interests, public interest groups, and other claimant organizations with narrow or incidental concerns in the specific domain.

A closer look at a specific event in the course of existence of one "policy domain" will give a better picture of how this informal interorganizational network operates. This is a "snapshot" of a particular policy issue in the context of the ongoing policy domain of U.S. energy policy, which involves the White House, several federal Departments, congressional oversight committees, public interest and professional organizations, and energy corporations as ongoing members in the core network.

U.S. Energy Policy: The Windfall Profits Tax

In 1979 the Carter administration was confronted by the sudden rise in world oil prices, which resulted from the drop in oil supply after the recent Iranian revolution. An energy policy was needed that would neutralize the negative impacts of fuel price escalation on the national economy and trade balance. To be implemented, any policy would have to mobilize enough support to overcome the opposition of the big oil corporations, which were obvious gainers under the new status quo.

The administration's policy of deregulating oil and natural gas prices was already in progress, and any return to price control was unthinkable. Instead, President Carter presented his "price conservation" policy, which proposed a windfall profit tax on oil producers. The revenues from this tax would be distributed so as to reduce the price rise's negative distributive effects and enhance fuel conservation. One part would go to low income families to help them pay skyrocketing fuel bills. Another part was allocated to increase mass transit subsidies, so as to make this form of transportation more competitive and discourage more energy-intensive automobile use. The last part was designated for the new Department of Energy, to distribute in support of synthetic fuels research, and encourage the development of substitute forms of energy.

The policy domain was evenly split for and against these proposals. As expected, the major oil producers and their industrial associations were adamantly in opposition. Core actors in this group included Gulf Oil, Shell, ARCO, and the National Resources Council. The opposition also included most large manufacturing corporations, who were active participants in the core network, such as Allied Chemicals, Boeing, Chrysler, General Motors, TRW, Union Carbon and U.S. Steel.

Supporting the proposed policy were the executive agencies which had been actively involved in its development: the White House, the Department of Energy and the Office of Management and Budget. Other federal agencies, such as the Department of the Interior and the Department of Housing and Urban Development were also part of the core network, and lobbied congress in favor of the Administration's policy. Other blocks mobilized in active support included environmental and consumer organizations, such as the Environmental Policy Institute, the Public Interest, and the American Automobile Association.

Other energy producing sectors, each including active lobbyists, national industrial associations, and major corporate actors, were split for and against the policy. The coal mining corporations joined big oil to oppose the tax; the electrical and the nuclear industries were divided among themselves on this issue, and the small emerging solar energy producers were ardent supporters. The unions were also split, with the AFL-CIO and the ACAW in active support, and the Teamsters in active opposition.

The network operated through a variety of channels. These included informal links and alliances and indirect influence through the media. The formal arenas for interaction were the congressional deliberations on the Administration proposals, which included the

House and Senate oversight committees and subcommittees, and the joint Conference committee which drafted the final legislation.

The outcome was a compromise which reflected the relative influence of the various constituencies. Instead of the 70% windfall profits tax the Administration had requested, Congress authorized only 30% on new oil, with additional breaks to small independent producers. The tax was limited by a "sunset" provision that ended it in 1988 or when the sum of collected revenues reached $227 billion, whichever was sooner. In a sharp divergence from the original policy, most of the revenues were earmarked for corporate and income tax reduction, with much smaller shares than originally envisaged going to low income households and to mass transit. To appease "big oil", Congress refused to allocate any of the funds to the Administration's proposed Synfuels development project.

This description covers one event in the making of U.S. energy policy. Enactment of the Windfall Profits Tax illustrates how the actors in this "policy domain" — the informal policy networks of relatively permanent core participants and more peripheral occasional actors interact to produce particular policy outcomes. Laumann and Knoke assign a major role to these networks in the development of policy in the U.S., supporting their argument with a detailed analysis of health and energy policy.

Undoubtedly such networks are widespread and play an important role in determining what actions government will take on issues that are of critical interest to the participants. These largely informal networks, however, are only part of a larger class of policy making structures: "policy networks".[21]

Policy networks vary between countries, issues, and levels of government, ranging from the "ideal type" of structured political-bureaucratic decision making in a policy hierarchy (which may describe some policy sectors in more centralized European governments) to the largely informal network typifying policy-related interactions in the U.S. Each of these policy networks has its own mixture of bureaucracy, political and economic market interactions, and community or corporatist association. How these are combined in a specific policy network addressing a particular policy domain in a given society and level of government can only be revealed by looking at and analyzing the network concerned (Kenis and Schneider, 1992).

*   *   *

Unlike some of the cases that follow, all these cases were successful. Does this mean that informal links always work? Do these results suggest that coordination without hierarchy is always effective? It is tempting to agree, but we should be wary of coming to this conclusion.

There are two reasons to hesitate. One is that our positive impression may, in fact, be an analytical artefact: the result of the way in which research is done and history is written. Historical accounts and research findings are the products of selective attention,[22] so it is not surprising that successful cases of informal coordination are documented rather than failures.

One could argue that this should be true of formal hierarchical coordination as well, yet there are at least as many accounts of failed formal coordination efforts as there are of effective ones. But informal coordination is different: it does not deposit the institutionalized residue of formal operating norms and organizational frameworks that hierarchical coordination does.

Its failures are either undocumentable, because they are the result of the informal network not having come into existence, or not recognizably affecting individuals' and organizations' behavior. Or, if informal links did operate but were ineffective, unsuccessful in effecting positive changes, or produced negative outcomes, they are not memorable. Without the institutionalized evidence of their existence that formal coordination structures leave behind them, failed informal links and networks can be forgotten.[23]

The second reason is the contingent nature of our evidence. These cases of successful informal coordination are much too limited for any valid generalization. All they can do is to tell us about some conditions that might enable or constrain the formation of informal links and networks, and allow us to infer some factors which facilitate or inhibit non-hierarchical coordination.

Preconditions for informal links include environmental, interorganizational system, and individual attributes. The organizational environment has to be relatively stable and predictable. Slow, continuous, evolutionary change is acceptable; turbulent, rapidly changing, discontinuous, revolutionary or crisis situations are not. This is necessary for the norms of reciprocity to develop, which are the foundation on which the durable interpersonal relations rest, that make up successful informal links.

This seems paradoxical: after all, coordination without hierarchy is particularly appropriate to uncertainty, where more rigid, less adaptable formal structures fail. The resolution of this paradox is to distinguish between factors enabling the development of informal links, and situations encouraging their effective operation. Stability is critical for informal links to develop and persist. Where the stable context is assured, informal links can be highly effective in adapting to incidental uncertainty and addressing localized crises.

A small, simple interorganizational system — two to five organizations, say, linked through sequential, reciprocal or mutual interdependencies — will be more supportive of informal links and networks than a large, complex one. In the latter, decomposability of the interorganizational system facilitates informal links.

An interorganizational network that can be decomposed into a set of dyadic interdependencies — a few, like Larson's entrepreneurial partnerships, or many, like Chisholm's Bay Area transit system — is well suited to elicit informal links between pairs of organizational actors. But this degree of decomposability is not necessary for informal links to emerge. Functional or sectoral subsets of interdependent organizations may also enable informal networking covering these more limited parts of the system.

The pure informal network may be rare, and limited to relatively small and simple interorganizational systems. More widespread are largely informal networks, like the U.S. "policy domains", in which informal links are a hidden "iceberg" making up a social construct known to informed actors, and the formal channels and arenas (e.g., congressional hearings) are its visible peak.

Informal links are more common as supplements to formal coordination structures, as substitutes for formal communication channels that have failed, or as ad-hoc precursors to the development of hierarchical forms of coordination. Formal coordination structures often facilitate informal links, providing arenas for informal interaction between individuals in their organizational roles.

Individual characteristics are also important: informal links are unlikely between people separated by conflicting interests, incompatible values, or incomprehensible professional languages. Solidarity or associational bonds — common goals, shared cultural, educational, or professional backgrounds, or mutual task-related objectives — make informal links more likely and effective.

NOTES

1. This information is often entirely or partially absent, even from cases presented for their IOC interest. One description of an interorganizational network, Corning Glass' "global network" of allied firms (Alter and Hage, 1993: 3–4) is an example. Though we are told that this is an

interrelated group of closely linked businesses consisting of a set of partnerships and joint ventures between Corning and its foreign associates, we do not know how this network is coordinated and administered. Is there a section in Corning headquarters that serves as a coordinating unit, or do various divisions (e.g., R&D, production, marketing) have staff who serve as liaisons with their foreign counterparts, or are interfirm project teams organized around specific joint undertakings? The information provided on the meso-coordination structure is not supplemented by the detail on the complementary micro-structures that undoubtedly exist, without which this case cannot teach us much.

2. Many cases fail to follow this sequence through from its beginning to its conclusion; cases describing planning or implementation efforts, but which are too early to do more than predict success, are common. Without some description of concrete outputs or consequences (or the lack of expected results) any evaluation is impossible.

3. This is one reason why quantitative empirical analysis of the cases has not been attempted here. The large number of possibly significant variables, and the fact that numbers have to be arbitrarily assigned to nominal, not ordinal dimensions, makes the findings of such analysis (if it were possible) suspect as a methodological artefact.

4. Focusing evaluation on this pragmatic criterion runs the risk, which most analysts avoid, of instrumental goal-displacement, as in "The operation succeeded but the patient died". Evaluations based on outputs have later become controversial, e.g., the case of the urban renewal programs of the 1950s and 60s, which indeed succeeded in transforming significant parts of American and European city centers, but raised questions of: to what effect? who paid? and who benefits? (Anderson, 1964; Gans, 1968). But in evaluation, as in other areas, the best may be the enemy of the good. Because of these evaluation problems, many researchers have limited themselves to descriptive analysis. As a result, the existing literature on interorganizational coordination offers little information that can provide a valid base for prescriptions of "what to do" or "what to avoid" (Alexander, 1993: 334).

5. This implies a relatively rich and detailed account which is too often absent. Many other otherwise suitable case studies were unusable because they had a different focus (understandably, since they were not developed for the purpose of this study) and did not provide the necessary detail on IOC in general and coordination structures in particular. As a result, a greater proportion of the cases than I would like is based on my own field research and aggregation of diverse secondary sources (Alexander, 1980, 1981, 1983). Sources for other case studies were books, professional journals, and journals with a central focus or secondary interest in interorganizational coordination.

6. Of course, this description only fits an ideal type: the "perfect" market is as rare in the real world as the "perfect vacuum" in nature. Even organizations in markets are linked in various ways, from interpersonal informal networks to interlocking board memberships, as the review of micro-IOC structures will reveal.

7. Alter and Hage (1993: 2–22, 259–272), for example, argue that technological changes and growth in knowledge, leading to new forms of efficient production and increasing societal and cognitive complexity, place a new premium on informal non-hierarchical linkages and interorganizational cooperation based on mutual interest and trust.

8. Though this approach is not unthinkable.

9. See §5.1 below, pp. 118–121.

10. As defined by Alter and Hage (1993: 78–80). Some awareness of the apparently paradoxical intermeshing of non-hierarchical networks and hierarchical linkages is suggested by Alter and Hage's reference to self-regulation of non-hierarchical networks and a "surrender of sovereignty" by participating organizations (p. 79). Possibly their view limits hierarchy to external or mandated authority; in any case the model of IOC structures presented here allows us to explore these "non-hierarchical networks" in their real complexity.

11. Given prevailing instability, these examples, though current at the time of writing, may join the numerous cases in history (e.g., Haiti's Duvaliers, Nicaragua's Somozas, and Iran's Pahlevis) for the reader.

12. This is, in fact, the origin of the term "hierarchy", which literally means priestly rule and is derived from *hieros*, the Greek word for priest (Oxford English Dictionary, 1971: 272).

13. In some countries where state established religion prevails, as it does in Catholic Ireland, Saudi Arabia, and the Islamic Republic of Iran, for example, we witness the merging of religious and social-political ideologies, as we do in some political movements, such as the "Moral Majority" in the U.S., Israel's Jewish fundamentalist *Gush Emunim*, and Islamic fundamentalist movements like the Egyptian Muslim Brotherhood and the Lebanese *Hezbollah*.

14. For this discussion, informal linkages are differentiated from more formal and hierarchical ones by distinguishing between the roles in which the parties interact. The linkage is informal if the actors initiate the exchange purely in their task-related or organizational roles, like the child protection caseworkers, or the bus operator and the transit official, in the cases below. On the other hand, if one or more of the actors is participating in a designated coordinating role: as an interdivisional project manager in an organization, as a liaison in a joint venture, or as a member of an interagency task force, for example, we are no longer dealing with informal linkages, even though the media of interaction may be the same.

15. Chisholm calls the informal coordination structures he describes: "co-ordination without hierarchy", but a more accurate title would be "co-ordination next to/instead of hierarchy".

16. Chisholm describes the years he researched as "a time of great volatility and change in the Bay Area" (1989: 203) but this is only relative to later when the interorganizational system stabilized after its earlier formative period. Compared to truly turbulent situations, the Bay area organizational environment in the late 1970s was quite placid. Instability with rapid personnel turnover is a serous handicap for informal links, as suggested from the experience of human services systems (Jennings and Krane, 1993).

17. This interorganizational link is really in the grey area between informal and formal. Legally, board members are appointed in their personal capacity, and their organizational affiliation is irrelevant. In fact, such board members' organizational role is critical, and they usually resign their directorships when they change or lose their positions in their parent organizations (Mizruchi and Stearns, 1988).

18. If the only source of this information had been service provider staff, this might not be so surprising, since their evaluations of their own organizations' performance might be self-interested. But their positive assessment was confirmed by other respondents, including planning and funding agency officials, and elderly people at service locations.

19. My fieldwork was unlike Chisholm's, both in scope and orientation. His monumental project included at least 50 interviews over two years, aiming to identify and analyze informal networks, which he found in plenty. My study was more modest: an exploratory review taking three months, looking for IOC structures. Not searching for informal coordination links among operating agencies, I found none. Maybe this explains the different findings of the two studies. However, I was also not looking for the informal links I did find: the interlocking governance at the policy-planning-management level. Perhaps, therefore, the informal operating links Chisholm describes in San Francisco really do not exist in Milwaukee.

20. With the exception of the Commission on Aging, which was areawide and general (i.e., it covered the relevant client group), all the other organizations were limited and sectoral.

21. For some of the reasons given above, policy networks and domains are more of descriptive than normative interest. I have covered them here for completeness, although their prescriptive relevance (i.e., how to coordinate better, or how to design IOC structures) is low, because this type of informal network is in fact widespread and important.

22. This has been widely discussed in the philosophy of science and sociology of knowledge literature, and is too well confirmed to reference

here; for an interesting extension to the apparently rigorous and rational domain of "pure" physical science, see Mitroff (1974).

23. There are, of course, exceptions; for example, informal power elites, criminal conspiracies and economic cartels. However, perhaps these exceptions prove the rule: they have been documented either because the networks were only nominally or legally informal, but were actually quite durable and institutionalized, e.g., the Mafia (Salerno and Tompkins, 1969), or because their powerful impacts, as in the case of local power-elites (Mills, 1956) made them impossible to ignore.

CHAPTER 5

Formal Coordination:

Micro-Structures in Action

Most coordination structures are different from the informal links and networks we have discussed. They are formal ways in which coordination is institutionalized, but they appear at different levels on the scale of organizational scope and complexity.

At the lowest level are what I have called micro-structures. These are the most direct forms of formal linkage between the decision centers of the organizations making up an interorganizational system. At higher levels meso- and meta-structures appear. A symptom of the varying scope and complexity of coordination structures is the existence of several IOC structures at different levels in one interorganizational system. We will see many examples of this, with micro-structures "nested" in meso- and meta-structures, but never the reverse.

Though they are all formal and hierarchical, in contrast to the informal links already reviewed, the other IOC micro-structures vary in how hierarchical they are. The least hierarchical is the liaison or boundary-spanner, with the interorganizational group and the coordinator at intermediate levels of hierarchy. The most hierarchical is the coordinating unit, which may have all the attributes of a formal organization.

5.1. The Liaison and Boundary-Spanner

One might not see much difference in their behavior between some of the people we have observed networking in informal roles, and someone working as a liaison between two organizations, or a boundary-spanner in an interorganizational network. The difference is that the liaison and boundary-spanner are acting in assigned formal roles, in which their task is to coordinate the actions of two or more interdependent organizations.

This task might be part of, or incidental to a person's other duties. In each of the Swedish prisons Mathiesen (1971) describes, for example, there were several boundary-spanners. The Governor was the general formal boundary-spanner between the penal institution he headed, and the other organizations making up its relevant interorganizational network.[1] The main ones with which he interacted were the Ministry of Justice and the Prison Bureau.

Some other officials were more specialized liaisons in their domains. The prison chaplain was involved in transactions with private organizations and religious charities. Social workers had formal links with private charitable organizations and area firms, and with more distant local welfare officers through the National Welfare Association, to find work for parolees and discharged prisoners. Other prison officials, such as psychiatrists, had similar formal liaison functions. These boundary-spanners, then, were the way in which the prison organization interacted with its organizational environment.[2]

Many interorganizational networks are linked by no more than liaisons (if they are primarily dyadic) or boundary spanners in their member organizations, who are in these roles as an integral part of their assigned functions in their organizations. In this way, Macdonald's Director of Franchise Operations and his assistants, on the one hand, and the managers of its franchised outlets on the other, would be the links turning the corporation and its franchisees into an interacting interorganizational network.

Or United Airways's Vice President for Finance and its officials charged with investor relations are boundary-spanners linking the organization to its network of banks and financial institutions: major insurance corporations and pension funds. These links are through their interactions with those organizations' boundary spanners: their customer account managers and investment portfolio executives. Or the University of Minnesota's Assistant President for Development and her staff might fill boundary spanning roles that assign several interorganizational networks as their domains: one may be responsible for corporate and foundation donors; another for linking the university with its alumni organizations; a third for interacting with his counterpart boundary spanners in public federal and state agencies which are sources of research and educational grant funding.

Some boundary spanners actually fill full-time designated roles with the sole functions of external representation and collecting and processing environmental information. A corporate VP for Public Relations, a professional association's Director of Congressional Relations, and an agency's Community Relations official are examples. Aldrich and Herker (1979) suggest that such boundary spanning positions tend to be created in organizations that are larger and internally more differentiated by function. Organizational mission and technology also makes a difference: there will be more designated formal boundary spanners in people-processing organizations, while manufacturing organizations with long-linked technologies will have the fewest.

The focus here is on the IOC role of the liaison or boundary spanner, i.e., as a channel for formal communication, interaction and coordination between his or her organization and another or several (sometimes many) other organizations. Another aspect of the boundary spanning role: the task of collecting and processing information for the organization from its relevant environment, has been the subject of some research.

Tushman (1977) looked at boundary spanners in R&D labs both as intraorganizational liaisons and as specialist "gatekeepers": processing information from the larger organization and its environment relating to the lab's professional concerns and its technical operations. This environment is not limited to organizations with which the boundary spanner's organization has some direct interaction: its interorganizational networks. So this aspect of the boundary spanner's role might seem less relevant to his IOC function. But coordinated action may also result, as spontaneous adjustment based on the information which the boundary spanner has provided.

Boundary spanners often link organizations in quite specialized functional interorganizational networks which are concerned with a particular mutual activity. An example in the public sector is the network described in Mathiesen's (1971) account of Swedish penal institutions. Here the mutual concern is finding employment for released and paroled prisoners; the network consists of the prisons, major firms in the areas around the prisons, local Welfare and social services departments in other areas, and the National Welfare Association. Boundary spanners are the penal institutions' social workers, local employers' managers or personnel officials, and other local governments' Welfare officials.

Public sector agency boundary spanners are active in interorganizational networks in areas such as client referrals and processing, grant and program development and funding, procurement and purchasing, and contracting and supervising third-party service providers. Similarly, in the private sector, functional areas such as investment and finance, manufacturing and subcontracting, advertising and marketing, purchasing, and personnel generate their interorganizational networks which modify the perfect market. These consist of more durable ongoing interactions between liaisons or boundary spanners in their task related roles. The purchasing agent described below is an example.

Chicago Area Purchasing Agents as Boundary Spanners

In classic economics buying a product is a simple market decision. The real world is not so simple. An analysis of Chicago area businesses found that their purchase decisions are a more complex process, one that links the buying firm with its suppliers in what is essentially an informal interorganizational network.

The purchase decision involves several actors. One is the firm's purchasing agent, who is in fact its boundary spanner, or what Spekman (1979) called a "boundary role person". Another is an informal group in the company, the "buying task group", made up of the responsible decision makers in the firm's relevant departments — production or manufacturing, R&D, engineering, quality control, sales management, etc. — who have to approve any acquisition. This "buying task group" is, in fact, the purchasing agent's constituency in the organization: the consumer of the price and product information he or she provides, and the executor of the purchasing agents' recommendations. Finally, the suppliers' sales staff who interact with the purchasing agent complete the linkages in this interorganizational network.

Spekman's sample covered 220 firms in eleven industries, and the decision process he reviewed involved the purchase of commodities in 21 different classes, ranging from edible fats, through steel plate, to metal fasteners. Though these were all market transactions, the fact that many of them were repetitive purchases over extended periods of time turned the buying and selling firms into an interorganizational dyad, linked by the buyer's purchasing agent and the supplier's sales staff as boundary spanners.

The purchasing agent's boundary spanning role, Spekman found, was also the basis of his power in the organization, as indicated by his ability to control the purchase decision. Though the actual decision was made by the relevant member of the "buying task group", the purchasing agent's expertise — her ability to collect and filter critical information — turned the authorizing official into a rubber stamp for her recommendations most of the time.

* * *

Boundary spanners and liaisons in a wide variety of roles are an important IOC micro-structure. They may be the sole links connecting relatively informal and non-hierarchical interorganizational dyads and networks, or they may act in their formal roles to supplement or interact with other IOC structures. The corporate executive who is a member of another corporation's Board, the elected official heading an interagency task force, or the agency staffer serving on another agency's governing commission or advisory committee are all examples of the latter. They are boundary spanners or liaisons between their organization and others, where another IOC structure, an interorganizational group, provides one arena for their mutual interaction.

5.2. The Interorganizational Group

The interorganizational group is one of the most common ways in which IOC is structured. Interorganizational groups have many names. The ad-hoc committee, the interagency task force, the corporate Board of Directors, the agency governing Board or Commission[3] are all interorganizational groups.

Based on her analysis of interagency Federal Regional Councils, Derthick (1974: 197–202) aptly states some of the limitations of the interorganizational group as a coordinating structure. Such bodies, she found, are reluctant to invoke the authority which is the reason for their existence. But it takes nothing less for them to fulfil their tasks: mediating disputes between the powerful line agencies that make up the interorganizational system they are supposed to coordinate, facilitating relations between central and local government, and effecting operational coordination between governmental units delivering public resources and services.

The Federal Regional Councils were interorganizational groups at the regional level: ten high level interagency committees originally established in 1972 by the Nixon administration, and abolished by the Reagan administration (after a negative OMB evaluation and review) in 1983. Like many interorganizational groups they were politically too weak for their job, though they had some value as ad-hoc networks to exchange information and concert federal responses to extraordinary local crises or disasters (Gage, 1984).

Interorganizational groups also frequently appear as an IOC structure at the central level of government. An example of such a group was the Public Expenditure Survey Committee (PESC) in the U.K. This group was charged with coordinating long-range capital expenditures and budgeting between government ministries (Heclo and Wildavsky, 1974). Unlike many other interorganizational groups, PESC was both powerful and relatively successful. Its demise was the result of its growing too strong for its own good, threatening the special status of the Treasury in the British bureaucracy.

Rather than the broad fiscal coordination that was PESC's mandate, more limited program coordination was the task of another central government interorganizational group: the Interministerial Coordinating Committee (ICC) that managed Israel's Project Renewal up to 1987. This case offers a striking demonstration of the advantages and limits of the interorganizational group.[4]

"Project Renewal" in Israel: 1978–1985[5]

In 1978, Prime Minister Begin proclaimed the initiation of "Project Renewal" (PR). PR was unveiled as a cooperative effort between the Israel government and the Jewish communities of the diaspora, in an ambitious program to attack poverty and revitalize Israel's deteriorated urban neighborhoods.

Immediately following the Prime Minister's announcement, a struggle for control of the program began between the government, and the Jewish Agency (JA) representing the Jewish communities abroad. Who would control the government's share of the program was also in dispute, with two ministries, the Ministry of Housing, and the Ministry of Labor and Welfare, each claiming primacy. Another issue was the respective roles of local government, and neighborhood residents. A guiding ideology of participative democracy could imply a leading role for local neighborhood organizations, which local government strongly opposed.

It took nearly 18 months to settle all these conflicts, in an organizational structure established by a formal cabinet resolution in June 1979. This structure reflected the compromises without which no resolution would have been possible. It also minimized the potential costs of any reorganization, relying as much as possible on existing institutions.

Formally, a cabinet-level committee, chaired jointly by the Deputy Prime Minister and the head of the JA, directed the program. Under this group (which met infrequently) PR was administered by another interorganizational group, the Interministerial Coordinating Committee (ICC). The ICC, too, was jointly chaired, by the head of the Social Policy Team in the Deputy PM's office, and the head of the JA's PR team.

The ICC provided overall direction for PR; implementation occurred through regular program delivery channels: the relevant government agencies and divisions of the JA. But planning and program initiatives would come from the local level: the ICC would only guide, review, and allocate funds between proposals.

At the local level, PR was run by a Local Steering Committee (LSC). This was an interorganizational group, too, made up of central and local government agency officials, and residents. Usually the local government chief executive was ex officio chairman. There was an ICC administered program requirement of neighborhood representation, which was more rigorously enforced over time.

Complementing the LSC was a local project management team headed by the Project Manager (appointed by the Housing Ministry) and the LSC Coordinator (appointed by the ICC and paid by the Deputy PM's office). This ambiguous arrangement was also a compromise between conflicting ministries.

PR funding was shared between the government and the Jewish communities of the diaspora, whose contributions were channelled through the JA. In a novel arrangement each community, or groups of smaller communities, "adopted" a renewal neighborhood, assuming responsibility for funding, learning its problems, and participating in planning.

The ICC had no budget of its own, and was supported only by a small (4–6 persons) professional staff who were formally part of the Deputy PM's office. The ICC received each LSC's plans and proposals, and circulated them for review to the relevant agencies. On conclusion of this process, the ICC Budget Committee assigned approved program elements to the various government agencies or the JA for funding and implementation.

Members of the ICC: representatives of ministries, public agencies and JA divisions, devoted a great deal of time to their work on the ICC. Though they continued to be affiliated with their parent organizations, they became a team over time, often submerging their different professional backgrounds and their agencies' conflicting interests. This was a positive development, but it had some less intended results.

PR was launched with high expectations of immediate action. Deployment delay meant that any longer wait for completion of protracted planning would erode any credibility that PR had left. So a "fast track" planning process was prescribed, identifying immediate action projects for the first budget year. Nevertheless, the program was slow to get off the ground.

Local conflicts due to the vague assignment of functions often paralyzed action until they were resolved. Activity in the social sector had to await the establishment of some central-local channels of communication and funding. This was less the case in the physical arena (housing and infrastructure) where Housing Ministry projects were already under way before PR began.

In the earlier years of the project, implementation frustrations were common. Later, mutual learning speeded action, but throughout the life of PR the slow disbursement of funds indicates implementation problems. One reason was the lack of advance planning and limited local capacity. Sometimes this resulted in uncoordinated action, such as the approval and budgeting of facilities construction, without ensuring that an appropriate site was available or while the optimal location was still being debated.

Another reason was the time needed for ICC review and approval. In this process the ICC was simply a channel between the central government agencies who retained the prerogative of professional review and enforcement of standards. Every proposal had to be approved and budgeted by all the relevant agencies. Even when the ICC Budget Committee finally assigned project funding to the appropriate organization, that agency did not necessarily consider itself bound by the ICC's decision, or committed by its representative on the ICC, if the project conflicted with its own priorities.

A third reason was the need for other authorizations and permits, such as plan approval from District and Local Planning Commissions, and building permits from local governments. This increment of complexity had not been foreseen when PR was blended into the existing system with minimal realignments of power and authority.

Implementing agencies, too, were slow in transmitting funds; often several months to a year lapsed between ICC approval, and the actual disbursement of funds. This delay mainly affected social programs in the earlier years. Physical projects funded by the experienced Housing Ministry moved ahead much more smoothly.

Central-local coordination also took time to develop. Many of the early delays, slow deployment and low activity levels were the result of vertical coordination breakdowns, and caused by several flaws in institutional design. One was the decentralization built into PR, which ignored some basic realities of Israeli center-local relations. These have always been very centralized. High dependence of local on central government, and a flow of competence from the periphery to the center, made the lack of confidence of central personnel and institutions in their local counterparts a self-fulfilling prophecy.

In a praiseworthy innovation,[6] PR created in the LSC a focus of local initiative. Neither the central government nor the ICC was going to tell the local community what it must do. However, while the locals could propose, the ICC and central government would dispose. The LSCs had no discretionary resources or entitlement funds until late in the program. The ICC's review and approval process, combined with traditional distrust of local officials, resulted in a flow of all decisions to the center. This created an information and decision overload with which the ICC, with its minimal staff, was ill equipped to cope. At the same time, the ICC resisted any expansion of its staff and powers that would turn it into a coordinating unit.

Some of the distrust of local capacity was warranted. The LSCs began slowly, sometimes beset by domain conflicts. They rarely fulfilled the horizontal coordination functions for which they were designed, often meeting only sporadically. Real decisions and coordination of actions took place informally, in small-group executives made up of the Project Director, a few officials and professional consultants. Local planning was often weak; exceptions were sites in the large cities, which benefitted from large and experienced municipal renewal corporations. Many programs were developed almost entirely on a sectoral basis, with intersectoral coordination limited to proforma packaging and LSC approval of the neighborhood action plan.

Over the life of PR, central-local coordination improved dramatically. In part this resulted from the routinization of the new procedures and those funding and implementation channels (mainly for social programs) that had not existed before. In part, local project administrations learned to be much more adept at responding to the central institutions' demands. Though, in the early stages of the project, they perceived PR as an unfulfilled promise for the future, involving immediate bureaucratic burdens, they gradually saw the effort as worth while in terms of the additional PR generated resources.

PR had deliberately been created with a "sunset" provision, with the expectation that its projects and programs would become institutionalized as regular government-funded activities. JA programs and funding were phased out after their 5-year intended life-span. With project phase-out, some of the LSCs disbanded; others reconstituted as community action agencies.

In its first years PR's administration was dominated, through the ICC, by the ICC's government co-chair, an American-educated administrator-academic. Changes in the governing party coalition which removed his patron, the Deputy Prime Minister, led to the appointment of a Housing Ministry official as the government co-chair in his place. As PR was phased out and ongoing physical and infrastructure projects again became a growing proportion of PR activities, the Housing Ministry had an increasingly prominent role. At this point the ICC was dissolved, but its government co-chair continued to run the project from the Housing Ministry's Renewal Agency, where she had been before.

PR is considered a qualified success. The original plan proposed investing $1.2 billion in 160 slum neighborhoods, of which half was to come from diaspora donations, and half from the Israel government. Later the project was scaled down; by 1986 82 neighborhoods were included in PR and about $660 million had been spent. But this figure may include several distortions that reflect on its accuracy.

One is that in 1986 PR was still in progress, though beginning its phase-out. Expenditures later in the project are based on budget projections that are more inaccurate because of the implementation lag referred to above. Another distortion is budget displacement: some preceding government programs were folded into PR; others came to be supported by PR for activities which might still have been funded. Though budget displacement has been assessed at "under 40%" it has been significant.

PR's physical programs produced substantial tangible results in public facility construction, infrastructure improvements, and housing. 30% of the dwellings in PR neighborhoods received cosmetic improvements; and 10,000 housing units were subsidized for enlargements and major improvements.

PR supported education, cultural, and recreation programs, and special programs and services for youth and elderly. Economic efforts had low priority in the early years, but by 1985 PR assisted manpower centers in 31 neighborhoods, serving about 10,000 residents, and provided funds for several vocational schools. Health funding, while only a small part of the PR budget, supported 40 dental clinics, and early childhood outreach, screening, diagnosis and counselling programs.

Impact evaluations have concluded that the changes attributable to PR basically amount to a halt in the trend of deterioration that would otherwise have continued unabated. Only a few areas enhanced their status relative to other urban neighborhoods. In the words of one evaluation: "PR did not cause revolutionary results" (Alterman, Carmon and Hill, 1985: 6/186).

In the light of proclaimed goals and expectations, this seems disappointing. But a view in terms of PR's actual inputs and investments, puts these impacts in a different light. Over the first six years of its duration, PR spent an average of about $245 per year on each neighborhood resident. Of course, this average conceals wide variations: targeted programs meant that some households received much larger subsidies, while others received none. Still, this figure gives some sense of the actual scale of PR, in terms of which its modest results look quite positive.

Evaluation of PRs organizational structure is almost totally negative. If PR succeeded, it was in spite of its organization, not because of it. PR's organization maximized the use of coordination structures that were "low-cost" in terms of reorganizing existing institutions or committing new resources or authority: interorganizational groups at the central and local levels, supported locally by a coordinator. In a conscious decision, all PR-related projects and services were delivered through existing agencies and organizations. Rather than simplifying administration, however, this structure created unanticipated and undesirable complexities and implementation delays.

In retrospect, as one informed observer has suggested, this may have been a mistake. A different form of organization: a coordinating unit with more power and resources than the ICC, or a new organization, a Neighborhood Renewal Authority with an earmarked budget and planning and implementation powers, might have been more effective.[7]

But these alternatives may have involved costs in reorganization and commitment that in reality were unacceptable. In these terms, the interorganizational group as used in PR has significant advantages. It is less formalized, demands fewer resources, is transient, and requires little reorganization. The organizers of PR had these clearly in mind.

Obviously, they were less aware of its problems. Even an interorganizational group needs staff and resources to cope with its information and decision load. As a project grows, this load may exceed the capacity of an interorganizational group's limited personnel. This happened to the ICC.

With a separate identity, staff, and budget the ICC would have turned from an interorganizational group into a coordinating unit. Its members resisted such changes, afraid of turning the ICC into another bureaucracy. Probably PR would have been better run if the ICC had been formed as a coordinating unit to begin with, or if it had transformed itself into one before it was too late.

Another problem for the interorganizational group is the tension between its members' bonding, and their affiliation with their own organizations. As organizational delegates become part of the group "team" and acquire a personal stake in the mutual project or program, their ties to their home organization may weaken, undermining their representative legitimacy. This happened in the ICC, and may be why its decisions were sometimes ignored. Noted in other interorganizational groups (Bars, Baum and Fiedler, 1976), this may be a problem that cannot be resolved.

Ultimately, PR's weak coordination and its complex organization nearly doomed it to failure. That PR succeeded as much as it did is partly due to the political commitment that the project generated in the course of its delivery. This political commitment to PR was not so much the commitment of its initiators (as demonstrated by their real organizational and material investment) but more that of the constituencies which acquired a stake in its success.

PR also succeeded through a process of mutual adaptation and learning. This was apparent over the course of the project: implementation became much more effective over its later years than when PR began. PR's first stages involved a learning process for all the parties involved.

The ICC gradually grew and formalized its operations, and later even acquired some control over budgets. There came to be some real decentralization, with LSCs getting small discretionary budgets. The LSCs adapted to the ICC's expectations and central agencies' requirements in designing their proposals. They came to function more effectively, too, and became arenas for more genuine resident participation. Planning and implementation became more professional and more effective.

But this also had its costs. With local initiatives more constrained by central direction, PR's revolutionary aspirations to decentralization and democratic participation were compromised. This experience prompts several conclusions about institutional learning.

On the one hand, learning is important. Learning should be taken into account in institutional design. An aspect of this is the time needed for organization, deployment, and planning. In complex programs this can be long, so expectations cannot shortly be followed by action. In PR the time from its initial announcement to the first on-site action was two years, and real program activity took nearly four years to peak.

While they are common, such delays are unexpected by politicians and public alike. Growing pressure in PR for immediate and visible output worked to the detriment of systematic planning and often diverted action from less visible but more important long-term developmental objectives. This could be avoided by more realistic timetables and less inflated expectations; but this may be too bitter medicine for elected politicians to swallow.

On the other hand, the nature of the learning experience must also be taken into account. The more radical a program is, and the more it aims to change the status-quo, the more learning may be necessary to master the process of effecting change. Yet a paradox remains: the more such learning is successful, the more it may dilute just what made the program innovative in the first place.

*   *   *

In central government interorganizational groups are sometimes used as general intersectoral coordination structures. Examples are Britain's PESC, and national planning commissions, as in the Netherlands (Faludi and v.d. Valk, 1994) and in Israel (Alexander, Alterman and Law Yone, 1983). They are very common in sectoral coordination: interagency committees or task forces focusing on a particular policy, issue or program. The ICC coordinating Project Renewal in Israel is one example; others are the Federal interagency committees and task Forces set up in the U.S. for policy issues and programs ranging from the Low Income Opportunity Working Group coordinating welfare policy (Hopkins, 1993) to the DHUD-chaired interagency committee in the Model Cities program (Frieden and Kaplan, 1968). Such interorganizational groups exist in most countries' central government bureaucracies and operate in almost every sector.

At intermediate levels of government — the region, province or state — there are also interorganizational groups charged with vertical (central-local) and horizontal (intersectoral) coordination. In the U.S. the River Valley Planning Commissions and the Federal Regional Councils (Derthick, 1974) were such groups, and many existing Regional Planning Commissions are little more than interorganizational groups.[8]

Such groups exist in many other countries as well. One example is the Regional Economic Policy Commissions (REPCs) and Boards (REPBs) which operated in Britain in the mid-60s (Alexander, 1981).

Coordinating Regional Development: The REPCs and REPBs

British regional development policy dates back to the depression years, with the enactment of the Special Areas Acts of 1934, 1936 and 1937. Ever since then, the concentration of wealth, employment, and economic growth in the South-East, with a resulting polarization of resources and decline of peripheral regions, has continued unabated. Interregional disparities have persisted with varying intensity up to the present. Regional development policy, then, has been the response to regional problems that are symptoms of inadequate adjustment of depressed areas to changes in the spatial economy of the country as a whole.

By October 1964, the beginning of the period of this case, regional development was the subject of a diverse array of programs and regulations. One of these was the Town and Country Planning Act of 1947, which was the statutory framework for stringent land use controls. Others were the system of Industrial Development Certificates (IDCs) and the Advanced Factories Program, which channelled the location of industry, and the Local Employment and Finance Acts of 1963, which provided grants and accelerated depreciation allowances to firms locating in designated high unemployment areas.

Already in 1962 a Regional Development Division had been established in the new Department of Trade, Industry, and Regional Development, to coordinate more effective deployment of all these tools.

Through 1963–64 this unit, together with an interdepartmental steering group, prepared several model regional planning documents, and several regional coordinating structures were set up.

The Labor government which took over in October 1964 stepped up these efforts to coordinate regional development policy and programs. At the central level, this function was put under one of the new "super-ministries", the Department of Economic Affairs (DEA), which emerged from a government reorganization. England was divided into eight planning regions. Each region was to plan and coordinate its regional development, under its Regional Economic Planning Council (REPC) and Regional Economic Planning Board (REPB).

The REPBs were advisory bodies, made up of thirty knowledgeable persons from industry, academe, the professions and local govern-

ment, appointed on a part-time basis. Government departments continued to administer their respective regional development programs,
but they were now to be coordinated through the REPCs: working
groups of senior government officials. Central government departments also set up regional offices, but these received little delegated
authority, nor were the REPCs given any executive powers. Consequently,there was no noticeable shift in power between Whitehall and
the "provinces".

Local authorities continued to transact their business with London,
ignoring the regional level. Government departments too, each with
its own vertical hierarchy straight to Whitehall, bypassed the regional
coordination machinery. They had clear statutory responsibilities,
which enabled them to evade the DEA, whose lack of formal authority
limited its power, and whose vague goals inhibited its effectiveness.

In October 1969 the DEA was abolished in another government
reorganization. In its place the new Ministry for Local Government
and Regional Planning took over the regional coordination apparatus,
while an expanded Ministry of Technology inherited the Ministry of
Trade and Industry's industrial development programs.

The Town and Country Planning Act of 1968, with its "structure
plan" requirements, provided a new incentive for Local Authorities
to cooperate with the REPBs. As a result, joint planning teams were
often set up to develop "strategic plans", but apart from that the
REPBs and REPCs acquired little more substantive power. For example, they had no input into the budgeting process, which is a government's most potent expression of its decision commitment.

Expenditure plans continued to be articulated on a sectoral basis,
without anything like a "regional budget". Instead, selective relaxa-
tion of deflationary policies, such as tax deferrals for investments in
special development areas, in effect reallocated resources to depressed
regions. Growing development expenditures in the areas of greatest
need were in response to increasing unemployment through the late
60s and early 70s. But on the whole national regional development
policy emerged through a series of piecemeal adjustments, with little
evidence of any overall strategy.

New changes in 1970 concentrated power in the central government
and in the regions. Another consolidation of ministries produced three
ministries involved in regional policy and programs: the Departments
of the Environment (DEA), Trade and Industry, and Employment.
With their increasing fund of experience, the REPBs also grew more
cohesive, and the regional coordination apparatus had some tangible

impact on central government decisions by articulating and communicating regional interests.

Through this period, Britain's investment in regional development programs: industrial location controls, investment incentives, and the decentralization of office employment, was significant, and resulted in some stimulated regional development. For example, by 1972 some 90,000 jobs had been transferred away from London. However, much of this effect must be credited to the regulatory component of regional development policy. In terms of the long-run impact on interregional imbalances, the evidence is mixed, and perhaps the best that can be said is that regional development efforts prevented even greater inequalities.

The organization of regional development policy described here produced somewhat better coordination within each of its two main sectors: infrastructure, and location. But little was achieved in knitting the two together into a concerted regional policy and coordinated implementation program. The REPBs and REPCs represented a "separation of power from responsibility", and squeezed a new quasi-level of administration in between the central government and the Local Authorities, each with its statutory powers and responsibilities. Even the regional controllers which several Departments established were managers at most, without any policy responsibilities.

There was widespread disappointment with the REPBs and REPCs, which completely failed to live up to expectations. They cannot be credited with any of the successes, such as there were, of regional development programs, which would probably have had the same impacts without their ineffectual coordination efforts. Their failure can be ascribed to three main causes.

First, the coordinating bodies never received statutory powers suited to their responsibilities, both at the central (DEA), and at the regional levels (REPBs and REPCs). Next, none of the reorganizations significantly changed the distribution of power between existing institutions. The centralized power structure persisted, with Whitehall retaining its monopoly on policy making, and subregional units — departmental branches and Local Authorities, continuing to be vested with implementation powers.

Finally, the low priority given to regional planning and coordination, and a lack of direction from central government, produced a "credibility gap" between the professed aspirations of the regional apparatus and its actual capability to influence central decisions. As a result, Local Authorities had little incentive to pay attention to the

REPBs and REPCs, or to their plans. In fact, "the advent of regional planning was more apparent than real" (Wright and Young, 1975: 259).

This case, like the former one, is another illustration of the weakness of the interorganizational group as a coordination structure in relation to its tasks. The British REPBs and REPCs also recall Derthick's verdict on the U.S. regional interorganizational groups which were inadequately empowered to discharge their responsibilities.

The similarity is striking between these American, British, and Israeli experiences: low political commitment seems make the "low cost" of the interorganizational group as an IOC structure attractive. But neglect to equip these groups with resources and authority commensurate to their horizontal (intersectoral) and vertical coordination (between levels of government) tasks limited the group's effectiveness, in each case, and led to its substantial failure.

*   *   *

In another case a regional interorganizational group produced somewhat different results, but there were also significant differences in the issues and the circumstances. This case is in the context of physical planning in the Netherlands, presented in Mastop's (1983) description of planning of the Dommeldal area.

The Dommeldal Planning Steering Group

The Dommeldal is a small river valley in the southern Netherlands, stretching from den Bosch, where the Dommel joins the Meuse, to the Belgian border. The area contains thirty three municipalities, two of which, Eindhoven and den Bosch, are cities forming the core of metropolitan areas. The local governments in these areas had formed inter-municipal authorities. Development in the Dommeldal was creating management problems, and there were ongoing conflicts between agriculture and nature preservation.

The province of North Brabant, in which the Dommeldal is situated, encouraged interaction between the Dommeldal city-regions to develop a strategic framework for the area's development. As a result of the Provincial planners' initiative, an interorganizational group — an informal Steering Group representing the Province and the two city-regions — was created to elaborate a strategic plan for the area's physical development that had been completed by the late 1970s. Originally, the Steering Group's task was envisaged as formulating agreed upon regional policy and a detailed statutory plan that would commit all the relevant agencies to its coordinated implementation.

This group produced a plan that included as its central proposal the creation of a valleywide special purpose authority. When neither the plan nor its proposed implementation framework won the necessary endorsement from the involved governments or other interests, provincial planners made another effort at stimulating intergovernmental coordination. A new Steering Group was formed, this time including government agency and other local government representatives, and chaired by a member of the Provincial cabinet (the Provincial Executive Council).

However, this interorganizational group had no statutory powers: it was a consultative arena only. The Steering Group had no staff of its own, and depended on provincial staff and consultants for staff support, information and data analysis. Through some years of interaction the Steering Group achieved little more than the adoption of several policy proposals by the relevant participating agencies. By the time it was dissolved it had not succeeded in completing the statutory land use and development plan for which it had been established.

On its face, this looks like a failure. But in fact, the Steering Group made a significant contribution to coordinating action between various agencies involved in the area's physical development. In serving as an arena for interaction, it enabled the informal coordination of overall policies among the participating agencies, and established an ongoing network for information exchange.

The elaboration of the area strategic plan, that was the Steering Group's task, also resulted in the adoption and implementation of several of the plan's most important elements, in the form of selected strategic infrastructure and developmental projects. The parties' negotiations on the Group resulted in agreed statements concerning agriculture and landscape preservation, which were adopted as part of their policies by the relevant line agencies. Parts of the Group's plan were taken up by the Provincial planners and incorporated as "infill plans" into the Provincial structure plan, giving them directive authority. Thus, while the Steering Group failed in its formally assigned task, it essentially acted as an informal enabling network that accomplished many of its substantive objectives.

Mastop's conclusions focus on the distinction between this group's alternative assignments. Formally, it was to produce a structured plan that incorporated an explicit implementation scheme which demanded formal prior commitment from all the relevant authorities. The Steering Group, as it was authorized and constituted, proved unequal to this task.

But it did produce a different kind of plan, one that in fact elicited coordinated action. This "plan" was not a formal document, but represented a negotiated elaboration of the existing strategic plan. In this view, the planning process is more important than the plan, which is seen is no more than a frame-setting basis for negotiated implementation.[9]

* * *

At the local level interorganizational groups frequently coordinate quite large and complex interorganizational networks, in both the public and the private sectors. In the public sector these may be intergovernmental or interagency groups; in the private sector they may be task forces combining representatives of firms and public agencies, as in the cases below.

Interagency Planning Teams in Berlin

In the mid-1970s the planning system in the city of Berlin was reorganized to focus on a number of selected policy issues. These included education, environmental protection, foreign worker integration, restructuring the hospital system, planning and construction of housing, social services, and traffic.

Each issue became the domain of an interorganizational group, to which city government agencies and other relevant organizations seconded members of their staff. There were ten such "planning working groups", which were charged to develop proposals which the organizations in the network would implement. Another interorganizational group was formed to review and adopt these proposals: a "planning committee" (planungsauschuss) made up of representatives of the city's mayor, senate and council and the Land legislature.

In a detailed analysis of these groups' performance, Bars, Baum and Fiedler (1976: 99–183) found problems, many of which were intrinsic to this attempt to restructure a bureaucratic hierarchy. One problem was the capability of the planning teams, to which some agencies, with little sympathy for their mission and less confidence in their potential, seconded their weakest staff.

Another problem was the integration of diverse team members into an effective working group. The six more successful teams had some traits the others did not. They had a better command of the relevant information and developed a keener awareness of their members' mutual interests. They went through a learning process which enhanced their capability for innovation, improved their abilities to form a consensus, and helped them in conflict resolution.

As these groups entered their active working stage, their assigned roles were often incompatible with their hierarchical context. Planning teams disagreed on goals and means with specific agencies that had divergent orientations and different problem-solving patterns, and frequently competitive relations developed between project teams and functional units.

These conflicts affected the teams' coordinating capability: functional "line" agencies resisted accepting their projects, developing competing parallel proposals of their own, and addressing the team's proposals slowly or not at all. Some agencies branded preliminary proposals as incompetent, and disputed the teams' standing to address specific issues.

Team members also faced role and loyalty conflicts. Some agency staff who were team members were cut off from their organizations' internal information flow and excluded from agency discussions. Many confronted competing demands on their time and energy from their agencies and the planning team.

Problems also arose in the authorization and implementation of the teams' projects. Planning subcommittees of the *planungsauschuss* were the locus of these decisions. They soon encountered the limits of the interorganizational group as an arena for consensus formation and conflict-resolution. There were many non-decisions and outright rejection of proposals that would have had tangible effects on interests to which city government was sensitive. Some politically plausible and feasible proposals, however, were also eliminated in the planning committees, when they were vetoed by the responsible line agencies.

The decision making limits of the planning subcommittees could only have been overcome by modifying the substantive content of the proposals, to arrive at negotiated agreed solutions. But these bodies made up of political officials lacked the competence or information processing capability for this type of interaction.

At best, the planning subcommittees served as arenas for political conflict resolution. The approval of any proposal that transcended one organization's domain, over other agencies' opposition, depended on someone's readiness to take on an active supportive role. Advocacy became important, and sometimes issues were taken beyond the planning subcommittee into the broader public arena, through leaks to the media and other public relations strategies.

The Berlin planning experience showed many attempts at adoption and implementation of proposals which failed to overcome the resistance of entrenched interests and agencies. This was the result of the limited conflict-resolution capacity of the interorganizational groups: the planning committees. But in some conflict situations, when the project teams took on active roles as promoters of their proposals, this pattern was broken, and several planning teams succeeded in getting their proposals implemented.

As the process continued, the planning committees' influence on organizations' actions weakened, and fewer project issues were found that could be sustained through bureaucratic opposition. Ultimately, in reaction both to their "successes" and failures, the planning committees were gradually disbanded.

Bars and his associates found that the interorganizational group can improve coordination between interacting functional organizations. It can enhance mutual learning about the task or problem at hand, and provide an interactive capacity that is otherwise lacking. On the downside, interagency teams can create tensions between themselves and the functional units making up the interorganizational network. This is especially likely when the teams themselves come to work as integrated groups and develop well conceived and innovative proposals, raising the level of conflict in the process of plan or program development.

The outcomes of this effort highlight the limits of the project team form of interorganizational group that was adopted here. The team was designed as a kind of non-bureaucracy within a bureaucracy. This ambiguous way of structuring the planning system really demands a kind of "meta-planning": the interorganizational group as a coordination structure requires selective use.

Some problem situations, which involve conflicting interests, may be better served through a conventional hierarchical process with clear domain assignments. Planning and coordination through interagency teams, even when they represent organizations whose interdependencies are high, are likely to fail when the participating functional units perceive that they have only limited action space. This perception may be due to high interconnectivity with their external environment (e.g., linkages to active interest or political constituencies, statutory responsibilities, etc.), lack of discretionary resources, or the momentum of ongoing activities and programs. Another situation unsuitable for interorganizational groups is the highly ramified, extensive, and complex problem area which a temporary unit such as a project team cannot master in the limited time at its disposal.

On the other hand, a project or planning team's chances of success are enhanced if the problem enjoys a high profile and its solution commands some political commitment. In this situation the increased pressure gives the group's work higher priority, and its proposals command the attention of the relevant political decision making levels.

* * *

Just as in central government, interorganizational groups frequently appear at the local level too, to coordinate action between agencies and government organizations operating in a particular sector. Such local councils, committees or task forces can be found in sectors ranging from air pollution abatement to transportation. In human services they are common, as in the case that follows.

Intergovernmental Bodies Coordinating Human Services

Local interorganizational groups have often been set up in the U.S. to deal with problems of coordinating human services program delivery. Agranoff and Lindsay (1983) looked at six such groups: policy boards made up of local elected officials, agency administrators, and some officials and staff of relevant private client and service delivery organizations. The programs in their domain were funded from a variety of sources: some local funds, some funding from formula-based federal programs: Title XX (education), Community Development Block Grants, and General Revenue Sharing, and some categorical grant programs such as the training and employment services funded under the Community Education and Employment Act.

In the various localities the groups took different forms. In Dayton, Ohio, there was a complex structure with three separate groups: planners, executives, and policymakers. The human services policy board in Columbus, Ohio, was a commission with some seconded staff, governed by a cabinet of local agency executives. In Pueblo, New Mexico, there was a citizen manned Human Resources Council in the local Council of Governments, supported by some agency staff. Baltimore, Maryland had a multi-tiered structure headed by a group of public agency directors and authorized signatories, who, with additional officials, formed several policy teams, with a third level of staff. In Seattle, Washington, the board was made up of agency directors, and was staffed by shared personnel. It is interesting to note that none of these is a "pure" interorganizational group; each is at a different level of organizational autonomy between the "pure" group and a fully formed coordinating unit.

The formal structures of these intergovernmental bodies evolved as they attempted to arrive at domain consensus among the participating agencies, and to address jurisdictional questions while handling specific operational issues. These included technical issues which involved extensive staff level interaction and "gut work". Agronoff and Lindsay found that all the groups they observed used adaptive approaches rather than rational planning techniques to address these issues. The successful proposals were developed in a selective process which was quite political, identifying issues on which the relevant agencies could agree, shaping the problem to arrive at a shared consensus, and then pursuing practical solutions.

Difficult issues were avoided, sometimes by simply postponing agenda items that threatened unacceptable conflict. But many tasks were successfully completed. These included the development of administrative tools to improve service delivery and enhance inter-program coordination, such as standard needs and capacity surveys, and unified application processes.

Agranoff and Lindsay's evaluation reaches some striking findings about how interorganizational groups such as these should work together. They advocate a managerial focus that seeks solutions to specific issues, rather than attempting interagency coordination of programs as a general or comprehensive strategy.

The successful efforts they observed involved a process with the following steps:

1) Recognition of the constitutional-legal and organizational-structural context, involving fragmented systems with jurisdictional overlaps;

2) Consciousness of the political nature of the tasks and the diffusion of power in the system: "put politics up front";

3) Addressing the technical elements of problems with the assistance of specialists such as planners, community center directors, and program heads, and dealing with the "nuts-and-bolts" of substantive issues;

4) A task orientation involving a clear focus on the problem at hand and a mutual willingness to make adjustments to solve that particular problem, rather than hollow attempts to "work together" or more "pseudo-arenas" for interagency coordination such as joint boards, task forces, or requirements for co-ordinated or comprehensive planning.

Their conclusions cite Seidman's (1980: 215) assessment which found that federal interagency committees are effective only when they are assigned appropriate tasks within their competence, tasks which they have the motivation and authority to complete. The successful groups were not required to revise basic intergovernmental arrangements or amend basic public policies, but simply to agree on specific work that needed to be done, and they decided on concrete actions that could be implemented on a phased time schedule. The ineffective coordinating groups were unsuccessful because they were assigned problems which they were inherently incapable of solving.

* * *

Interdependencies between local organizations in the private sector are often handled by interorganizational groups as well. Such interdependencies may be the same kind of mutual interests that have traditionally produced collective public action. A dynamic process leads to the general perception of interdependence that generates the relevant interorganizational network and its IOC structure (Logsdon, 1991: 25–30). This is the same process described in the structuration theory of IOC in Chapter 3 above. The following case shows how this process formed an interorganizational group to coordinate action in the private sector.

Hazardous Waste Contamination in Silicon Valley

Around 1980–81 five firms in Silicon Valley (Santa Clara Co., California) discovered small leaks in their hazardous waste disposal systems. They did not think this was much of a problem. Formally, there were no regulations or disclosure requirements covering this phenomenon, so they were not exposed to any legal or statutory liability. And substantively, they believed that a clay barrier under the valley floor protected the deep aquifer on which the water supply depended from any contamination. The affected firms' stakes in the issue, therefore, were low, and their perceived interdependence was nonexistent.

But the stakes were raised in January 1982, when a drinking water well was closed, due to TCA contamination from a nearby semiconductor plant. This tarnished Silicon Valley's semiconductor firms' image as a "clean industry", and put pressure both on manufacturers and local government with regard to the industry's presence and legitimacy. Public and corporate officials realized their mutual interdependence in this area, and recognized that this was a common problem that needed a regional remedy. Such a remedy would involve agreed upon uniform standards for hazardous waste storage and disposal, which would afford the necessary public protection and eliminate any potential "freeloaders" who might otherwise enjoy a competitive advantage. An interorganizational group was formed to deal with the problem. This was a public-private task force which included responsible public officials and representatives from participating businesses. The Task Force developed a model Hazardous Materials Storage Permit Ordinance, that was adopted by local governments in the affected area. This ordinance was so successful in controlling the problem that it subsequently became the basis for State and federal environmental standards (Logsdon, 1991: 33–34).

* * *

The interorganizational groups reviewed here include some successes and some failures. The failures have several factors in common. One is low political commitment, making an IOC structure attractive that demands low investment in reorganization, and little or no reallocation of power and resources. The other is an assignment of significant responsibility to commit powerful agencies to modify their actions in support of the mutual task or goal. This combination of high expectations with a relatively weak and "low cost" IOC structure has defeated the efforts of many interorganizational groups to effectively perform the comprehensive coordination tasks they were assigned.

This IOC structure, however, does not have to fail. The successful cases suggest that the interorganizational group can be an effective IOC structure, if it performs to more modest goals. As John Friend concluded his review of British regional strategy teams and intergovernmental working groups: "authorities should be highly selective in attempting to introduce formal machinery of inter-agency working, concentrating on limited and tangible tasks which would not be seen as too threatening to the primary responsibilities of the agencies concerned" (1980: 267).

Interorganizational groups can coordinate complex interorganizational networks, when their resources fit their tasks. If the group does not have control over resources on which organizations in the network are dependent, or a grant of authority over those organizations to support its mandate, it is unlikely to be able to get powerful line agencies to alter their priorities or change their behavior. But the interorganizational group can produce coordinated action in several other ways.

One is as an arena for essential information exchange among representatives of interdependent organizations, producing (if nothing more) some mutual adjustment that would not have occurred otherwise. The interorganizational group also enables or facilitates informal networking which can sometimes be critical for an interorganizational system's interaction. The corporate Board with its interlocking Directors and the agency Commission's representative membership serve this purpose, as we have seen. Perhaps most important, if it is not burdened with impossibly high expectations, the interorganizational group can coordinate participating organizations' actions to solve specific problems in a process of negotiated (rather than mandated) implementation.

5.3. The Coordinator

An individual can be appointed whose only, or main function is to coordinate the activities of the members of an interorganizational system related to their common project. If the IOC task were related or incidental to his functional role, he would not be a coordinator, but a liaison or boundary spanner. The coordinator is often used together with other IOC structures.

The local Project Director in Israel's Project Renewal (PR), described above, is an example. Together with the Local Steering Committee, an interorganizational group, he coordinated the agencies and organizations involved in developing the local action plan, and later in the execution of approved projects and PR funded program delivery. But the PR Project Director was the only person at the local site level who had full time and exclusive responsibility for coordinating program planning and implementation.

Another example is the federal member of the interstate Regional Commissions in the U.S., who had the special task of coordinating between the region and the federal bureaucracy. Given the federal agencies' resistance to any interference, and the Commissioner's lack of authority, his failure was a foregone conclusion (Derthick, 1974: 65–72, 195–197).

We must be careful to distinguish between the independent coordinator, which is the IOC structure discussed here, and the person heading a coordinating unit, which we will come to next. Unlike the coordinating unit, the coordinator has no staff and often no resources except the power of persuasion or some authority. Such authority could be conferred by the appointing organization, or delegated by the organizations in the relevant interorganizational network.

Cases of such delegated authority to an independent coordinator are rare. More usually such coordinators are "nested" in the kind of complex set of IOC structures that will be discussed later. One example is the "client relations specialist" in Florida's interagency integrated social services delivery system (Polivka et al., 1981), a role which coordinated the various human services delivered under different agencies' programs.

The case manager in many human services sectors is this kind of coordinator. An example is the general case manager in Pittsburgh's "Single Point of Contact" (SPOC) program, which was set up in 1988 under the Job Training Partnership Act.

The General Case Manager in Pittsburgh

SPOC was designed for coordinated delivery of medical benefits, welfare and supportive services, basic skills and vocational training, and job placement services to targeted welfare clients. Staff of the involved agencies are collocated at the local welfare office, the "Single Point of Contact", and the program is run by a Local Management Committee (LMC). The LMC is headed by the Executive Director of the Allegheny County Assistance Office, and includes local executives of the other involved agencies: the Pittsburgh Partnership, the State Job Service and Office of Vocational Rehabilitation, and an education representative.

The job training and placement services delivered to each SPOC participant in the employability development plan (EDP) phase of the program are coordinated by a general case manager. These services make up one phase of the client's movement through the SPOC program, which is designed to end the participant's dependence on welfare.

The general case manager is part of the direct service team, and provides assistance and advocacy to the participant. This begins with clients' intake meetings with SPOC staff and their assessment, goes on through their training, job search, and placement, and only concludes at the end of the follow-up period. The general case manager's role is to deal with any of the problems that may come up in delivery of these services by the participating agencies, and to ensure the client's smooth transition from one program to another. This coordinator role is essential for effective implementation of the EDP, to provide continuity of services for participants and to integrate service delivery under several different programs (Farley and Misechok, 1993: 176–179).

But, though the coordinator here is authorized to intervene in the interaction between SPOC clients and service delivery agencies, she is not independent or acting alone. The coordinator role, the general case manager, is linked to several other coordination structures. He is part of an interorganizational group, which monitors clients' progress through all phases of the program, and she works with several primary case managers, who accompany particular program services. He is also "nested" in another meso-IOC structure: the SPOC program itself which links an interorganizational network of participating agencies governed by its LMC, an interorganizational group.

* * *

Coordinators who do not have the authority they need to carry out their tasks are more common, as suggested by some of the cases reviewed next. Like the interorganizational group, the coordinator, almost by definition, is low on the scale of organizational autonomy. Perhaps for this reason, the independent coordinator is rare, and the cases that follow may suggest why this IOC structure is seldom used alone.

Coordinator of Government Activities in the Galilee[10]

The Galilee in the north of Israel stretches west from the Lake of Galilee to the Mediterranean, and north from the Jezreel Valley to the Lebanese border. Though rich in historical associations, the region's development has been a source of public concern since the State's independence.

Several of the region's characteristics constrain its development. While its rugged landscape gives the Galilee unusual recreational and tourism potential, agricultural land and industrial sites are limited. At the same time, national priorities forbid relegating the region to extensive use as a natural reserve, recreation area, and the water catchment area it already is today. These priorities demand development to support a significant Jewish presence in the Galilee, to balance the substantial and growing Arab population.

Accordingly, national policy and development plans have recurrently included proposals for providing the infrastructure for Jewish settlement and at the same time enhancing the environment and services of the Arab sector. From time to time these proposals surface on the national agenda, generating a spurt of activity which later subsides to its normal level on the threshold of national consciousness as other priorities intervene.

One of these peaks occurred in 1975, when the Rabin government established an Interministerial Committee for the Development of the Galilee as an expression of this issue's priority. Chaim Bar-Lev, the Minister of Commerce and Industry, headed this group on the strength of already chairing the existing cabinet committee on development areas. The executive arm of the new committee in coordinating government initiated development activities in the Galilee was to be a newly created post: the Coordinator of Government Activities in the Galilee.

It is interesting to note that this was actually a watered-down version of a much more radical proposal based on several successful Israeli precedents: a regional development authority. Though this idea was mooted in the cabinet, it foundered on Bar-Lev's opposition, who saw it as a threat to his existing powers, both as minister and as chair of the development committee.

The Coordinator of Government Activities in the Galilee was originally an official of the Ministry of Commerce and Industry, and responsible to the Minister in the latter's capacity as chair of the Interministerial Committee. In the following *Likud* administration this committee was headed by one of the two Deputy Prime Ministers, and on the initiative of the Coordinator serving at the same time, he was placed directly under the Deputy PM.

As representative of the Interministerial Committee, the Coordinator's task was to coordinate the development plans and activities of all governmental and public organizations in the Galilee. These included the respective District Offices of ministries such as Housing and Construction, Interior, Tourism, Transportation, etc., other public agencies such as the Jewish Agency and the Lands Authority, and public bodies such as the Center for Directing (Immigrants) to Development Towns.

But the Coordinator was not given any explicit authority over the other functional ministries and public agencies. He had only a small staff: two assistants, a clerk and a secretary. In the absence of any powers or resources, the Coordinator was constrained to invoke the potential sanction of the Interministerial Committee in cases of non-compliance, or the intervention of another, lower level interorganizational group made up of the Directors of the relevant ministries. This rarely happened, since the Coordinators were generally content with a role limited to information exchange, effected through meetings of senior regional officials under their auspices.

The first Coordinator resigned after several months, frustrated by a task he saw as impossible without any authority or resources. David Reuben, his successor, filled the position through the remainder of the Rabin administration, simultaneously serving as Bar-Lev's Advisor on Development Areas. A new Coordinator, Chaim Chacham, took over with the new *Likud* administration in 1977, serving until October

1979 when he left to become Assistant to the Minister of Finance. After a half-year's gap the next coordinator, Amos Lotan, was appointed in March 1980.

The Coordinators' backgrounds varied: Lotan came from the army and some later experience in his family business, while his predecessor was a career bureaucrat. Reuben was another "outside" political appointment, returning later to his law practice. In spite of these differences, all the Coordinators were acutely conscious of the limitations of their role, and each in turn tried to change his terms of reference or amend his source of authority.

In 1977 Chacham, on assuming his post, commissioned an exhaustive study of the region's needs, which included an analysis of his role's organizational status. This review concluded that the Coordinator's success would depend on his ability to concert development plans for the region, to coordinate action among the relevant public agencies, and to implement ongoing monitoring and control of public activities in the Galilee. These prerequisites for effective coordination are, of course, a tautology.

However, the consultants identified another prerequisite: a horizontal link between government agencies in the form of a joint regional body whose decisions would commit its members. No such body came into being, but a close parallel exists, and was in place even at the time of the quoted report. This is the District Committee for Planning and Building, which is chaired by the District Commissioner (an Interior Ministry official who supervises local government in the District), and includes representatives of all the relevant government and public agencies and local government. Among this body's statutory functions is the coordination of public development activities (Alexander, Alterman and Law-Yone, 1983).

The District Committee's effectiveness in coordinating regional development has been very limited, for reasons falling beyond the scope of this case.[11] But this did not prevent the District Commissioner and his planning staff from asserting what they viewed as their coordination functions. As a result, they resisted any cooperation with the Coordinator, and tried to replace his activities wherever they could.

For his part, the last Coordinator in this case saw the development of comprehensive regional development plans as a major part of his charge. This mission obviously duplicates that of the Interior Ministry's District Planning Bureau (which staffs the District Committee). The Coordinator's tendency to invade the planning domain, which already shows in the 1977 consultants' report, seems to suggest that there were no plans for development of the Galilee. In fact, the reverse is true, and if coordination of development is conspicuous for its absence, it is not for a lack of plans.[12]

Most of what the Coordinators did was to convene meetings of regional government officials from time to time. These meetings served mainly as an arena for the exchange of information, a useful function no doubt, but one that the District Committee fulfilled just as well. Through the six months that the Coordinator's post was vacant there is no evidence that these meetings were missed. On the whole, it does not seem that the Coordinators succeeded in carrying out their assigned task, nor that the creation of this post had any tangible impact.

Successive attempts to redefine the Coordinator's role, and to give some substance to the incumbents' assignments and responsibilities, suggest some of the reasons for this failure. The Coordinator had no statutory responsibilities, and no authority except of the vaguest kind that flowed from a source whose own control over other powerful functional ministries and line agencies was itself almost nonexistent. He had no resources of his own, or any incentives he could offer to other organizations to concert their decisions. Given his total lack of power or resources, the Coordinator's failure was inevitable. Indeed, the long survival of this role, in the absence of any results to warrant its existence, is a tribute to bureaucratic inertia.

* * *

Program or project coordinators are quite common as liaison devices within organizations to integrate operations that cut across the functional or sectoral lines of departments or divisions, or in matrix forms of organization (Mintzberg, 1979: 162–163, 165–168). They seem to be more rarely used to coordinate project related activities in a set of organizations or among separate government agencies. One such case is the local coordinator of the British General Improvement Areas program.

Local Authority Coordinators in the British GIA Program

Urban renewal in Britain has always been a complex undertaking, involving both the public and private sectors. The initiating, planning and implementing agency has been the Local Authority (LA), sometimes in partnership with private developers. The LA's implementation powers include condemnation and compulsory purchase, the reclamation of derelict land, the acquisition and clearance of slum dwellings, and the enforcement of needed home rehabilitation and repair by delinquent landlords. Central government set the statutory context for plan preparation, review, and approval, and provided a large part of the funding.

By the mid-1960s, just as in the U.S., cumulative critical reactions to urban renewal, which had been oriented predominantly to clearance and reconstruction, stimulated a shift to neighborhood revitalization. Another factor contributing to the new emphasis on conservation and rehabilitation, was the substantial amount of public housing built since the war, which fundamentally changed the nature of the "slum" problem. In Manchester, for example, 82,000 housing units had been cleared over 25 years, and the LA had built 104,000 Council Homes.

The Housing Act of 1969 reflected this new orientation, giving the LA broad discretion to declare any predominantly residential area a General Improvement Area (GIA), subject to minimal statutory limitations. In the GIAs property owners were eligible for grant assistance of up to 50% or 75% of approved improvement costs, of which between 75% and 90% was covered by central government funding. The Act covered a wider range of repairs than before, and increased the LAs' claims to central government subsidy by extending to 30 years the expected life of affected dwellings. The LA, for its part, usually committed itself to providing needed improvements in the GIA's infrastructure and physical environment, for which government grants were also available.

With enactment of the statute, the Department of the Environment (DOE) issued several circulars which were much more specific about central government's intentions. They identified the objectives of the GIA program as effecting environmental and housing improvements in deteriorated areas, while protecting existing tenants to avoid "gentrification". The local organization of the GIA program was expected to be centralized and coordinated, since the program had been designed based on a pilot project involving several LA departments. Accordingly, the DOE advocated setting up a formal coordination apparatus, for "centralization of the direction of the work".

In his survey of 75 GIA projects Roberts (1976) found little evidence that this advice had been followed. Centralization at the senior elected or appointed official level was unusual. Most common was an interdepartmental working committee, responsible to the LA's chief officers. 45% of the responding LAs had four or more committees involved in program supervision, and one reported as many as eight.

In terms of centralizing control over program implementation, 47 out of 75 LAs made no changes, six located the program mainly in one department, seven established a special section of a department, and fifteen used coordinators. Nine of the coordinators were hired consultants, while six were in-house "troubleshooters".

The overall results of the GIA effort were disappointing.[13] This was undoubtedly partly due to the program's aims, which were vague and somewhat unrealistic to begin with, and which were also defeated by other, contradictory, elements of government policy. But the program's ineffectiveness also had to do with its organization and coordination. As Roberts (1976: 111) concludes:

> In so far as GIAs have failed to achieve the objectives set them, it is not unreasonable to lay some of the blame on (the LAs') failure to establish what was clearly regarded as a vital ingredient of the policy.

However, Robert's evaluation discovered a clear relationship between a LA's achievements in the program, and the degree to which it had effected coordination of its efforts. In his sample, 85% of the successful GIAs had a central coordinator or "troubleshooter", while this IOC structure was used by only 54% of his sample as a whole. This comparative assessment of the respective effectiveness, in the same context, of two different IOC structures, is interesting and unusual.

As in many of the cases reviewed above, various combinations of interorganizational groups proved relatively ineffective. But a larger proportion of coordinators were successful in fulfilling their task of concerting the planning and implementation of the GIA program among the LA's responsible departments. Though the sources do not provide details, we can assume that with the appointment of the more effective coordinators went an appropriate delegation of authority over the GIA-related decisions and actions of the respective LA agencies.

* * *

Though they both have little organizational autonomy, interorganizational groups and independent coordinators are used to coordinate complex interorganizational networks with reciprocal and mutual interdependencies. Unlike the interorganizational group, however, the coordinator cannot be an arena for information exchange among the members of the interorganizational network, though she could create such arenas to stimulate useful interaction. Nor can he be an arena for negotiating program implementation among participating organizations, another role the interorganizational group can perform.

To manage simple tasks between interorganizational dyads or very small simple systems a coordinator is overqualified: a liaison or boundary spanner can do that as part of his other task-related functional responsibilities. When the undertaking is more complex, or a recurring process is involved which calls for a more differentiated and specialized role, a coordinator is often "nested" in an interorganizational system together with other IOC structures.

The project manager, common in the construction sector and in many complex manufacturing industries such as aerospace and weapons, is one such coordinator. Project managers very effectively coordinate tasks in large and complex interorganizational networks which sometimes include hundreds of technical planners, expert consultants and subcontractors. The case manager in human services is another example, illustrated by the general case manager in Pittsburgh's SPOC program.

But they are not independent coordinators: they are "nested" in a multi-tiered system of IOC structures in which the responsible agency, prime contractor or manufacturing corporation is the lead organization, with hierarchical links (by mandate, contract or interagency agreement) to the other actors which give the project manager control over them. The project manager's effective performance is the result of a combination of authority and resources intrinsic to this kind of interorganizational system.

The independent coordinator is usually in a different situation: not "nested" in a hierarchical system, but floating in a loosely linked network. And his essential function is not simple task-related coordination, or coordination through information exchange or negotiated implementation. It is comprehensive multifunctional hierarchical coordination of a complex interorganizational system.

It seems that an independent coordinator's resources and authority are seldom equal to this role. When they have been, as in the GIA case presented above, it may be because of a particular set of factors. His mission was relatively narrow and clearly defined, limited as it was to a particular program and its related projects. The interorganizational system was relatively small and quite hierarchical, consisting mainly of the Local Authority's Departments involved in the program which were all, ultimately, subject to the Council's governance. In this sense, this IOC role was more like that of an intraorganizational coordinator, or a project manager, roles that are far more common and usually more effective. Finally, this coordinator succeeded due to the combination of a hierarchical interorganizational system and an appropriate grant of authority over its members.

Given the independent coordinator's mission, her empowerment with the necessary authority and resources are a necessary condition for her success. As we have seen, this is rare, and it may be why the coordinator is more usually found as one element of a "nested" combination of IOC structures. Another common way to address the coordination challenge is to provide the coordinator with resources and organizational autonomy equal to the dimensions of his assigned role: instead of just appointing a coordinator, to create a coordinating unit.

NOTES

1. The evidence that the Governor and other specialists were acting in formal boundary-spanning or liaison roles is the fact that prison regulations prohibited communications other than these assigned channels (Mathiesen, 1971: 39–40).

2. The focus of Mathiesen's attention in this case, in fact, are not these roles, but the supplementary informal network. His conclusions highlight the importance of informal interpersonal interaction with external organizations. He found that the bureaucratic constraints limiting interaction to formal channels were dysfunctional: they gave an air of conspiracy to informal transactions that were really positive, and inhibited the free internal flow of communication.

3. Here, interorganizational groups that are governing bodies of organizations will not be covered. These are cases of "nested" IOC structures, i.e., the interorganizational group is part of a hierarchy which includes other coordination structures, and it is supported and staffed by the organization it controls. This review covers interorganizational groups that are relatively "pure": they stand alone in their interorganizational system and have no or only limited organizational autonomy (see pp. 64–65 above).

4. "Project Renewal" in fact included several other IOC structures too, which are referred to in the case below. In this sense, the ICC as a central interorganizational group was really part of a hierarchical IOC system, like the U.S Model Cities program (see pp. 258–263 below).

5. Alexander (1989); this case study is based on fieldwork (Alexander, 1981) and other sources (Alterman, 1987, 1988; Alterman, Carmon and Hill, 1985; Carmon, 1987; Hofman, 1986; International Committee 1985).

6. This, and the neighborhood resident participation requirement, was copied from the U.S. Model Cities program.

7. In the same sector, the British New Town Corporation (see pp. 289–290), and Israel's earlier Lakhish regional development project (Alexander, 1978) are successful precedents.

8. This refers to those RPCs that have a governing Commission but little or no staff; sometimes they are staffed by another local government agency. Other RPCs are in fact coordinating units with substantial organizational autonomy and resources (sometimes based on taxing powers), where the interorganizational group — the governing Commission itself — is only part of the organizational hierarchy.

9. For more on this aspect of planning and its relation to IOC, see Faludi (1987), Alexander and Faludi (1989), and Alexander (1992: 51).

10. Alexander (1980b); this case covers the period from 1975 to 1980.

11. These are partly connected to the way the "planning game" is played by its governmental actors in Israel (Alexander, Alterman and Law-Yone, 1983), and partly linked to the District Committee's organizational context and historical evolution (Alexander, 1980b).

12. Since the mid-70s, the District Planning Bureau, the Israel Lands Authority, the Ministries of Commerce and Industry, Housing, Tourism, and Transportation, and the Settlement Department of the Jewish Agency, each prepared a comprehensive development plan for the Galilee. There is even some coordination between the plans, though each reflects its agency's professional orientation and institutional interests. What they all had in common was their total failure to affect their authors' or any other agency's activities on the ground (Alexander, 1987).

13. This was expressed in a 1973 White Paper evaluating the GIA program, and by a House of Commons Expenditures Committee.

CHAPTER 6

Coordinating Organizations:

Organizations as IOC Structures

6.1. The Coordinating Unit

The coordinating unit is an organization or organizational unit which exists for the sole (or major) purpose of coordinating decisions and actions in the relevant interorganizational system. It has greater organizational autonomy than the interorganizational group: generally the coordinating unit will have its own identity and enjoy "ecological autonomy" in the form of a distinct location and its own offices. It will have its separate operational budget, if not control over other funds, and is staffed by its own personnel.

In contrast to the lead organization and single organization IOC structures, the coordinating unit does not have any "line" functions, or implement any of the tasks it is charged with coordinating. But like the "single organization", it may have all the attributes of an organization.

The coordinating unit may be within a larger organization. It can be housed in a government agency, like the Employment and Training Administration, which coordinates the interorganizational network involved in federally funded job training and placement programs, is

153

in the U.S. Department of Labor. It can be part of a firm or corporation, like the project office in aerospace manufacturing or the headquarters of a hospital holding corporation.

It can be "nested" in another IOC structure, as the administrative unit of the mutual organization that identifies the interorganizational network it coordinates: trade associations such as the National Association of Manufacturers or the Tobacco Institute, professional organizations such as the American Bar Association or the Royal Institute of British Architects, and promotional networks such as the AFL-CIO. Or it can be a separate and relatively free-standing organization, such as the U.S. Office of Management and Budget, the Appalachian Regional Commission, the North West Energy Corporation, the Cincinnati United Fund, the European Commission for Regional Development and many others.

Coordinating units can be differentiated in several ways.[1] One way is according to what they are supposed to coordinate. In this fashion we can distinguish between units coordinating organizations that depend on the same medium — usually money (funding) or people (personnel or clients); units coordinating organizations that share a common function, for example in sectors such as collegiate athletics, elementary education, nuclear energy, or transportation; units coordinating organizations operating in the same area: often planning coordination at a national, regional or local level, and coordinating units dedicated to a specific task: coordinating the implementation set of a particular program or project.

Of course, these distinctions somewhat arbitrarily focus on what seems to be a coordinating unit's main purpose. In reality, most units are mixtures of these types. For example, the Health Management Organization (HMO) is a form of coordinating unit that has evolved in the U.S. to manage the transactions of an interorganizational network which includes hospitals, physicians in individual and group practices, area employers — businesses, corporations, and public agencies, and sometimes financial institutions (Fennell and Alexander, 1993). The common purpose of these organizations is the provision of third-party paid health services, so we could properly call the HMO a functional coordinating unit. But the HMO carries out its coordinating task, which is to modify participating organizations' behavior so as to ensure the most cost-effective service delivery, through its control of resources: the flow of money from the payers to the service providers, and the assignment and referral of patients.

Money is a powerful incentive for affecting organizations' behavior. Therefore, it is not surprising to find coordinating units which are charged with controlling funding in many interorganizational networks. Almost every government has such a coordinating unit, from the Office of Management and Budget in the U.S. federal government, to the Mayor's Budget Bureau in the city of Aalborg. These coordinating units' power to control the behavior of the other members in the interorganizational network is the result of their delegated authority over the flow of funding, a resource on which all the other organizations are critically dependent.

Other organizations are coordinating units in less hierarchical, more loosely linked interorganizational networks, but also on the strength of their control over essential resources. Their transactions with member organizations are less on a basis of authority, and based more on exchange: compliance in return for the continued allocation of the needed resource. The United Way is an example of such a coordinating organization.

Coordinating Charity: The United Way

The United Way came into existence in response to unrestrained competition in soliciting charitable donations for worthy causes. This was especially troublesome when many different charities would approach large corporate employers in an area and ask for formal access to their employees to engage in systematic solicitation of donations. On the one hand, the managers felt uncomfortable selecting among the competing fundraisers and preempting their staff's choices among the objects of their charity. On the other hand, it was impractical to give unrestricted access to any organization that wished to approach the firms' employees in their workplace.

To solve this problem, groups of charitable organizations and corporate employers formed the United Way. The United Way is an organization that exists in most U.S. cities and metropolitan areas with the task of coordinating workplace solicitation by fundraisers and charitable organizations. Each area's United Way is governed by a Board that represents the prominent member organizations in its interorganizational network: charitable organizations and foundations, volunteer organizations, and major corporate employers. The organization, however, is not limited to the Board (which would make it an interorganizational group), but is a true coordinating unit managed by an Executive Director and a sometimes quite large administrative staff.

Organizations wishing to solicit donations in area workplaces do not receive separate access to the large firms and corporate plants and offices that represent a major source of their funds, but are referred to the area's United Way. On becoming members of the United Way, such organizations agree to participate in the United Way's "combined campaign", which is a single annual solicitation among all the area's large employers, and to forgo any attempts at separate solicitations.

Corporate and employee donations to the United Way's "combined campaign" have been allocated among member organizations and charities in various ways. Originally, all the donations were distributed from a consolidated fund, with members' shares allocated according to a formula determined by the Board. This allocation could be quite political and controversial, since United Way funding represented a significant proportion of some organizations' revenues.

United Way Boards were more than willing to abdicate as much of this decision as possible, and soon donors were given the option, and encouraged, to designate all or a proportion of their donations for particular causes or beneficiary organizations. With advances in information processing technology, these options were continually widened, but there is still a residual fund of unrestricted donations which the Board allocates among members, and which continues to represent a substantial proportion of the combined campaign funds.

Competition for funds among United Way member charities and interest organizations is intense, and their relative power is indicated by the degree to which they can influence the Board's allocations in their favor. An analysis of one United Way organization found that power among its 45 member agencies was linked to their respective resource dependency. Those agencies that had strong outside constituencies and alternative sources of funding tended to get more positive funding decisions than the organizations which were more exclusively dependent on United Way support (Provan, Breyer and Kruytbosch, 1980).

The United Way has not been entirely successful, however, in retaining control over its interorganizational network. In the 1970s a growing number of funding agencies which supported "alternative" causes, or more radical or progressive objectives, grew dissatisfied with their share of United Way funds. They claimed that the United Way's allocations of its undesignated "combined campaign" were influenced by a conservative orientation that reflected the views of corporate management which represented the large donors and employers.

After fruitless attempts to change the United Way's funding formula internally, some of these organizations resigned from the United Way. Several resumed direct funding campaigns with varying degrees of success. A number of them joined with other agencies that shared their goals and ideologies, and which had stayed outside the United Way, to consolidate their solicitations into an "alternative" combined campaign which has successfully broken the United Way's monopoly on workplace solicitation in a number of sectors and locations.

With this qualification, however, the United Way has been very effective as a coordinating unit. Its interorganizational network has grown or remained stable over a considerable period of time, and it has essentially succeeded in accomplishing its purpose: to assure and distribute a steady flow of charitable donations from corporate and employee donors to a network of participating charitable and funding agencies, in a consolidated campaign that has largely eliminated competitive workplace solicitations.

*   *   *

Functional coordinating units are legion. They are found in every country and in all functional areas, from air pollution abatement to zero-defects manufacturing. They exist in government at all levels: in international and multinational intergovernmental bodies, in central government ministries, federal departments and as independent authorities, in regional, Provincial and State agencies, and in special purpose and general local governments. One example is a local unit of a federal agency coordinating emergency management and civil defense.

Coordinating Local Emergency Management: The CD Agency

The U.S. Federal Emergency Management Agency (FEMA) is charged with the organization of civil defense and the management of federal intervention in local crises and disasters. FEMA's local Civil Defense (CD) offices are essentially interorganizational coordinating units, because they depend on an extensive and diversified network of other organizations to accomplish their tasks. The CD agency's functions include hazard assessment and mitigation, and assuring emergency preparedness, response and recovery.

The CD agency's organization set can be as large as a hundred organizations. They include the local general government and its various agencies, local special governments (such as the School District, water and sewerage utilities), other relevant area and regional

government agencies (e.g., public transit, regional parks, etc.), and
State and federal government agencies. The set also includes military
bases and units in the area, State National Guard units, the utility
corporations, area hospitals, and civic and voluntary organizations.

David Sink (1985) evaluated the effectiveness of CD agencies as IOC
units, and found that two environmental factors had significant impacts on their performance. One was dependence: the degree to which
the local CD agency's decisions and action were constrained by its
bureaucratic and administrative context. The other was uncertainty:
the degree of stability and change in the environment, and the perceived predictability of future events.

Cross-tabulation of these factors yielded four types of contexts to
which CD agencies adapted in different ways. The most supportive
environment was one of low dependence and little uncertainty, giving
the CD agency maximal freedom of action. These were powerful
coordinating units with ample funding for their tasks and well endowed with the necessary authority to mobilize other organizations
in their relatively small and stable domains.

Where dependency was still small uncertainty could be high, for
example if the CD agency was operating in a larger area and dependent on multiple units of government. Another intermediate condition
existed in predictable environments of low uncertainty, but where
dependence was high, as in the case of resource scarcity due to
inadequate funding or lack of access to other organizations' critical
resources. Finally, the least effective CD agencies were the ones in the
most constraining environments, where dependence and uncertainty
were both the highest. This was the case, for example, in large metropolitan areas, where CD agencies enjoyed little authority and were
dependent on many large and well organized suburban governments
and metropolitan organizations.

*   *   *

Not limited to the public sector, functional coordinating units exist as
public-private partnerships as well, for example the local development corporations active in downtown development (Frieden and
Sagalynn, 1989). They also operate in networks of voluntary and
quasi-public organizations, for example school and higher education
accrediting organizations (Lyttwak and Hylton, 1961: 399). The area
of intercollegiate athletics in the U.S. provides one case of such a
coordinating unit.

Intercollegiate Athletics: The NCAA

The U.S. National Collegiate Athletics Association (NCAA) is a mutual organization: an interorganizational network linking the athletics programs of its member colleges and universities. It has a complex organizational structure, made up of its participating members which are arranged in two membership categories, which elect an Executive Board and a governing Council. It is interesting to trace the evolution of the coordinating unit that runs the NCAA today.[2]

The NCAA was founded by thirteen colleges which agreed on its constitution in 1906. The incentive for this interorganizational network was its members' common desire to standardize the rules for intercollegiate football, in the face of prevailing confusion over existing rules of play, exacerbated by the impact of the recent deaths of several players. The colleges created the NCAA to provide mutual support in the face of mounting public pressure, and as an arena to agree on rules which would eliminate pregame negotiations and protect the players.

Some organizations already existed in the field of amateur athletics. The same problems that generated the NCAA had led to the formation of an interorganizational group, the Football Rules Committee, which was soon absorbed in the NCAA. There was also the Amateur Athletic Union (AAU): a coordinating organization for club-affiliated athletes. The AAU controlled and continues to regulate international events, and there is some overlap between it and the NCAA, producing competition between the two organizations which continues to this day.

Local football conferences, which had been formed in the 1890s, included the "Big Ten", the Chicago Conference, and the Southern Intercollegiate Athletic Conference. The NCAA's organizational structure successfully integrated them into its network as an intermediate level of its hierarchy, initially supplementing them by seeking to influence nationwide practices rather than local ones; later it absorbed them completely.

Under its first constitution the NCAA membership was divided into several geographic districts which made up the unit of representation. Each district elected a representative to the Executive Board which governs the organization, originally made up of three officers and four other members. The NCAA was a loosely linked interorganizational network, whose members retained all their autonomy. Though the Board and committees could promulgate rules, under the original constitution no rule was binding on a member institution that formally objected to it. Since the NCAA rules were freely available to all, the only incentive linking the participating colleges and universities was the solidarity of mutual support.

This soon changed in the years of the NCAA's expansion, beginning in the mid teens.[3] Several environmental factors contributed to the Association's growth. The rebirth of the Olympic Games, which stimulated the development of many athletic programs in the U.S., combined with a concern for physical conditioning engendered by the recruitment needs of World War I. The growth of college athletic programs through the 1920s paralleled the expansion of the national economy. The construction of new stadia on university campuses proceeded apace, and attendance at college football games exploded.

But expansion brought problems, together with its benefits. Colleges' indebtedness generated pressures to increase their athletic revenues. Schools whose attendance depended on their athletic reputations made rehiring their well-paid coaches dependent on winning. Increasing press coverage of collegiate sports and growing public interest provided welcome attention, but also generated alumni pressure for winning performance. This intensely competitive environment resulted in recruiting abuses and the subsidy of amateur athletes which repeatedly produced public scandals.

The Association's membership has consisted of two kinds of schools. One kind are the larger universities which combine more resources with a more acute need for athletic revenues; these are called the "University Division" schools. The other kind, which make up a substantial majority of the membership, are the smaller universities and colleges, who value athletics for their participative competition and support their athletic programs more as a supplement to higher education than for the funds they generate. The conflicting interests of these two groups concerning rules enforcement and revenue distribution reflected their divergent orientations on the relative values of education and athletic competition.

Reflecting the growth of the 1920s, the NCAA restructured its organization. The Executive Board was expanded in 1921, and a separate Council was established to deal with nonfinancial issues. The Council was made up of an elected representative from each district, and five delegates-at-large elected by the entire membership. In 1928 the Board size was increased again, and the Council was also expanded.

During this period, too, the NCAA gradually transformed itself from a network loosely linked through some governing interorganizational groups, into an interorganizational system that was run by an emerging coordinating unit. The organization acquired some full-time support staff, and the governance structure elaborated to reflect the Association's increasing complexity.

Standing committees were formed to develop and monitor rules in each sport. To the existing one for football, the Association added rules committees for basketball (1909), track (1910), soccer (1912), baseball (1913) swimming (1914), volleyball (1918), boxing and wrestling (1920), gymnastics (1927) and fencing (1931). Standing committees also handled championship tournaments, publications, Olympic sports, and records. In 1949 the evolution of the NCAA into a coordinating unit culminated with the appointment of a full-time Director to manage the organization and supervise its staff.

In the early 1930s, economic collapse put a temporary brake on the expansion of intercollegiate athletics as an enterprise, but left a residue of organizational problems. Member institutions were concerned with gate receipts, the costs of competitive recruiting and athletes' subsidies, and the need to maintain their alumni support. Technological advances, too, created problems and opportunities which increased the complexity of interorganizational control.

The initiation and spread of radio combined with post-depression decreases in attendance, to generate heated controversy over the effect of broadcast coverage of football games on revenues (later, this was repeated with the advent of television). At the same time, highway construction and rapidly increasing automobile use vastly expanded the major institutions' catchment areas. Competition grew heated between member schools for two critical resources: athletes and prestige. Prominent schools' athletic recruitment expanded from its local base to become nationwide, and clear channels for acquiring and increasing their prestige were created with the establishment of national championship competition in various sports.

Championship tournaments not only gave prestige to the winners; they also produced revenues. After subsidizing transportation costs for competing teams, substantial receipts remained. The Executive Board, dominated at the time by representatives of the major schools, decided that these funds, after deduction of administrative costs and a percentage for the Association, should be distributed between the competing institutions. This decision reflected the NCAA's character as a loosely linked network, but it was not to be repeated later.

Responding to the problem of rules enforcement was probably one major factor that changed the NCAA's character from a loosely linked network to a much more formal and hierarchical system coordinated by the Association. The original constitution's fundamental principle of member autonomy was reiterated in the 1909 constitution, and member conferences often included non-NCAA affiliated schools. Early attempts at strict enforcement of eligibility rules ended in failure, and all through the 1930s members felt free to ignore rules that limited their competitiveness. In 1935, for example, the S.E. Conference decided against limiting athletic scholarships in a move that was widely imitated, although it was counter to national NCAA policy.

As a result of recurrent abuses, however, the question of enforceable rules was frequently debated, with contrary positions taken by the major universities, who were opposed, and the smaller colleges, who favored stricter enforcement. The central organizational group, made up of NCAA officials and administrative staff, threw the decision to the opponents until the 1930s, when some tentative experiments with enforcement were made. However, obtaining compliance with Association policy and rules remained a problem, as long as the only legislated sanction was expulsion, which was only a limited deterrent.

By the late 1940s public disclosure of unethical practices in recruiting and subsidizing athletes had become a constant embarrassment, and there was growing pressure for some outside intervention and regulation. In 1946 the major conferences met in Chicago to draft one more program that would control eligibility, recruitment practices, and payments to athletes. This was as ineffective as the previous attempts had been, and there were again repeated scandals.

Finally, in 1951 the NCAA drafted legislation that would make its rules binding on all its members, and made noncompliance subject to penalties. This was approved at an Association meeting of the entire membership. This legislation also institutionalized NCAA dominance of intercollegiate football, forcing all the schools in its affiliated conferences to become members.

This decision was the culmination of a long evolution. The smaller colleges had always been interested in restricting recruitment costs and competition, but they had been successfully opposed by the more prominent universities, who feared losing their autonomy and falling under the Association's control. A third interest group had meanwhile emerged: the NCAA officers and staff who, in a process typical of voluntary organizations, formed a group that was considerably more cohesive than the Association's loosely linked membership.

The members' conflicting interests were also reflected in their attitudes to organizational change, which slowed administrative development. For example, when it was proposed to hire a full-time Director, the smaller schools who favored tougher rules enforcement agreed. They were also for expanding the Association staff to improve its capacity for monitoring and enforcing compliance. But the large universities resisted these changes, correctly expecting them to constrain their mutual competition.

The adoption of binding legislation was the result of a coalition between the smaller schools (who were also a majority on the governance bodies) and the NCAA officials and staff. The latter had come to be convinced of the need for rules enforcement, though they were themselves mostly representatives of large universities. Ultimately, even these institutions were prepared to sacrifice some of their independence and choose self-regulation when they were confronted with the escalating costs of unbridled competition and the threat of outside intervention.

There was another major factor which was responsible for the NCAA's evolution from merely a forum for interorganizational communication and debate into a unit which coordinated the network members' interactions in areas of critical interdependence. It was the Association's success in gaining control over resources, on which its membership was dependent, that gave it the ability to coordinate the member institution's actions.

This took several forms, beginning with the members delegating to the Association the representative responsibility in regulating radio broadcasting of athletic events, and in controlling members' access to Olympic competition. But it peaked with the advent of television, and the revenue potential of televised coverage of intercollegiate football. With the opportunity of substantial income, political conflict arose between the large competitive schools who favored individually negotiated contracts with the networks, and the smaller schools seeking central administration of contract negotiation with revenue sharing provisions.

By the early 1950s, when this issue arose, the NCAA leadership was dominated by its administrative core and the smaller schools which made up a majority of its membership. These members, with lesser athletic reputations than the large universities, feared that television coverage would cut their attendance and reduce their revenues. This was the basis for the Association's decision to become the administrative agent for all its members' television coverage, by creating a special committee which approved, negotiated, and administered intercollegiate sports appearances on network television.

Today, the NCAA's administration of the contracts for the television broadcast of major intercollegiate football games gives it control over a critical resource. This "substantial revenue provided the strongest financial linkage between the association and its members." (Stern,

1979: 257). But the NCAA coordinates its members through its control of other resources too: athletic talent, through its binding recruitment and subsidy rules, competitive prestige, through its administration of national championships, and Olympic participation, in its gatekeeper capacity for potential Olympic contenders from the collegiate arena.

In his analysis of this process, Stern (1979) found that changes in the network's linkages and rules gradually gave the NCAA — in effect, the coordinating unit that manages the network — control of resources essential to the member organizations. This made the colleges' athletic programs critically dependent on the NCAA and gave the NCAA administration total dominance over intercollegiate athletics. It was the NCAA's success in capturing resources that has given it the powerful coordinating role it continues to enjoy to this day.

*   *   *

There are many kinds of functional-sectoral coordinating units. One kind are the regulatory agencies coordinating organizations which are interacting in mandated frameworks. These may be agencies, like the U.S. Securities and Exchange Commission, that regulate markets: in this case, the stock exchanges. Or, like the Federal Communications Commission, their regulatory role may be the result of their power to allocate common pool resources: here, assignment of frequencies in the electromagnetic spectrum that is in the public domain.

Another kind of coordinating unit is also operating in a mandated framework, but its link to the interorganizational network is through its control of resources: funds and sometimes delegated authority. Government agencies or bureaus coordinating public projects or programs are this kind of unit.

A different form of functional coordinating unit are government agencies providing coordination between line agencies at the program or service delivery level, for example the Education Service Agencies (ESAs). These were designed to enhance the delivery of specialized services, by providing an arena for School Districts to cooperate with each other in providing these services.

Weiss (1987) evaluated ESAs in nine groups of local School Districts and found that several variables accounted for their relative effectiveness. Their ability to offer funding mattered, but was not as critical as exchange theory seems to suggest. Nor did common professional or political activities seem to have much to do with successful or unsuccessful outcomes. The ESAs' legal mandate was not decisive by itself in eliciting the interdistrict coordination that was intended, but worked when it was reinforced by political consensus, good prior interorganizational relationships, and shared values.

A common aspiration to a "better quality of education" was the reason most frequently cited for cooperating with other Districts. The main reason for some of the ESAs' failure was their inability to instill any sense of pressing need for coordinated special services delivery among members of the interorganizational network concerned. These findings are quite a striking confirmation of the "structuration theory" of IOC discussed in Chapter 3.

Functional-sectoral coordinating units may also appear outside mandated frameworks. Common problems in a particular domain may link a set of organizations into an obligational network: a network in which interdependent organizations are mutually committed through contracts or agreements. Such a network may be coordinated by what Trist called a "referent organization."[4] An example is the N.E. Energy Corporation, which was created as a coordinating unit by several New England utility corporations to handle issues of cooperative plant and infrastructure development and energy allocation between members (Trist, 1983).

Obligational interorganizational networks in the private sector are common. Their number is growing, as a way to obtain the benefits of cooperation without incurring the transaction costs of hierarchical integration (Alter and Hage, 1993: 2–43). Coordination units in these networks are common, too. In construction, for example, the project office in the prime contractor's organization is such a coordinating unit. This exists in complex manufacturing networks as well, as in the aerospace industry (Wren, 1969). Construction management firms show how this type of functional coordinating unit in an obligational network has emerged as a separate and distinct type of organization.

Functional-sectoral coordinating units are also frequently found in promotional interorganizational networks: groups of competing organizations linked by a common sectoral interest. Some forms of these networks are often controlled by coordinating units: the central administrative offices of trade union federations such as the AFL-CIO, for example, or of trade associations such as the National Association of Manufacturers or the Petroleum Institute. Professional and disciplinary organizations, such as the American Bar Association or the Royal College of Surgeons, are also such networks and are coordinated by their central organization.

The last type of coordinating unit is the one linking an interorganizational network that has a common territory or area as its mutual bond. Such units are common in planning and development. Statutory settlement and environmental planning, and land development control, provide a mandated framework for coordinating units in many countries at various levels of government.

At the national level a ministry such as the Department of the Environment in the U.K., and a sub-ministerial agency, such as the Netherlands' *Rijkplanologiese Dienst*, are such coordinating units.[5] Areawide coordinating units at the intermediate level — regional, State or Provincial — are common too. These may be charged with planning and coordinating development in a given territory; for example, the District Planning Commission in Israel, the German *Siedlungsverband Rurkohlenbezirk*, and the California Coastal Development Commission.[6]

Some area coordinating units are not part of a mandated statutory framework, but have come into existence to address problems specific to their designated territories. The following case is an example.

The Appalachian Regional Commission[7]

Appalachia, a depressed region in the eastern U.S., is linked by a common history and culture which developed along its spine of the Appalachian hills. Its population, about 9% of the nation's, has consistently been undereducated and underemployed, and income is well below the national average.

The 1950s saw unprecedented outmigration which combined with a tragic flood in Eastern Kentucky to generate concern. This was the basis of a report of the Eastern Kentucky Regional Planning Commission which called for a regional federal development agency and an interstate development authority. An ongoing dialogue between the governors of the Appalachian States[8] also promoted consciousness of a common regional agenda. While consisting mainly of a concerted appeal for more federal support, it matured into a demand for a comprehensive development program based on major additions to the area's infrastructure, and including natural resource development, tourism and industrial components and social and community programs.

In the fall of 1960 this group took on a formal identity as the Conference of Appalachian Governors (CAG) representing eight states: Alabama, Kentucky, Maryland, N. Carolina, Pennsylvania, Virginia and W.Virginia. CAG successfully made Appalachia's needs one of the issues of the 1960 presidential election. But for the first two years of the Kennedy administration CAG's pressure only produced special treatment for their area by the new Area Redevelopment

Administration, which had been created to administer a national program for depressed areas.

Finally, in April 1963, the President's Appalachian Regional Commission (PARC), made up of federal and State representatives, and chaired by the Secretary of Commerce, was appointed. PARC's program was the basis for the Appalachian Regional Development Act (ARDA) which Congress passed in the spring of 1965. ARDA provided over $840m over six years in highway construction, and $252.4m over two years for other development projects.

PARC's original proposal called for a new organization: a chartered corporation in which the federal government and the Appalachian States would be partners. This was amended, after some objections, to propose two bodies: a joint federal-state planning commission, and a federally chartered development corporation. With the latter killed in Congress, the Appalachian Regional Commission (ARC) remained as the sole coordinating unit to implement ARDA's projects and programs.

ARC is made up of one federal member (with Assistant Secretary status, appointed by the President) and a representative from each State. The federal member, together with one elected state member, serve as co-chairs of the Commission. The ARDA gave ARC the functions of planning, program and project development, and establishing spending criteria and priorities. But the Act withheld authority to make any direct expenditures, which continued to flow through the States and federal line agencies.

To promote the region's economic development, ARC was also expected to coordinate the deployment of federal and private funds, and to "serve as a focal point and coordinating unit for Appalachian programs." To do this, however, ARC received no overriding authority or any independent resources.

Through its first two years ARC planned development programs and lobbied, with some success, for additional appropriations for the region. During this period it performed mainly a "brokerage" function on the region's behalf, and ARC staff became a resource that enabled Appalachian communities to tap the existing grant-in-aid system for their benefit.

In 1967, however, ARC succeeded in gaining new powers through amendments to ARDA, which gave it control over Appalachian expenditures by appropriating funds directly to ARC for ARC proposed projects and programs. This resolved previous conflicts with federal agencies, which had resisted coordinating their activities in the region with the Commission.

Since this change ARC has functioned in many ways like the coordinating unit in any other federal agency administering grants-in-aid. The Commission meets monthly in Washington to determine policy, spending guidelines, and fund allocation between States. ARC personnel staffs the Commission and reviews State submitted program and project proposals. As a coordinating unit, ARC has no "line" functions: programs and projects are implemented by the responsible public agency, and monitored by the appropriate federal oversight agency. Besides its coordinating function, ARC serves as the region's advocate in Washington, and its staff provide technical support for the region's State and local officials.

ARC's effectiveness was enhanced by several developments. By the end of its first year, when the number of proposals grew too large to be reviewed at the Commission's regular meeting, an executive committee was formed and given review authority. This executive committee, made up of the federal co-chair, ARC's Executive Director, and a delegated States' regional representative (a full-time appointed official), had the additional merit of reducing backstage "logrolling" between States, though some open trading still takes place.

Another change was the governors' delegation of their roles on ARC to lower-ranking representatives. This facilitated interstate negotiations and compromises, by reducing political pressures on the Commission. The decision-making system which emerged was based on a series of allocation formulas for the various programs, developed by ARC staff. Where these formulas proved too rigid to accommodate States' competing interests, they were supplemented by formal bilateral trades of categorical funds between States, and by discretionary reallocations by the executive committee.

ARC's dual federal-state role is reflected in its organizational headquarters structure, which is jointly headed by the federal co-chair and the States' regional representative. Each has a veto over decisions, and each has the same access to Congress and control over ARC's staff. However, this has had some divisive impacts too, as ARC evolved into what is, in fact, an agency with two heads.

Evaluation of ARC's performance is difficult. One of its goals was to improve intergovernmental decision making, through a more decentralized planning process. The plan that ARC developed essentially proposed a growth pole policy, so its effectiveness could be assessed by the conformity of public investments to the plan. By this criterion ARC can claim some limited success, though no one can say that these investments might not have been the same in the absence of ARC and its development strategy.

ARC's success in restructuring regional planning and decision making has also been limited. States are still the basic polities in the development game, and their policies have not adjusted more than the minimum needed to fulfill federal assistance requirements. As in other grant programs, ARC's planning is passively accepted by States and localities as another channel for receiving federal aid. The actual impact of regional programs is questionable, and they seem to have little effect on Appalachia's economic performance.

But these questions are secondary to the main issue here: what has been the impact of ARC as a coordination structure? In other words, are the effects of ARC's activities different from what they would have been under a different program planning and delivery system? One way of attempting such an evaluation is to compare these effects to the estimated costs and benefits of an alternative structure: direct grant administration by a federal agency.

One positive impact claimed for ARC is a more rational public decision making process with its related social and political benefits. Most of the Appalachian States would not have pursued the comprehensive planning process that they did without ARC, and ARC successfully reconciled federal, State and local interests. Public programs and projects in Appalachia have been better coordinated in space and over time than they would otherwise have been, and are more consistent with State goals and priorities that were articulated in plans which, but for ARC, would not have come into existence.

Another positive impact is the benefits resulting from federal funds. ARC undoubtedly attracted a far larger share of federal support than the region would otherwise have received, including federal investments well beyond the direct appropriations for the Appalachian program. It is impossible to estimate what proportion of these investments might have been attracted to the region under an alternative form of organization. But ARC's planning and operating costs over its first four years have been estimated at between $1.6 million and $4.9 million, representing between 0.3% and 0.8% of total State and local investment in the Appalachian program over this period. Federal funds devoted to Appalachia over these four years totaled nearly $360 million. If only 5% of this amount is the increment attributable to ARC compared to any alternative, this still represents a very positive benefit-cost ratio.

Finally, the clearest evidence of ARC's success is its continued political support and survival. In the early 1970s ARC looked like an exemplar for potential imitators, but more detailed observation suggested that some of its advantages, compared to other forms of decentralization, may have been the result of special circumstances, and so may not be easily replicated (Derthick, 1974: 106–107, 224–230).

ARC's success as a coordinating unit may, at least in part, be due to its particular configuration, which fitted it especially well to become the arena for resolving conflicting interests between States and the federal government. Its mandate and geographical distribution, too, equipped ARC well for generating the congressional constituency which has been a powerful factor in its growth and stability.

*   *   *

Organizations sometimes also emerge as coordinating units of interorganizational networks outside a mandated framework. By creating the perception of mutual interests and interdependence among potential members, the coordinating organization can create such a network where there was only a fragmented interorganizational field before.

Rubin (1984) describes such a case in his review of "meshing" organizations and other types of coordinating units, which he distinguishes from coordinating organizations operating through authority in mandated frameworks. These organizations elicit coordinated action in the interorganizational network through negotiation in different ways: through dyadic interaction between the coordinating unit and other agencies in joint project or program implementation, or through simultaneous interaction with other members of the network (for example, in joint planning arenas) in defining common goals.

The County Planning Agency as a "Meshing" Organization

"Twin Rivers" a wealthy suburban Illinois county abutting the metropolitan area of Chicago, faced several problems as a result of the fragmented development of its individual municipalities. Its population had tripled within two decades, its local governments were locked in annexation wars, and its towns were experiencing rapid and undirected growth.

Strip commercial development on major highways was creating visual blight and transportation hazards. Uncoordinated development produced incompatible neighbors, as when the less desirable industrial and commercial areas of one municipality expanded to the edge of another's elite residential development. Development was swallowing up open space, which would rapidly disappear with the existing rate of urbanization. Infrastructure development was fragmented, without coordinated planning of water, sewerage or transportation, and area municipalities were unable to respond to State and federal demands for their planning responses in areas such as transportation and open housing.

Previous coordination efforts had failed. The County Board, which had jurisdiction over one third of the county's population and half of its area in its unincorporated areas, could not initiate any coordination among the municipalities, which considered the county their rival. The multicounty regional planning commission was distrusted as a tool of the threatening neighboring Chicago metropolis. Recognizing their mutual problems and interdependence, the "Twin Rivers" municipalities established a Mayors'-Managers' Conference which met periodically to formalize intergovernmental coordination, but this interorganizational group did not accomplish much.

The foundation was laid for the County planning agency to become a "meshing" coordinating unit when the Board hired a planner and two secretaries in 1969 to draw up a "701" countywide land use plan.[9] In a series of moves the county planner transformed his agency into the "Twin Rivers Regional Planning Commission" (TRRPC), which grew from its original staff of three to twenty three, including seventeen professionals, and a budget of over $0.5 million.

The planner's first move was to broaden his political base and legitimate his agency's coordinating role. Legally, the planning department was an agency of the county, regarded as a competing unit of government by many municipalities. Recognizing the danger in this perception, the county planner conditioned his contract on his reporting to a special supervising Commission. This Commission was made up of individuals reflecting the distribution of power in the area: elected politicians, leaders of the county professional managers' association, and members of the county's economic elite. Though the county Board appointed its members, the Commission's recommendations were almost always followed, and the agency's reports were not published as county documents, but appeared over the Commission's signatures.

In another move, TRRPC leveraged its mandate to prepare the county land use plan, into a tool that enabled it to interact with, and eventually influence, the implementation of several other important activities. The data that the TRRPC collected and processed for its comprehensive land use planning became a valuable resource for the individual municipalities in preparing their specific plans, and finally the coordination of municipalities' plans was effected by their use of a common data set.

The land use planning in which TRRPC was engaged also gave its staff information and expertise which were transferable to other areas, assets that TRRPC exploited to the limit. Its control of pertinent data enabled TRRPC's involvement in coordinating Community Development Block Grant (CDBG) allocations, planning the towns' "fair share" housing distributions, and developing the county's "208" environmental plan.

TRRPC's baseline data also enabled it to obtain contracts for area transportation planning from three substate agencies, which again gave the organization leverage to expand its coordinating role. When the local Mayor's-Manager's Conference learned of these contracts, it assigned its share of technical responsibility for highway planning to TRRPC. In its negotiations with individual municipalities to coordinate their transportation plans, TRRPC's role was enhanced by its other transportation planning responsibilities and its knowledge of other municipalities' plans.

In the course of preparing its "701" plan, TRRPC also developed a political constituency. TRRPC staff met with all the area's homeowners associations, numbering several hundred, and all its local governments. The coalition which emerged from these interactions proved invaluable in support of TRRPC's open space policy of creating a greenbelt to limit and direct urban growth in the county, and for the establishment of a Forest Preservation District.

As it expanded its functions, TRRPC's command of information combined with area municipalities' distrust of outside government agencies to give it another coordinating role: as a "buffer" and mediator in local governments' interactions with state and federal agencies. TRRPC came to handle all their contacts with the Department of Housing and Urban Development, the Illinois Department of Transportation, and the multicounty regional planning agency which had federally assigned signoff and coordination responsibilities (known as A-95 from the relevant OMB regulation).

In this coordinating role TRRPC sometimes represented both sides. For example, the regional A-95 agency had delegated its water quality planning responsibilities (called "208" planning) for the area to TRRPC. One small city requested approval for the construction of a new sewage processing plant, but the regional agency feared that this would promote the city's growth. TRRPC was also the city's contract planner; in this role it credibly reassured the regional overseer that no growth was planned. The new plant was only intended to process the current load; its additional capacity did not provide for new residential construction, but only for hooking up dwellings currently using septic systems to the sewerage network.

During its infancy TRRPC was confronted with absorption into the County's Public Works Department. The Director successfully fended off this threat, and later TRRPC itself initiated the takeover of several related county offices. The first was the county zoning department, known as "maps and plats". This was also an advantageous acquisition because the fees for its services made "maps and plats" self-sustaining and even a modest profit center. Later, the county was convinced to establish a County Development Department under the TRRPC, which included the planning, zoning, "maps and plats", and community development units. These additional functions gave the TRRPC welcome legitimation in a range of areas, and linked it to implementation agencies; for example, TRRPC came to staff the zoning board and was thus involved in critical land use implementation decisions.

In multiplying its functions, TRRPC also expanded its fiscal base. Over the period of 1975 to 1979, 11.5% of TRRPC's budget came from its transportation planning contracts, 18.7% was CDBG funded, 9.3% was 701 funding, 3.2% was "208" planning fees, 5.4% was paid by eight municipalities under planning service contracts, and just under 1% was paid under contracts with CETA and the Census Bureau. The balance of the agency's budget, just under 50%, was appropriated by the county. These diverse sources of funding reduced the agency's dependence on any single constituency, and enhanced its coordinating power.

TRRPC's successful coordination of its areawide interorganizational network resulted in a comprehensive land use plan for the whole county which was adopted by county government and many of the area's municipalities. Local plans in the county were modified and periodically adjusted to coincide with the county plan's provisions. A coordinated transportation plan was prepared for the region and approved by all the relevant participating agencies and units of government.

The agency also initiated subcounty agreements which curtailed strip commercial development, and created a standing forum for county municipalities to react to federal and state initiatives which might affect them. TRRPC's urban growth policy and its open space program became the coordinating framework for the county's local governments' regulation of their individual development, and the TRRPC was instrumental in obtaining general agreement to establish the county's Forest Preserve District.

This agency's experiences suggest some rules that would improve the chances of successful cooperation:

- Focus on activities offering potential economies of scale, but which also produce outcomes that are useful to each member of the interorganizational network — in this case the individual municipalities;

- Identify as cooperative projects, undertakings that capitalize on network members' distrust of outside agencies;

- Create (if it does not already exist) an advisory interorganizational group representing the network: a Board or committee, for political protection;

- Diversify the coordinating unit's resource base: find different sources of funding;

- "Capture" other bureaucratic agencies that are noncontroversial;

- Maximize "meshing" and "reticulating" activities: dyadic interactions between the coordinating unit and other network organizations;

- Wherever possible, depoliticize: define actions as merely technical;

- Be prepared to take some political "heat" to protect your allied organizations and political supporters (Rubin, 1984).

*   *   *

Coordinating units have a relatively high degree of organizational autonomy. They can be distinct units within a larger agency, organization or corporation, or they are themselves separate organizations. Their effectiveness, which varies considerably, does not seem necessarily associated either with their autonomy or their power.

We can find highly autonomous and powerful coordinating units that are very effective. One kind are the powerful governmental regulatory agencies which have successfully structured important sectors and markets. On the other hand, there are some autonomous coordinating agencies which seem potentially powerful but are quite ineffective; many planning agencies illustrate this case.

But coordinating units can also be effective with relatively little authority and slender resources. This is shown in the case of the County Planning Agency which succeeded in turning itself into the "meshing" organization for its areawide interorganizational network, and is true of many coordinating units in obligatory networks, such as the N.E. Energy Corporation Trist described.

Though often interorganizational groups face the same tasks as coordinating units, generally coordinating units handle larger interorganizational networks, with more complex interdependencies, than less autonomous IOC structures, such as the liaison or coordinator. The interorganizational networks which have to be coordinated, however, and the coordinating unit's mission, vary widely. They range from the four or five School Districts linked in a mandated framework, which were coordinated by the Educational Services Agencies to deliver a few specialized educational services, to the enormous and ramified network of federal agencies which cover almost every aspect of human endeavor, that is coordinated by the U.S. Office of Management and Budget.

If it is not clearly associated with autonomy or power, the effectiveness of coordinating units may be related to their "fit" with their tasks and their interorganizational networks. What the cases of successful coordinating units seem to have in common is the way in which their structure, authority, and resources matched the coordination tasks and the network that was to be coordinated.

"Fit" occurs in one of two ways. The institutional design of the coordinating unit: its own organizational structure, the authority it has to modify the behavior of members of its network (mandated, or by contract or agreement in obligatory and promotional networks) or the resources it controls as incentives for compliant performance, can be appropriate for the characteristics of its network and the type and range of coordinated tasks.

This prescription is a tautology, of course: how does one know what "appropriate" is, before the coordinating unit is in operation? Neither research nor experience have succeeded in producing a general blueprint for good institutional design. There are undoubtedly cases in which coordination units have been created which perform very well from the start, and undergo little or no modification during their operation: the United Way is an example. But these cases are either rare or seldom documented.

The other, more usual, way in which coordinating units get to "fit" their tasks and environment is in a process of adaptation. This process is the subject of many of the prescriptions that are the product of positive evaluations or successful experience. The prospective coordinating unit can adapt a potential interorganizational network to match its own capacity: it can select organizations in its environment and initiate interactions with them, finding appropriate tasks that will stimulate these interactions. This is what the "meshing" organization, the county planning agency, did.

This form of adaptation to achieve a successful fit is the subject of prescriptions such as: "Identify needs for ... coordination and emphasize the value of interorganizational collaboration", and "identify potential ... partners and seek linkage with those who are most compatible" (Whetten and Bozeman, 1991: 89–90). Task-related prescriptions, too, such as Rubin's (1984: 295–6) suggestion to focus on projects that combine the need for resources (e.g., . information or expertise) controlled by the coordinating unit, with the prospect of products useful to network members, address this adaptive process.

Other forms of adaptation present themselves when the relation between the coordinating unit and its interorganizational network is already determined: by a mandated framework, or by obligatory or promotional links. The coordinating unit can adapt its mission and tasks to its capacity and power. This is the sense of prescriptions to: "Recognize limits and set reasonable goals" (Whetten and Bozeman, 1991: 95), adapt the organization's mission to its constitutional, legal, and structural context (Agranoff and Lindsay, 1983: 229), and to focus on well-defined and specific tasks within the coordinating unit's area of competence (Seidman, 1980: 215).

Finally, effective coordination units adapt their structure and resources to the demands of their interorganizational network and mission. When these do not match, coordination units usually fail. There are two types of such failures. "Crises of competence" occur when a coordinating unit has adequate authority to initiate actions, but lacks the resources to follow their implementation through. A "crisis of legitimacy" happens when a coordinating unit is well endowed with resources, but not with the necessary responsibility or authority to support its involvement in a particular domain (Lehman, 1979: 95–96).

Some coordinating units succeed because they have adapted their organization, authority, and funding to the scope of their interorganizational network or the dimensions of their task. The NCAA case illustrates how a coordinating unit has done this: it changed its organizational structure, received more binding authority from its membership, and gained control over critical resources to eventually dominate its field.

The Appalachian Regional Commission is another good example of adaptive "fit". It modified its internal organization to enable more effective decision making, it obtained substantial additional funding from Congress, and it received new authority under legislation it sponsored that increased its control over the powerful federal line agencies in its interorganizational network.

6.2. The Lead Organization

Another meso-IOC structure is the lead organization. This describes one way of coordinating an interorganizational network, in which one organization, in addition to its line functions, is responsible for coordinating the activities of all the other organizations. The lead organization is distinguished from the coordinating unit by the fact that the latter has coordination of the network as its sole purpose, while coordination may be incidental to the lead organization's functional tasks.[10]

In the intergovernmental context the lead organization is a common IOC structure, usually under a mandated framework. Ministries or Departments responsible for programs involving extensive networks of other agencies and organizations — other sectoral departments, state or provincial agencies, local governments and their agencies, and contractors and service providers — are in fact lead organizations.

Some examples are the U.S. Department of Housing and Urban Development in the Model Cities program (Alexander, 1980) and in the Urban Information Systems interagency committees (USAC) (Kraemer and King, 1979), the Israel Ministry of Housing and Construction in Israel's development towns program (Alexander, 1980), and the U.S. Department of Labor in the CETA- and JTPA-funded employment training and placement programs (Williams, 1980; Jennings and Zank, 1993). There are many more, in almost all countries of the globe.

Intergovernmental networks at the local level may also be coordinated by lead agencies. For example, for the Los Angeles Century Freeway project, the California Housing and Development Commission was designated as the lead organization. As it happened (like other similar cases), the commission's mandate was too weak for it to function effectively, and it was replaced in its coordinating role by other IOC structures (Mandell, 1984).

Another mandated framework produced a more successful case of a local lead organization. The framework was a state work-welfare initiative in Wisconsin: the Work Experience and Job Training (WEJT) program enacted in 1986 as a forerunner to the JOBS program, which designated the county welfare office as the lead organization. Kenosha County, Wisconsin was a pilot site for the project, and its welfare agency offers a good illustration of this IOC structure.

The Kenosha Co., Wisconsin, WEJT Program

The original model for program coordination envisaged bringing together all the major actors: the welfare office, the PIC, the Job Service, the local technical college, and community organizations. Under the nominal responsibility of the county welfare agency, they were to improve job-readiness and increase the labor market participation of the county's welfare recipients. But interorganizational linkages were too weak for effective action, and massive confusion, client loss, and interagency scapegoating ensued.

In response, the county welfare office shut down operations in 1987, while it restructured the interorganizational network to create a functionally integrated program. This process took four years, but at the end of that time it succeeded in assembling a model program that attracted wide attention.

The main coordination tool used was collocation of core functions under one roof. These include income maintenance (delivered by the county welfare office under the AFDC program), JOBS case management, employment-related functions delivered by the Job Service, and several other services. Physical proximity facilitated client access and enabled unified case management.

The system includes a shared computerized information bank, into which public assistance applicant data is entered, and which automatically computes eligibility and benefits for all major assistance programs. Client intake is handled by a JOBS case manager, working with an economic support or welfare specialist from the county welfare office's staff. This is followed by an interagency-sponsored orientation, after which the participant enters a 5-month course which includes motivational classes, job-search skill training, vocational explorations, in-depth assessments, and preparation of an individual employment development plan.

Case management teams made up of an economic support specialist (a member of the welfare office staff), two JOBS case managers, and a Job Service specialist, work out of the same office, sharing telephone lines and workstations linked into the integrated information system. This integrated case management ensures effective coordination of services delivered by other agencies that are not in-house: vocational training at the technical college, for example, or on-the-job training through a PIC-affiliated firm. The same facility offers on-site child care, training rooms, and other services. Additional planned services include child support personnel, basic education programs, additional JOB service staff, and selected PIC placement-related activities.

Although the model is not yet fully developed, every indicator suggests that it is very effective. Participation rates are well above JOBS program requirements, and the performance of clients processed through the program is encouraging. Welfare caseloads dropped by 20% from their 1986 peak, in spite of the closing of Chrysler's Kenosha plant, which was the area's major employer. Today, more than 80% of Kenosha County's new AFDC and general assistance clients exit (if only temporarily) within their first 30 months on welfare (Corbett, 1993).

These results are due to the program's excellent design and effective implementation. But this experience, after the program's initial failure, also suggests that these would not have happened without the county welfare agency taking its lead organization responsibilities seriously. The lead organization contributed the institutional design of the integrated program format, and it developed strong links with the other participating agencies that enabled it to effect some radical reorganization. This included other agencies seconding and collocating their staff for teamwork in the new integrated one-stop facility, participating in joint planning and training, and blending their previously separate client monitoring data into a common client and program information system. Unquestionably it was these changes, implemented by the participating organizations at the lead organization's initiative, that turned this program into a success.

*   *   *

The linking of interorganizational production networks through contracts and subcontracting is another way in which lead organizations operate, in the public and private sectors alike. In the private sector this IOC model is widespread; examples are the prime- and subcontractors in the construction industry, and subcontracting networks in sectors such as automobile production, aerospace, computer hardware, electronics, fashion apparel, light machinery, and publishing.

This is the way in which public projects that involve extensive private sector procurement are also coordinated, on what is in effect the interface between the public and the private sectors. The agency implementing such a project is not really acting as an organization in the sense we usually understand, but as the lead organization coordinating the activities of an interorganizational network of other agencies, contractors, and suppliers. The Apollo moon-landing program, in which the National Aeronautics and Space Agency (NASA) was the lead organization, is a case that illustrates this IOC structure in all its scope and complexity.

NASA and the Apollo Program

The event that led to the creation of NASA was the Russian launching of the first spacecraft, *Sputnik*, in 1959. NASA was formed as a loosely linked organization of four preexisting centers that remained relatively autonomous. The "mother center" at Langley, Virginia, which became NASA's headquarters, was originally the National Advisory Committee for Aeronautics (NACA), an aeronautic research laboratory that had been established in 1917. The other units were the Lewis Research Center at Cleveland, Ohio, responsible for propulsion systems, the Ames Research Center in California which did wind testing, and the Edwards High Speed Flight Station which was transferred from the Air Force.

NASA's creation was simultaneous with the definition of its lunar mission, and in 1959 an interorganizational group, the Goett committee, was formed to plan the steps toward manned space flight. These resulted in the Mercury program which successfully orbited the first astronaut, John Glenn, around the earth, as a first stage towards space flight and lunar exploration. But U.S.-Soviet competition in space continued, and a possible technology gap was exposed when the Russian spacecraft *Vostok* orbited the earth. The American response was to initiate the Apollo program, which President Kennedy announced to Congress in his famous speech on April 12, 1961, setting the goal of landing a man on the moon within the decade (Murray and Cox, 1989: 60–65).

Even before Kennedy's formal announcement, NASA began planning for its new mission. This meant making some basic decisions, which involved simultaneous exploration of technological and feasibility alternatives. Should there be one spacecraft, which would follow a direct route to land on the moon after its earth launching? Or was an indirect alternative preferable: an earth orbit rendezvous, or a lunar orbit rendezvous between the spacecraft and a lunar lander?

An ad-hoc internal planning group, the Fleming committee, was called together to deliberate this question. It had twenty members, representing NASA headquarters and its other centers, and selected the direct route. NASA administration, uncomfortable with this decision, set up another group to consider other alternatives in more depth. This eight-man group, headed by a member of the Lewis Research Center, favored the lunar rendezvous option, which was adopted as the Apollo mission plan.

In late 1961, as NASA scientists and engineers proceeded with more detailed design of the Apollo system, the system was decomposed into its major components to bid and assign the major hardware contracts. The first was for the guidance and navigation system; this was given to MIT Instrumentation Labs, which had already been working with NASA as consultants.

For the command module, there was vigorous competition in the aerospace industry, and fourteen firms bid on NASA's specifications. In a rigorous review process these were narrowed down to five consortia: General Dynamics-AVCO, General Electric-Douglas with Grumman Aircraft and STL, Martin-McDonnell with Lockheed, Hughes Aircraft and Chance-Vought, and North American. The NASA selection board ranked Martin highest on its formal evaluation criteria, but ultimately North American was awarded the contract, based largely on its experience and its long association with NASA and its predecessor, NACA.

In 1962, subcontractors were selected for four spacecraft systems. Collins Radio was awarded the contract for telecommunications, the Garrett Corporation received environmental controls, Honeywell subcontracted for the stability and altitude control system, and Northrop's Radioplane Division was assigned the parachutes and earth landing equipment. At the same time another major component was put out for bid; this resulted in the Grumman Corporation receiving the contract for the lunar lander.

When the Apollo program was in full swing NASA, which retained basic system design and engineering responsibilities, was coordinating an interorganizational network made up of thirty four firms: major manufacturers contracting for over $5 million of work. They included the prime contractors (who experienced some consolidations and changes after the initial contracts were awarded): North American Rockwell, AC Electronics, MIT Instrumentation Labs, Grumman, and General Electric, and thirty three subcontractors for all the systems and components of the spacecraft, including the command module, the lunar lander, and the boosters and rockets.

NASA itself expanded considerably to cope with its lead organization responsibilities and run the Apollo program. It also underwent some internal reorganization, and initiated significant organizational innovations. The Apollo program tasks were assigned between the NASA units which included several new centers.

The Johnson Manned Spacecraft Center in Houston, Texas, created for this program, supervised the spacecraft development and manufacture, and associated ground input equipment, planned missions, and was responsible for flight control and developing mission control equipment, and flight crew selection and training. The Marshall Space

Flight Center in Huntsville, Alabama, designed and developed the Saturn launch vehicles and supervised their production. The Kennedy Space Center at Cape Canaveral, Florida, had responsibility for developing and operating the launch and industrial maintenance facilities there, and for providing the associated ground support for assembly, testing, inspection, checkout and launching at the launch site (Brooks, Grimwood and Swenson, 1979: 33–65, 399–405).

The Apollo program not only originated technological innovations; NASA had to create some organizational innovations as well. One of these was what was popularly known as "Mission Control". This was the Flight Control unit in Houston, Texas, which supplanted the previous rudimentary control center that existed for the Mercury program. NASA's Flight Control for Apollo centered on a newly devised feature: the Mission Control Operations Room (MOCR), which collocated all the by now quite elaborate and highly differentiated control systems in one space.

MOCR contained rows of specialized controllers at adjacent consoles and monitors, allowing instant interaction and response to mission problems and crises, which did in fact occur. Tel Comm (communications systems), O&P (operations and procedures), the Flight Director and his Assistant, the Flight Activities Officer (representing Flight Crew Operations, whose task was to check actual mission activities' consistency with crews' training routines) the Surgeon, CapCon (communications), EECom (life support systems monitoring), GNC (guidance, navigation and control) and others occupied desks in the MOCR, as did similar functions for the lunar module. Monitors for the Saturn rocket and the booster system also had their stations in the MOCR: Booster, Retro, FIDO, Guido, and others. MOCR was devised so as to ensure coordinated interaction between all the various functions and system controllers: its function was to monitor and manage each mission in real time (Murray and Cox, 1989: 270–281).

The Apollo program was NASA's golden age; though coordinating such a complex undertaking was a monumental task,[11] NASA effectively discharged its lead organization responsibilities, adapting its own organization and managing the extensive network of contractors to bring the program to a successful conclusion.

The culmination of almost ten years' effort came on June 20, 1969, at 4:17:32 Eastern Daylight Time, when the lunar landing module headed in on its final landing approach between two boulder-strewn fields on the moon's surface, towards a relatively smooth area pocked only with some small craters. As the module's pads touched the lunar topsoil a contact light flashed on the control console, and the crew reported to Mission Control back on Earth. "Houston, Tranquility Base here", said astronaut Armstrong: "The Eagle has landed" (Lewis, 1974).

*   *   *

The success of a lead organization operating in a mandated framework depends on the strength of its mandate and its willingness to use its authority to impose sanctions or allocate resources. The lead organization in a production network, on the other hand, is very likely to be effective, if it has the resources to purchase the services or products it needs from contractors and suppliers. While this is a necessary condition, it has to be coupled with the ability to manage and coordinate the interorganizational network. This involves designing and deploying other IOC structures to plan joint action, monitor performance, assure quality and compliance with specifications, and adapt participating organizations' behavior to unanticipated contingencies.

6.3. The Single Organization

The distinction between the lead organization and the single organization, as IOC structures, depends on the degree to which all the relevant activities are internalized. It is the difference between an organization that has some line functions, but that has as an important part of its role the coordination of an interorganizational network to carry out other important activities, as NASA was in the Apollo program, and the single organization entrusted with the execution of a complex undertaking — a program or project, for example, the British New Town Corporation, in the planning and development of a new community (Alexander, 1980; Herbert, 1980) — in which outside actors are more peripheral.[12]

Identifying a single organization as an IOC structure seems paradoxical, but it is not when we recognize that the role of IOC structures is enacted in the context of dynamic processes. The case of U.S. planned community development shows how illusory this apparent paradox is. The 1968 New Communities program, a non-administered program in a complex interorganizational system of public agencies, developers and financial institutions, was created to stimulate the construction of large comprehensively planned new communities (Alexander, 1992). Thirty years earlier, Roosevelt's New Deal administration addressed the same problems and the same interorganizational system in a different way. A new federal agency was created as a subunit of the Resettlement Administration to plan and build new towns in the Greenbelt Towns program (Arnold, 1971). This IOC structure was a single organization.

The same sector offers many examples of the single organization IOC structure: Britain's New Town Corporation (Alexander, 1980), France's *Etablissement Public d'Amenagement* (Rubinstein, 1978) and Malasia's Federal Land Development Authority (Turner, 1978) are some. Another arena where this IOC structure is popular is regional development. The U.S. Tennessee Valley Authority (Derthick, 1974: 18–45) was a trend-setting example; other cases are Venezuela's *Corporacion Venezolana de Guyana* (CVG), and Israel's Lakhish Regional Administration (Alexander, 1980).

Single organizations may be formed by merger of existing organizations in the hierarchical integration explained by transaction cost theory (Williamson, 1981, 1991). This refers to coordination in the private sector, where we can distinguish between several kinds of mergers (Pfeffer and Salancik, 1978: 114–131). One kind is the classic vertical integration that merges firms linked by symbiotic interdependence. For example, corporations in the petrochemical industry integrate plastics production with the refinery operations which generate byproducts that are its raw materials.

Another kind of merger is between competitive or commensally interdependent organizations. The multihospital systems that formed in the late 1970s and early 1980s are an example. Here, government regulation and purchase of services created a supportive environment for horizontal integration, which offered benefits of scale in the form of increased Medicaid payments, while externalizing the costs of merger (interest on financing, and asset depreciation) by allowing cost-plus accounting (Arnold, 1991). Merger can also be a response to a thrust for diversification; the diversified conglomerate is an example.

In the public sector we find the same types of mergers. The U.S. Department of Housing and Urban Development (HUD) was formed by putting several separate symbiotically interdependent agencies, including the Federal Housing Authority (FHA), the Federal National Mortgage Agency ("Fannie Mae") and the Public Housing Authority, under one hierarchical cabinet department.

The Minneapolis Community Development Agency is example of the second type, where state legislation merged two different agencies carrying out similar activities in a "horse and rabbit stew". These were the large Housing and Redevelopment Authority, with nearly 500 staff, with the little Industrial Development Commission. The Minnesota Department of Energy, Planning and Development is a case of the third kind of merger, combining relatively diverse predecessor agencies in a loosely coupled organization. Another example of this almost random "garbage can" type of merged organization is the U.S. Department of Health and Human Services (Hult, 1987).

An organization may also be created as an IOC structure for a particular undertaking. In the private sector, this may be as a vehicle for a consortium, joint venture, or partnership between firms. Such an organization may function largely as a coordinating unit, as in some of the cases discussed under interorganizational networks.

Or the new organization may be a pool in which network members invest resources to carry out a task in which they share a common interest. An example is Switchco, set up by a network of twenty Independent Financial Advisor firms in Britain's insurance industry, to develop and support electronic trading between companies in the network and their intermediaries (Knight, Murray and Willmott, 1993: 982–987). Or it may be the framework for a public-private partnership, for example: the downtown development corporations that proliferated in the U.S. in the 1980s (Frieden and Sagalynn, 1989).

In the public sector, too, new organizations are constantly being created as IOC structures for special projects or programs. They may be for large and complex sets of activities, or relatively simple and small ones. An example of the former is the CVG, formed to undertake the development of the Guyana region of Venezuela.

The Corporación Venezolana de Guyana[13]

In 1950 the population of the Guyana region of South-Eastern Venezuela was only about 4000, but its agricultural and industrial potential was recognized. The new civilian-military junta under Romulo Betancourt created the *Corporación Venezolana de Fomento* (CVF) to explore the feasibility of exploiting the area's huge iron ore deposits in combination with the region's cheap hydroelectric power. But the next administration allowed the CVF to atrophy, giving the development task to a politicized unit close to the new dictator, Pedro Jimenez, the Office of Special Studies, which became notorious for its corruption and inefficiency.

At the same time, however, Jimenez created another, very different, organization for the Caroni Dam: the *Comision de Estudios para la Electrificacion del Caroni* (CEEC), headed by an engineer, Major (later General) Rafael Alonzo Ravard. He gave this unit a reputation for technical competence that assured its organizational autonomy and enabled it to survive the fall of the Jimenez regime. The newly elected · Betancourt administration made the development of Guyana a cornerstone of its national development program, and formed a Presidential Commission, headed by Ravard, to design a permanent organization to implement the CVF's development program. On December 30, 1960, the *Corporación Venezolana de Guyana* (CVG) was established, with Ravard as its president.

With a program that enjoyed high government priority and wide popular support, and as the only operational agency answerable directly to the president, the CVG had a unique power base. This enabled it to overcome a regional agency's usual problems of managing relations with powerful sectoral and partisan ministries. The CVG also enhanced its status by limiting its activities to development programs that reflected broad national priorities rather than narrow regional interests.

The development program included the planning and construction of a new city, Ciudad Guyana, for a target population of a quarter of a million by 1975. The new city was to be based on an industrial complex including hydroelectric powered steel and aluminum production, and would be a growth pole for agriculture-based development of the regional hinterland. During planning and implementation, the city's population targets were constantly raised, finally reaching 600,000 by 1980.

The CVG encouraged the State legislature to create a municipal district for the planned city, and later assisted the local government in providing municipal services. But relations between the CVG and the city council were not all sweetness and light: the city complained that the CVG continued to exercise paternalistic authority and to cream off profitable activities such as development of the commercial center. In turn the CVG argued (probably correctly) that the local government lacked technical competence, and suggested it focus on meeting its low-income residents' service needs.

A CVG-created urban development subsidiary undertook land acquisition and disposition, site development, infrastructure and services planning and promotion, and project financing. In the course of the program, the CVG changed, from an organization focused on planning and direct implementation, to an indirect actor promoting development. This transformation did not occur without friction.

CVG owned almost all the land in the planned city, after acquiring about 40% of the land in the Caroni district. This gave the CVG unusual control over development, but also made land management a burden diverting attention and resources from other issues. Ciudad Guyana also had to avoid the image of a "company town", which would discourage private investment. CVG's flexible land disposition policy, which included phased release of commercial land, and development partnerships, minimized these problems.

In its economic development strategy, CVG focused on a few large-scale industrial and infrastructure projects, in which it played the role of promoter and developer to recruit foreign investors and local capital. Projects included the Guri Dam hydroelectric power complex, the Orinoco Steel Mill, and other iron ore processing and aluminum production plants. The results of these efforts have been mixed, but on the whole CVG's record in this sector has been quite good.

However, in other areas the CVG has been less successful. These include light industry, commerce, social infrastructure, and services. This is partly due to these sectors' lower priority compared to primary and heavy industry, and partly due to CVG's unwarranted confidence in the unassisted market to develop these areas. In spite of incentives which included government plant and equipment financing, an expanding local market, and fully serviced industrial parks, light industry (apart from construction materials) has been slow to develop. Housing, commercial and personal services, and transportation have also lagged behind the expanding population's needs.

CVG's effectiveness in leveraging its own investments is critical to the success of its program. On this criterion reality fell far short of expectations: instead of the planned fivefold leverage, investors only contributed a half-dollar for each CVG dollar. Major projects calling for advanced technology, and limited to two-party negotiations with one of a few large corporations were quite successful. But CVG has been less effective in more complex undertakings involving more extensive networks of other national agencies, city government, and small to medium businesses.

The CVG went through several phases of coordinating its relevant interorganizational network, especially other public agencies. Until 1965 it pursued a direct-action model, internalizing all essential functions. Partly, this was due to the difference between its tasks and "normal" public services, which are budgeted for an existing population. Estimates for CVG's developmental activities, by contrast, are based on planners' dreams, as viewed by other public agencies which preferred to withhold their investments in Guyana until its growth was manifest.

However, the same agencies reacted angrily when they saw development in progress, and CVG invading sectors under their jurisdiction. While CVG's charter gives it the task of coordinating public agencies' activities in the region, its lack of any enforcement powers forced it to seek their cooperation. This was less urgent in the early stages of the program when the GVG could "do it yourself", but later it became crucial.

At this stage the CVG had to abandon its separate path, which was linked to an image of technocratic secrecy, instead becoming a promoter of its plans and programs to encourage other functional agencies to take part. This process culminated in 1965 with the integration of the Guyana program into the national plan, and the earmarking of other sectoral funds for investment in the region.

Other aspects of CVG's IOC strategies also changed. Originally, CVG saw itself in a hierarchical relationship with other public agencies: its coordinating role required them to follow its plans and development strategies, and limited them to implementation. GVG was reluctant to reveal its longer-range plans, and focused its activities in areas that did not need other institutions. For example, for several years CVG neglected public education in Ciudad Guyana, just providing some support for parochial schools. However, over the long run this proved untenable, and the Ministry of Education had to become involved in developing an acceptable educational system.

The Corporation's administrative style was dominated by technical, nonpartisan expertise, giving it the prestige and appeal of technology in a developing country. CVG oriented its activities to technical, rather than "people" sectors: heavy industrial development rather than light industry, commerce or services, and large-scale food production in the Orinoco delta rather than land reform nearer to Ciudad Guyana. It postponed addressing issues such as public education and social welfare which are politically volatile and demand few technical skills.

Through this period this administrative style resulted in a division of labor with other government agencies and partisan political bodies which sustained the CVG's base of support. Its focus on noncontroversial programs with a high technological content, and its low public profile, allowed others — often the President — to claim credit for the development program's benefits, but also rallied them to defend the CVG against partisan attack and political controversy. This style succeeded in assuring the CVG's survival and power for nearly a decade, into its next period of transition.

Given the expanding scale of the Guyana development program and the increasing complexity of managing a growing regional society and economy, this transition has been smaller than might have been expected. The trend of increased openness and cooperation with other public agencies continued, as did CVG's tendency to even the imbalance between its primary industry development priorities and the need for adequate services for the increasing population. But while CVG's newer Division of Human Services expanded its systematic operations, and enjoyed higher budgets based on growing oil revenues, CVG's main focus continued to be the state owned high technology industries and its new major projects planned for the national development agency, CORDIPLAN.

Two surveys, one in 1965 and one in 1975, show some of the results of CVG's development program. Ongoing migration has made Ciudad Guyana a city that has remained close to its rural background, but its development has not been responsive enough to its population's needs. The CVG's development strategy emphasized the corporate sector which now provides over half the city's employment, with a shift over time from white-collar to more blue-collar jobs. But there has been little structural change since the steel mill and public works projects of the 1960s, and high uncertainty in employment still persists. Unplanned jobs in the informal economy of the barrios have been important in taking up the slack for the growing core of shanty people in the city.

Formal housing programs have not served a large proportion of the population, and self-help was encouraged by CVG (in the form of sites-and-services projects) and has received growing emphasis. Initially quite low quality construction, many informal areas have been rebuilt to standards comparable to subsidized housing. But CVG's planning never addressed the problem of new immigrants and of construction workers remaining after project completion, and its transportation policy was linked to its misconceived housing policy.

Education is improving but the average level is still low, and rising standards are excluding and marginalizing an increasing proportion of the population which is unstable due to employment uncertainty. There is still a low level of health services and infant mortality is high, though CVG formulated a 5-year health plan. Generally, human services in the region suffer from lack of coordination and purpose.

As an organization created to develop the Guyana region, CVG has been a success. CVG's administrative style ensured its power and survival in a turbulent and uncertain environment, and its development strategy was effective in promoting and implementing industrial development and some agricultural growth in a previously almost totally unexploited region. Guyana's development has provided gainful employment for a population today that did not exist before, and made a significant contribution to the national economy. But CVG has been less apt at managing a more mature and complex society and providing for the needs of a growing immigrant population.

In the CVG the Venezuelan government created a single organization to undertake all the activities needed to implement its regional development policy. Not all, of course, were internalized, though the CVG focused on programs which were contained as much as possible within its own range of competence. But the Corporation remained dependent to some degree on the cooperation of other organizations in its environment.

As the complexity of urban and regional development increased, with a growing and heterogeneous population, and as technological infrastructure and economic base development were gradually supplanted by social development and human services, interdependence between the CVG and its interorganizational network increased, and the issue of coordinating its diverse activities grew more critical. At this point the adequacy of this single organization IOC structure becomes questionable, and perhaps in a better adaptation to its new environment the CVG should have behaved more like a lead organization or a coordinating unit.

*   *   *

Creating a single organization can also be a response to the problem of coordinating diverse activities with a common purpose (a program, project, a shared set of users or market) at a relatively small scale. A family development center in Baltimore, Pennsylvania, is an example, where a new organization was formed so as to bring together social services and housing programs for a particular clientele.

The Lafayette Court Family Development Center

Lafayette Homes is a Baltimore public housing project with 805 dwelling units and almost 2400 residents, all of whom are poor, and many on public assistance. Half the population are children, suffering from stunted development as a result of inadequate prenatal care, poor nutrition, abuse, and neglect, and with high teenage dropout, pregnancy, and drug addiction rates.

In 1986, as Baltimore entered its annual phase of planning its Community Development Block Grant (CDBG) financed programs, the Housing and Community Development Commissioner had an idea. He wanted the Housing Authority, which was under his jurisdiction, to be more than just a landlord for public housing, like

Lafayette homes, but to become an instrument for addressing some of the residents' problems. Indicating a willingness to appropriate funds for implementing an appropriate intervention strategy, he challenged his three deputy commissioners (who were respectively responsible for the Housing Authority, CDBG programming, and training and employment programs funded under the JTPA) to devise one.

Planning took about five months. First they prepared a three page concept paper presenting the outline of the Family Development Center. This was used as a prospectus to enlist the support of other organizations and constituencies: the health commissioner, the social services director, the school system, the project tenants, and others. As planning continued, eleven organizations participated in designing their components of the Center, with the understanding that the new organization was not to duplicate existing services or replace current service providers. They included city housing and tenant services, health, employment development, social services, recreation and youth agencies, the Baltimore PIC, the public school system, the Lafayette Homes Tenants Council, the Residents' Advisory Council, and Morgan State University. Each was represented by a high level staff person on a planning committee, and for programs needing licensing, the responsible individual was brought into the planning process at an early stage.

The plan was to offer the best services to the project residents through an organization that would be a single access point. With the exception of Head Start, none of the services was closely available, but the city had a rich array of service providers and the planning process tapped their expertise. The availability of funding for physical renovation and the operating infrastructure took some pressure off participating organizations. The Center needed four sources of funding: CDBG provided a $1 million initial grant and $600,000 in annual support. Title XX Day Care set aside funds for 250 day care slots, with the first year deficit covered by CDBG, and later years' by the Housing Authority. Job training costs were funded from JTPA funds and JOBS, and CDBG underwrote the front-end costs of the clinic. Clinic operations were paid for through a funding pool fed by Medicaid reimbursements.

The lead organization implementing the plan was the Office of Manpower Resources, the JTPA administrative entity, which had considerable experience in program development and contract negotiation. This stood the development of the Center in good stead, since there was no central control over the funding streams for any of the services which were to be included. Interagency agreements had to be negotiated (not all were complete by the time the Center opened, but they soon followed) but the bonding that took place through the planning process made the successful conclusion of signed agreements possible.

Figure 3 below shows the organization of the Family Development Center. Its staff is headed by a Director, and it is formally part of the Office of Employment Development (formerly the Office of Manpower Resources). The solid lines show direct supervisory authority; the dotted lines indicate a relationship governed by a written agreement.[14]

The Family Development Center brings several delivery agents together on one site to provide exclusive services to its members: residents of the Lafayette Homes project. The Center has a case management system to access its services, which operate subject to agreements established by its Advisory Board. The Advisory Board is convened by the Director, and includes representatives of all the service providing agencies.

A large complex made up of nine converted apartments and an added on portable facility houses most of the Center's activities, and three floors of an elementary school opposite were renovated for additional literacy and day care services. The Center occupies nearly thirty thousand square feet of floorspace. The Center's main direct function is case management, which provides the point of entry to all its services. There are three case managers, who have two functions. The first is to develop a comprehensive plan of service for each member family unit. Next, they essentially perform a brokering function: ensuring priority access to needed services, arranging members' enrollment in the designated programs, and advocacy or mediation to resolve any problems.

The Center's services include adult education, provided through a video-disk learning lab and computer-assisted courses for remedial reading, preparation for the high school equivalency diploma (GED), and college matriculation through community based courses offered by Morgan State University. Child development services include Head Start activities for infants, toddlers and their parents, full-day child care for 100 three- to five-year olds that offers a program of discovery learning, developmental assessment, parent workshops and other activities, and a school-age child care program for 150 children offering peer tutoring, homework assistance, and activities such as music, arts, and sports.

An on-site health clinic with a nurse-practitioner and available physicians provides health and dental screening, well-baby clinic

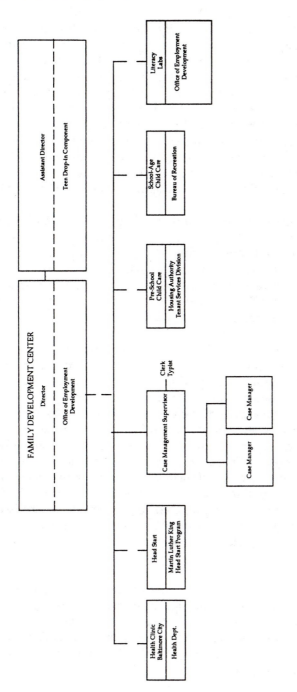

Figure 3. Organizational structure of the Lafayette Court Family Development Center (Harris, 1993, p. 195, Fig. 13.2).

services, nutrition counseling, family planning, health education, and referral for diagnosed health problems. The Center has a teen drop-in center, providing an informal setting for peer interaction, structured social activities, and counseling-case management linked to outside services such as alternative schools, work experience, and job placement. The case management system is also members' point of intake for JTPA and JOBS training and placement programs, and provides family support in the form of assistance with problems of violence, substance abuse, eviction, and other crises. Case managers refer members to appropriate services through their links with the Family Services Unit of the Department of Social Services and the City Health Department.

Any or all these services are deployed as part of the comprehensive plan of service for the family unit, which is aimed at family development. This includes consciousness-raising, developing a structured plan to address the family's future, developing the individual member's skills, and developing the family's self-sufficiency and independence. In July, 1991, the Center began its fifth year of operation, in a unique collaboration between city agencies, local service providers, and multiple funding sources.

It is too soon to identify the Center's effects on its clientele and its environment, but early impacts included high participation, movement toward the long-term goal of economic independence for Lafayette Homes residents, successful provision of comprehensive services, and a synergistic effect of combined services. A Johns Hopkins Institute for Policy Studies evaluation found that families' participation in employment and training activities far exceeded similar levels for control groups. The Center's programs have given the nearby elementary school, which was slated for closing, a new lease of life, and school reports show that students entering after its child care programs are much better prepared for first grade. There is every indication that the Center is working, and will achieve the goals for which it was created (Harris, 1993).

*   *   *

Coordinating organizations' activities by forming a single organization, either through reorganization or merger of existing organizations, or by creating a new organization, is not a "low cost" approach. It usually demands a greater investment of political and material resources, than other, less hierarchical, IOC structures such as the interorganizational group.

These investments suggest that organizations are formed for undertakings that enjoy relatively high priority, to achieve objectives backed by significant political commitment. Indirectly, that may be one reason why single organizations have been quite successful,[15] by comparison with other IOC structures that are lower on the continuum of hierarchy and institutionalization.

The organization, as an IOC structure, is often a meso-structure in a "nested" IOC system. Many of the examples here show this: OPEC, actually a federated cartel governed by an interorganizational group; Airbus Industrie: a framework for an international joint venture, managed by a coordinating unit; the CVG, an organization with its own subsidiaries, that perhaps became a lead organization; the Lafayette Court Center, an organization at the brink of being a coordinating unit, containing a coordinating unit (its case management system) and governed by an interorganizational group (its Advisory Board).

NOTES

1. No reasoned taxonomy of coordinating units is intended here, but simply a heuristic presentation framework. For an interesting typology of governance structures that includes coordinating units, see Hult and Walcott (1990: 41–48, 71–78).

2. The NCAA is really a complex "nested" combination of IOC structures; its meso-structure is a mutual organization, governed by several interorganizational groups and managed by a coordinating unit. Here the focus is on the last, and on how the coordinating unit evolved in a loosely linked interorganizational network.

3. Membership in the NCAA continued to grow as the following table shows (Stern, 1976: 248):

Year	No. member schools	No. member conferences
1906	38	–
1916	95	6
1926	148	4
1936	191	19
1941	220	22
1951	368	24

4. Trist's "referent organization" is not limited to coordinating units, but is in fact an IOC structure, that includes coordinating units, interorganizational groups, and single organizations.

5. Many countries (e.g., Australia and Israel, to name but two) have national Planning Commissions, but these are interorganizational groups and not coordinating units: they have no "ecological autonomy", no separate operational budget and no staff of their own.

6. The lack of any systematic comparative research on these coordinating units, given their number and frequency, is surprising. To knowledgeable observers, it is clear that their effectiveness varies widely. Some single case studies, e.g., of Israeli District Commissions in the context of the statutory planning system there (Alexander, Alterman and Law Yone, 1983), and of the California Coastal Development Commission in the context of U.S. coastal zone management (Lowry, 1985), and anecdotal evidence suggest that their success seems to depend on their statutory authority and how they manage to deploy it in a political arena which often includes other powerful actors and interests.

7. Alexander (1980c) based on Hansen (1970: 61–83), Rothblatt (1971) and Derthick (1974: 76–107).

8. These vary depending on how the region is defined; the core states are Kentucky, Tennessee and W. Virginia, with "upstate" parts of Alabama, Georgia, Maryland, New York, N. Carolina, Ohio, Pennsylvania, S. Carolina and Virginia; later Mississippi was included in the region, mainly for political reasons.

9. "701" was a U.S. Department of Housing and Urban Development funded program to support local comprehensive land use planning.

10. Consistent with this definition, lead organizations may have internal units (an agency, division, department, bureau, or office) which are coordinating units. For example, in the Model Cities program the U.S. Department of Housing and Urban Development was the lead agency, and its Model Cities Administration was its coordinating unit for the program (see also pp. 258–263 below).

11. The coordination failures described in the Preface (see pp. x–xi) give some idea of how complex this task was.

12. This may be a fine distinction in some cases that in reality are quite ambiguous: the New Town Corporation, for example, depended extensively on consultant and contract services. How extensive must such a network be for an organization to be a lead organization rather than a single organization? In such cases it is probably more useful to think of this distinction as an analytic convenience. When we are focusing on IOC as integrating the diverse functions of an interorganizational network we would think of the IOC structure as a lead organization. When the focus is on the internal integration of functions we would describe the IOC structure as a single organization. Thus,

the New Town Corporation might be viewed as a lead organization in looking at its interorganizational network made up of local governments, consultants and contractors. On the other hand, it is a single organization when we consider its internalization of the otherwise separate functions of new towns financing, planning, government and development control, and land disposition and development.

13. This case covers the period up to 1975 (Rodwin and Associates, 1969; Appleyard, 1976: 9–14; Macdonald, 1980).

14. This organizational structure raises some doubts about what kind of IOC structure the Lafayette Court Family Center is. Its linkages (by interagency agreement) with the relevant organizations in its network suggest that it might be a coordinating unit, while the degree of internalization of its functions, their location on its premises, and its organizational autonomy make it look like a single organization. Like many organizations in reality, it is probably a blend of the two. It is worth remembering that the IOC structures are ideal types, useful for analysis but not always encountered in their "pure" forms.

15. Not all organizations are successful, of course. Here the reference is to single organizations as IOC structures, and to their effectiveness in this role by comparison with other IOC structures, as distinct from their success by other measures such as task performance, goals achievement etc. (Alexander, 1992: 227–239).

CHAPTER 7

Mutual Organizations:

IOC in Interorganizational Networks

7.1. Types of Interorganizational Networks

In the last few years, interorganizational networks have been the subject of growing interest. But there is still some ambiguity about what they actually are. One of the first to look at them, Howard Aldrich, defined them as hierarchical loosely coupled systems of organizations (1977: 32), in contrasting interorganizational networks with more hierarchical and tightly linked organizations and interorganizational hierarchies.

At the other extreme, Alter and Hage define networks as "unbounded or bounded clusters of organizations that, by definition, are nonhierarchical collectives of legally separate units" (1993: 46), and which are "in a normative sense, both nonhierarchical and self-regulating" (1993: 77).[1] What all observers agree on, however, is that interorganizational networks are a distinct form of organization that is neither a market nor a hierarchy. Networks are "institutional arrangements that are intermediate between markets and hierarchies" (Koenig and Thietart, 1988: 10) and can include elements of both (Powell, 1990). Sometimes the interorganizational network itself is formalized as an organization: Koenig and Thietart call this a "mutual organization" (1988: 10–12).

Interorganizational networks and mutual organizations take many different forms. Alter and Hage (1993: 44–80) have developed a typology which arrays these various types of networks on several dimensions. One is the type of cooperation linking the network members: is it competitive, that is, does the network combine similar organizations in the same sector (such as firms competing in the same market), or is it symbiotic (i.e., complementary organizations or members operating in different sectors)? Another dimension of the typology distinguishes between obligational networks (i.e., organizations linked by agreement or contract to perform tasks that are part of a common undertaking) and promotional networks (linking sometimes competing organizations in the same sector to promote a shared interest vis a vis their common environment). Finally, interorganizational networks can be divided according to the medium and objective of their cooperation: friendship and support for solidarity, information to pursue knowledge (scientific or technological objectives), goods, services or people (processing or production objectives), money in pursuit of economic objectives, or power to attain political goals.[2]

Table 2 shows the various kinds of interorganizational networks and mutual organizations arrayed on these three dimensions. At the extremes we find some of the completely nonhierarchical and largely informal networks which were discussed in Chapter 4: friendship-solidarity networks (such as the Child Protective Services' caseworkers' network), and some policy networks, like the ones affecting U.S. health and energy policy.

But under the solidarity objective we can also find quite hierarchical networks, including cultural associations and federations of sports organizations. These are mutual organizations, such as the NCAA, in which member organizations are coordinated through highly formalized rules and regulations which are mutually agreed upon by a hierarchical governance structure, and administered through a coordinating unit.

Another way of looking at interorganizational networks identifies different kinds on the basis of their structural characteristics: how large are they? how centralized? are they complex or simple? how different are their member organizations? how are these linked and what is their degree of connectivity? Some other traits are also relevant: how dependent is the network on external resources? and what are the scope and volume of its task?

Analyzing interorganizational networks, Alter and Hage found that they fell into four basic categories, which reflected the four possible combinations of vertical resource dependency (low or high) and task scope (narrow or broad). The first kind is a small, simple network with low centralization, and narrow task scope. Growth of this network may transform it into the second type, with higher vertical dependency, but still quite low complexity and differentiation (for example, electronics supply networks). Technological innovation can change it into the third type: still small and with low resource dependency, the network now has broad task scope, is highly centralized, and has high complexity and differentiation; research consortia are an example. The fourth kind is a moderately sized, complex and highly differentiated network with broad task scope and high external resource dependence, like the Japanese automotive supply networks[3] (Alter and Hage, 1993: 106–258).

7.2. Cooperative Networks: Consortium to Cartel

A wide variety of interorganizational networks exist primarily to exchange information. These range from quite informal ones, such as computer networks and "billboards", through more formalized and hierarchical data retrieval networks such as electronic catalogue and data search services, and interlibrary federations which share holdings information and exchange circulation privileges.

Relatively informal scientific and technological research networks are also subsumed here under competitive-promotional networks. Sometimes these appear as more formal mutual organizations, such as the British Industrial Telecommunications Supply Association (ITSA). The ITSA, though formally a trade association, really existed as a common network for prospecting and diffusing information on technological innovations that might be of interest to firms in the industry (Carney, 1987). Research networks can also evolve into more hierarchical R&D consortia, obligational networks like the one in the case that follows.

High T_c Superconductivity Research in Germany

In the German Federal Republic, research in the specialized area of high T_c superconductivity was quite advanced. Several universities and scientific institutes and laboratories were carrying out basic research, and a number of industrial corporations had active R&D programs. Their common interest and interpersonal information exchange linked them in an informal network, which was intensified by the nature of the topic, in which scientific basic research was closely

Table 2. A Typology of Interorganizational Networks

Medium (objective) of cooperation	Type of interorganizational network		
	Competitive/ obligational	Competitive/ promotional	Symbiotic/ obligational
Friendship/ Interaction (SOLIDARITY)	Social networks activities Networks:: recreational, cultural ,(e.g., sports club federations)		
Information (KNOWLEDGE-SCIENTIFIC-TECHNOLOGICAL)		Professional/ Scientific/ Disciplinary Associations Educational Associations (e.g., collegiate accreditation networks) Information Networks (e.g., Interlibrary Federations) Research Networks	Information/ Data Retrieval Networks (e.g., computer communication networks/ "billboards". Data/info. retrieval subscriber services R&D Networks
Goods/Services/ People (PROCESSING/ PRODUCTION)	R&D Consortia Purchasing/ Procurement	Prime/ Subcontractor Networks (e.g., manufacturing Networks Purchasing/ Marketing Cooperatives Joint Ventures Consortia	Construction Program/Project implementation "sets" Human services Networks (e.g., client referral networks, health serv. networks, blood banks) Joint Ventures Consortia

cont'd

Table 2, cont'd

Medium (objective) of cooperation	Type of interorganizational network		
	Competitive/ obligational	Competitive/ promotional	Symbiotic/ obligational
Money (ECONOMIC OBJECTIVES)	Consolidated campaigns (fund raising)		Corporate Networks (equity participations director interlocks)
	Investment consortia *gurupu*		
			Keiretsu
	Corporate Networks (equity participation, director interlocks)		
		Cartels	
Power	Lobbying	Trade Associations alliances	
			Trade Union Federations
		Advocacy coalitions	
		Policy networks	
		Political/ ideological movements	

After Alter and Hage, 1993, Figures 2.1, 2.2, pp. 51, 60, 61.

bound to technological development and potential industrial applications.

Another actor in this network was the Federal Ministry for Research and Technology (BMFT), which had four programs through which funding support was provided to high T_c superconductivity research. The universities and corporations involved in this research were also active members of the policy network which attempted to influence the BMFT's research program and its funding priorities. One of the questions which exercised BMFT research policy was the relative priority of basic scientific research (which was done primarily by universities and scientific institutes) and the more applied research carried out by the corporate R&D units.

In 1987 BMFT policy favored basic research, and its research program which was announced in September 1987 formed fifteen interdisciplinary research groups made up of primarily university-based investigators, and in addition funded studies in fifteen scientific institutes. At the same time there was a significant decline in the industry share of the federal superconductivity research budget.

Hoechst was the German corporation with the most active interest in high T_c superconductivity research and applications. Hoechst's R&D unit was the focus of another network of intensive information exchange, which was managed by a special in-house task force. The Hoechst superconductivity research task force forged collaborative links with several research laboratories and institutes that specialized in this area, and with a number of other firms pursuing parallel investigations.

The BMFT's program announcement sparked an intensive lobbying effort spearheaded by Hoechst and involving its network, to influence the BMFT to expand funding support for an industry-based superconductivity R&D program. This effort, based on arguments about German international competitiveness in superconductivity development and applications, succeeded, and the BMFT announced a program soliciting applications for industry-based R&D support.

Interfirm competition, however, must have inhibited communication in this instance, because the BMFT received very similar applications from several corporations. The BMFT saw little point in funding several parallel competing industrial research efforts; rather, it was interested in encouraging collaboration between firms in the industry. The HTS Committee, an interorganizational group serving as an advisory committee on superconductivity research to the BMFT, became the arena for bargaining between the members of this interorganizational research and policy network. Representatives of all the firms which had submitted proposals, and who were the major actors in German superconductivity research, were members of the HTS committee.

The result of this process was the formation of a research consortium for German high T_c superconductivity research, as a joint venture of the corporations that had been competing for BMFT funding. The federal funding designated to support industry-based superconductivity R&D underwrote this consortium, which became the unit coordinating corporate research in this area and integrating university and institute-based basic research with corporate R&D (Jansen, 1990).

* * *

The consortium is quite a common form of mutual organization. Carney (1987) suggests that different conditions in the interorganizational network and its environment affect the specific network form or type of mutual organization that evolves, and that the consortium is the result of symbiotic interdependence. By contrast, organizations linked by commensal interdependence form associations or joint ventures.

Four cases in the British telecommunications sector illustrate this. One of the consortia was Project Mercury, an alternative communication network linked by optical fibers, in which three organizations participated. One was Barclay's Bank, which provided financing and was one of the network users. The second was British Petroleum (BP), another user, which also invested capital and provided needed expertise in dealing with government regulation. The third was Cable & Wireless, which provided the technology.

The other consortium was Cellular Radio Ltd., which linked several telecommunication firms with different specializations. Its main purpose was to develop a common cellular-radio technology and to obtain an operator's license from the government. The member organizations in both these networks were linked by symbiotic interdependencies, and both consortia were formed to carry out a common strategy of technological innovation.

These consortia varied in their institutional integration, which was quite high in Project Mercury, but relatively low though increasing in Cellular Radio Ltd. Though the case descriptions are incomplete, it is interesting to note the different types of IOC structures employed. In Cellular Radio Ltd. a new organization was formed, whether as a coordinating unit among member organizations, or whether to integrate functions that were previously diffused among them is unclear. Project Mercury did not have anything like this, but, judging from its higher level of integration, its organizations must have been linked by at least one, if not several, IOC structures.

The two other interorganizational networks emerged to manage commensal interdependence. One was System X, a joint venture between several firms that supplied electronic switching equipment for British Telecommunications (BT). In the face of BT's system of competitive bidding for these components, the member firms formed a joint venture to develop System X and "capture" this market by freezing out potential competitors by creating incompatible terminals.

The other was ITSA, which linked firms sharing a common market in a trade association to prospect potential technological innovations.

Joint ventures, consortia and other kinds of mutual organization are forms of obligational networks linking competitive organizations with a common medium (goods, services, or people) of processing or production. These include purchasing consortia and procurement networks, for example, federations for common purchasing or marketing such as agricultural cooperatives.

Hospitals linked by joint purchasing agreements or patient referral arrangements are another case of this type of network. In the U.S., these have become widespread in response to cost-containment efforts in the health services delivery system. An example of such a network is American Hospital Supply, which was formed to be the common purchasing agent for a large number of hospitals. Some of these are again linked in other cooperative networks, such as the Voluntary Hospitals of America which incorporates over thirty hospitals. Characteristic of the network, rather than hierarchical or market links between the organizations, is the purchasing agreement, which does not itemize prices, but stipulates that prices charged must be "competitive" (Thorelli, 1986: 45).

Obligational interorganizational networks of collaborating competitors also form to process money and pursue common economic objectives. Examples are the investment consortium, partnerships, and networks of firms linked by equity participation. Aerospace and automobile manufacturing today offer dramatic examples of such networks, which link firms competing in the same global market in cooperative ventures.

Boeing-Japan links Boeing with two Japanese consortia, the Japan Aircraft Corporation and Japan Aircraft Development Corp., and three Japanese heavy industry conglomerates: Mitsubishi, Kawasaki and Fuji. International Aero Engines combines Pratt & Whitney (U.S.A.) with Rolls-Royce (U.K), Japan Aero Engines, Motoren-und-Turbinen Union (Germany) and Fiat (Italy). Ford Motors owns 25% of Mazda, General Motors holds 42% of Isusu's shares, and 5% of Suzuki's, and Chrysler has 12% of the equity in Mitsubishi. Ford has joined Nissan to build minivans in Ohio, and assembles Mazdas in its plant in Mexico, while General Motors exports Toyotas to Japan from its plant in Concord, California (Alter and Hage, 1993: 5; Powell, 1990: 320–321).

Cartels are another form of mutual organization which links organizations that compete in one market in an obligational network. Historically cartels have been networks of firms combining to control a market, and they have rarely been successful over the long haul. An effective cartel needs some special conditions, and its specific form of organization does not seem to be one of them. A rare example of a durable cartel is the De Beer's diamond conglomerate, which has successfully controlled the global production and price of diamonds for nearly a century (Chivers, 1956). Another form of cartel is the network of producer countries combining to affect the market for their resource. The Organization of Oil Producing Countries (OPEC) is such a cartel.

OPEC: A Successful Cartel[4]

The cartel is a mutual organization of economic units (firms, corporations, or countries) which decide to cooperate, rather than compete, in a particular market. There are different kinds of cartel, but few of them survive for long or prosper in a free market. The most extreme cartel is to form a monopoly. This is rare because all the actors have to give up their individual control, and merger demands unanimous consensus.

A profit-sharing cartel does not involve merger, but it also presents problems. All the participants have to agree on pricing, production quotas, and the allocation of profits. Such agreements are difficult to arrive at and even harder to maintain. Various actors have different interests, and the structure of the market offers many incentives for opportunism. Low cost producers are tempted to exceed their quotas, and high cost producers hesitate to shut down their redundant plant, in case their partners try to renegotiate profit allocations in the future.

Another type of cartel is the market-sharing cartel. Here the partners agree to limit output and distribute market shares. In the oil market this type of cartel is called *market demand prorationing*, and it prevailed in the U.S. for many years. Some of the same problems exist: each partner can become a rival if he decides to exceed his quota. Production limits have to be balanced with potential demand to make prices low enough to discourage entry by potential competitors, but high enough to give the members an incentive to participate.

Finally, the price-fixing cartel simply sets a market price. In theory consumer demand then determines supply. In fact, the price fixing cartel also has to project demand, and allocate market shares and price differentials (reflecting product and cost variations) among its members. This is the most common arrangement. The price-fixing cartel does not even have to come to a formal agreement; they almost always use a form of price leadership, in which a dominant member (usually the one with the largest market share and the lowest production costs) initiates price changes.[5] In OPEC, which is a price-fixing cartel, there have been several price-leaders, but since the late 1970s Saudi Arabia has filled this role.

OPEC is a classic case of quite an effective cartel. But oil is an almost unique commodity: its extraction costs are very low, and there are few technical constraints to quick adjustment of its supply to changes in demand. This makes large inventories unnecessary, while above-ground storage is expensive. As a result, a global petroleum delivery system has evolved which has only enough slack to accommodate predictable seasonal changes in demand. Scheduling between production and final sale to the consumer is tight, so that even a relatively small disruption in supply can set off a major crisis.

The distribution of oil reserves, unlike many other commodities, is also highly concentrated. OPEC controls nearly 70% of the world's petroleum reserves, and OPEC member countries are the source of over three-quarters of (1980) global oil supply. While there are alternative energy sources (natural gas, coal, nuclear fission, geothermal, solar, etc.) substitutability for oil is quite limited, especially in the range of prevailing prices. Conservation can reduce and has affected demand, but it is burdensome and implementable only in the long run.

Consequently, the demand for oil is quite insensitive to price changes, and in transportation it would remain high even at prices well in excess of today's. In many countries additional gasoline taxes have already raised fuel costs to over $120 per barrel[6] without appreciably reducing demand. This contrasts with other commodities, few of which have this type of concentration or enjoy the same urgency of demand.

While oil has most of the necessary requirements for successful cartelization, these are not sufficient to explain OPEC's success. After all, they existed well before 1960 when OPEC was only founded, and continued up to the 70s, when OPEC's impact, though it was already active, was quite limited.

Before the foundation of OPEC, the world oil market was also largely controlled by a cartel, but a different one. This was essentially a market-sharing cartel in which the major corporations which dominated global oil production and marketing[7] allocated market shares among themselves through a system of voluntary prorationing, and kept prices at levels that would maximize their profits.

Although commercial oil extraction was subject to a government concession, the producing states' revenues were limited to relatively small royalties and taxes. The majors minimized these by shifting production between countries, and by invoking complex bookkeeping formulas relating nominal extraction volumes to low taxes and royalties.

However, in the 1940s producing countries began to make concession renewals contingent on profit-sharing. In the first such agreement, Venezuela obtained a 50–50 split of profits. This reduced the oil majors' take from Venezuelan oil, and they shifted production to the middle East. In response, Venezuelan officials suggested to their mid-Eastern counterparts that profit sharing would be a good idea for them too. At the same time, they offered attractive concessions to smaller independent corporations which were new in the market. The resulting overall expansion of production led to a steady fall in global oil prices through the 1950s, which would have been even greater but for the majors' voluntary prorationing, and import controls in the U.S.

A 10% price reduction in February 1959, unilaterally posted by the oil companies, finally stimulated a collective reaction in the exporting countries that went beyond individual protests. A meeting of the "First Arab Petroleum Congress" was convened in Cairo in April 1959, to which Venezuela and Iran were also invited. The Congress ended in a "gentleman's agreement" to adopt common policies, and created a "Petroleum Consulting Committee" which would meet yearly. This committee would coordinate oil producing governments' negotiations with the majors so that they would all raise their shares of oil profits to 60%, (as Venezuela had done) in any new agreements.

But soon the oil exporting countries realized that stronger measures were needed, when another unilateral price cut was announced in August 1960. Representatives from the leading oil producers: Iran, Iraq, Kuwait, Saudi Arabia, and Venezuela, met in Baghdad through September 9–14, 1960, and founded OPEC as an intergovernmental federation to coordinate their policies, as stated in the second Resolution passed at this meeting:

> The principal aim of the Organization shall be the unification of petroleum policies for the member countries and the determination of the best means for safeguarding the interests of the member countries individually and collectively. (Danielson, 1982: 151)

The five founding members of OPEC controlled 67% of known petroleum reserves, produced 38% of the world's oil, and exported 90% of the oil transferred in international trade.

OPEC's immediate aims were stated in other Resolutions. These were intended to restore and maintain the previous posted price of oil. To accomplish this, the member states agreed to stand together against the oil majors, if the latter tried to shift production between countries, or to break their common front by offering one country higher prices than others.

Membership in OPEC soon expanded, and by the mid-1970s it consisted of its present thirteen members: Algeria, Ecuador, Gabon, Indonesia, Iran, Iraq, Kuwait, Libya, Nigeria, Qatar, Saudi Arabia, United Arab Emirates and Venezuela. OPEC is governed by a conference of its members' representatives, which meets twice each year to set policy. The regular summer meeting is in Vienna, OPEC's headquarters; the winter venue rotates among member states, and extraordinary meetings are convened as needed. Conference decisions, which are binding on member states unless appealed by a special procedure, require a unanimous vote of all attending delegates.

OPEC is run by a Board of Governors, one from each member country, and headed by a Secretary General who is appointed by the Board. The Secretariat does little more than organize information. It consists of a small professional staff in five departments, which carry out technical and economic research, and provide information services and public relations.

While OPEC succeeded, initially, in preventing any further drop in prices, it failed to boost market prices to their earlier levels. With higher posted prices than world demand would sustain, these became little more than the formal basis for computing government revenues. The oil exporting countries were back to receiving a fixed sum per barrel, though their take was higher than before. As oil prices declined through the 1960s, it became obvious to OPEC governments that they could not increase their oil revenues any more at the major oil corporations' expense. By 1970 this realization led OPEC to initiate a major restructuring of the global oil market, into the form that it still retains today.

Libya was the price leader initiating this change, when its new revolutionary government asked for a price rise from $1.80 to $2.20 per barrel. To support its demand it imposed production cuts on its largest independent producer, Occidental Petroleum, which finally capitulated. This was followed by price negotiations between OPEC and the oil industry, and areawide agreements for North Africa and the Persian Gulf. The Tripoli and Teheran agreements, concluded in early 1971, raised oil prices by 30–40%.

Libya's nationalization of its oil industry stimulated another significant change, which was finalized in agreements between OPEC states and the oil companies through 1972–74. Oil exporting governments claimed and received participation (at rates ranging from 25–60%) in ownership of their product, which the extracting companies agreed to buy back from the host states.

This was the first step in a radical transformation of the relationship between oil producing states and the oil extracting companies. The countries now really own their petroleum products, which the corporations extract and sell under a form of contract called "service contracting". In this arrangement the oil companies receive a fixed price per barrel of oil for their extraction services, irrespective of the market price. They in turn buy the oil from the host countries at negotiated prices related to global market prices, while the host governments are responsible for financing the oil extractors' exploration, infrastructure and other investments.

The "Geneva Agreements" of 1972 and 1973, in which OPEC raised oil prices by 35¢. per barrel, marked another significant change. These relatively small price hikes were important, because they compensated OPEC members for inflationary erosion of their revenues. Since then OPEC has aimed, and often succeeded, in maintaining the real price of oil (in terms of the purchasing power of its members' revenues), though the technical details of how to establish real prices have remained a troublesome issue.

In 1972–73 rapid increases in the world demand for oil produced marked increases in spot prices for oil, localized shortages, and a general sense of an impending energy crisis. But the next large increase in world oil prices came following the Arab oil embargo which accompanied the Yom-Kippur War of 1973. Though the embargo was ineffective, reduced production by OPEC members coupled with high global demand gave OPEC the largest price increases in history, allowing it to raise the posted price by 70% in October, 1973, and more than doubling the price of crude oil in January, 1974.

More modest price hikes through the later 1970s were related to shifting supply and demand, and revealed diverging interests among OPEC members. Some producers, with Saudi Arabia in the lead, feared energy substitution in response to high price increases, based on their large reserves. Others were more interested in high current revenues. These conflicts of interest have continued up to the present, and while OPEC has generally succeeded in finding a consensual formula, divergences in member states' revenue goals have often evoked imperfect compliance.

The Iranian revolution in 1978, which interrupted its oil exports, sparked the next oil crisis and another series of major price increases, to $18 per barrel by June 1979. Through the 1980s OPEC was less effective in maintaining real oil prices, in the face of slowing global demand, and some of its members' production resulting in excess supply.

One result of these pressures on world oil prices was OPEC's adoption of formal production quotas in March, 1982, though production shares had been a frequent topic of informal discussion and agreements. But now conflicts that had previously been buried in OPEC conferences were apparent for all the world to see, when one member or another (often Iran) exceeded his quota so as to increase his current oil income. However, price unity has consistently been maintained, even when Saudi Arabia and other producers have had to reduce production below their assigned shares to avoid a glut which would put irresistible pressure on the posted price.

Danielsens' conclusion, true in 1982, still appears to hold today:

> OPEC is a price-setting cartel which seems to be cohesive enough to prevent nominal contract prices from declining when markets are weak, but ... it is not strong enough to substantially raise prices except when political turmoil brings about sharp production cutbacks. It is this degree of cohesion which has resulted in the relative success of OPEC. (Danielson, 1982: 198)

How can we account for this cohesion to which, apart from other favorable circumstances, we can attribute OPEC's success? It can be explained, in part, by invoking the structuration model of coordination: the essential ingredient has been the participating actors' knowledge.

The combination of a number of circumstances in the late 1950s produced an awareness, which did not exist before, of the oil exporting countries' interdependence. In a few of the oil producing states' a number of prominent officials came to realize that they could not promote their governments' separate interests without coming together to develop a common policy.

Venezuela's experience, in attempting to implement its separate profit-sharing agreement in the face of the oil majors' resistance, contributed to that awareness. The unanticipated collective results of a few countries' independent initiative in bringing new independents into the market (an oil glut that reduced global prices) was another important element. This knowledge led to the creation of OPEC as an oil producing countries' price-setting cartel.

OPEC's first, but, in terms of its limited early objectives, successful, confrontations with the major oil corporations taught it a critical lesson. OPEC learned that its members did not have to be passive objects of the majors' pricing policies. The knowledge that OPEC officials acquired: that collective action gave its member governments power over global oil prices, is the source of OPEC's cohesion to this day.

It is this knowledge which produces OPEC's unanimous policy, even when some governments believe that it contradicts their states' immediate or short-term interests. It is this knowledge that gives some of the more radical member states the leverage that allows them sometimes to defy OPEC's decisions, and to force more moderate members (like Saudi Arabia) into de facto compromises. Ultimately, OPEC's cohesion and success are the result of its members' knowledge that carrying out a common agreed upon policy will serve their individual long-term interests.

Even if inadvertently, OPEC's lean organizational structure undoubtedly contributed to its success. Intimate face-to-face interaction between government decision makers, that takes place at the OPEC Conferences, enhances their consciousness of their mutual interdependence. The fact that the Conference is directly responsible for OPEC policy that has to reflect a unanimous consensus, and is binding on member governments, means that its members' knowledge is relatively unencumbered by any bureaucracy or organizational culture of OPEC itself. Finally, this knowledge is reflected in the mission given to OPEC's small Secretariat: to be a clearing house for the collection and dissemination of relevant information.

OPEC is emphatically not a coordinating unit that controls its members' actions. Since they are all sovereign states, this would be difficult, though not impossible.[8] Rather, as an intergovernmental federation, OPEC is in fact a loose but formal interorganizational network, in which the Conference is an IOC structure: an interorganizational group that provides the arena for interaction between member states' governments and coordination of their oil production and pricing policies. In the light of OPEC's experience, it appears that little more than its members' knowledge of their mutual interdependence is needed to ensure the cohesion necessary for its survival and relative success.

*   *   *

Promotional networks of competing organizations are also common. These are often mutual organizations: professional, disciplinary and scientific associations, educational networks (for example, intercollegiate accrediting organizations), and trade associations. Trade associations spanning several sectors, and trades union federations, such

as the American Federation of Labor-Congress of Industrial Organizations (AFL-CIO) and the National Association of Manufacturers in
the U.S., the *Deutscher Gewerkschaftenbund* (DGB) and the German
Manufacturers' Association, have been called "peak federations":
higher-order networks that perhaps constitute a new interorganizational form (Franz, Rosewitz and Wolf, 1985: 540–541).

7.3. Networks for Processing and Production

Networks involving obligational links between symbiotically interdependent organizations are common too. These include interorganizational networks formed to produce goods and deliver services, and
people-processing networks. Examples of the former are the complex
formal subcontracting networks coordinated by a prime contractor
lead organization, widespread in sectors such as construction, automobile and aerospace manufacture.

Less formal but no less extended production networks involving
subcontracting links are also frequent in innovative sectors and craft-
like industries: home construction, publishing, and the film and re-
cording businesses are examples. Sometimes these also have a local-
cultural dimension, like the garment industry and high fashion links
in Milan and New York, and regional economic sectors such as textile
production in Baden-Wurttemberg and light industry in Emilia-Ro-
magna (Powell, 1990: 306–311).

Another form of the obligational symbiotic network is the "implementation set" of organizations linked by a common project or program (Hjern and Porter, 1981). Such a set can include organizations
linked by a common product; national blood banks coordinating a
network of supplying organizations and linking them to user hospitals are an example. It can also be structured around the delivery of a
particular service or related services.

A relatively recent case of this type is the interorganizational network for health services delivery. This links providers: physicians'
group practices and hospitals, with consumer organizations: employers and third-party payers such as insurance corporations, through
mediating units such as HMOs (health maintenance organizations)
and PPOs: preferred provider organizations (Fennell and Alexander,
1993: 95–97).

This kind of interorganizational network could also be considered
a "people-processing" network. These are common in human services: education, health, and social welfare. The networks of child and
youth service agencies in Texas, interacting through regional councils

(Van de Ven, Walker and Liston, 1979) are one example. State networks of agencies offering coordinated health, employment and training services to welfare clients (Jennings and Krane, 1993) are another. Farnham County, Maryland, has an interorganizational network to provide for the chronically mentally ill (CMI), which illustrates how such a network is structured and works.

The Farnham Co. CMI Community Support System

Many of the older chronically mentally ill (CMI) patients in American communities were discharged from psychiatric hospital wards and clinics in the deinstitutionalization programs of the 1960s. The baby boom added a new cohort of young adult chronic patients who are different from their predecessors, combining severe functional deficiencies with a tendency to reject medical and mental health services. Revolving-door patients who refuse to stay in therapeutic programs, and either seek crisis help in emergency facilities or end up in jail, they are a problem that few communities are equipped to address.

A group of parents of young CMIs in Farnham County confronted this problem in early 1981. The county Mental Health Center had denied residential care to these patients, but was prepared to cooperate if the parents' group would "take the lead". Over the next few years this group created a new coordinating organization, the Alliance for the Mentally Ill (AMI), which developed the necessary linkages between organizations providing specialized services.

Several factors made this possible. The perception of need was enhanced by the closing of several state institutions, which severely strained local resources. State and federal funding was newly available, tied to the number of discharged CMIs and the development of community service plans for them. Local resources included the core of committed parents and families, access to a good residential facility, and the community's willingness to accept a local property tax add-on earmarked for mental health services. A small core of local professionals shared the families' vision of community mental health care, and mobilized their own resources in support.

The network making up the community CMI support system consisted of five organizations. A regional hospital provided periodic inpatient treatment for CMIs when necessary. The Community Mental Health Center was responsible for developing a service plan for each CMI patient and monitoring patients' drug treatment. AMI coordinated services for each CMI patient referred to it by the Center, for the duration of the patient's stay in the community. Some of these serv-

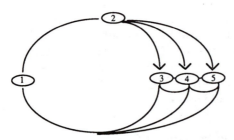

Community Support System
1. Regional State Hospital
2. Community Mental Health Center
3. Alliance for the Mentally Ill (3 levels of residential living)
4. State Vocational Rehabilitation

Figure 4. The Farnham County CMI Community Support Network (Alter and Hage, 1993, p. 147; Fig. 4.4).

ices: residential living, a sheltered jobs program, community job placement, and recreational programs, were provided by AMI. For other services AMI referred patients to programs in the community. The State Vocational Rehabilitation Office provided assessment and job training, and the State Public Aid Office paid out patients' Social Security benefits.

This interorganizational network and its linkages is shown in Figure 4. Partially, it operated under a mandated framework of State regulation, and had some quite formal links. The state hospital controlled the timing of patients' discharge and their financial reimbursement, and other aspects of their treatment were determined by state regulations. An interagency agreement between the hospital and the Center specified referral procedures, reimbursement rates, and payments schedules. Another written agreement, between the Mental Health Center and AMI, assigned their respective roles and formalized their mutual expectations. These parts of the treatment process, then, were hierarchically coordinated, and needed little or no informal interaction between agency staff.

Coordination of the community-based part of CMIs treatment was effected in various ways. The patient's service plan, developed by the Community Mental Health Center, provided the directive framework. AMI caseworker staff coordinated each CMIs services, delivered by AMI and other programs. Task integration among program workers was usually effected through dyadic communication, but sometimes team meetings were called to cope with emergency situations.

This interorganizational network was dependent on an array of resources. It required a new organization, the AMI, which functioned as a lead organization, delivering some services directly and coordinating others. It was funded by a combination of federal and state grants and a local tax increment, without which the network would disintegrate and the new services it provides would cease. Apparently Farnham County's CMI community support network is successful, and has accomplished its founders' goals. Without it, they said, "their adult children would be ... drifters and homeless" (Alter and Hage, 1993: 144-148).

*   *   *

The joint venture is another form of interorganizational network, in which organizations link up for a specified purpose, and invest trans-action-specific assets. This mutual organization is different from other types of interorganizational systems, such as prime-subcontracting networks: all the parties in a joint venture act as principals and agents at the same time. They may be competitors, pooling their resources for more effective positioning in a market, or they may be linked by symbiotic interdependence, where their resources complement each other. Two joint ventures in the European aerospace industry illustrate both these types.

The Concorde and Airbus Industrie: Joint Ventures in Aerospace

The development and production of the Concorde was a British-French joint venture, in which competing firms combined to strengthen their competitive edge in what at the time looked like a promising global market for supersonic aircraft. The participating firms were the British Aircraft Company (BAC) and Sud Aviation, both entering the venture with heavy state support.

The Concorde project, however, was not a true mutual organization. Instead, the partners deployed resources as necessary for the program, which was supervised by a joint standing committee which had a rotating chair. This relatively weak interorganizational group delegated more and more of its work to an Administrative and Technical Subcommittee which was also made up of BAC and Sud staff, but who were seconded full-time to the Concorde project.

One of the subcommittee's major responsibilities was selecting subcontractors among British and French concerns. It was presented with candidates by BAC and Sud, and had to make its choices conform to a 50–50 rule that ensured equal assignment of work between the two countries. The dual structure of the governing committee and subcommittee was reflected at the project's production level, too. This structure proved to be very inefficient, producing conflicts and delays which culminated in a crisis in 1964.

While the international cooperation on which the venture was premised worked better at lower levels of the project, coordination of tasks was poor, and the joint venture never really performed as an integrated organization. Its organizational shortcomings, while perhaps not the only cause, were reflected in the project's failures: its significant delays and massive cost overruns.

Another European joint venture in the aerospace sector, Airbus Industrie, was also motivated by the participants' desire to be more competitive in the global market. Unlike the Concorde venture, however, the relevant demand was not the rather speculative market for supersonic aircraft, but the existing and potential users of intermediate distance air transportation, whose number was rapidly growing. Unlike Concorde, too, Airbus was better organized and much more successful.

Several European aerospace firms were aware of their respective parallel and competitive efforts to penetrate this market, and concluded that cooperation would be to their mutual benefit. Organization of the joint venture involved intergovernmental negotiations, which included intensive political haggling about allocation of the respective tasks and shares of the enterprize between the participating countries. The agreement which emerged was a compromise between the British, French, and German participants, which awarded the main part of the engine to the British Rolls-Royce company, the airframe to France's Sud Aviation, and parts of the engine and other systems to Deutsche Airbus, and several other manufacturers.

In 1971 Airbus Industrie was set up under French law as a *groupement d'interet economique*, a French form of nonprofit corporation. This was not a merger of the participants' assets, but essentially a coordination device: a framework for the IOC structures that would manage the joint undertaking and coordinate the actors' deployment of their resources as needed for the project. Airbus Industrie was governed by a Board of Control that acted like a corporate board of directors, and included representatives of the partners in the joint venture. The enterprise was run by a Manager, who was appointed by the Board, and a small management team. Airbus did not have its own staff: its personnel were seconded and continued to be employees of the member firms.

Airbus' power to influence its parent firms' actions was very limited. Ultimately, its effective coordination of the tasks involved in the common project was based on its ability to persuade the participating firms to accept its work assignments. The incentive held out to the partners was minimizing overall project costs, in which all had a common interest. The Airbus management had the professional expertise to present a cogent case, and developed the personal commitment to the project that made their arguments persuasive. Airbus was successful in producing an aircraft that has continued to be very competitive in the market niche for which it was developed.

The contrast between Concorde and Airbus is enlightening. Concorde's failure (also due to of some unanticipated developments in the global market environment) is partly attributable to its poor organization and management. The governance of the joint venture was highly politicized, and top management became deeply involved in internal policy. As a result, many issues were pushed upwards for resolution, and relatively trivial decisions had to be made at the ministerial level of participating governments. The powerlessness of the project management together with the centralization of decision making increased the time needed to resolve problems, causing delays and escalating costs.

Decision making in the organization became rigid and lost flexibility. There was a lack of coordination with firms in the industry, and within the project there were conflicting interests. The absence of shared goals, the lack of a clear organizational identity, and the weakness of the incentives to elicit any real commitment from participants, contributed to the Concorde venture's poor performance.

Airbus, on the other hand, succeeded because professionals were put in charge. While they had to use persuasion to implement their decisions, they had the commitment to become real champions of the project. The venture had a clear organizational identity, but Airbus' management developed a relatively decentralized style of decision making (perhaps due to the quite loosely linked structure of the interorganizational network focused on the project) which worked well. Participants' roles were clearly defined both in the original agreement and through the course of its implementation, and they shared a common view of their mutual goals.

The project had a simple and powerful reinforcing mechanism, which management deployed to full effect. This was that all the shareholders were partners in the venture's successful outcome, giving them an incentive to cooperate in minimizing the costs of their contributions and maximizing their effectiveness. Outside suppliers and subcontractors were engaged on the "fair return" principle which also elicited good performance. Decision making was adaptable, and the conflicts that were inevitable were satisfactorily resolved within the organizational structure (Koenig and Thietart, 1988: 14–28).

In comparing the organizational structures of the Concorde venture and Airbus Industrie, note the IOC structures nested in each of these interorganizational networks. Concorde had a multilayered set of interorganizational groups: the Standing Committee (perhaps also an interministerial committee — if not, at least an ad-hoc group at the subcabinet level) and the Administrative and Technical Subcommittee. The dual nature of the binational partnership was never satisfactorily resolved, and was reflected in the dual structure of each of these groups. The Concorde is another case in which interorganizational groups proved to be a weak and ineffective coordination structure.

Airbus Industrie was essentially a coordinating unit. It is an organization that was created to integrate the tasks involved in developing and producing a competitive aircraft, tasks that were performed by the organizations making up the network involved in the joint venture. Though also governed by an interorganizational group (as many coordinating units are), its being a coordinating unit gave Airbus Industrie organizational autonomy and identity which the Concorde venture lacked. Even with relatively decentralized decision making in a loosely linked network, Airbus' organizational identity summoned up the commitment of its staff to mobilize the members of the network and coordinate their effective performance.

*   *   *

Semiformal linkages, such as interlocking corporate directorships, and formal ones, such as equity participation, also connect ramified interorganizational networks of firms and corporations. These may be competitive networks, like the investment consortia mentioned above, and the international networks of competing firms based on shared ownership, to which we pointed in the automobile and aerospace industries.

Japan's *gurupu* (one present form of the pre-World-War II *zaibatsu*) are also equity-linked networks of diverse corporations in a variety of sectors (Alter and Hage, 1993: 60, 62). In this way they are like the western conglomerate. But the conglomerate usually has a formal holding corporation which has final ownership and acts as a coordinating unit to concert its network companies' strategic positioning to conform to a common financial policy. The *gurupu's* network, however, is more loosely linked.

The Japanese *keiretsu* are another descendant of the *zaibatsu*. Sometimes they are distinguished from *gurupu* by emphasizing their members' symbiotic and complementary interdependency, and the vertical rather than lateral links between them (Alter and Hage, 1993: 61–62). But in fact the *keiretsu* involve both kinds of interdependency in a complex pattern of linkages which is worth more detailed examination.

Japanese Interorganizational Corporate Networks: The Keiretsu

During the Meiji period up to World War II Japanese industry evolved into a well-differentiated set of highly integrated interorganizational networks. These were the *zaibatsu*: financial-industrial conglomerates which were family-held through a holding corporation that controlled an extensive loosely linked network of direct and indirect subsidiaries. The U.S. occupation after the war took deliberate measures to break up the *zaibatsu* and curtail their directors' power.

Nevertheless, networking remained ingrained in Japanese industrial organization, related, perhaps, to some intrinsically cooperative traits in Japanese culture (especially when contrasted to American competitive individualism). Today "the Japanese corporate network represents a well-ordered structure of relationships among highly differentiated firms" (Gerlach, 1992: 135). In the *keiretsu* this structure takes a typical form of several loosely linked core corporations, each with its own network of subsidiaries, as shown in Figure 5.

The *keiretsu* have evolved as interorganizational systems in which diverse firms manage two kinds of symbiotic interdependencies. One is financial, represented by the dispersion of investments and the flow of profits, in which banks and financial institutions play a central role. The other is functional, reflected in vertical links in a particular industrial sector between major manufacturers and primary suppliers. The relative importance of these interdependencies is shown in the form of the interorganizational network. The *keiretsu* could be structured as a laterally linked and functionally nondifferentiated network; what Gerlach (1992: 114) called a "nonhierarchical clique". Or it could be more focused on investment links, and structured as a "bank centered clique", as illustrated in Figure 5 above.

Gerlach (1992) analyzed three kinds of intercorporate links to discover how the *keiretsu* network is really structured: bank borrowing, equity ownership, and interlocking directorates. His analysis used data from sixty Japanese industrial firms and financial institutions. Thirty of these, he found, could be clearly identified with one of six *keiretsu*, whose membership ranged between four and eight companies: Dai-Ichi Kangyo, Fuji, Mitsubishi, Misui, Sanwa, and Sumitomo.

The *keiretsu* turns out to be more like the "bank-centered clique": financial institutions hold central positions in these interorganizational networks. The majority of the directorship interlocks and the intercorporate equity ties suggest that network links are financial, rather than vertical links within industrial blocks. The centrality of individual financial institutions is reinforced by the fact that their ties

1a. Prewar *zaibatsu* ownership and control patterns.

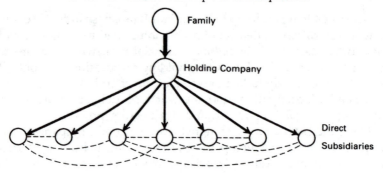

1b. Postwar *keiretsu* ownership and control patterns.

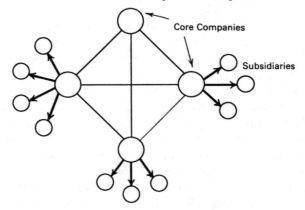

Figure 5. The Japanese *Keiretsu* (Gerlach, 1992: pp. 110, 114): 1. the *Keiretsu* interorganizational network (p. 110); 2. alternative forms of network organization (p. 114); a. the "non-hierarchical clique"; b. the "bank-centered clique".

are directed primarily to the firms in their related industrial blocks, rather than to other financial corporations. Individual firms of similar types share similar positions in the various *keiretsu*, making this the typical alliance form of the Japanese corporate network. Besides the interorganizational links forming corporate networks like the *keiretsu*, other IOC structures are also deployed, including formal interorganizational groups such as "Group Presidents' Councils".

Keiretsu, then, are "hierarchical cliques among structurally differentiated firms in which banks hold a special role ... as coordinators of

2a. The *keiretsu* as a nonhierarchical clique.

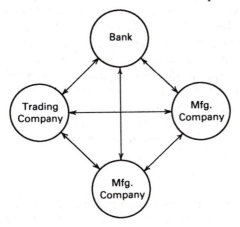

2a. The *keiretsu* as a bank-centered clique.

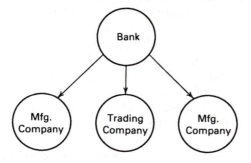

specific subsets of affiliated firms" (Gerlach, 1990: 135). In terms of our definitions, we can view the *keiretsu* as a loosely linked interorganizational network in which a central financial institution acts as a lead organization.

The interorganizational networking of Japanese industry has been widely analyzed as a major contributor to Japan's successful economic development. Some observers have contrasted Japan's loosely linked intercorporate networks with the more rigid organization of Western and especially American integrated industrial hierarchies, to partially account for Japanese dominance of global markets over the last two decades.[9]

A closer look at *keiretsu*, however, suggests that these are not as different as they superficially seem. The American corporation that looks like a vertically integrated hierarchy rarely internalizes all its production systems, let alone other important functions such as finance and marketing, but is really only the lead organization in an interorganizational network. Japanese intercorporate coordination is not simply the product of loosely linked groups of firms based on sociocultural norms of cooperation, but of another kind of hierarchical interorganizational network. It is not enough, then, to juxtapose "networking" with "hierarchy" to explain the one's success or the other's failure. Rather, to learn from this comparison, we need more detailed analysis of the IOC structures in each case and their respective performance.

*   *   *

Interorganizational networks are perhaps the most common IOC structure at the meso-level. What is noteworthy is their diversity and range, from completely nonhierarchical informal linkages (like the Child Protection agencies' caseworkers' network) to well-structured and quite hierarchical networks such as the Farnham County community metal health system or the Japanese *keiretsu*.

While networks and mutual organizations are a form of organization that is distinct from the market and the organized hierarchy, they can incorporate both these types. Organizations in networks are linked by combinations of hierarchical authority, market prices, and solidarity based on trust (Bradach and Eccles, 1989). These various linkages are also reflected in different IOC structures nested in most networks.

In some networks, it is clear, the organizations are linked by no more than informal interpersonal contacts between members; these tend to be solidarity-based associations. The discussion of nonhierarchical coordination in Chapter 4 covered this type of network: social-interpersonal networks, policy advocacy coalitions, and policy issue networks.

Many nonhierarchical informal networks, however, often include some formal elements and arenas of interaction: for example, the interagency agreements and interorganizational groups in the San Francisco Bay Area transit network. Policy issue networks, too, focus on formal interactive arenas, for example, congressional committees and comments to regulatory agencies. In some cases policy networks are quite structured around a hierarchical bureaucracy, as in the German *politikverflechtung* that Kenis and Schneider (1990) refer to.

Most linkages are more formal and become more hierarchical as member organizations' stakes in the mutual transactions increase. The least hierarchical is the loosely linked network of organizations interacting through boundary-spanners (often in dyadic links) around specific mutual tasks. The procurement network linking trusted suppliers to their customer through customer account executives and purchasing agent, and the financial networks in which recurring transactions link investors to seekers of capital through brokers, financial institutions' account executives, and interacting corporate directors, are examples.

Mutual organizations, such as the informal entrepreneurial partnership, joint ventures, consortiums, and cartels use boundary spanners too, as well as other micro-IOC structures. In these networks we find coordinators as project managers, interorganizational groups as interfirm or interagency task forces and governing boards, and coordinating units in the form of mutual organizations.

Interfirm and intercorporate networks in the private sector, public service networks connecting government agencies, nonprofit organizations and private suppliers in the public sector, and networks of other organizations are also hierarchically linked, as we have found. Equity participation, mandated frameworks, and formal agreements and contracts are the bases for these links.

Interactions between the organizations in these networks are again managed by various IOC structures. One of these we have found is the lead organization: in the *keiretsu* network, the construction and manufacturing project, and the local community human services network. Another is the coordinating unit, as in the public program implementation set, and as the mutual organization in athletic, cultural, educational, and professional associations, trade associations and trade union federations. Again, these networks are often linked through interorganizational groups: interlocking boards, councils of Presidents or Directors, Councils of Governments, commissions, committees and task forces.

NOTES

1. The IOC structures presented here, which show various degrees of hierarchy, enable a closer examination of interorganizational networks and how they work. This lets us avoid defining networks as hierarchical or not, and instead explore how hierarchical they are by identifying the micro-IOC structures (from informal links to coordinating units) that link their member organizations.

2. This is a modification of Alter and Hage's typology.

3. Alter and Hage draw some broad generalizations from their empirical data which is based on a survey of fifteen networks of local social service organizations. This is why factors such as vertical dependency (which is related to state control) and a voluntary or involuntary clientele are more prominent than they would be if their sample were made up of, say, electronic supply networks, research consortia, or corporate partnerships. However, their normative conclusions, suggesting a "fit" between effective ways of administrative and task coordination, and network type, are interesting and well supported for the kinds of networks they studied (Alter and Hage, 1993: 234–258).

4. Based on Danielson (1982), Sampson (1982) and Seymour (1980).

5. This is convenient in countries (like the U.S.A.) with anti-trust legislation, where cartel members try to present their price changes as spontaneous mutual adjustment in a "free" market (Bowman,1989: 32–68).

6. 1982 data.

7. These were the firms known as the "Seven Sisters", currently named: Exxon, Mobil, Texaco, Socal, Gulf, Shell and BP, together with the Compagnie Francoise des Petroles.

8. This is demonstrated by the quite successful existence of an alternative model: the European Union (EU), successor to the Common Market and European Community established by the Treaty of Rome. The EU has developed a complex of institutions that do coordinate and in a significant measure control the decisions and actions of its member governments (Medefind, 1975; Bulmer and Wessels, 1987; Wistrich, 1990).

9. A more complete explanation includes Japanese government-business links as well (Johnson, 1982; Murakani, 1982; Okimoto, 1990).

CHAPTER 8

From Markets to Hierarchies:

Meso-Structures for IOC

═══════════════════════════════════

8.1. New and Artificial Markets

In theory, the perfect market is the ideal coordination structure. Without any formal links, all the organizations in the market — buyers and sellers of goods and services — interact and coordinate their behavior by spontaneous mutual adjustment, reacting to the market's signals: price and demand information.

Goods and services are not only economic. Market-like exchanges use media other than money. Political markets involve bargaining and negotiation between participants, who are interest groups, political parties, elected officials, units of government and public agencies. In these markets, the participants exchange information, support in the form of money and votes, and material benefits in transactions that take place in various political arenas (Ilchman and Uphoff, 1969; Buchanan and Tullock, 1967; Wildavsky, 1979).

There are other such quasi-markets. In the health services area, for example, Fennell (1980) describes a "market" in which the sellers are hospitals, but what they are selling are not health services. The "buyers" are not patients, but physicians who exchange their affiliations with hospitals for various packages of benefits and amenities. Milner (1980) analyzed a group of hospitals which made up a "market", in which one medium of exchange was patient allocations. These transactions were mediated through the area's ambulance services, who delivered patients according to a set of informal norms agreed upon between the hospitals, ensuring that most indigent patients were diverted from the high-status hospitals, and steering some paying patients to the lower-status hospital.

What all "perfect" markets, economic and other, have in common is that spontaneous mutual adjustment is how the participants' actions are coordinated. In reality, markets are rarely if ever perfect: they are modified in many ways. We have already seen some of these ways: dyadic links between organizations, mediated by liaisons or boundary spanners (like the Chicago-area purchasing agents), to handle recurrent transactions; informal interorganizational networks (such as the ones linked by interlocking directorates); and more formal obligational and promotional networks (e.g., subcontracting and trade associations) managed by organizational groups and coordinating units. Later, we will discuss still other ways in which coordination structures modify or supplement the market: mutual organizations (joint ventures, alliances, and cartels), mandated regulatory frameworks, and hierarchical integration.

Markets are also modified on the interface between the public and private sectors. Here, rather than the spontaneously existing and mutually adjusting "perfect" market, we find new markets that have been created by privatization, and markets in which government is such a major actor that mutual adjustment merges into public policy. In these cases, then, it is a *managed market* that coordinates interactions between the participating organizations. Unlike the perfect market, managed markets can be and are the subjects of institutional design.

Service contracting by public agencies is one example of a managed market. Public demand for the service, sometimes by privatization which externalizes services previously delivered in-house (Savas, 1982; Donahue, 1989; Kamerman and Kahn, 1989) creates the market, or may significantly modify a market that already existed. Public policy structures the market, too. Ideally, this would be unnecessary: the agency would simply be entering an existing market as one buyer among many, of a service offered by many competing suppliers.

It is a managed market when this ideal is absent. Sometimes, this is why the public sector was involved in this area in the first place.[1] The choice among private suppliers of the service may be limited, creating a "small numbers" phenomenon that inhibits competition. A specific supplier or contractor may have a claim resulting from asset specificity: unique expertise, a common language and trust, or capital investment to offer the specific product or service. The public agency's transaction costs to manage simple market procurement may be high, due to recurrent transactions and the risk of supplier opportunism.

These circumstances demand modification of the competitive market. One form of such a managed market is relational contracting: limiting solicitation, modifying competitive bidding by bargaining, and substituting negotiation for competitive selection of contractors. This is a common way of managing markets.

Relational contracting can be employed in noncompetitive markets when there are only a few suppliers, and has the merit of lowering the agency's transaction costs by avoiding the formalities of competitive bidding. However, this may be offset by higher costs for monitoring and evaluation. It also handles uncertainty well, giving the parties more leeway in implementation, but this flexibility also risks politicizing the agency's relationship with the contractor (De Hoog, 1990: 320–329).

Another form of managed market is cooperation: a mutual undertaking linking the public agency with one contractor. Conditions favoring a cooperative relationship are low resources in time or funds, limited expertise in the public agency, and very few suppliers — sometimes limited to one source. In this form of procurement, the government and the contractor are in a partnership that makes maximal use of the contractor's expertise, based on free sharing of relevant information.

The cooperative contract is a flexible agreement, often covering a long-term transaction; multi-year contracts are frequent. It may include performance incentives, and often depends on professional norms as ways of ensuring effective delivery and limiting possible opportunism. This model's advantages are its use of contractors' expertise, its adaptiveness and flexibility, and its emphasis on long-term project management and performance.

But cooperative contracting is a closed process, risking complacency without the stimulus of competition, and giving the supplier an opportunity to use his expertise to manipulate and ultimately control the transaction. Human services is one area in which such cooperative agreements between public agencies and third-party providers are common; research and development (e.g., in defense and health technology) is another (De Hoog, 1990: 329–334).

Arms procurement, in fact, is a striking example of how managed markets can take various forms, marking the shifting boundary between the public and private sectors. In various countries, differences in national political and administrative cultures have produced several answers to the question of how best to manage the relationship between potential sole-source suppliers of military technology and a monopsonistic government.

While cooperative contracting in a supposedly still somewhat competitive market is the norm in U.S. defense procurement (Melman, 1970; Gansler, 1980), some countries (e.g., France and Sweden) have much more direct and open public involvement in their arms industries, including part ownership of major defense contractors (Ardagh, 1982: 44, 73–4; Adams, 1989: 60, 75–79). Other countries (e.g., Israel and Brazil) have publicly owned core defence industries that act as lead organizations in a network of smaller private subcontractors (Branco, 1984: 84–88; Peres, 1970: 110–111, 121–135; Sachar, 1987: 249–252).

Each of these models has its flaws; the corrupting relationship between military procurement officials and contractors in the U.S., and the defense industry's manipulation of pertinent information, has been repeatedly documented. On the other hand, in other countries dissatisfaction with the results of heavier public involvement in arms production has resulted in a growing push to privatization.

Privatization can be another form of managed market, when withdrawal from public ownership and control of a service creates a market where none existed before. This involves a major exercise in institutional design.[2] One example of such a managed market is Britain's privatization of local public transit.

Privatizing Britain's Local Bus Services

Up to 1985 local bus services in Britain were almost all provided by public enterprises. Many local transit services were owned by the (English) National Bus Company (NBC) and the (Scottish) SBC. These public holding corporations combined longstanding public operators with some private companies which the government bought out in 1969. In addition, each metropolitan county owned its own Passenger Transport Executive (PTE), which operated a large bus system that was sometimes supplemented by services offered by NBC or SBG subsidiaries.

All this was transformed by the British Transport Act of 1985. Implementation of the Act, which began on 26 October 1986, introduced three major changes to establish a competitive market for local transit services. The first was to practically abandon government control over entry into the transit business. Any firm wishing to run local bus services simply has to give the local authority 42 days' notice of its intention.

The second change was to compel local authorities to divest themselves of their publicly owned transit services. This could be done through sale, and many public corporations were in fact sold, either to private businesses or through labor or management buyouts. Or it could be done by reorganization: "spinning off" the transit corporation as a separate "for profit" enterprise. The third was in the government subsidy for public transit, which was drastically reduced. While local authorities were permitted to continue their previous subsidy of supplementary transit services (for example, to retain nonprofitable routes), the Act required them to award all contracts through competitive bidding.

The new market immediately modified the way transit services were organized. The stimulus of competition and potential profits generated many new service providers. In the first year of the Act most of these were small firms. In the second year about a dozen holding corporations evolved which owned bus operators in several counties. Most of the holding corporations started out as small firms or as previous NBC or SBG subsidiaries.

Various competitive strategies emerged between the large incumbent corporations and the new challengers. What many had in common was to keep per-unit costs low by reducing drivers' wages, controlling overheads, and using flexible workrules to make operations more effective. But there is little evidence of new entrants' exploiting their relative cost advantage over the incumbents by drastic fare reductions.

The large incumbents' strategies were to exploit their size, though they enjoyed few economies of scale that gave them any cost advantage. But they could and did cross-subsidize routes, and could offer riders the convenience of travel cards entitling them to unlimited travel in a large service area. On the other hand, they were handicapped in competing for subsidized service contracts, because the new entrants would enjoy a bidding advantage if they could attract riders from the incumbents' routes.

Several longer-term effects of this new managed market have been noted. Contrary to some expectations, there was no drastic cutback in routes: 80% of the prederegulation mileage was registered on deregulation day, and the percentage has been steadily growing since. But fewer off-peak and low-density services have been registered on a commercial basis.

The introduction of competition has effected perceptible service improvements, offsetting the effects of major cuts in public subsidies. These service improvements seem to be the principal result of greater cost-effectiveness attributable to reduced labor costs and competitive subcontracting, since fares continued to increase faster than inflation. Though there has been some loss in transit ridership since deregulation, this has not led to increased automobile use. Competition also encouraged innovation, most of which has been in subsidized services. One innovation is the widespread replacement of larger and double-decked buses by 12–15-seat minibuses.

How successful has the transformation been of Britain's bus transit services from a publicly owned system to a managed market? One's evaluation depends on one's perspective. In one way bus riders have been losers: they are paying higher fares. These, however, are not so much the result of privatization as of the subsidy cuts that went along with it. But passengers have also benefitted from service improvements which are a direct result of the competitive market. Labor ended up a big loser in wages and working conditions. The overall gainers have been British taxpayers, who ended up paying far less in transit subsidies than they did before the Act (Gomez-Ibanez and Meyer, 1990).

                                        *   *   *

Artificial markets are also created in the context of mandated frameworks or obligatory networks. Products of institutional design, artificial markets are intended to elicit spontaneous mutual adjustment among their participants. Their coordinated outcomes reflect a supply-demand equilibrium in response to prices for a newly formed "commodity". The auctions of such publicly allocated "commodities" as frequencies in the electromagnetic spectrum (regulated by the Federal Communications Commission) and offshore oil concessions (by the U.S. Department of the Interior) are examples of such artificial markets.

Elinor Ostrom (1990) has suggested such markets as effective coordination structures[3] to allocate these "commodities" in what she called "common resource pool" situations. These are situations in which a group of people or societal units — households, firms, organizations, or communities — are commensally interdependent on a limited resource.[4] A result of this interdependency can be a mandated framework regulating the use of the relevant resource; for example environmental regulations covering the use of natural resources such as air and water.

Another result can be an obligatory interorganizational network of the interdependent parties. Examples of such a "common resource pool" organization are the Water Replenishment Districts set up by landowners in several California counties. These originated as voluntary associations to apportion groundwater utilization among members, and to share information and enforcement costs. Ostrom's case of "bidding" for fishing areas among members of a Turkish fishing cooperative shows how an artificial market can be created as a coordinating structure in an interorganizational network (Ostrom, 1990: 103–177).

Artificial markets have become quite popular in mandated frameworks as an alternative to controlling actions through regulation. One type of such a market is the "internal market" in a production or service delivery system. In the business sector, accounting transactions between separate "profit center" divisions of a corporation or conglomerate are a familiar example. In the public sector, such internal markets exist too; for example, the exchange of patients and reimbursements among local Health Authorities in Britain's National Health system (Mullen, 1991).

Another example is the use of Transferable Development Rights (TDRs) in the context of land development control in the U.S. The "market" in TDRs is created by the local zoning ordinance which enables property owners to trade development rights among themselves. In this fashion the political burden[5] of compensating owners for reductions in the value of their land due to lost potential development opportunities is shifted from the local government authoring the zoning plan. Instead, the artificial market enables compensation of the "losers" by those property owners whose land values are enhanced by the new zoning (Platt, 1991: 234–237).

The area of environmental regulation is another mandated framework that offers an example of an artificial market. This is the exchange of "rights to pollute" which was enabled under the regulations to abate point-source (mainly industrial) air pollution in the U.S.

Tradeable Emission Rights Under the U.S. Clean Air Act

Under the Clean Air Act of 1970, the federal regulations controlling point-source air pollution set maximum allowable levels of particular pollutants, and divided the country into geographic areas with specified "attainment levels". When pollution in a particular area reached its specified maximum, no further industrial development that could be a source of additional pollutants was permitted in that area.

Giving in to considerable political pressure from economic development interests and States with substantial nonattainment areas, Congress amended the statute. As a result, the Environmental Protection Agency (EPA) relaxed these regulations, to create an artificial market which would allow existing polluters to sell their emission rights to firms wishing to construct plant in a nonattainment area.

EPA's "Offset Policy" provided that a new major facility could enter a nonattainment area (like California) if it could obtain emission reductions from existing polluters that would at least offset or exceed its new pollution. Though the new policy did raise some problems of measurement and monitoring, it opened the door to competition which offered the prospect of ultimately improving pollution abatement efficiency.

In this new artificial market the "commodity" traded was the capitalized value of their pollution "rights" to existing firms in nonattainment areas. These values depended on their technologies and production costs and efficiency. Potential entrants into an area went "shopping" for emission rights which they would buy from the lowest bidders. So, for example, a petroleum corporation wanting to build a new refinery in New Jersey that would emit hydrocarbons could not do so unless it bought out fifteen Trenton area dry cleaners.

The market was not quite free: implementation of the policy also depended on prescribed offsets set by the regulators. These could become a "moving target", as in the 1978 case of SOHIO's California refinery. While not formally obstructing any purchase of emission rights, the California pollution control authorities increased the required offset until SOHIO gave up, and shipped its oil for refining to Galveston, Texas, as a less expensive substitute.

In another case the market worked better. When Volkswagen was considering Pennsylvania as a location for a large plant, which offered welcome employment to an economically hard-hit area, the State of Pennsylvania came to the rescue. To enable the plant's construction in a nonattainment area, the State provided the required emission offsets by changing from petrol-based asphalt to a water-based compound for its highway construction and repair.

In the 1977 Amendments to the Clean Air Act the offset mechanism was modified to allow less than one-to-one offsets, and they permitted certain pollution increments in cleaner air regions. EPA also encouraged extension of the artificial market in tradeable emission rights, including a proposal to enable individuals to "bid" for them as intermediaries. Perhaps this was due to EPA's sense that the market was not clearing as well as it could. In fact, data suggest that most transactions are between parent companies and their subsidiaries or between organizational affiliates.

Another EPA proposal was for State environmental agencies also to establish such "markets". But States were not enthusiastic about this idea. They did not adopt the market mechanism EPA advocated, preferring instead to continue the regulatory allocation of offsets, which gave more play to discretionary political power (Yandle, 1989: 77–98).

*   *   *

While markets, then, are a wonderful way of effecting coordinated action, they often also need institutional design to make them work. Sometimes, to make a market, a "commodity" has to be created, which interested parties will want to exchange. The market must be managed to ensure and maintain the conditions for effective competition, or to modify the transactions between buyers and sellers where the competitive stimulus is feeble or absent.

Ensuring competition includes intervention to enable entry or access to the market for organizations and individuals who are potential buyers or sellers, and to facilitate the transfer of pertinent information between all the actors so that the market will clear. This also demands institutional design responses including regulation, organization or reorganization, and channelling or modifying public subsidies. We have seen examples of all these in the artificial and managed markets reviewed above.

8.2. Mandated Frameworks

Mandated frameworks are another meta-IOC structure within which other IOC structures are always found. Raelin called this a "mandated network."[6] The mandated framework is distinguished by the legal-political mandates, which are the basis for its interorganizational relations, from other networks based on voluntary exchange, solidarity-association, or direct hierarchical links (Raelin, 1982: 243–244). While exchange-based networks tend to have symmetrical interactions between their member organizations, and formal hierarchies have extreme asymmetries of power dependency of one unit on another, the mandated framework is somewhere between these poles (Raelin, 1980: 57–60).

Interorganizational networks based on legal or political mandates take a wide variety of forms. They can be networks of organizations interacting in a regulatory framework, or in a planning context, or implementation sets of organizations structured around a particular program or project. These are often mixed: many mandated frameworks include elements of several of these types, and contain a variety of interorganizational networks and other IOC structures.

For example, U.S. air pollution abatement policy was articulated in the Clean Air Act of 1970 and later amendments. This is the mandated framework for a variety of interorganizational interactions and several IOC structures. The legislation identified the federal Environmental Protection Agency (EPA) and state EPAs as coordinating units, and established several programs that combine regulations and incentives to coordinate the behavior of relevant organizations. The EPA issued regulations setting attainment standards in identified regions for specific pollutants, and enabling the exchange of emission rights between existing and new industries in nonattainment areas.

This mandated framework, then, links interorganizational networks made up of the federal EPA, state environmental authorities and other state agencies, local governments, developers, and industrial and commercial firms which emit point-source pollution. It created coordinating units at the federal and state levels, and embraces programs such as point-source pollution abatement which include regulations and funding incentives for state planning and coordination, and a managed market in emission rights in nonattainment areas.

Mandated frameworks are most apparent, perhaps, in their regulatory aspects. The regulatory context of mandatory frameworks is a set of norms and rules that has been established by a series of social-political decisions resulting in legislation, public policy allocating resources, sanctions and incentives, and administrative regulations. Statutory land use regulation, which exists in most countries, and which includes land use planning at several levels and local development control such as zoning, is one case (Patricios, 1987). Environmental regulation, for instance the framework covering the collection and disposal of hazardous waste (Goggin et al., 1990: 22–23), is another. Most areas of human activity, in which there is some public interest, are covered by a regulatory mandated framework that coordinates the activities of the relevant organizations. The issue of urban development in flood-prone areas is an example.

Floodplain Development Management in the U.S. and Australia

There are two reasons for government intervention in regulating floodplain development. One is the public interest in reducing people's exposure to flood risks, and the losses that go along with them. The other is based on the fact that one public response to these risks has been to provide government subsidized insurance against flood-caused damage, and compensation to eligible firms and households for flood disaster losses. The federal government's interest in reducing its flood insurance and disaster assistance costs has made the control of flood plain development an issue that transcends local boundaries.

In the U.S. the management of floodplain development has always been a local government responsibility, but communities had no interest or incentives to limit construction in floodplains, which often offered good sites for industrial and commercial construction, and sometimes the most attractive locations for residential development. Several federal attempts (e.g., through the Tennessee Valley Authority and the U.S. Geological Survey) offering incentives for local government capacity building to enhance communities' consciousness of the risks and real costs of floodplain development were failures: few cities and townships took advantage of them. In 1968, with the enactment of federal flood insurance, the issue of limiting floodplain development became more urgent for the federal government.

After 1968, local governments were required to develop and implement floodplain management plans that would limit construction in areas that were defined as floodplains in terms of the regulations, to be eligible for federally financed flood-damage insurance. Floodplain management was to be integrated with local comprehensive land use plans and zoning. The control of construction in floodplains was to be coordinated with local development policy, as reflected in the delimitation of water and sewerage service areas by the local government or the responsible utility district.

This floodplain management program was premised on the potential sanction of withholding federally financed flood-loss insurance from noncomplying localities. In fact, local responsiveness was limited, because the government was unwilling to incur the financial costs of systematic monitoring, or the political costs of deterrence by withholding post-disaster assistance from the residents of noncomplying jurisdictions.

In 1973, with the costs of federal flood insurance and disaster assistance escalating, the floodplain management program was significantly strengthened. Funds were budgeted for local government assistance, that would give municipalities and townships an incentive to develop floodplain management plans and would give them front-end funding for monitoring and implementation capacity-building. The sanctions were stiffened, and federal and state monitoring and enforcement capacity was enhanced, so that federal insurance was in fact withdrawn from noncomplying municipalities.

The program still cannot claim universal compliance with flood-plain management requirements, and implementation of develop-ment controls has been rather weak. But the combination of planning incentives, technical assistance, encouragement of intergovernmental cooperation between local and county planning and zoning and public works departments and water and sewerage districts, and enhanced deterrence through strengthened monitoring and enforce-ment capability, has been more successful than the previous reliance on unsupported regulative deterrence.

The Australian state of New South Wales (NSW) had the same reasons as the U.S. to control floodplain development, and began to regulate floodplain planning and management in 1977. Its floodplain management program was based on the American 1968 model, but it also was not very effective. In 1984 NSW modified its program with some major changes in its regulative design. Instead of its prior reliance on deterrence and sanctions, which the state lacked the moni-toring capacity to enforce, the new format emphasized intergovern-mental cooperation.

Complementing the existing sanctions, the program included sev-eral new capacity-building elements. The state produced and distrib-uted a floodplain development manual that clearly spelled out the floodplain management planning process and the required standards for insurance eligible development. The program included planning assistance funding to local governments and offered them direct technical assistance in floodplain planning and management. Inter-governmental coordination was encouraged through the creation of local floodplain management committees, which became eligible for funding to support their planning and implementation activities.

Two more elements demonstrated the new state commitment to a cooperative model of floodplain development control. One was tax relief and incentives for land that remained vacant as a result of its floodplain location and consequent constraints on its development. The other was a waiver of municipalities' liability for any actions they took in connection with floodplain development control that were consistent with state guidelines.

The modified mandated framework for floodplain development in NSW has been quite effective. Review of the U.S. and NSW experience lets us compare two types of mandated frameworks, one emphasizing deterrence through regulation, the "deterrent form", the other combining regulation with incentives for cooperative action: the "cooperative form". Where the objectives of the deterrent form are to ensure adherence to prescribed standards, the cooperative form aims to achieve broader policy goals, such as (in this case) balancing the social and economic costs of floodplain development with its immediate benefits. The deterrent form relies on monitoring and enforcement to invoke the prescribed sanctions and penalties; the cooperative form deploys additional instruments: public education, technical assistance, funding for planning, intergovernmental cooperation and implementation.

Each form of mandated framework is also premised on different assumptions about organizational behavior. The deterrent form assumes that any cooperative commitment is lacking, while the cooperative form assumes more intrinsic willingness to cooperate among lower level governments, and a mutual commitment to common goals of rational floodplain development. Their emphases also differ: the deterrent form focuses on regulating adherence to prescribed standards, the cooperative form emphasizes capacity-building of lower level governmental agencies.

Both forms also have their weaknesses and potential for failure: neither usually provides the complete answer to the problem that stimulated the public policy in the first place. In the deterrent form, local interests and politics weaken strict adherence to regulated standards, and effective implementation demands a real investment in monitoring and enforcement. The cooperative form falls short when the local units' commitment to the program, even with the incentives provided, is lacking, and fails to deal adequately with recalcitrant jurisdictions (Burby, Keiser and Moreau, 1988; May and Handmer, 1992).

*   *   *

This case is quite typical of mandated frameworks. Though we began by thinking of floodplain development control as a regulatory framework it embraces much more. It includes government programs of flood disaster assistance and a non-administered program of federal (in the U.S.) or state (in Australia) flood loss insurance. The behavior of the state and local governments, public agencies, developers, landowners, firms and households which are interacting in the context of this mandated framework is coordinated by several other IOC structures, including coordinating units (the state agencies administering the regulations and programs) and interorganizational groups, for example the NSW floodplain management committees.

Concerted action of the network of organizations interacting in the context of a mandated framework may not be the result of regulatory constraints alone. The mandated framework may require them to undertake joint planning as a way of ensuring coordinated outcomes. Mandated planning, plan review and comment by affected parties, and plan approval by designated oversight bodies, are common IOC tools which are part of mandated frameworks.

Mandated frameworks with a major planning component are universal. They cover defense and national security, economic development, environmental management, land development and urbanization, human services in education, health, and social welfare, and transportation, infrastructure and utilities networks. The case of planning a light rail transit system for Hennepin County, Minnesota, illustrates how a mandated planning framework works to integrate a network of diverse organizations and produce coordinated action.

Hennepin County Light Rail Transit Plan

Hennepin County, Minnesota, is one of the seven counties making up the Minneapolis-St.Paul metropolitan area. Development in this area is controlled by an advanced system of regional planning under the Metropolitan Council, which was created by the state legislature in 1967. In 1984 the legislature also formed the Regional Transportation Board (RTB) to conduct mid-range transit planning implementing Metro Council's transportation policies for the metropolitan area, and to provide for effective transit services.

But Minnesota statutes placed light rail systems in the domain of the county railroad authorities, making the Hennepin County Regional Railroad Authority (HCRRA) the lead agency for light rail transit (LRT) planning when the development of an LRT system was mooted in the mid-1980s. In 1987 legislation, the Minnesota legislature mandated a LRT planning system that would ensure coordination between the affected agencies and units of government. It prescribed that the preliminary and final LRT plans developed by the HCRRA are to be reviewed by the Metropolitan Council and the RTB, and must be approved by all the affected cities and towns.

It was obvious that only an inclusionary planning process would ensure the consensus needed to get the prescribed approvals. HCRRA developed a LRT planning structure made up of seven corridor committees (one for each of the possible LRT routes), four advisory committees (on downtown, finance, land use, and technical matters), and an Intergovernmental Advisory Committee (IAC) governing the planning process. The IAC included all the county commissioners, and representatives from the affected cities, regional transportation agencies, community organizations, and the legislature. 180 people were members of one or more of the planning committees.

At the IAC's first meeting on September 15, 1987, the co-chair launched the comprehensive LRT planning study which was to answer four questions: Where to build LRT? How to build it? How to pay for it? Who will operate it? However, this directive was flawed by its failure to include any evaluation of alternative modes to LRT, such as busways or reserved highway lanes for high-occupancy vehicles.[7] The planning timetable was very tight: just over 19 months. To meet this deadline, the corridor advisory committees had only three months to complete their part of the work. Conflicts over a variety of issues created delays in the committee reports, and the final LRT System Plan was adopted by the HCRRA only in June 1988.

One of the areas of conflict was over the corridor alignments and their impacts on neighborhoods in four of the seven corridors. In the southwest corridor, a high-income neighborhood organization (VOTERS) opposed the proposed route. Two inner-ring suburban cities claimed, in support of the route, that it would provide valuable transit service and boost development. An alternative corridor running down Nicollet Ave. was suggested and initially supported by the adjacent inner-city district representative. But the area's neighborhood association, and the Nicollet Avenue merchants contended that Nicollet Avenue was too narrow to support the LRT lane without diverting other traffic into neighborhood streets, with undesirable effects, and proposed a tunnel instead. This was adopted by the committee, whose recommendation retained the rest of the original route over the opposition of VOTERS.

The proposed South Corridor route used the abandoned Soo Line railroad right-of-way, which generated resident opposition because this would separate a high school from its athletic fields and disturb many adjacent homes. The committee yielded to this opposition and substituted a route on Interstate Highway I-35W right-of-way. In the Northwest Corridor, the West Broadway alignment was favored because it would serve a larger transit-dependent population and stimulate the street's revitalization. But merchants opposed it, fearing a loss of parking, and proposed an alternative which the committee adopted.

At the University of Minnesota a conflict also arose between the proposed alignment which was technically and financially preferable, but which provided poorer service to the campus, and a University-offered alternative on the major arterial running through the campus. The committee's recommendation reflected the University's position, and was consistent with all the committee's proposals which adopted the least controversial solutions.

Another area of conflict was the question of at-grade or subsurface service through downtown Minneapolis. Intensive lobbying by tunnel advocates argued speed, safety, and winter comfort. Favoring street level service were cost considerations, and merchants' arguments that removing another source of traffic from the streets (in addition to the existing skyway system) would turn downtown into "a ghost town, especially after dark". The surface option was supported by a consultant's feasibility study commissioned by the City of Minneapolis, endorsed by the City Council's Transportation and Public Works Committee, and finally recommended by the Downtown Advisory Committee.

The last issue was the location and number of stations. This raised the question of basic transit philosophy and goals: should the LRT be a high-speed service with limited stops for suburban commuters, or should it be designed to serve a more urban transit-dependent population and have more frequent stops? Suburban representatives of course favored the former, arguing the LRT's potential to compete with automobile traffic and reduce highway congestion. Central city representatives advocated the latter, promoting the development potential of LRT stations and arguing that LRT should serve the city and inner-ring suburbs which housed 70% of its potential riders. The Metropolitan Council endorsed the latter position as more compatible with its regional policy.

But this conflict was never resolved in principle. Rather, debate on the location of stations continued in each advisory committee, whose hearings were taken over by neighborhood residents opposing stations in their area. The advisory committees had to decide on station locations based on a tradeoff between each additional station's neighborhood impacts, and its increased ridership potential offset against the loss in travel speed it causes.

All the proposals and advisory committee recommendations were combined into fifteen alternative scenarios which, besides their common "system core", varied according to the location and length of corridors and the existence of a downtown tunnel. The scenarios were ranked according to their comparative performance on effectiveness criteria such as patrons per vehicle mile, and efficiency criteria such as total annual cost per annual patron.

Evaluating the scenarios and comparing their rankings on the various criteria, the IAC selected the option which, while not optimal, served the most important corridors and generated an adequate level of ridership. This plan, estimated to cost $481 million in its first stage, was adopted by the HCRRA on June 21, 1988. Hennepin County's LRT planning process also stimulated similar activities in other metropolitan counties, two of which adopted their own LRT plans.

In 1990 the state legislature mandated the Regional Transit Board to consolidate the county plans into a regional LRT plan. This plan included nine corridors and was estimated to cost $1.3 billion. In February 1992 the Metropolitan Council adopted a Regional Transit Facilities Plan which integrated LRT with other transportation modes and recommended only one corridor connecting the cities of Minneapolis and St.Paul. For later construction this plan recommended the Hennepin County South Corridor, and called for analysis of other alternatives. Meanwhile funding sources for capital construction are being explored, with the metropolitan area governments and agencies asking the legislature to enact an earmarked sales tax or some other source of revenue, which the legislature has so far refused (Rafter, 1992).

By contrast with some previous cases, the interorganizational groups involved in the Hennepin County LRT planning process were quite successful. It is possible that their effectiveness as arenas for conflict resolution is partly due to the fact that the mandated framework within which they were operating made consensus among the involved parties a necessary condition for carrying out the project, combined with the all the actors' common interest in having some LRT system implemented.

The elaborate hierarchy of IOC structures in this mandated framework is also noteworthy, from the interorganizational groups (the advisory committees and corridor committees) at lower and intermediate levels (the IAC) to the coordinating units at intermediate (the county planning units, such as the HCRRA) and upper levels (the Regional Council). Some other experience suggests that this could have been an administrative nightmare; in fact, it seems to have worked quite well. This is almost certainly because they were all operating within the same mandated framework (the relevant federal transportation planning and funding programs, and the state enabling legislation) which included a clear assignment of domains and responsibilities.

But, if effectiveness is to be judged by plan implementation,[8] this framework was also flawed. The fact that, as it filtered up through the planning process, the scope and cost of the proposed LRT system was constantly reduced, until it was stalled due to the state legislature's refusal to vote the necessary taxes, suggests that user interests were overrepresented in the planning system as it was designed. While the interaction of the interorganizational network produced proposals on which all the affected parties could agree, it did not work as well in generating consensus and commitment on how to pay for them. It remains to be seen if this problem will be overcome.

*   *   *

Another way in which a mandated framework may be structured is as a policy, program or project that mobilizes an "implementation set" of organizations (Hjern and Porter, 1981). This is particularly true of public agencies and organizations involved in intergovernmental implementation. A few examples are U.S. hazardous waste disposal policy, family planning services, and municipal waste water treatment (Goggin et al., 1990), legal aid services (Kessler, 1987), food stamps (Milward, 1982), employment, training and vocational education (Jennings and Zank, 1993), and coastal zone management (Lowry and Eichenberg, 1986); European river pollution abatement (Schleicher, 1985) and infrastructure networks such as Toronto's metropolitan transit system (Frisken, 1991) and German highway planning and construction (Garlichs and Hull, 1978).

These terms — policy, program and project — share the idea of a joint undertaking to achieve some mutual goals; they differ in their respective levels on the continuum of abstraction, ranging from the policy at the broadest and most general level, to the concrete and specific project (Alexander and Faludi, 1989). The policy or program, then, is a type of mandated framework that forms an interorganizational network joining sometimes thousands of agencies and organizations in areas of activity defined by legislative mandates and linked by the flow of government funding (Brinton, 1992: 62–71). Programs vary widely in their forms and operation depending on their objectives, functions and context, so no one case can be a proxy for all programs. But the U.S. Job Opportunities and Basic Skills (JOBS) program illustrates how this form of mandated framework works as an IOC structure.

The U.S. JOBS Program

The JOBS program was created in 1988 under the Family Support Act, as a modification of the Aid to Families with Dependent Children (AFDC) program. The program's goal is to end welfare clients' dependency by giving them the education, training and skills they lack and to enable them to enter the employment market. It is administered by the Administration for Children and Families in the U.S. Department of Health and Human Services (HHS), which has written the regulations prescribing eligibility and mandating program planning, coordination, and operations, and monitors compliance. Federal JOBS program funding is allocated by legislated formula between states and communities, and requires matching state contributions. The legislation creating the program also required its coordination with other existing employment and training programs. The most important of these are the programs established under the Job Training Partnership Act (JTPA), which are administered by the Department of Labor. The JTPA also mandates a variety of IOC structures to assure coordinated delivery of its employment and training services and other related programs.

One of these is the state job training coordination council (SJTCC), a coordinating unit[9] which is charged with developing a plan that identifies state-level coordination activities, setting standards for program coordination by the Service Delivery Areas (SDAs) and monitoring their implementation. The SJTCC also allocates funds set aside for encouraging coordination efforts, and reviews and approves related agency plans for employment and vocational education.

Another is the local Private Industry Council (PIC), an interorganizational group containing a majority of employer representatives, and including representatives of local education agencies, the employment service, labor unions, rehabilitation agencies, economic development agencies, and community organizations. Each PIC draws up a biennial plan that identifies its employment and training activities and resource allocations in its SDA, and describes how they will be integrated with JOBS and other employment-related programs.

The JOBS program also includes several coordination mandates. One is a requirement for state-level coordination between JOBS activities and other employment and training programs. This is effected by submitting the state JOBS plan to the SJTCC for its review and comment, and consultation between the state agencies administering the JOBS and JTPA employment and training programs, and the state education agency. In many states the JOBS and JTPA programs are administered by the same department, sometimes even the same division. This agency may be a state department of human services, social services, or public welfare (Jennings, 1993).

Planning the program involves decisions about the program components that will be offered, allocation of funds, and service delivery contracting. Planning varies from completely centralized at the state level, to almost totally local and decentralized planning in various combinations. For example, in one state the state agency coordinating the program signs contracts with the state education agency and the state employment service to provide education, job readiness, job development and placement services. Decisions on SDA involvement, what optional services to provide from the state-developed menu of possible options, and the details of operational relations between service providing agencies are decided at the local level.

The community level actors in the JOBS program include the local welfare office responsible for the AFDC program (which can be the county office of the state welfare agency, or the county welfare department), the PIC, the administrative entity of the JTPA service delivery area (SDA), the local school system and community colleges, the local office of the state employment service, community-based organizations and for-profit contractors. The delivery of program services takes place in three phases.

Client diagnosis and supervision, the first phase, begins with determination of the potential client's eligibility, after which the client goes through a needs assessment that varies from extensive, in-depth assessment of education, aptitudes and literacy, to simple cursory math and reading skills tests or just an informal assessment by the caseworker. Based on his or her "job readiness", an employability plan is developed for each client, determining placement in a basic educational context, a skill training program, or assignment to job placement. This initial phase is the primary responsibility of the local social service agency, though sometimes client assessment and case management are contracted out to other agencies, community organizations or third-party providers.

The second phase is removal of employment barriers. This includes referral for adult remedial education supported by JOBS program funds, in local schools, independent school districts, community colleges or adult learning centers. Clients may also be referred for life-skills training that includes goal-setting, time management, communications, networking etc. to another outside partner which may be a community college, the employment service, a community organization, or a for-profit contractor.

Another barrier is lack of job skills. Training in job skills is usually provided by the SDA, but often paid for by JTPA funds. JOBS clients get reassessed when entering the JTPA program to determine if they have the needed basic education. If they do not, they are referred back; if they do, they are assigned to a job skills training program in an appropriate technical educational institution or to on-the-job training or wage subsidized work experience with one of the firms on the PIC's roster.

Finally, clients are ready to enter the work force. In many communities placement has been a relatively low priority because most JOBS clients have needed more education or training. Various arrangements for job placement services exist in different communities. In some, collocated social service and employment service staff share placement responsibilities, using the directly available state job data bank. This gives the SDA a relatively minor role. Some JOBS clients are placed through their JTPA-funded training provider or with their on-the-job training or work experience firms.

In some communities, agreements between the local job service office and the SDA structure the placement process. Job-ready welfare recipients get training and placement services from JTPA providers, paid for with JOBS funds. In other communities, one agency (the employment service, the welfare office, or a contractor) is the designated gatekeeper for JOBS clients' entering the workforce, with other agencies contracting for services that are paid for through the lead agency.

The JOBS program also provides for necessary support services, such as child care and transportation, for its clients who need them. This is either done by contracting with service providers, or by referring and reimbursing eligible clients who procure these services. This may involve another state agency in managing a voucher system, or the use of another resource and referral organization to identify vendors, manage a data base system, and disburse payments.

Local level coordination between the diverse agencies and organizations involved in the JOBS program varies from the formal to the informal. A major coordination tool is contracts, often used between public agencies, and always with not-for-profit and for-profit service providers. Between public agencies nonfinancial interagency agreements often lay out the framework for cooperation. These contracts and agreements may be the result of bilateral negotiation, but more often they are the product of multiorganizational planning involving formal interagency coordinating bodies: planning task forces or coordinating councils. These are interorganizational groups representing all the involved agencies and organizations.

Other coordination tools are often used at the operational level. These include collocation of staff, common referral and tracking procedures, and joint staff training. Regular communication is an important aspect of coordination, and is sometimes formalized through a designated interagency liaison or coordinator. For example, in two counties the social service agency created a JOBS program education coordinator, whose tasks were to interact regularly with local education providers, address individual clients' problems in education programs and monitor their progress, and link case managers with education providers. Regular meetings between program managers also facilitate communication. Shared electronic information systems are another coordination tool, but are rare (Jennings and Krane, 1993).

The scope and complexity of this program is striking. It involves an interorganizational network that includes government and public agencies at all levels and in several sectors, community organizations, firms and businesses. This network is coordinated through a complex set of IOC structures that includes lead organizations, coordinating units, interorganizational groups, coordinators and liaisons, using joint planning, budget control, contracts and agreements, collocation and other coordination tools.

In terms of its results, JOBS has been a qualified success, though the low job-readiness of most of its clients has shifted its focus from job skills and placement to more basic education and training. Consequently, the program's original output criterion of clients successfully moved off welfare and into the employment market shows rather disappointing figures.

The program's coordination, too, between its various service delivery agencies and with other related services such as vocational education, has been less than perfect, in spite of the mandated coordination requirements and the funds set aside to support coordination efforts. This is inferred from the fact that barriers to coordination are still identified, and reforms to improve coordination are still called for. Thus, for example, all the IOC structures, and all the mandated interagency planning and coordination, have only rarely produced elementary operational coordination features such as standard integrated eligibility screening and instruments, "one-stop" client intake and assessment, and joint electronic data banks and information processing (Jennings and Zank, 1993; Zank and Jennings, 1993).

*   *   *

A special kind of program is the *non-administered program* (Levine, 1972). In this type of mandated framework the interorganizational network is indirectly coordinated by invoking appropriate stimuli: incentives, sanctions, or both, to change what organizations would do if they were simply interacting in the market.

However, even non-administered programs require some monitoring and supervision: the self-administered part of the U.S. income tax system, a classic non-administered program, is actually run by a substantial bureaucracy. On the other hand, there is no denying that mobilizing the taxpayer's and firm's own actions in response to the system of tax legislation and regulations allows the administrative superstructure to be much smaller than it would otherwise have to be to run a program of this scale.

In the United States, besides the managed market advocated by neoconservative scholars, the non-administered program has been the darling of neoliberal economists and political scientists. Most categorical grant programs, for example, were designed on the assumption that the prospect of funding for a prescribed activity or purpose would bias decisions by firms, organizations, or local governments in a desired direction. This was the idea behind programs from Head Start (support for preschool education for poor and minority children) to Hill-Burton (federal subsidies for hospital construction).

But the pure non-administered program is rare; more often it has to be supplemented by some bureaucratic apparatus, including other IOC structures, to ensure that its conception is matched by its execution (Williams, 1975: 541–542). Decision adjustments to tap available grant funding, for example, have to be formalized as proposals which require review and, when demand outstrips resources (which is usually), selection on the basis of predetermined criteria. Program implementation to achieve designated objectives has to be ensured by drafting and administering a complex set of regulations, which can become quite a coordination problem in itself (Rabinowitz, Pressman and Rein, 1976).

To succeed, this IOC structure needs an adequate grant of power to the organization setting up the non-administered program. The responsible agency must have, and be prepared to use, authority in the form of a credible threat of sanctions in cases of non-compliance, as is the case, in fact, in the U.S. income tax system. Or the program must deploy enough resources to provide an incentive for organizations to adjust their behavior in the desired direction, or both.

Some non-administered programs which failed to meet their objectives due to the lack of federal enforcement are the U.S. Community

Development Block Grant (CDBG) and Concentrated Employment and Training Act (CETA) programs. In both, local implementing agencies accepted formula-distributed funds. But local governments used their political clout to neutralize pressure and threats of sanctions by the federal departments (Housing and Urban Development, and the Employment & Training Administration) responsible for ensuring compliance with the statutory mandates (Williams, 1980). The U.S. New Communities Development program was another non-administered program which failed, this time partly because its financial incentives were inadequate to outweigh its administrative complexities (Alexander, 1981).[10] A similar case is the German *Standortprogramme* (STOP) program.

Coordinating Planning in Germany: the STOP Program

The STOP program responded to perceived deficiencies in the development planning process, both at the Land[11] and at the local level. The Land plans were poorly implemented due to weak vertical coordination, while local plans were vague, based on poor information, and supported by inadequate organization. As a result, an effort to reduce complexity emerged, by limiting detailed plans to small areas only within each municipality.

This planning concept was introduced in the early 1970s in North Rhine-Westphalia, where it was linked to Land-prescribed special objectives and procedures. These plans were called *Standortprogramme*, and were intended to concentrate the municipality's mid- to long-term development planning and implementation measures. They would also make the Land's public investment policy much more effective, by focusing resources on a few areas. The incentive for local governments to adopt STOP was its link to the Land's funding for housing, industrial development, education, and transportation.

STOP had three objectives: to concentrate public investment within municipalities; to institutionalize vertical coordination between the Land and local authorities; and to promote horizontal coordination among functional agencies at the local, regional and Land levels, and between the public and the private sectors. The STOP format was prescribed in the Land guidelines, enacted in 1971. It should be a development plan for a limited area (contained in a radius of about 1 km. from public transportation stops) indicating proposed patterns of housing, jobs, commercial services and public institutions. Its horizon should be between five and ten years, and it should be integrated into the municipality's comprehensive plan.

The guidelines mandated interaction between the local authorities and the public in the course of plan preparation, with inputs from relevant regional and other public agencies. Regional and Land consultation and approval was required at various stages of the planning process, and the Land Minister of the Interior had to approve the plan to give it statutory validity.

Many local authorities began the STOP process when the guidelines were published in 1971, hoping to simplify their grant applications and get more funds. For many of them, especially rural communities, this was their first attempt at development planning. But in many areas, especially the larger municipalities, selecting action areas raised political conflicts, and there were constant attempts to evade this requirement. Some large cities identified many areas, and small communities sometimes wanted to include their whole territory.

Though the regional authorities resisted these efforts to dilute the basic concept of STOP, there were also objective obstacles. These included economic stagnation, slower population growth, suburbanization, and the shortage or cost of centrally located urban land. Sometimes topography, too, inhibited identification of a limited development area. These problems combined with regional agencies' administrative inexperience to make the whole program suspect to local authorities, who began to see STOP as limiting their autonomy. At the same time, their incentive to participate was undercut when, in 1972, the Land modified its requirement of STOP as a prerequisite for all funding applications, and made it mandatory only for especially complex or costly projects.

When they began STOP, most municipalities set up interdepartmental working groups to effect horizontal coordination. These interorganizational groups were a rather weak form of institutionalization. Even less reorganization took place at the regional and Land levels. Land ministries refused to give up their independence, and continued to use their own sectoral criteria in reviewing grant applications, without giving any preference to proposals included in a STOP. The public participation prescribed in the guidelines was generally neglected.

The results of this effort were disappointing. By 1977, only 160 of 200 local authorities had initiated the STOP process, and most of these were smaller towns. Only about 40 STOPs had been submitted to the Minister of the Interior for approval, and only five of these had been approved. The low approval rate was mainly due to unrealistic population projections which were developed to support costly project proposals.

Approved STOPS did not speed up the flow of funds to the local government, and grant applications still had to be pursued separately with each ministry as before. STOPs produced few changes in local development policy, since they usually included investments that had been planned anyway. But they did improve local horizontal coordination, and gave many municipalities valuable experience in development planning.

A 1976–77 review resulted in revised Ministry of the Interior guidelines which were issued in February 1978. These only regulated the STOP process and simplified the procedures, rather than indicating planning objectives, as the previous guidelines did. They also limited the STOP requirement to areas needing special coordination measures, and exempted rural districts completely. The new STOP guidelines were a significant retreat from the original program aims of concentrating planning and investment, and from its coordination goals.

In retrospect, it is obvious that the STOP failed for several reasons. The main reason was that it increased the formal interlocking of different levels of the political structure, without providing sufficient incentives for the participants to come to grips with this increment of procedural complexity.

This was reinforced by other factors. Local governments' resistance to the Land's centralizing tendencies was backed up by local power (at least of inertia) which was underestimated by the Land authorities initiating the program. At the regional and Land levels, STOP failed to institutionalize the horizontal interagency coordination that might have provided an incentive for local participation. The responding group shifted from the larger cities, which were the program's initial target, to smaller rural communities for whom STOP's concentration goals were less relevant. Objective changes in the planning environment, which the program was too inflexible to accommodate, also inhibited achievement of its goals.

*   *   *

As we have seen, the mandated framework is a meso-IOC structure that always embraces other IOC structures: programs, projects, lead organizations, coordinating units, interorganizational groups, coordinators and interorganizational liaisons. Even the mainly regulatory framework needs monitoring and enforcement, and non-administered programs include other IOC structures to invoke the sanctions and deploy the resources on which they depend for their effective implementation.

Although other factors undoubtedly play an important role, some of the successes and failures of the mandated frameworks we have reviewed are attributable partly to their institutional design. What IOC structures are used at which levels of the interorganizational network, and how they are equipped with resources of authority or funds, clearly effects the observed outcomes.

But there are no simple solutions; the relationships are quite complex. Interorganizational groups were effective, for example, in the Hennepin County LRT planning process, because they operated in a clearly defined mandated framework which gave them powerful incentives to arrive at the consensus they needed to succeed. In another planning framework, the STOP program, local interorganizational groups contributed little towards improving coordination, because their incentives were incommensurate with the difficulties of their task. Nevertheless, we may be able to say something about the institutional design of mandated frameworks, if we learn more about the other micro- and meso-IOC structures of which they are composed.

8.3. IOC Systems

IOC structures are often parts of "nested" IOC systems, as we have seen. Sometimes these IOC systems emerge in associational interorganizational networks. Often they are designed into mandated frameworks. An example of the first kind is the NCAA: a federation of collegiate athletic programs governed by an interorganizational group, which grew to be managed by a coordinating unit.

Less formal interorganizational networks may also in fact be coordinated by IOC systems. For example, the hospice care network in two Maryland counties, which was made up of seven organizations, included a coordinating unit (Hospice care, a voluntary private organization created for this purpose), an interorganizational group (a interagency team representing member organizations), and coordinators: caseworkers from Family Social Services, a participating agency (Alter and Hage, 1993: 141–142).

Another case of this type is the policy issue network. Though apparently informal loosely linked interorganizational associations, many policy issue networks are actually quite complex IOC systems. One common element in many such networks is the "policy broker", a kind of (often informal) coordinator who plays a critical role in forming and maintaining the network (Kirst, Meister and Rowley,

1984: 249–250). Various policy issue networks are linked by different IOC structures.

One such network was a group advocating the teaching of scientific creationism; this network was essentially linked through an organization that acted as its coordinating unit (rather like the NCAA described above). Another network was a coalition of interest groups looking for ways to increase school financing. This coalition was led by the Ford Foundation acting as a lead organization. A third network was concerned with competency testing for high school graduates. This was a truly informal network, but it too had its IOC structure: a cadre of experts and individual politician-promoters who acted as boundary-spanners between their organizations, interacting in meetings, exchanging information through the media, and advocating their positions in speeches and papers (Kirst, Meister and Rowley, 1984: 251–255, 257–259).

Many mandated frameworks are designed as IOC systems: hierarchies of different IOC structures at the various levels of the system of organizations encompassed by the mandated framework. Regulatory mandated frameworks offer many examples of IOC systems. Statutory land use regulation and development control is one, with local, and district, provincial or regional planning agencies as coordinating units governed by their planning or zoning commissions (interorganizational groups), and national planning commissions or councils (another interorganizational group) staffed by a coordinating unit, either a separate agency, such as the Netherlands' *Rijksplanologiese Dienst*, or a unit in a ministry or department, such as Britain's Department of the Environment or the Planning Administration in the Israel Ministry of the Interior.

Another such mandated framework is environmental regulation and management. The issue of river water pollution, for example, has generated different mandated frameworks with complex IOC systems in Europe and the U.S.A. These IOC systems include an interstate commission (an interorganizational group) and coordinating unit for the Ohio River valley, a complex combination of two organizations (the RV and RTV) forming the *Ruhrgenossenschaften* to manage the German Ruhr valley's water resources, and coordinating organizations governed by interorganizational groups in France: the "Financial Basin Agencies" (Schleicher, 1985: 520–527). The area of state environmental management in the U.S. also offers a case of complex IOC systems combining various IOC structures.

State Environmental Management in the U.S.

The mandated framework of environmental regulation in the U.S. is hierarchically structured to encompass the federal, state and local levels. At the federal level, the Environmental Protection Agency (EPA) was created in 1970 to integrate environmental management, and be the *lead agency* in this area for the federal government. While the EPA is a comprehensive agency, it is also internally segmented, partly along programmatic and partly on functional lines. This case, however, focuses on environmental management at the state level, which falls under overlapping mandated frameworks of federal and state legislation.

State environmental regulation soon came to be burdened by a proliferation of permits and their increasing segmentation into specialized activities. This stimulated several state efforts to coordinate their environmental management, which usually took the form of reorganizing the relevant state agencies and their permitting process. All environmental programs, which had been the responsibility of the state public health department or a Department of Health and Human Relations, were assigned to a new organization which would be the *coordinating unit* for environmental management. The previous form of administration has survived only in about fifteen small southeastern and western states.

Reorganization followed one of two models. One was the environmental "superagency", such as the New York Department of Environmental Conservation (founded in 1970), and the Washington Department of Ecology (1971). The second model was the "mini-EPA", copying the EPA's format and name, e.g., the Illinois EPA (IEPA), also created in 1970.

By 1982 twenty seven states had set up procedures for coordinated permit review and approval. These consisted of a master permit information form, joint interagency applications and hearings, and one-stop permitting. Several states created a *coordinator* role: a "permit expediter". These measures provided some regulatory relief for permit seekers, but they did not produce the functional integration and comprehensive review of permit applications that had been hoped for.

Illinois' attempts to integrate environmental management are revealing. The state created a quasi-judicial body, the Illinois Pollution Control Board (IPCB) with broad powers for rulemaking and adjudication, as a *coordinating unit*. The members were appointed with a view to maximizing their individual discretion and their professional diversity, so that the Board was more likely to adopt a comprehensive perspective and take cross-media (air, water, waste, etc.) impacts into account.

However, ten years after the ICPB was established, there were still critical cross-media problems. Among IOC structures formed to address these were the Toxics Project Team and Advisory Committee, two *interorganizational groups*. The Toxics Project Team was internal to the IEPA and its membership cut across program boundaries, while the Advisory Committee was made up of IEPA and outside experts. Their report recommended several projects which made up an Integrated Toxics Control Structure, involving all IEPA divisions, to coordinate and integrate permitting for toxic waste discharge, processing and disposal.

These IOC systems' record of program implementation and performance is spotty. In Washington state, its Environmental Control Procedures Act encountered stiff political opposition, and consequently had only limited application, even though a strong agency had been created to implement it. New York's State Environmental Quality Protection Act also had some administrative problems, and suffered from funding shortages. But it ultimately won general acceptance, and its mandated permitting procedures are now standard throughout the state.

The IPCB's effectiveness was limited by shortages of staff, which were exacerbated when the Institute of Environmental Quality, which gave the Board research assistance, was dismantled. Weak mutual support between the ICPB and the IEPA also caused problems. Later, these were overcome, and the IPCB obtained more staff to carry out its mission. Today, the ICPB is regarded as well administered and competent.

Overall, in spite of their respective shortfalls, the IOC structures put in place to coordinate environmental management in these three states were quite effective. All made major contributions in fostering communication among the organizations involved, and produced better interactions between the agencies responsible for environmental control of the various media. Unquestionably, environmental management is better integrated than it would have been without them (Rabe, 1986).

*   *   *

Another type of mandated framework is the one that is intended to concert organizations' actions by prescribing coordinated planning. Complex IOC systems in mandated planning frameworks are common. One example is light rail transit planning in the Minnesota Twin

Cities metropolitan area, presented above, which involved an elaborate hierarchy of interorganizational groups and coordinating units. The Century Freeway project in south-central Los Angeles is another.

The Los Angeles Century Freeway Project

In October, 1979, a consent decree was negotiated between the U.S. Department of Transportation and its Federal Highway Agency (FHWA), and Caltrans, its state counterpart, and the Center for Law in the Public Interest (CFLPI), an advocacy organization which attacked the project's Environmental Impact Statement. This turned a simple freeway plan into a more complex project in which the California Department of Housing and Community Development (HCD) was designated as the *lead organization* for the planning process, supported by the Housing Advisory Committee (HAC), an *interorganizational group* representing the localities affected by the proposed freeway. Under the HCD, the planning process was to be managed by a Steering Committee, another *interorganizational group*.

In the event, the CFLPI's attempt to transform the traditional loosely coupled transportation planning system into a more hierarchical network, with the HCD as a central "coordinating agency", failed. The actual lead agency in the process, Caltrans, reasserted its role when the other actors perceived that HCD had no power to enforce its decisions, and lacked the expertise to make its arguments persuasive. "(I)t was the relationship among the cities and Caltrans, and between Caltrans and FHWA, based on shared norms and values, which effectively changed how ... the network would be put into operation" (Mandell, 1984: 673).

Unlike the HCD, the HAC did retain its role, partly owing to its legitimacy as representing important local interests, and partly because it learned to interact directly with Caltrans, switching HCD out of their loop. Caltrans never lost its central position in the network, since the cities were dependent on Caltrans for their highway funding, and it enhanced its own power by recognizing HAC's claims and supporting its legitimacy (Mandell, 1984).

*   *   *

Mandated frameworks often have a legislated and funded program as their base. Such frameworks also have complex IOC systems. One case is the Job Training Partnership Act (JTPA) program in the U.S. Among its IOC structures are an interorganizational group at the federal level, the Low Income Opportunity Board (later the Economic

Empowerment Task Force), a coordinating unit in the federal Department of Labor, and interorganizational groups at the state and local levels: the State Job Training Coordinating Councils and the Private Industry Councils (Jennings and Zank, 1993).

Another striking example is the U.S. Model Cities program, where an extensive network of federal, state and local government agencies, community organizations, and private contractors, consultants and service providers were involved in program and project planning and implementation. This program included an innovative IOC system which was designed to replace the bureaucracy's traditional functional decentralization with a form of political decentralization that would empower local communities.[12]

The U.S. Model Cities Program [13]

In 1965 disenchantment with conventional urban renewal, a rediscovery of urban poverty, and a city hall backlash against the radical Community Action Agencies (CAAs) combined to stimulate the creation of the Model Cities program. This was the sense of the presidential Task Force, which recommended a "demonstration program" in about 66 cities. The proposed program would concentrate public investment in deteriorated central city neighborhoods, coordinate federal programs, and mobilize local initiative and leadership.

This program held out the promise of federal reform: a streamlined grant application process, earmarked funds from functional programs, technical assistance from other federal bureaus, and a new local agency that would be the sole point of entry for all federal resources to the demonstration neighborhood. Its funding, of $2.3 billion over five years, was estimated in an optimistic budget context which projected economic growth that would make $4 billion available for domestic spending.

On November 3, 1966, the Demonstration Cities and Metropolitan Development Act was passed, but with some changes in the proposals. Congress authorized only $900 million over two years, and required nearly 140 eligible cities. The Secretary of HUD was denied the power he sought to earmark other programs' funds; indeed, he was warned that they were sacrosanct. The legislation omitted to specify how the program's coordination goals were to be achieved, and one of the few concrete proposals in this line, a federal *coordinator* at the local level, was dropped.

Through early 1967 HUD staffed its new Model Cities Administration (MCA), and reviewed the first round of grant applications. Review panels included representatives of other agencies: the Office of Economic Opportunity (OEO), the Department of Health, Education and Welfare (HEW), and the Department of Justice, so as to enlist their support and coopt them for eventual coordinated resource allocation.

At the same time the local Demonstration City Agencies (DCAs) were being set up according to HUD guidelines. The DCA was to combine policy-making and implementation responsibilities, and was governed by a Board combining citizens and local government officials and an advisory Neighborhood Council made up of elected or appointed residents. It had an Executive Director who managed its administrative and professional staff. The DCA's success depended on finding mutual interests between city hall and neighborhood poverty groups; we shall see how this condition was met.

Meanwhile, in Washington, HUD's new MCA was trying to augment the program's resources by obtaining review authority over other federal programs. It succeeded with its first targets: other HUD bureaus, but achieved only limited results in its negotiations through the Interagency Committee, which had been set up to concert Model Cities policy. HEW agreed in principle, but evaded its commitment in practice, since most of its funds were legally restricted and channeled through states. OEO got into a standoff with HUD, each wanting its local agency, the CAA or the DCA, to have final authority over the other's programs. Finally they compromised on mutual review, but many CAAs reneged on this agreement. Labor, too, refused to limit its local officials' authority by giving the city mayors and DCAs any review or veto powers.

By early 1968 75 cities had been approved for planning funding, and by the end of 1968 another 75 of the second round of applications were approved, bringing the number of Model Cities to its total of 150. Under the new Nixon administration a new undersecretary, Floyd Hyde, took over the MCA. Hyde was aware of the problem of Model Cities' underfunding because of HUD's failure to obtain the "earmarking" of other program funds that was part of the original proposal. Aggressively setting out to change this, he succeeded in committing other HUD bureaus, HEW and OEO to earmark $62 million of their 1969 funds. But much of this amount might have been spent in these areas anyway. Later, as White House support for the program eroded, there was a good deal of footdragging in the standing Assistant Secretaries Working Group, when it came to making any new commitments.

The administration's enthusiasm for the program waned as the idea of revenue sharing emerged as a replacement for categorical grant programs, and several presidential task forces evaluated the program, threatening its survival. Meanwhile, by June 1969 the first 35 cities with approved plans began to receive their first action-year grants. Some projects were approved incrementally to as to expedite funding, while other elements were held up for revision to meet HUD requirements.

While MCA was hurting at the federal level, the new DCAs were also facing problems. One was citizen involvement, which led to a good deal of pressure on local government from HUD. But even when a genuine desire for citizen participation existed, there were objective obstacles to involving poor citizens: they lack experience, a longer time-horizon, and the capacity to assign priorities when means are limited. Another problem was recruiting qualified administrative and professional staff, which created a conflict between residency requirements and job descriptions. Residency requirements had to be relaxed, and by Spring 1971 MCA required DCAs to develop resident recruitment, training and employment plans as part of their programs.

The local program mix was a problem too. Model Cities had been created in reaction to the physical thrust of urban renewal, but now DCA Boards learned the drawbacks of social and economic development programs: long startup times, limited direct effects and diffuse indirect impacts. Physical projects, on the other hand: housing, infrastructure, open space or recreational facilities, are immediately observable by all. Elected neighborhood boards acquired the same political instincts as city officials: they discovered that there is a larger instant political payoff in a cheap tree-planting project that produces few real benefits, than in an employment training program for which they will not be around to take credit. As a result, Model Cities came increasingly to resemble the urban renewal it was to replace.[14]

Different local DCAs developed different kinds of relationships with city hall, depending on the type of planning system they had (resident or staff dominated, or parity), their resident characteristics, and their organizational environment. These relationships were crucial to the DCAs effectiveness. Most successful, but rather rare, was the "parity" relationship, reflecting a coalition between strong equal partners in the city administration and the neighborhood organization.

By 1971 Model Cities was under serious threat of replacement by Special Revenue Sharing, and was only extended by heavy city lobbying in Congress. Meanwhile, the expected shift was reflected in a HUD reorganization, which merged the MCA with the Urban Renewal Administration under Hyde, now as Assistant Secretary for Community Development.

In mid-1971 twenty cities participated in a new program experiment, called "planned variations", which was launched in response to difficulties in implementing HUD guidelines. This gave cities more discretion, allowing them to extend Model Cities type planning throughout their territory, giving local chief executives signoff over all federal programs, and streamlining Washington's review and approval procedures. Though this reform, too, was defeated by bureaucratic resistance and failed to live up to expectations, it was continued through a second year, and extended to another twenty cities. In January 1973 Model Cities was halted by a federal moratorium on several HUD programs, and with passage of the Housing and Community Development Act of 1974 it was effectively killed, to be merged into the new Community Development Block Grant program.

The Model Cities program has generally been judged a failure. This is less because of its lack of tangible impacts, though these were disappointing, as because of the gap between the program's promise and its performance. What happened? There is little evidence that this outcome was due to a lack of political commitment: the eventual appropriation and spending of funds was more or less consistent with the original targets. But the program's diffusion and its gradual change in emphasis from focusing on poor neighborhoods to general assistance for cities was a displacement of its original goals.

As a vehicle for coordinating federal agencies at the local level, and for reforming the federal grants-in-aid system to make it more responsive to local priorities and the needs of the poor, Model Cities achieved little. The existing structure of federal agencies effectively defeated its efforts, and cities helped by failing to organize to spend their allocated funds in time.

Local DCA implementation was slow for several reasons. Slow HUD approvals of detailed projects was one. DCAs' inability to cope with the prescribed planning process was another. Cities also failed to streamline their own internal administration, losing valuable time in cumbersome internal decision making and review. Finally, DCAs were often defeated by the complexity of mixing Model Cities supplemental funds with other categorical grant programs, a form of coordination for which Model Cities had been expressly designed.

As a coordination effort, the Model Cities program failed at both the federal and local levels. The "earmarking" of other funds was never achieved to the extent planned, because HUD never received the lead agency powers that were part of the original program design.

Consequently, other agencies had little incentive to cooperate in the Model Cities effort. Federal interagency coordination in processing grant applications was also weak, and the devolution of real decision-making authority to the local level of DCA Boards or city executives remained little more than a promise.

The IOC system devised for the Model Cities program was to effect three types of coordination: concerting the decisions of the various federal agencies (central horizontal coordination), ensuring that local actions complied with program requirements (vertical coordination), and coordinating planning and implementation between all the relevant organizations at the local level (local horizontal coordination).

At the meso-scale, Model Cities was designed as a *non-administered program*: rather than legislation mandating certain behavior, the availability of federal funding was to be the incentive for local units to propose and carry out actions promoting national objectives. HUD was designated the *lead organization*, and an *interorganizational group*, the Model Cities interagency committee, was set up to effect horizontal coordination at the federal level.

HUD formed the MCA as the program *coordinating unit* with vertical coordination as its main task. The DCA was the local *coordinating unit* and implementor of all the Model Cities neighborhood programs. It was also designed to be the arena for integrating the interests of area residents, other local institutions, and local government, but the latter claimed and eventually received the DCA's authorizing powers.

As a non-administered program, Model Cities had the potential to succeed: the participation of nearly 150 localities suggests that the expectation of substantial funds, at least, was enough of an incentive. But the program's actual performance was inhibited by several factors. The failure of earmarking eliminated a source of substantial funds, and the remaining funding was dispersed over a much larger number of sites than originally planned.

Also, as suggested before, the non-administered program is rarely as unadministered as it seems. Here, too, it was actually coordinated by the MCA, which had a mixed record of performance. It took several rounds of regulations and guidelines to "get the bugs out" of the program's administrative system, and just about when this was accomplished the program was killed by the Ford administration's moratorium. Also, in looking for the right balance between centralization and decentralization in its relationships with the DCAs, the MCA was biased towards the former, and as a result a growing volume of paperwork inhibited the DCAs in their timely disbursement of funds.

The lead organization IOC structure that was to effect horizontal coordination at the federal level was a total failure, since HUD had neither the power to coerce nor the resources to tempt other federal agencies into surrendering any of their autonomy. The weakness of HUD's role is reflected in the micro-structure adopted to effect inter-agency coordination: the interorganizational group, armed only — for other agencies — with the (inadequate) power of persuasion, or — for other HUD bureaus — with the ultimate and rarely invoked sanction of the Secretary's authority.

The DCAs' achievements in coordinating local program planning and implementation varied, depending to a significant degree on the specific context and configuration of each. To the extent that they were effective, this was related both to their perceived inducements in prospective funding and to their signoff powers over other programs in their neighborhoods. The CDA's performance was also linked to their staff/citizen/city hall interaction, which, when it was successful, gave the CDA the legitimacy it needed to aggregate these participants' different interests.

*   *   *

Mandated frameworks for implementing legislated programs are another area where IOC systems are frequently found. State-level implementation of education programs for handicapped children in the U.S., legislated in 1986 amendments to the statute, is an example. The federal law required a "Single line of authority in a lead agency designated by the Governor for" administration, resource allocation, interagency dispute resolution and formal interagency agreements.

The IOC system for education programs for the handicapped in most states included an interorganizational group: an Interagency Coordinating Council with state agency officials and citizen repre-sentatives as its members, and its chair was sometimes designated the State-level coordinator for handicapped education programs. Some respondents to a survey which was part of an evaluation of this program even suggested strengthening parts of this system, for exam-ple, creating a state Office for Children which would have interagency and program coordination responsibilities — in effect, a coordinating unit (Harbin et al., 1992: 103–105, 113).

Finally, mandated frameworks often have complex IOC systems for operational coordination. Florida's reorganized integrated human services delivery system is one example. It included two interorgani-zational groups: the cross-program staffed case team, and the case planning committee for children; a coordinating unit: the relevant DSS supervising unit; and coordinators at several stages: the lead case-worker assigned to a case, and later the "client relations specialist" (Polivka et al., 1981: 362–364).

Another example is the U.S. JTPA education, training and job-placement services, which are coordinated by a lead organization, the designated SDA, and a specially created coordinating unit, the Private Industry Council which is governed by an interorganizational group. In addition, several areas have created special IOC structures to coordinate interagency service delivery, including new organizations and integrated case management (Jennings and Zank, 1993).

In both interorganizational networks and mandated frameworks, the overall design of their IOC systems seems to have little to do with their success or failure. What the examples do show, however, is that the system's performance depends on the effectiveness in its role of each of the IOC structures that make up its parts. What we can say about this is one of the subjects of the concluding chapter.

NOTES

1. There can be several reasons for this. Some kinds of service, e.g., utilities, are "natural" monopolies. Others have a significant "public good" character, such as education or health services. Often, commercial suppliers of a particular good or service are few or absent because it is unprofitable, or can only be made to pay with additional public subsidy, due to high costs, low demand, or both. Thus, retail stores flee low-income neighborhoods because their potential customers lack buying power, commercial operators will run peripheral bus lines only with subsidies to supplement low fare receipts, and utilities are reluctant to connect distant users because of their high marginal costs.

2. Today the salient example of this, of course, is the marketization of the command economies of Eastern European countries and the previous U.S.S.R.; see, e.g., Bolan (1991).

3. She does not call them that, but, in terms of our definition, that is what they are.

4. The classic illustration of "common resource pool" interdependency is Garrett Hardin's (1968) "Tragedy of the Commons", which describes how the individual rationality of maximizing exploitation of common land by each cattle-owner led to exhaustion of the resource through overgrazing.

5. Though downzoning does not imply a legal liability for compensation (Boselman, Callies and Banta, 1973: 246; Platt, 1991: 196–201).

6. I have not adopted Raelin's term, so as to avoid confusion with interorganizational networks: a mandated framework is a meta-IOC structure within which interorganizational networks and other IOC structures can be nested.

7. This was in violation of the U.S. Department of Transportation mandated planning process, which requires formal consideration of alternative transportation modes.

8. Conformity of reality to plans is a common way of assessing plans' effectiveness, but implementation is not necessarily the only gauge of how well a plan worked (Alexander and Faludi, 1989).

9. I have called the SJTCC a coordinating unit, though formally it is an interorganizational group, because it is staffed by the state agency administering the JTPA programs. The PIC is subject to similar ambiguity: some PICs are really bare-bones interorganizational groups, others are staffed by a county agency, and still others have their own organizational autonomy with an executive director and staff.

10. For a more detailed presentation, see p. 20 below.

11. The German equivalent of the Australian, Brazilian, Indian or U.S. state, or the Canadian or Netherlands' province.

12. See Porter and Olsen (1976) for the distinction between political and functional decentralization. This aspect of the Model Cities program was subsequently imitated by others, e.g., Israel's Project Renewal (see pp. 122–129 above).

13. Alexander (1980), based on Frieden and Kaplan (1975), Kaplan (1971), Haar (1975) and Rapkin (1979).

14. These observations, from personal contact with several California Model Cities programs, are confirmed by the Congressional Research Service's (1973: 69–73) note that Model Cities was moving from a "software" to a "hardware" approach. Note the resemblance of this process to Israel's Project Renewal described above.

III.
SYNTHESIS

Theory and Practice

CHAPTER 9

Integrating What We Know

9.1. What Is IOC and How Does It Happen?

There is no one "true" definition of IOC. Rather, views of IOC vary, we have found, depending on their theoretical premises. Intuitively, people have often regarded coordination as something to be achieved: a form of desired behavior that would ensure successful action. This is the view Wildavsky scorned when he said: "Coordination is one of the golden words of our time".

Still, this attitude is quite widespread. Persons of undoubted wisdom, including academics, professional administrators, and elected officials, implicitly subscribe to this view, which informs the conclusions and recommendations of prestigious bodies such as National Commissions and Presidential Advisory Task Forces.[1]

But what is really so wrong with this view of coordination? The problem with a definition that does little more than associate coordination with effective action is that it distracts us from coming to grips with the important questions. If coordination itself is just a positive attribute of organizational behavior or interorganizational relations, how can IOC be an object of enquiry? If all coordination is good, and more coordination is better than less, how can we look at coordination, distinguish between different kinds of coordination, and learn which are more effective and why?

This definition, then, is problematic not because it is untrue, but because it is counterproductive. This finding gives us a clue on how to evaluate the other definitions of IOC which we have encountered. Perhaps we should not be looking for a definition of IOC that is true, or more correct than any other, but for the one that is most useful in eliciting productive questions, stimulating enlightening research and analysis, and ultimately producing better action.

Another view of coordination is based on exchange theory, and focuses on voluntary transactions between organizations. In this view coordination is a property of decisions: a decision is coordinated if it takes all the relevant information in the organizational environment into account and makes the appropriate spontaneous adjustments. There are several problems with this definition too, but it also has some advantages.

It shares the flaw of the previous definition, of associating coordination with success. Thus, we can only know if a decision was really coordinated when all the evidence is in, rather than determining if coordination was an intrinsic attribute of the decision or not. Another problem is this definition's inclusiveness: how many decisions, by this standard, are uncoordinated?

This definition's advantage, however, is that it recognizes spontaneous mutual adjustment as a form of coordination. As a result, the market also comes to mind when we are thinking about IOC, instead of only the more hierarchical kinds of coordination implied in the traditional view. But this is not enough to outweigh the problems of this approach, if there is another way of defining coordination that is broad enough to embrace market coordination through mutual adjustment, yet not so inclusive as to make every decision a coordinated one.

There are alternative definitions of IOC, less exclusively based on exchange theory and premised also on contingency theory. These see coordination as a process, a linkage between actions, or a relationship between organizations. All are correct, but each is limited to a particular aspect of IOC and neglects others.

Mulford and Rogers (1982) define IOC as an interorganizational process of creating new rules or norms for collective action, or using existing ones. This definition also has the merit of including mutual adjustment (as a use of existing decision rules), but then has the same problem of indeterminacy as the previous definitions. It has the advantage of highlighting process, but at the cost of neglecting structure.

Viewing IOC as the emergence of linked chains of actions emphasizes interdependency, an important aspect of coordination, but leaves
other questions unanswered. The issue of intent remains open: is any
complex interlinked action system coordinated, or must it be deliberately structured to handle the interdependencies? Indeterminacy also
troubles Hall's (1977) definition of coordination as a relationship
between organizations: the degree to which each organization takes
other organizations' activities into account. Any group of organizations which has taken other organizations into account enough to
prosper, or even survive over time, would have been considered
coordinated.

Other definitions of IOC focus on just the aspects these definitions
neglect: intent, direction or control. Typically: "Coordination means
getting what you do not have" (Dunsire, 1978). But these definitions
again have the flaw of being partial: with their implications of coordination as an exercise of power, they neglect the possibility of spontaneous mutual adjustment and coordination through voluntary exchange.

Structuration theory offers a way of viewing IOC that integrates
process and structure, intent and action. It suggests that IOC is a form
of social structure: a set of rules and norms that enables and constrains
action, and which is itself enacted: created, sustained or transformed
by action.

What mediates between structure and action is the actors' knowledge of the structures that form the society in which they live. For IOC,
the critical stimulus is organizations' interdependence: knowledge of
their interdependence is what motivates people in organizations to
link up so as to coordinate their respective organizations' actions.
*Interorganizational coordination, then, is a set of organizations' recognition
and management of their interdependence, by creating or using IOC structures to decide on their actions together.*

The reason for IOC, the emergence and use of IOC structures, and
the quality of ensuing action are all encompassed in this definition. It
recognizes mutual adjustment as a form of coordination, when the
market is considered as an IOC structure. But this view does not
associate IOC with successful outcomes; rather, action is coordinated
if it is the result of intended coordination. Not any action which takes
the organization's environment into account is, by this definition,
coordinated. To qualify as coordinated, organizations' actions, even
their mutual adjustments in political or economic markets, must be
the result of deliberate interactions with other organizations.

This means, for example, that a firm's market behavior, simply responding to aggregate price, demand and supply information, is not a coordinated decision, because no deliberate or structured interaction with other organizations is involved. On the other hand, the same firm might adjust its production, for instance, on the basis of market demand information it received in its trade association newsletter, and raise its prices after learning that one of its inputs would cost more, at a supplier's board meeting which one of its executives attended as a director. These actions would already be coordinated with other organizations in the sector; and if the price raise, for example, was following a recognized but informal price leader in an industry cartel, they would be coordinated indeed.

Or a neighborhood association, leafletting its members to vote for one of its officials who is a candidate in the upcoming local election, is simply acting spontaneously in the political market, logically expecting that her position as an alderperson will yield some positive benefits. But the same action may be coordinated, if the association is acting as a member of a policy coalition, and its official's election is part of a common strategy to place its people in positions from which they can affect public decisions to advance the coalition's aims.

This definition of IOC also integrates the alternative explanations we have seen for the emergence of IOC and IOC structures. IOC structures evolve in a cyclical process much like the one which Campbell and Lindberg (1991) described for governance regimes of economic sectors, which are of course IOC structures too. At some point in this process perceived anomalies or pressures for change in the existing situation stimulate a consciousness of interdependence between organizations. This may take the form of recognizing issues that cannot be addressed without involving all the organizations needed to solve the problem, or challenges that demand multi-organizational action to achieve a mutual goal.

Recognition of their interdependence in the relevant organizations sets off a search for a way of linking them and managing their interactions: new IOC structures or changes in existing ones. The stimulus or pressures for change may be recognition of organizations' resource dependence (as premised by exchange theory), or it may be the result of environmental changes, as suggested by contingency theory and organizational ecology. Such changes include new societal decisions expressed in legislation, or mandates that sometimes involve radical transformation of the organizations' environment. Or the recognition of interdependence may involve a consciousness of high costs of the status quo, and the potential for reducing transaction costs by changing existing IOC structures, as suggested by transaction cost theory. Often, as many of the cases show, new or transformed IOC structures are the result of a complex combination of several of these factors.

It is clear that all the antecedents of IOC involve organizations' recognition of their interdependence. IOC is more easily accomplished among organizations which are predisposed to recognize their mutual interests in concerted action. IOC is difficult, and may be impossible, to bring about among organizations whose interdependence is really quite small, or whose relations and characteristics obscure the interdependence that may in fact exist between them.

If interdependence is objectively weak or absent, IOC may in fact offer few or no benefits, and setting up IOC structures may involve costs which, even if they are low, offer few prospects of offsetting gains. But organizations' failure, owing to inhibiting factors in their own characteristics, or because of their historical relations (such as competition or domain conflicts between them), to recognize mutual interdependence that does exist, may have serious consequences.

The challenge for someone thinking of promoting coordination among organizations, or considering appropriate IOC structures to effect IOC between them, is to distinguish between these two situations. Is there no IOC because of weak interdependence between the organizations concerned? Or is the absence of IOC the result of decision makers' "false consciousness": the failure of responsible officials and staff to recognize the interdependence that really exists between their organizations, and the potential that appropriate IOC structures could offer for more effective action?

In the former case, the effort to initiate IOC is misplaced. In the second case, the advocate of IOC must assess the feasibility of changing attitudes, to create the recognition of interdependence which, as we have seen, is an indispensable prerequisite for IOC. Sound assessment of the antecedent factors promoting and inhibiting IOC will help the potential advocate pick an arena that offers some chance of success.

These factors include organizational characteristics: to what extent are the concerned organizations outward-looking, innovative, decentralized, diverse, adaptable, and with people already in boundary-spanning roles? Or are they rigid, formalized, hierarchical, centralized, bureaucratic, single-task oriented, and self-focused, with little openness to or interaction with their environment?

Another set of factors makes up the real and perceived relationship between the benefits and costs of IOC. These include whether IOC is seen as reinforcing or undermining the organization's critical values;

to what extent it advances or threatens the interests of salient groups in the organizations or stakeholder constituencies; and what are the real and perceived costs of the needed IOC structures. Such costs, in terms of resources and the political costs of reorganization and reallocation of power, are compared to IOC's expected benefits.

Interaction potential between the organizations making up the possible action set or interorganizational network is also based on several positive or negative factors. Actual interdependence, commensal or symbiotic, is one. Common or complementary tasks, technological linkages, and processing or production interactions, are expressions of these interdependencies. Coordination incentives, including resources or authoritative mandates, is another. The history of organizations' relationships and pervious interactions is also important. Common goals and values, complementary rather than overlapping domains, common professional or disciplinary "languages", similar or complementary tasks, and structural and technological consistency will also enhance the interaction potential between organizations.

Contextual factors constraining or enhancing the potential for IOC include environmental stability or change, predictability or uncertainty. The relation between these is complex and relatively unexplored. However, it seems that a certain amount of "looseness" is likely to facilitate IOC, while a very stable and predictable context may inhibit it. On the other hand, too much turbulence and uncertainty will make IOC much more difficult, because effective IOC structures depend a great deal on a durable framework of mutual expectations and reciprocal obligations among the interacting organizations.

Anyone wanting to promote IOC among several organizations in a given environment needs to know to what extent the organizations recognize their mutual interdependence, or, if not, how easy it will be to create this consciousness among them. A systematic assessment of these factors will help potential IOC advocates make a sound judgement on whether this is a promising arena for investing their efforts, and what are the prospects for their success.

9.2. Thinking About IOC

As we have seen,[2] speculation and research into IOC over the last three decades have spawned a bewildering variety of concepts, models, and theories. Perhaps this is partly because IOC as a concern has transcended the boundaries of particular disciplines or literatures. IOC has been the topic of theory and scholarly analysis, while IOC experience has been shared in case studies drawn from practice.

To make future thinking and research into IOC more productive, a conceptual framework that offers some logical ordering of all these ideas and terms might be helpful. Such a framework is proposed here (see Figure 6 below), to array the concepts and terms which we have encountered, in a three-dimensional space.

One dimension is the level of abstraction, from the most specific and concrete at one end, to the most general and abstract at the other. The other dimension is the degree of institutionalization, which in a way subsumes formality and hierarchy.[3] This dimension is not shown as a continuum; rather, it is divided into two parts: formal and more institutionalized, and less institutionalized-informal. The third dimension (the "depth") distinguishes between structure (describing relationships) and process, that deals with activities or behavior.

Beginning at the most abstract level, the concept of *interorganizational contexts* describes the interorganizational system preceding or resulting from IOC structures. Where IOC is absent, or where it is limited to partisan mutual adjustment or informal linkages alone, they can be laterally linked "feudal" fields. Examples of such fields are a relatively free market, or an oligopoly, or an environment dominated (like some policy areas) by a few large independent and only loosely interacting organizations. With the introduction of formal IOC structures, they can be "mediated", like many of the interorganizational networks we have seen. At the hierarchical extreme is the "guided" or controlled interorganizational field, such as the multi-hospital "empire" or the diverse conglomerate.

A source of confusion is some writers' use of the term "interorganizational network", to mean roughly the same as "interorganizational field". In this conceptual framework interorganizational networks are defined as one type of IOC structure, so they appear at a lower level of abstraction than the interorganizational field.

Coordination strategies is another term that has been loosely used, with examples ranging from the relatively abstract, like cooperation or control, to quite concrete ones, such as contracting or budget review. Where other elements of this framework are essentially structural (that is, they describe elements or relationships between them), coordination strategies describe processes or behavior.

In the sense that this term has been used, coordination strategies often overlap with other concepts. For example, contracting can be quite a concrete coordination strategy: a process or a form of organizational behavior. At the same time, a contract is an IOC tool. The

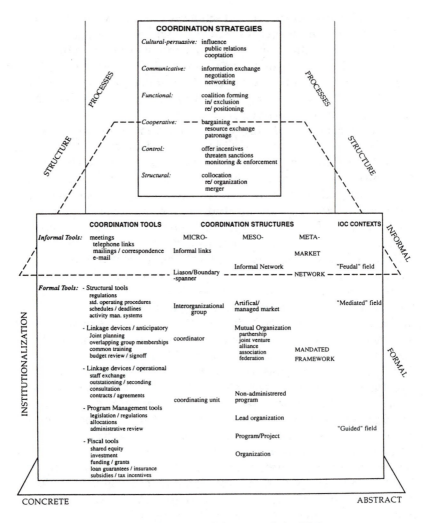

Figure 6. Conceptual framework for IOC.

conceptual framework presented here distinguishes as clearly as possible between strategies and tools, both on the dimension of abstraction-concreteness, and as process or structure.

Coordination strategies are processes or forms of organizational behavior, and often (though not always) they are more general and abstract than the specific coordination tools many of them apply. Coordination strategies have different media of action. Cultural or persuasive strategies involve compatible values; an example is professional cooptation. Negotiation and public-relations are communicative strategies; coalition-forming or exclusion are functional strategies; and bargaining, resource-exchange, and patronage are instances of cooperative strategies. Control strategies include resource incentives and sanctions, while structural strategies include organization, reorganization, contracting and competition.

Coordination structures describe the relationships or linkages between organizations that have evolved (in the case of informal links or networks) or that have been designed (in the case of formal IOC structures) to bring about IOC. They are the linking mechanisms that transform uncoordinated or less coordinated interorganizational fields into more coordinated ones.

Coordination structures can also be arrayed on the dimensions of relative abstraction and institutionalization. An IOC structure's abstraction corresponds to its level of organizational scope and generality: higher-level IOC structures are more abstract, lower-level ones are more concrete and specific. As we have seen, these traits are reflected in IOC structures' "nesting", and the ways in which they can combine to form IOC systems. Micro-structures can be found within meso- and meta-structures, meso-structures form parts of meta-structures, but the reverse is impossible.

Meta-IOC structures include the market: spontaneous and preexisting economic and political markets, modified and managed markets, and newly created or artificial markets. In the market, transactions between organizations are voluntary, based on resource exchange mediated by price. At the opposite extreme is the mandated framework, in which IOC is the result of hierarchical authority, and coordination is effected by command, monitoring, and control. Between these is the interorganizational network: a linkage between organizations that may combine elements of price, authority, and trust.

Under interorganizational networks we find informal networks, and various kinds of mutual organizations as meso-structures: federations, associations, alliances, consortia, joint ventures and partnerships. Meso-IOC structures under mandated frameworks include planning frameworks, programs and non-administered programs, projects, lead organizations and new or merged organizations. Any of these can include, as micro-IOC structures: informal links, boundary-spanners and interorganizational liaisons, coordinators, interorganizational groups, and coordinating units or organizations.

Coordination tools are the specific elements of organizational action, interaction, or behavior that enable IOC. Meetings, telephone calls and shared mailings are examples of tools in informal linkages.

Formal IOC tools address the three basic coordination problems of feedback, guidance, and control. They include structural tools such as regulations, standard operating procedures, and schedules. Linkage devices may be anticipatory, such as joint planning, overlapping board memberships, common training, and budget signoff. Or they can be operational: staff exchange, "outstationing" or seconding personnel, consultation or team management, contracts and interagency agreements. Program management devices are another kind of structural tool: defining roles and domains through legislation, regulations, and resource allocations, and ensuring compliance through monitoring and administrative review. Fiscal tools, working through resource exchange, include shared equity, financing, categorical and formula-based grants, loan guarantees, insurance, subsidies, and tax incentives.

This framework provides a clearer picture of IOC and how the concepts used to describe and explain IOC fit together. It allows us to understand what interorganizational fields, IOC strategies and structures, and coordination tools are, to tell one from the other, and to connect these concepts to each other in an overall logical relationship.

For example, in a particular case and time we might find a "feudal" field of loosely interacting, relatively independent organizations. Something happens in their environment to start a search for a closer form of linkage: a new interdependence perhaps resulting from their common need to adapt to market changes (for example, technological innovations or state regulatory intervention), or from a perceived opportunity to achieve some mutual goals through concerted action. Facilitating conditions: relatively decentralized organizations, domain consensus, complementary tasks and technologies, open the organizations to a common recognition of their interdependence.

The organizations coalesce into an "action set" or an "implementation set" around a common purpose, and collaborate to develop some IOC structures to manage their interdependence. In the process of this collaboration the interacting organizations may already invoke IOC strategies such as cooptation, bargaining, financial incentives, or legislative mandates.

At this stage, IOC may take the form of informal IOC structures: informal links between a few boundary-spanners in the participating organizations or an interorganizational group; for example, a joint planning team, an interfirm committee, or an interagency task force.

They will use informal rather than formal IOC tools: ad-hoc meetings, telephone contacts, information exchange through electronic mailings or correspondence.

This process transforms the interorganizational field into a mediated or guided field, depending on the IOC structures the organizations adopt to manage their longer-term interactions. They may continue as a relatively informal interorganizational network, with the interorganizational group that started out as a planning team, becoming the body linking the member organizations and managing their interactions, using primarily informal coordination tools.

Or the organizations may decide to form a mutual organization for their common undertaking: a federation, a consortium, or a joint venture. This IOC structure may be supported by other micro-structures: a board to govern the federation or a coordinating unit to direct its members, an interorganizational group to coordinate the consortium, or a new organization to undertake the consortium's common functions and contract special tasks out to members, a coordinator to manage the joint venture, or several liaison roles to handle the partners' interactions.

Various IOC strategies may be invoked: cooperation or control, structural changes in member organizations, negotiation and information exchange, depending on the needs and circumstances. Formal IOC tools are necessary to set up the IOC structure, sustain it, and implement IOC among the network members: contracts or inter-agency agreements, joint planning, equity participation, common staff training and exchange, collocation of operations, and other tools may be used.

The change that set off the transformation of the interorganizational field may join the organizations in a mandated framework. As a result, they may find themselves linked to a lead organization, involved in a common planning process, or participating in a joint program or project. For a particular action set of organizations, related to a specific policy, domain, or mission, these meso-structures may even exist in combination, or follow one another over time. Again, IOC in these meso-structures is likely to be implemented by one or more micro-structures: a coordinating unit in the lead organization, an interagency group concerting program-related operations, or a project coordinator.

Coordination in mandated frameworks is likely to involve more command-related strategies relying on authority, but success may need cooperative strategies as well. Formal IOC tools will be used in both: legislation and regulations, formal agreements and contracts, monitoring and administrative control such as plan approval and budget signoff in the former, resource allocations or fiscal incentives, joint planning, shared training, staff exchange, collocation, teamwork, and informal tools in the latter.

This description of IOC illustrates how the conceptual framework presented here can work. By integrating the concepts which previous writers have used to describe and account for IOC, this framework makes it easier to think about IOC, and provides a coherent explanation of what IOC is and how it happens.

9.3. Effective Coordination: IOC Structures and Their Fit

As we have seen, systematic study offers few answers to the question: how can IOC be effective? Researchers have been reluctant to assess the outcomes of IOC efforts, and without evaluation it is impossible to address this question. Cases presenting experience in practice offer some information that usually tells us if the undertaking was more or less successful, but their diversity and the way they are presented limits rigorous analysis that would establish a clear association between IOC structures and their effects.[4]

One thing is evident: there is no one "best" IOC structure. No single IOC structure, among all the ones we have reviewed here, clearly shows a higher proportion of successes to failures than the others. Each of the IOC structures has been more effective in some situations, and less effective in others. This conclusion can lead our search for improvements in IOC effectiveness in several different directions.

Perhaps IOC structures make no difference in the results of efforts to achieve better action through IOC. One possible implication of this failure: to find an IOC structure that is more effective than others, could be that there is little or no association between the kind of IOC structure adopted, and the outcomes of the IOC effort. This might be because IOC structures are only one of many factors affecting organizational behavior. These interact in complex ways which are still poorly understood, to produce the results of interlinked organizational actions that we see. Either the influence of IOC structures on outcomes in this interaction is absolutely low or zero, or the effects of some other factors are so much more powerful that they make the role of IOC structures insignificant.

To accept this possibility means admitting that our exploration of IOC structures, as a way of making IOC more effective, has been on the wrong track. If IOC structures make no difference in the outcomes of IOC, they are, for all practical purposes, irrelevant. But there are two reasons to think that this conclusion is mistaken. The first is that it is wrong to infer that, because a simple relationship between IOC structures and IOC outcomes has not been found, no association is there. The search may well be warranted, for a more complex account of IOC structures' relation to IOC effectiveness than the explanation that the "one best form" has failed to provide.

The other reason is the evidence of experience. Too many cases demonstrate the existence of some relationship between IOC structures and the success or failure of the undertaking, even if it is difficult to make a simple connection. These are the cases where the contribution of the "right" IOC structure to the success of the mutual effort is apparent, where IOC structures adapted to become effective in carrying out their tasks, or where an enterprise failed or came close to failure because of inappropriate IOC structures, and it is clear in retrospect what other IOC structure would have worked better. These evaluations, even if somewhat intuitive or anecdotal, suggest themselves too often for the denial of any connection between IOC structures and outcomes to be plausible.

Another response to the failure to find "the best" IOC structure is to look for a more complex, perhaps contingent, relationship. If we could develop a model that related the success of IOC efforts to the kind of IOC structures used through a few intermediate variables, we would have the answer to our question, in the form of a statement: If a, b, c, then use IOC structure x; if d, e, f, then use IOC structure y.

At first glance this approach is very appealing. All it needs is to develop or find case data on which to test alternative hypotheses identifying possible factors which might be part of the link between IOC structures and their effectiveness. These could include contextual differences (for example, the stability or turbulence of the organizational environment), relevant characteristics of the interorganizational network (its size, diversity, complexity, and relative autonomy or dependence), variations in the problem or task (its orientation, scope and complexity),[5] and the different IOC strategies and tools that were employed.

There are several limitations to this approach, however, that make it less attractive than it seems. It is more appropriate for descriptive analysis (for which, in fact, it has usually been applied) than to data that includes evaluation of outcomes. This is because evaluations cannot, by their nature, be as "hard" and objective as this kind of analysis demands, and so the apparently significant quantitative results may, in fact, be a statistical artefact.

Another limitation is the number of possible variables and the probable complexity of their interaction, that have to be included for the findings to be of much interest. Consequently, even the successful applications of quantified empirical analysis are still flawed, for our purpose. Many have only limited generalizability, either owing to small samples covering only a particular subset of interorganizational networks, or because their analysis includes only a few selected variables. Most offer descriptive-explanatory findings that have weak or no normative implications. Empirical analysis applying statistical techniques to quantified data has not fulfilled the hope of yielding practically applicable conclusions.

Some of these limitations do not apply to the information about IOC structures and their effects collected in the cases here: for example, the sample of cases and contexts, while not random or systematic, is quite large and diverse. But other limitations do: the outcome evaluations in the cases are "soft", and would be overspecified if they were translated into quantified assessments. The cases, drawn as they are from diverse sources, do not all cover an identical set of variables, or provide the kind of information that can be reliably be transformed into numerical data. Consequently, we have to adopt another approach if we want to learn something from the IOC experiences reviewed here.

A possible approach is suggested by some of the findings and partial conclusions that emerged from our exploration of particular IOC structures. Reviewing coordination units, for example, two observations were striking. One was the way in which those IOC structures which were successful, evolved to adapt themselves to their environments, so that they fitted their contexts much better than at the time they were created. The other was the degree to which a coordination unit's effectiveness was related to the correspondence between its form (its governance, organization, authority and resources), its context (such as the number, diversity, and kinds of organizations in its network) and its tasks, which could range from coordination by negotiation and persuasion based on information or resource exchange, to effecting powerful agencies' compliance with legislated mandates. Implicit in these findings is the idea of "fit".

Relating effectiveness to the "fit" between IOC structures, their tasks, and their contexts, is also compatible with our present purpose. The objective of this effort to integrate theory and research into IOC with the observation of experience, is not so much to develop a better description of IOC than those which other writers have proposed. Nor is it to offer a model that can give practitioners a formula for more effective IOC. This aim is denied not because it is undesirable — on the contrary — but because we understand enough about the complexity of IOC to know how unlikely we are to achieve it.

Rather, the purpose of this inquiry into IOC, and our focus on IOC structures in particular, is to make IOC more effective, by improving institutional design. IOC structures have been suggested as a building block for institutional design, and explaining their effectiveness in terms of "fit" is an excellent way of putting this concept to use as an institutional design tool. This is because finding an exemplar or prototype (here: the IOC structure), and forming it to fit its context and purpose, is just what design is about.[6]

As used in design, "fit" is not the precise, algorithmic correspondence that could be expressed in a systematic normative model. It is different, too, from the contingent prescription that would be generated by a multivariate explanation of IOC effectiveness, if such an explanation could be found. "Fit" is a qualitative term, and describes the kind of appropriateness to context and task that is discovered in trial-and-error or in the kind of "thought experiment" that is part of the planning or design process. But "fit" may be just the way we were looking for to account for different IOC structures' performance in the various cases we have observed.

Reflection on the cases we have reviewed, and others, suggests a "fit" theory of IOC structures' effectiveness. The more effective IOC structures succeeded because they fitted their environments and were appropriate for their missions, or they adapted themselves to their contexts. The failures were IOC structures that were incompatible with their contexts, or inadequate for the tasks with which they were charged.

Comparing some cases, this becomes obvious. The ARC was a coordinating unit that had a major burden of concerting the actions of powerful federal line agencies, and coordinating mutual development policy among the participating states. It succeeded because it modified its structure and acquired the resources that enabled it to fulfil its coordinating tasks. The ICC in Israel's Project Renewal was in a situation that in many respects was very similar. But some of its characteristics as an interorganizational group made it too weak for its coordinating role, and in retrospect it seems that if it had adapted to the dimensions of its task and turned into a coordinating unit, it might have been more effective.

The British REPBs and REPCs had no less ambitious roles to the ARC's and the ICC's, in coordinating regional development. They also failed because, as interorganizational groups, they were inadequate for their mission, and had neither the authority nor the resources to influence the other agencies in their action set. In the Netherlands, however, another interorganizational group, the Dommeldal valley planning task force, succeeded, even though it was no better equipped than its British and Israeli counterparts. But this group's performance was called effective relative to much more modest aims: serving as an arena for information exchange and negotiation that ultimately resulted in some coordinated action. It failed, on the other hand, if judged by its more demanding formal mandate.

Coordinators, too, have succeeded or failed, depending on their fit with their contexts and tasks. Charged with coordinating powerful ministries, and lacking any authority or resources apart from his title, the failure of the Coordinator of Government Activities in the Galilee was predictable. In a similar role, and in an environment that was not significantly different, the Regional Administrator of Israel's Lakhish regional development was much more effective. Partly this was due to his support by a coordinating unit, and partly due to the Prime Minister's backstopping his authority over government line agencies (Alexander, 1978). With less authority and resources, however, coordinators have also been effective at a more limited scale, and at more narrowly defined tasks, as the examples of the Pittsburgh case managers and the British local GIA program coordinators show.

To say that effectiveness of IOC structures is related to their fit implies that the results of IOC efforts depend, to a perceptible degree, on an IOC structure's appropriateness to its task and context. For this statement to be meaningful, however, and more than a tautology, it must be elaborated. Which characteristics of an IOC structure are the ones that modify its fit? What are the relevant dimensions in the IOC structure's environment that affect its performance? And how do these interact so that some IOC structures are more successful than others in particular situations and for specific tasks?

Institutionalization, Cost and Commitment

IOC structures have some intrinsic characteristics. One of these is the structure's level of organizational scope and abstraction; we have used this to distinguish between meta-, meso- and micro-structures. Another is its relative degree of hierarchy and formalization, from the informally linked network at the one extreme, to the formal organization and the mandated framework at the other. These attributes really reflect another, deeper, characteristic: institutionalization.

Institutionalization has been described in a variety of ways by sociologists, political scientists, and organization theorists. Social institutionalization has been defined as "a process of crystallization of ... norms, organizations, and frameworks, which regulate the processes of exchange" (Eisenstadt, 1968: 414–415). Political institutionalization is related to political stability and revolution, and to the emergence of political institutions as mediators of social values and needs (Huntingdon, 1968). Institutions are "socially constructed, routine-reproduced ... program or rule systems ... operat(ing) as relative fixtures of constraining environments and ... accompanied by taken-for-granted accounts" (Jepperson, 1991: 149).

Organizations, of course, are themselves institutions, and are one manifestation of institutionalization.[7] But studies of organizations recognize that institutionalization is a continuous variable, and that organizations may be more, or less, institutionalized (Meyer and Rowan, 1991). In general, degrees of institutionalization indicate relative vulnerability to social intervention (Jepperson, 1991: 151–153). A highly institutionalized organization or structure of norms (for example, a total institution like a prison, or a prevailing set of rules, such as the U.S. constitution) takes a major social effort to change or abolish. Structures or processes that are less institutionalized, such as an interfirm partnership or an interagency task force, are much more easily set up, modified, and abandoned.

Indicators of organizational institutionalization include stability and durability, standardization of interorganizational contacts, hierarchy, and formalization of structure and interactions (Aldrich, 1979: 273–274; Ross, 1979: 29–30). When these characteristics are present to a high degree, then, an IOC structure is highly institutionalized. On the other hand, if they are weak or absent, the coordination structure would rank low on the institutionalization scale.

However, institutionalization alone does not necessarily make an IOC structure more powerful or effective. There are two reasons why. One is that power is associated with dependence and control; to be powerful, therefore, an actor needs authority or other resources (Lukes, 1974; Wrong, 1979).[8]

The other reason is that we are dealing with the intrinsic institutionalization that differentiates between IOC models, not with their actual institutionalization in specific cases. This may vary over quite a wide range, but at the range's extremes the variation in institutionalization is likely to go with a qualitative change in the IOC structure.

For example, the interorganizational group is intrinsically less institutionalized than the coordinating unit. However, some groups are more institutionalized than others. The lowest ones on this scale are relatively transitory, meeting only to address ad-hoc issues or problems, and have no organizational identity or autonomy. The Silicon Valley case offers an example. Others (for example, governing commissions or boards) have a clear identity, and enjoy staff support from another organization or unit.

But we can conceive of an interorganizational group which acquires a staff of its own, mobilizes the commitment of its members, and gains control of a budget to sustain its organizational autonomy and support its activities. At some stage in this process it would no longer be an interorganizational group, but would become a coordinating unit. This, in fact, is what happened with the NCAA and the ARC, and what did not happen to the ICC.

Meta-IOC structures, and most meso-structures, do not vary significantly between one another in their intrinsic institutionalization. Their within-structure variance is much greater. There is a vast difference, for example, between highly institutionalized markets like the New York Stock Exchange for shares, or Lloyds of London for insurance, and relatively uninstitutionalized ones such as the market for cosmeticians in Minneapolis, which is subject only to nominal State licensing of practitioners, or the restaurant industry in Frankfurt, where free entry is only limited by the cost of a city license and the approval of city health inspectors.

Mandated frameworks, too, vary widely, from the permanent, stable, and hierarchical structures of land planning and development control in countries such as France, Israel, the Netherlands and the U.K., to the short-term and changing contexts of World Bank assistance programs and non-administered categorical grant programs in the U.S. Interorganizational networks can also be more or less institutionalized, from totally informal ones like the child protection caseworkers' network, through ones that are linked by formal agreements and informal norms, such as the Bay Area transit operators' network, to associations that are completely institutionalized in the shape of formal organizations, like the NCAA, the National Association of Manufacturers, or the Deutscher Gewerkschaftenbund.

Lead organizations' institutionalization also depends on the form of their mandate, and their links with the organizations in their action set. The role of HUD in the U.S. Model Cities program was poorly institutionalized, based as it was solely on a weak legislative mandate, and operationalized in the form of an ad-hoc interorganizational group. NASA's role in the Apollo program, on the other hand, was highly institutionalized through formal planning, design, procurement and monitoring processes and contracts which regulated all the exchanges in this ramified contractor and subcontractor network.

It is obvious that meta- and meso-IOC structures' institutionalization is not an intrinsic characteristic. Rather, each of these structures is more or less institutionalized in every particular case, depending on the characteristics of the micro-IOC structures that make up its IOC system in that case. This is how we can account for the differences in institutionalization between the Chicago commodities market and the rice market in Bangkok, between the European Union's regional assistance program and the Wisconsin WIN program for mothers on welfare, and between Boeing's subcontractor network and the network of workshops making up the motorcycle industry of Bologna.

Micro-IOC structures, however, do differ in their intrinsic institutionalization, relative to one another. Ranked on an ordinal scale, the lowest are informal links, in which some individuals may act in boundary-spanning roles. Next is the designated boundary-spanner or interorganizational liaison, whether he is formally acting in that capacity, or whether these functions are part of her assigned functional role.

The coordinator and interorganizational group are intrinsically somewhat higher on the institutionalization scale, though the least institutionalized group may not be much more institutionalized than some formal boundary-spanners, and a titular coordinator may, in reality, be little more than a liaison between the organizations in his set. But in their more institutionalized forms, these approach the coordinating unit and the organization, the IOC structures which are the most institutionalized of all.

A previous analysis of fourteen cases of IOC in regional development, new towns, and neighborhood revitalization, evaluated the performance of twenty eight IOC structures: informal links, interorganizational groups, coordinators, coordinating units, and single organizations. This study found a weak association between institutionalization and effectiveness (Alexander, 1981).[9]

While this conclusion has to be viewed with caution,[10] it suggests one possible dimension of "fit" of IOC structures. But it raises a question: why should there be any relationship (even a weak one) between institutionalization and IOC effectiveness? No obvious link presents itself to account for this association. It would be easier to answer this question if we could say that institutionalization is related in some way to better organizational performance, but this is not so.

There has been a good deal of study of the relations between organizational effectiveness and many of the attributes of institutionalization. These include structural formalization: centralization, formal interactions through rules and standard procedures, hierarchical controls, etc. Synthesizing these traits, organizations have been described as "organic" or "mechanistic". Often the former, less institutionalized, organizations have proved more effective, while highly institutionalized bodies, often bureaucracies, are more dysfunctional (Burns and Stalker, 1961; Crozier, 1964; Sofer, 1972).

Other studies have looked at these variables in relation to an organization's capability to function in more or less changing and uncertain environments (Lawrence and Lorsch, 1967), their internal adaptability, and their effects on staff and employee performance (Argyris, 1964; Bennis, 1966; Johns, 1973). None of their findings suggest any link between institutionalization and effectiveness; indeed, the accepted conclusion is that many of the characteristics associated with institutionalization, if they exist to a high degree, are often dysfunctional.

How, then, can we explain the finding of this analysis, that IOC models may be more effective if they are more institutionalized? All we can do is suggest one possibility, and see if it is plausible on the basis of evidence from the experience of our cases.

This hypothesis involves two factors. One is another dimension of IOC structures: their relative cost. Cost does not necessarily, or only, mean cost in material resources: money and other concrete assets. Cost includes the mobilization of individual and organizational attention, and the trauma of change and reorganization. There is also the cost of deploying political power: authority, control over resources on which others depend, and influence through communications, the media, and political, social or moral stature or charisma. Any or all of these may be needed in setting up a highly institutionalized IOC structure, to effect the reorganization and reallocation of resources and authority that are involved.

Nor are costs limited to these start-up costs. In adopting a more institutionalized IOC structure, the responsible actors are accepting a corresponding increase in their vulnerability to failure. A prominent and identifiable coordination unit, or a new organization, is a visible symbol of the common undertaking: the project, the plan, the joint venture or partnership, and becomes associated with program accomplishment, with all the attendant risks.

Less institutionalized IOC structures — giving a boundary spanner some additional responsibilities or calling him a coordinator, setting up an interagency committee to meet from time to time in the depths of the bureaucracy, or forming an informal interfirm task force to explore a mutual project — are known to few besides those directly involved, and a small coterie of project or program aficionados. The lower profile of less institutionalized IOC structures makes them immune to the threats posed by the visibility associated with higher levels of institutionalization.

All these costs are held down with the adoption of less institutionalized IOC structures. Relatively uninstitutionalized boundary-spanners or liaisons, coordinators, and interorganizational groups, can be set up and given their coordination tasks with a correspondingly small investment of resources, authority, or power, and their accountability for failure is minimal. Reorganization is marginal and temporary, and prevailing distributions of resources and authority in the interorganizational network or action set can remain fairly undisturbed.

Many cases in mandated frameworks show this type of coordination. Legislative or executive fiat identifies a common goal, defines the arena in which coordination is to take place, and charges the appropriate officials with participation in the coordination effort. Sometimes a staff core is formed by transferring personnel on temporary assignment, or creating a few special positions. We have seen variations on this process in Britain, Germany, Israel, and the U.S.A.

The other factor is commitment, and the suggested link between institutionalization and effectiveness is based on the connection between costs and commitment.[11] To illustrate the link suggested by this hypothesis, let us compare IOC in British and American new towns programs.[12]

At the end of World War II, Britain was confronted with a massive housing problem. At the same time, a major development program presented the opportunity to take some steps toward realizing the utopias which had captured the imagination of opinion-molders between the two world wars. To address the housing crisis and realize these broadly supported aspirations for a better built environment, the new towns program was launched. A novel organization at the local level, the New Town Corporation, was formed to plan, develop, and manage the new towns.

The new towns' development was funded with money advanced by the Treasury, demanding an amount which was massive by any standard, and especially in the context of the austerity of the times. Creating the New Towns Corporations as the planning and implementation arm of the program called for a significant realignment of authority, involving a degree of decentralization almost unprecedented in British experience, while removing broad areas of activity from local governments' traditional jurisdiction. The readiness to accept the enormous material and organizational costs needed for this undertaking to succeed is evidence of the country's high level of commitment to this program.

The U.S. New Communities Development program, on the other hand, launched in the late 1960s as part of the Johnson administration's "New Society", emerged as a limited response to the demands of a narrow constituency. Few saw it as a solution to any pressing national or social problems. As a result it enjoyed a fluctuating, and generally low, priority in its competition for support and resources, and was vulnerable to short term changes in the political and economic environment.

The low political commitment to the program was reflected in its "low cost" IOC structures: a non-administered program added to the responsibilities of an existing unit in the Department of Housing and Urban Development. The program's effectiveness essentially depended on the capability of its grant and loan guarantee incentives to mobilize private developers to take the desired actions. Its failure had some outside causes (unforseen changes in the economic environment) but was largely due to flaws in its basic premise: a much larger organizational and monetary investment was needed to stimulate the changes in the land development market that the program's originators envisaged.

A critic could say that it is differences in social ideology and political context which are mainly responsible for the adoption of different IOC structures in two programs which are identical in their intended output: the development of planned new communities. But the U.S. offers control cases to refute this assertion: the federal "Greenbelt" program for constructing new towns in the 1930s, the Tennessee Valley Authority's program for housing their employees in planned new communities, and the Atomic Energy Commission's new community construction during World War II.

In these instances, when the federal government and its responsible agencies were confronted with an urgent problem, and were committed to giving its solution a high priority on their agenda, they behaved just like the British government when it launched its new towns program. They did not resort (as the U.S. did later) to mobilizing the market through non-administered programs, or to concerting the actions of involved line agencies through interorganizational groups. They took on the task of planning and delivering the projected program outputs directly through single organizations.

But it could still be possible that intrinsic differences between the U.S. and Britain were responsible for the differences between their post-war new communities programs that we observed, and that the American "Greenbelt" and war time housing programs were just "brief aberrations" (Corden, 1977: 66). In such a small sample this might be so, even though the cases match beautifully for the effects of functional sector (identical in all three), and sociopolitical context. This context was identical in the two U.S. cases, where different levels of commitment resulted in different IOC structures and different outcomes. It varied between the two single-organization cases (the British New Towns Authorities, and the U.S. Resettlement Administration) where commitment, IOC structures, and outcomes were similar.[13]

Why should commitment work through more institutionalized IOC structures to make IOC more effective? Commitment may work in three ways to enhance the chances of an undertaking's success. The first could be in creating a climate of expectation where successful achievement becomes a self-fulfilling prophecy. Looking back at some of the more successful efforts among those analyzed: the Airbus venture, the development of Stockholm's satellite communities, the Lakhish and Guyana regional development projects, the British and Israeli new towns programs, the revamped Kenosha County jobs program, and the Lafayette Court family center, we can see this process in action.

In each of these cases there was a sense of purpose in the organizations primarily involved and among the participating personnel. All were conscious of being actors in something that was innovative, "state-of-the-art", and non-routine. They knew that their task had high priority and enjoyed broad support from their relevant political and social environment. Their success or failure would have significant consequences, not least on their own careers and future.

In some of the cases where failure to achieve program objectives, or, sometimes, indeed, to accomplish anything at all, is as conspicuous as the success of the previous cases, we can see exactly the opposite. Often, such undertakings were mounted as hardly more than a token acknowledgement of some problem, or in a politically convenient obeisance to a particular interest or pressure group. Sometimes, the commitment between the parties to the joint undertaking was sufficient only temporarily to bridge between their conflicting interests.

Examples of such cases are the Berlin interagency planning teams, Britain's REPBs and REPCs and some of its local GIA programs, Israel's Coordinator of Government Activities in the Galilee, the British-French Concorde partnership, Germany's STOP program, and the New Communities Development program in the U.S. These were routine efforts to achieve somewhat better results by doing something a bit differently than it had been done before. Often, improved coordination was an end in itself, and there was little sense of urgency or immediate need for concrete program outputs. Actors in the interorganizational network were sometimes hardly aware that a new effort was under way, or if they were, it effected them only marginally.

The second way in which commitment may work is through the "implicative acts" which are its symptoms. These will have a direct effect on program performance, quite apart from the environment of expectations described above. Such acts include providing ample funds for the achievement of valued objectives, assigning organizational units of proven competence or individuals conspicuous for their talent to critical roles, and creating clear channels of authority, communication and resource allocation to avoid any roadblocks which might impede effective action.

It is unnecessary to illustrate the efficacy of such actions, and the cases we have reviewed provide plenty of examples. The adjustments to the preexisting interorganizational network, however, without which priority channels for critical programs or valued goals cannot be put into place, brings us to the third way in which commitment may work. This is indirectly, through adopting more institutionalized IOC structures, and being willing to incur the costs of equipping them with the tools of authority and control over resources adequate for the performance of their important tasks.

These effects of commitment explain the better performance of the more institutionalized IOC structures, a success that cannot be accounted for by their institutionalization alone. If institutionalization is just a symptom of a commitment which at once generates a positive climate of expectations and at the same time provides the material, organizational and political resources needed for accomplishment, then the more successful results of the more institutionalized IOC structures are not so surprising.

These conclusions can evoke both optimism and pessimism. Optimism, because they suggest that there is one way in which to improve the effectiveness of interorganizational coordination. That way is to have the commitment to the common goals, that the adoption of more institutionalized IOC structures for important missions or broadly scoped tasks seems to demand. The adoption of more institutionalized IOC structures in such situations could avoid the pitfalls that have dogged many coordination efforts in the past.

But this is not a novel prescription: it seems to be understood or intuitively sensed whenever policy is developed in interorganizational systems for addressing problems or goals which transcend the capabilities of any one of the existing organizations. When a group of organizations, or an issue-related network of institutions and interests, or a country's political establishment, are sufficiently committed to the realization of a significant program of action, they seem to know how to go about achieving their aim.

Acknowledging this fact exposes the pessimistic implication of our conclusions. When coordination efforts fail, perhaps it is not so much because their sponsors did not know how to go about it, but more because they did not want to succeed enough to accept the costs without which achievement is impossible.

This implication would transform, even distort, the thrust of this enquiry. Instead of some normative prescriptions for institutional design that could improve coordination between organizations, which this study was intended to provide, it would supply the makings of a political diagnostic tool. Look at how a project is coordinated, and you may be able to infer how committed its sponsors are to its ultimate success.

That is not what I set out to develop here, though it is not without its uses. If the appreciation of the link between the institutionalization of IOC structures and the commitment of their sponsors (individuals, executives, organizations, firms, political parties, or legislatures) becomes more widespread, it will become more difficult to mount token programs that express little more than a symbolic commitment to the objectives they pretend to promote.[14]

This gain in political sophistication might deter the fraud on client groups, stakeholders, issue-related constituencies, or particular political interests, which is implicit in projects and programs which have only cost their sponsors some public relations or media hype, or the drafting of a spectacular "plan" or an ambitious looking piece of legislation. If this is the only result of the present exploration of IOC structures, the ensuing savings in symbolic and material resources might still make it worth while.

But the learning potential of this enquiry is not yet exhausted. There are other dimensions of coordination structures and their settings which affect the IOC structure's fit with its environment. For those meso- and meta-structures where intrinsic institutionalization is irrelevant, the IOC structure itself may need other attributes to work well in its particular context. Contextual factors, too, are clearly important: the action set's organizational environment, the interorganizational network itself, and the IOC structure's mission. One IOC structure may fit a particular kind of environment and type of network better than another, and some IOC structures may be more suitable for some tasks than for others. What can research and the experience presented in the cases reviewed above can tell us about these aspects of IOC structures' fit?

NOTES

1. An example of the former is Alter and Hage (1993: 82–88); an example of the latter is the National Commission on Employment Policy (1991).
2. Especially Chapters 1 to 3 above.
3. Institutionalization is discussed in more detail later; for definitions see p. 285 below.
4. I attempted this in a comparative analysis of thirty two IOC structures that were used in fourteen cases (Alexander, 1992). This study is a source for some of the findings and conclusions developed below.
5. These are some of the factors that have been tested in empirical studies such as Paulson (1974), Hall et al. (1977), Van de Ven and Walker (1984), Alexander (1992), and Alter and Hage (1993).
6. This is, of course, quite a simplification, but elaboration would fill another book. I am using the term "design" here in its generic sense, which does not limit design to physical or spatial form-giving (as in art, architectural design, engineering, or urban design) but extends it to mean the development of alternative courses of action; for the relevance of design in this sense see Alexander (1982). A classic work by Christopher Alexander (1964) gives a good view of the role of "fit" in design; for more on the process of design, see Alexander (1982, 1987), and Cross (1987).
7. Institutionalization, as a property, is distinct from organization: organizations are one type of rule or control structure of several (e.g., regime, culture) which embody institutionalization (Jepperson, 1991: 150–151).
8. For the purposes of this discussion, I have adopted the conventional view of asymmetrical, or "integral" power. There is also "intercursive", "pooled" or "shared power" (Roberts, 1991), but this is so highly correlated with coordination itself that it would only add confusion.
9. This study evaluated thirty six IOC structures (see Alexander, 1992: 231–232), but they included several meso-structures: four lead organizations and four non-administered programs. Since these meso-IOC structures do not have any intrinsic levels of institutionalization, they are here excluded from the analysis, but this modification only reinforces the study's findings.

10. There are three reasons for this. 1) The study's generalizability is limited by the size of the sample and its scope: the cases are all in the area of regional and urban development, mostly in the context of mandated frameworks. IOC in other areas, such as intercorporate coordination in the private sector, or cooperation between community organizations and voluntary groups, might yield different results. 2) The association between effectiveness and institutionalization was found by quantifying two variables which are, at best, ordinal. 3) The effectiveness evaluations, though expressed in a score (from 1 to 5), are "soft", and it is open to question to what degree the interval differences in effectiveness ratings are accurate. The conclusion would be more robust, and less subject to the last two qualifications, if the association that was found had been stronger, but even with the quantification used institutionalization only explained part of the variance in effectiveness.

11. The term commitment is used here in its usual meaning; it is related to the verb: "to commit": "to engage or pledge by some implicative act (to a particular course)" (OED: 481). In tune with this definition, it is by the "implicative acts" related to a course of behavior intended to achieve a goal or solve a problem, that we can gauge the level of commitment. Commitment itself, or the degree to which decision makers see themselves as bound by a resolve, is also something continuous, rather than a matter of "all-or-nothing", and is related to other decision characteristics, such as specificity, and reversibility (Levin, 1972: 24–42).

12. For detailed case descriptions and analyses, see Alexander (1980c: 24–42).

13. Empirical analysis of the larger set of cases presented here, using similar methods to those of the previous study (Alexander, 1981), yielded no significant results. This was to be expected, given the complexity of the relationships and the number of other factors (some of which will be discussed below) which confound the search for a simple association between the three variables of institutionalization, commitment, and effectiveness.

14. For a discussion of coordination as a mere symbol of reform, see Weiss (1981).

CHAPTER 10

The Architecture of Institutional Design:

IOC Structures, Contexts, and Fit

10.1. IOC Meta-Structures

IOC meta-structures are the market, the interorganizational network, and the mandated framework.[1] We all know what markets are, and they have been rigorously defined. The network is something between markets and hierarchies, and may combine elements of both (exchange based on price, and actions based on command) with more informal transactions premised on mutual trust. The mandated framework is a structure for IOC that is based on authority. This may be political-societal authority premised on decisions that are recognized as legitimate, expressed as legislation, regulations, or public resource allocation. Or the authority may be legal-contractual, as a result of firms' or organizations' voluntary delegation of some of their autonomy in previous contracts or agreements.

As we have seen, each of these will contain other, lower-level IOC structures, and it is these that essentially determine the meta-structures' characteristics and performance. For example, an economic market such as the international market in commodities includes lower-level mandated frameworks at the national level (e.g., the laws and regulations regulating the U.S. commodities market) and coordinating units such as the U.S. Securities and Exchange Commission and the Chicago Commodities Exchange. Markets in political resources (e.g., the exchange of campaign contributions, media coverage, and votes for access or policy cooperation) or other assets (e.g., referrals of patients by physicians) may be similarly more or less institutionalized, with other IOC structures: mandated frameworks regulating elections and campaign contributions and coordination units such as Election Commissions, and HMOs mediating the procurement of health services.

Interorganizational networks, too, may contain mandated frameworks of interaction based on contracts (e.g., formal prime-subcontractor networks), informal links based on association and trust (such as entrepreneurial dyads or regional industries), and internal markets as arenas for exchange based on actual or notional prices of goods and services (e.g., conglomerates decentralized into profit centers). Each of these, in turn, will have other, meso- and micro-IOC structures to manage participating organizations' interactions: the lead organization and the coordinator or coordinating unit in the contracting network, informal links, boundary-spanners or liaisons in less formal networks, interorganizational groups to govern mutual organizations, coordinating units to manage organized associations, and organizations incorporating partnerships and joint ventures. We have seen examples of all these.

The mandated framework is also only the meta-structure for what may be a host of lower order IOC structures: the interorganizational network that is the relevant policy issue, action, or implementation set, the hierarchies of central and local governments and agencies, the program or project generating the framework and related resources, lead agencies and contracting networks, coordinating units in ministries and local governments, and internal markets for licenses or other scarce assets. The cases have shown examples of all these as well.

All this suggests that there is not much we can say about meta-IOC structures, without going into the details of each structure's IOC system. Looking at each of these meta-structures as an IOC meso-structure, however, in its own right (which each of them can be, as we have seen), the research we have reviewed combines with the case experience to offer some lessons.

Markets

No market can exist without an object of exchange that has a price: something to which both buyers and sellers assign a value. And anything that has a value to some potential buyer and seller can be the object of exchange in a market. This is the obvious basis for economic markets. When people understood this the foundation was laid for the idea of other, non-economic markets, for the privatization of mixed public-private goods and services (handling their public aspect by modifying the market), and for the design of artificial markets as IOC structures.

The necessary prerequisite, then, for forming a new or artificial market is the creation of value: assuring that the proposed object of exchange is assignable, divisible, and confers a benefit on the prospective buyer for which he is prepared to pay, i.e., to exchange for this object some other asset which the seller will value. We have seen how this is done for quite intangible assets, ranging from broadcast licenses to pollution points.

All markets are structured; in existing and spontaneous markets the structure has evolved as a set of norms of behavior and interaction that is implicitly understood and agreed by all the actors. In new markets (like the ones created by privatization) and artificial ones (such as the internal markets in mandated frameworks) this structure has to be designed and implemented through other IOC structures.

Elinor Ostrom (1990: 50–55) has described the way markets are structured by several generic types of rules, which essentially control the terms of entry, exchange, and exit. These include "position rules", which determine the role or roles participants must, can, or cannot fill to enter a particular position (e.g., buyer or seller) in the market, "boundary rules", characteristics that participants must or cannot have to enter these positions, and "authority rules", prescribing what the actors are allowed to do or are prohibited from doing independently.

Market structure also includes "aggregation rules": how multiple actor decisions are to be made, "information rules" prescribing the sharing of knowledge and communication of information, "scope rules" that identify the situations participants' actions must or should not affect, and "payoff rules": the rewards or penalties assigned to actions and outcomes. For them to be successful, the design of new and artificial markets has to be quite clear in specifying these rules, and how they are to be implemented. The appropriate IOC structures also have to be created to manage these interactions, and, perhaps as important, to adapt and modify the originally designed market structure to respond to inevitable unforseen contingencies.

Failure to fulfill all these requirements may jeopardize the whole enterprise. The case of U.S. emission rights offers an example: the lack of suitable channels for transmitting information between sellers and potential buyers limited the market largely to transactions between firms and their subsidiaries which were linked anyway, and political resistance has obstructed some possibly effective responses: the authorization of emerging emission rights brokers or middlemen, or assigning a more active mediating role to State environmental agencies.

The privatization of public bus transit in Britain succeeded, on the other hand, because the simple process designed by the Act was essentially self-executing. The principal goal of the deregulation, to save taxpayer money by drastically reducing subsidies, was achieved by cutting the link between local authorities and their transit operators, and creating a competitive market in bus transit services and subsidies. In the new mandated framework, remaining subsidies became discretionary and were provided by local authorities. These obviously had an incentive they previously lacked, to save money and promote efficient management of their now independent transit operating subsidiaries. A more complex mandated framework with stricter licensing and regulations might have avoided another predictable outcome: higher fares for transit riders, but to the government that passed and administered the Act this was a low priority.

Interorganizational Networks

These vary enormously, from large, complex, and diverse networks which host a complex IOC system of meso- and micro-IOC structures, to small informal ones in which members interact just through interpersonal links. Obviously, then, networks differ in their relative institutionalization. Other network characteristics include size: how many and what scale of organizations make up the network; complexity: the number of different sectors represented by member organizations, and their specialization and differentiation from one another; and structure: the centralization of links between organizations, and their relative interconnectedness.

Networks vary, too, in their openness. This depends on how much the network is differentiated from its environment, how intensive are members' transactions with their organizational environments compared to their mutual within-network interactions, and how autonomous the network is, or dependent for critical resources on outside organizations or its environment. We have also seen that interorganizational networks exist for different reasons: promotional networks to advance common interests (even of member organizations which may be competitors), and obligational networks for mutually agreed upon purposes. These include solidarity activities, exchanging information, processing and producing goods and services, and augmenting members' resources of money or power.

With the exception of the simplest informal networks, it is more useful to view the interorganizational network as part of the context of its lower-order IOC structures. Accordingly, the institutional design implications of these network variables will be developed later when we discuss meso- and micro-IOC structures. But there are two aspects of network structure that are worth addressing here: linkages and interdependencies.

There is clear evidence of a relationship between networks' institutionalization, the type and structure of network linkages, and the quality of an interorganizational network's fit. A network that can be disaggregated to a set of dyadic links can function very well as an informal network, with no or a relatively low level of institutionalization. This is "coordination without hierarchy", as illustrated in the case of the Bay Area transit operators.

Multilateral links between member organizations are more likely to demand more institutionalized networks, or at least (depending on the network's purpose and tasks) the creation of some arenas for interaction. These may still be quite informal (like the Child Protection caseworker's lunch meetings), or more institutionalized: from interorganizational groups like the human services interagency committee, or the *keiretsu's* Presidents' Council, to formal groups managing the network's interactions through coordinating units and organizational structures like the governing boards of the NCAA, the Trades Union Council, or the United Way.

The kind of interdependence between the organizations making up the network, is another aspect of the association between linkages and institutionalization. Interactions between organizations that reflect sequential interdependence can usually be handled quite effectively through dyadic links and, as we have seen, these do not necessarily have to be institutionalized. The degree and way in which these are institutionalized in some IOC structure depend more on the specifics of the link: its durability, the parties in the transaction, and the nature of the task.[2]

Reciprocal interdependence will demand dyadic or multilateral links, depending on whether there are two or more parties to the transaction, and on the complexity of the task. However, though it is possible, it is rare for reciprocal interdependencies to be handled by dyadic links, and their effective management usually requires more institutionalized IOC structures.

Pooled interdependence by its very nature involves multilateral links needing appropriate IOC structures. Again, these can range from relatively informal arenas for information exchange, negotiation and coordinated action by mutual adjustment: interorganizational groups such as task forces or governing boards, to highly institutionalized IOC structures mandating their decisions on member organizations, such as holding corporations, trade associations, and incorporated joint ventures.

This account suggests a weakly positive association between the prevailing interdependence in an interorganizational network, from sequential interdependence that demands the least institutionalization, to pooled interdependence requiring the most. But it is equally clear that this is not a simple or unidimensional relationship, but a complex one mediated by a host of other factors including network dimensions and mission or task characteristics.

It would be rash, therefore, to translate this insight into any kind of design prescription. The one prescription it does suggest, however, is to apply the principle of parsimony. In other words, in deciding how much institutionalization is needed for IOC structures in an interorganizational network, it is wise to remember the possibilities for quite effective coordination using informal interactions for sequential interdependence: this is the lesson of "coordination without hierarchy". The potential of less institutionalized IOC structures for managing even reciprocal and pooled interdependence should not be underestimated, too, when balancing the respective costs and benefits of alternative IOC structures.

Mandated Frameworks

Even more than the market and the network, the mandated framework is defined by its meso- and micro-IOC structures. These may run the entire gamut of possible forms, from internal markets through interorganizational networks to hierarchical organizations. When these occur as IOC structures in a mandated framework, all that they have in common is their existence in the context of an authoritative mandate, which is the ultimate source of their genesis, and may be the way they are changed or abolished.

To be effective, IOC structures in mandated frameworks have needs that are perhaps less acute in markets or networks. They have to be equipped with resources consistent with the scope and type of tasks they were created to perform.[3] Markets depend less on resources because they are premised on exchange of assets that have intrinsic or conferred value. Network transactions also do not have to be resource based: they can proceed on trust premised on solidarity or associational links between the parties. But IOC structures in mandated frameworks do not have these options: they need grants of authority, allocations of material resources, or both if they are to succeed.[4]

In his analysis of coordination in health services, Lehman (1975) described what happens when this requirement is not fulfilled. IOC structures that are given "empty" authority, but lack the material resources they need to function, encounter a "crisis of competence". On the other hand, IOC structures may be well funded, but lack the authority to intervene in the chosen domain: these fail in a "crisis of legitimacy".

Institutional design must take this into account, when IOC structures in mandated frameworks are formed or modified for particular tasks. It is particularly important for such an IOC structure to be equipped with the balance of authority and material resources that will enable it to develop the level of institutionalization that its context — its organizational environment and its interorganizational network or implementation set of organizations — demands. At the same time its resources — authority, funds, and other assets — must be appropriate to its assigned mission.

This looks, perhaps, like a typical "Monday morning quarterback" insight, or an observation so trite it is meaningless. But too many coordination failures (some described in cases above) suggest that either this is not as obvious as it seems, or that this maxim was knowingly ignored by sponsors who really lacked the commitment they proclaimed to the goals of their concerted effort. Be this as it may, the more detailed discussion of meso- and micro-IOC structures that follows will elaborate this prescription in a way that may be more useful when institutional design serves a project with real commitment.

10.2. The Interorganizational Network and Its Environment

If an IOC structure's effectiveness is related to its fit with its context, how do which structural characteristics have to fit what relevant aspects of the environment? One part of this question has already been answered, with some attributes of IOC structures that affect their performance: their relative institutionalization, and their resource endowment. The other part of the answer must identify those context dimensions that determine the IOC structure's fit. That is: what are the characteristics in the IOC structure's environment and the attributes of its mission or task that interact with the IOC structure's own traits to affect its success or failure?

The research and experience we have reviewed suggest some relevant context characteristics. One is the organizational environment of the coordination effort. Another is the action or implementation set of organizations or the interorganizational network that is the setting for the IOC system or structure. The nature and dimensions of the IOC structure's mission or task are also important. Reviewing these in turn, we can see how they affect IOC structures' fit, and extract some institutional design prescriptions from these observations.

The Organizational Environment

The organizational environment of an interorganizational system consists of the other organizations with which it interacts: the organizational field that is its setting, and the level of uncertainty and pace of change in the environment. Organizational environments range from turbulent, in which a few large organizations interact in a rapidly changing and highly uncertain context (for example, today's U.S. health policy environment, or the computer technology sector), to quite placid ones, in which a large number of small organizations interact in relatively stable and predictable ways, for example the classic market.

We have seen cases of each of the IOC structures, some of them more and some less effective, in different organizational environments. There is no evidence to suggest that any one IOC structure is more suitable for one type of organizational environment than another. The relative institutionalization of IOC structures is also in a complex relationship with their organizational environments, from which it is impossible to extract a simple picture of the ideal fit.

The low institutionalization of informal interorganizational networks, for example, gives them a flexibility and adaptability that are clearly advantages in more turbulent environments. These are among the reasons for the effectiveness of informal networks such as the Bay Area transit operators' or the Japanese *keiretsu*. On the other hand, some stability and predictability are necessary. Interactions must go on, to provide the expectation of future reciprocity which is often indispensable for trust to develop.

These conditions are not met in very turbulent organizational environments. As a result, though we might find strong association- or solidarity-based networks in such conditions (e.g., the kinship-based political networks in some countries, or political and ideological movements), informal promotional or production networks are unlikely to emerge or be successful. The resolution of this paradox can be found in the dynamics of interorganizational evolution over time: such informal networks need somewhat less turbulent environments to develop, but once they are in place they will be highly effective in settings where there is a great deal of uncertainty and change.

The very problems of developing effective informal links in very turbulent environments are perhaps the reason highly institutionalized IOC structures — often IOC systems with coordinating units or new organizations — have been the mode of choice for responding to perceived crises or major problems that are in urgent need of concrete solutions. The proliferation of new organizations and coordinating agencies in wartime, to address major postwar needs, and to confront economic crises (e.g., the U.S. "New Deal" agencies in the great Depression) illustrates this phenomenon.

It would be tempting to translate this observation into an institutional design prescription: when confronted by a crisis in a turbulent organizational environment, create a highly institutionalized IOC structure: a coordinating unit or a new organization. But the relative success of past cases of this kind may not be attributable so much to the IOC structure itself or the design of the IOC system. Rather, it may be a coincidental result of the combination of two circumstances: the perception (probably correct, in hindsight) that nothing short of a new institution would survive and work in such a turbulent environment, and the commitment to provide what was needed to solve the problem.

This observation does have an implication that is very relevant for institutional design. Highly institutionalized IOC structures formed in turbulent environments will not succeed without the necessary political, social or organizational commitment, and the resources of authority, expertise, and funds that are its concrete expression.

The Interorganizational Network

The interorganizational network is an important — perhaps the most important — feature of the IOC structure's context. The interorganizational network, action set, or implementation set which hosts the IOC structure has some characteristics which are clearly relevant to the IOC structure's fit with its context. They include the kind of interdependence on which the network is based, the network's structure, size, and complexity, and the network's autonomy: its openness to and dependency on its environment. The common purpose or task of the interorganizational set is also an important factor.

Some of these characteristics, such as the kind of interdependence linking the organizations, and the size and complexity of the network, are independent of the IOC structure. Others, such as the network's structure and autonomy, are associated with IOC structures. One kind of IOC structure, for example, may make a network more structured and autonomous, while another may leave it more loosely linked and more interactive with and dependent on its environment. The NCAA case illustrates this: with the evolution of the core organization from an interorganizational group into a fully institutionalized coordinating unit, the network itself — the NCAA as an association of participating organizations — became more structured and autonomous, and less dependent on resources from its environment that it could not control.

Combining these characteristics in a systematic way produces a matrix made up of six variables: type of interdependence (sequential, reciprocal, pooled, or a combination of these), network size, structure, complexity, autonomy, and mission. Some of these are combinations of related traits; for example, network structure includes the network's centralization, and its connectivity: the number and intensity of the links between member organizations. But even with this quite limited number of characteristics, it is clear that network "diagnosis" is too complex to enable a simple scheme of network types and their related "fitting" IOC structures.[5]

We can see, however, how these characteristics combine in various types of interorganizational networks. A small interorganizational set linked in sequential or (limited) reciprocal interdependence, unstructured, simple, quite autonomous and with quite a minor mission is one type.[6] Examples of this type are small, simple local human services organizations networks, such as the Special Needs Children Adoption network and the Maternal and Child Health Care network Alter and Hage (1993) observed in Maryland. This kind of network is also frequent in other, quite different sectors: entrepreneurial partnerships and small joint ventures, and local project implementation sets, for example planning and constructing facilities such as schools or libraries, and limited infrastructure projects.

Another type of network, that is still relatively uninstitutionalized, is also made up of organizations that are linked primarily by sequential dependence. But it is quite large, either made up of a greater number of small and moderately sized organizations, or a smaller number of larger organizations. It is also quite unstructured, but is more open and dependent on its environment, and also has a narrow and well-defined mission. Purchasing, procurement, and supply networks are often this type.[7]

Larger, more diffuse human services networks, such as the services for the Chronically Mentally Ill in Maryland that Alter and Hage (1993) describe, and the Milwaukee network of organizations serving the frail elderly, described above, are also this type. Large informal networks of interacting functional agencies, such as the Bay Area transit operators' network have these characteristics too.

Another type of network shares some of these characteristics, but combines sequential and reciprocal interdependence. It is also more complex: its component organizations are more heterogenous, specialized and differentiated. It has autonomy too, in a sense because it internalizes more of its relevant environment (though it may still depend on a market), and its mission has a somewhat broader scope. Examples of this type of network are regional crafts and locally specialized interfirm production networks.

Some networks, also combining sequential and reciprocal interdependence, and with similar autonomy and mission, are much smaller, more complex, and quite structured. This type of network may take the form of an organized consortium or joint venture, like the Airbus and Switchco cases described above.

A different type is the large network of organizations linked by sequential and reciprocal interdependence, which is at an intermediate level of complexity and mission importance. This type of network, unlike the previous ones, is highly structured and very autonomous. Formal production networks, linking a lead organization with prime- and subcontractors, are this type. Examples range from major construction to the U.S. automotive and aerospace industries, and public procurement networks like the NASA case described above.

There are smaller networks which are also linked by sequential and reciprocal interdependence, but they are at the same time more complex and less structured. Some research consortia and human services networks are this type,[8] which also includes less structured joint ventures and partnerships, such as the Concorde case described above.

Very different is the type of network in which member organizations are linked by pooled interdependence. This type of network is large, highly structured, of moderate to low complexity, quite autonomous, and has a mission of high to moderate importance. Many mature promotional networks are this type: trade associations and trades unions federations are examples. Formal associations of common interest or activity organizations, investment pools, data networks, and marketing cooperatives, such as the United Way and the NCAA described above, are this type of network too.

Similar to this type, but at much lower levels of autonomy and structuration is the network type that represents interest associations, advocacy coalitions, and policy issue networks. If structuration is regarded as an evolutionary characteristic, then this type of network is the ancestor of the type described just before.

Another type of large network is linked by a variety of interdependencies, is moderately structured, very complex, and quite autonomous. Its mission may vary, ranging in the intermediate levels between quite important to relatively minor. Moderately institutionalized production networks, such as the Japanese *keiretsu*, are this type.

The network type Alter and Hage (1993: 233) call "Type 4" is similar to the preceding one, but is more structured. It is also complex, but generally has a broader mission. Its main distinguishing feature is that it is very open and depends on its environment for critical resources. Some supply networks can be put into this type,[9] which also includes large networks of local human services organizations that are externally regulated by their sources of funding (Alter and Hage, 1993: 238).

A network type that is similar in structure and complexity to this one, but with other differences, includes the implementation sets of some mandated frameworks. Here organizations can also be linked through several kinds of interdependencies — sequential, reciprocal, and pooled. The network is moderately open, depending to some extent on its political and legislative environment. This type of network will also vary by size (from national to local, and also depending on sector) and the dimensions of its mission. The variations on this type of network include planning, program and project frameworks such as the Israel's Project Renewal, the U.S and Australian floodplain management programs, the Hennepin County transit planning project, the U.S. Model Cities and JOBS programs, State environmental management in the U.S., and the German STOP program described above.

These types are far from exhausting the combinations of various network characteristics. It is obvious, then, that systematic types of interorganizational networks or sets cannot be a vehicle for deducing the IOC structures that would be the most appropriate fit. If we are to talk about the fit of IOC structures with different interorganizational networks, it can only be under the network characteristics themselves. This, perhaps, is why institutional design cannot be formalized as a science, but can only be a more intuitive craft: because the designer is left to synthesize the combination of network characteristics and IOC structures that is discussed next.

10.3. Interorganizational Network Factors

Interdependence

We have seen that the kind of interdependence that links the members of an interorganizational network is often related to other network characteristics. Sequential interdependence opens the door to less institutionalized networks, pooled or combined interdependencies usually demand higher levels of structuration.

Combining the variable of interdependence with the principle of parsimony discussed above, one can say that the least institutionalized IOC structures will be most appropriate in interorganizational networks with sequential interdependence: informal liaisons or boundary-spanners, or designated liaisons or coordinators if necessary.

At the task or operational level, sequential interdependence can even be managed without direct interorganizational interaction at all, if appropriate IOC structures have previously set up standard operating, monitoring and feedback, and adaptive response procedures which the participating organizations simply follow. However, the extent to which this form of impersonal coordination is feasible does not only depend on sequential interdependence, but on other network and environmental characteristics as well.

Sequential interdependence is defined as a unidirectional link between two units. This is what makes it feasible and natural to manage sequential interdependence through dyadic relationships. As soon as the link is a two-way link we are no longer in the realm of sequential interdependence, but reciprocal interdependence. Reciprocal interdependence can involve a pair of units too, at the smallest scale, but it can and usually does involve more ramified networks. Thus, in simple dyadic networks, reciprocal interdependence can be managed by informal IOC structures, but as the number of member organizations rises, and the complexity of their interactions grows, more institutionalized IOC structures will be needed.

When the interorganizational set is still small, if relations are relatively simple, and tasks are limited and well defined, interorganizational groups can handle reciprocal interdependence quite well. Task-level teams are often an effective way of coordinating operations involving reciprocal interdependence. For administrative management and policy-level coordination involving reciprocal interdependence, interorganizational groups can be effective too.

Depending on other environmental and network characteristics, these can be informal groups, or they may need some institutionalization and resources. Complex reciprocal interdependence (for example, in some technologies and research enterprises) will demand more institutionalized IOC structures if these are to be a good fit in their networks and environments. This suggests that successful coordination of reciprocally interdependent organizations in larger, more complex networks and in more turbulent environments may call for a coordinating unit, or require formalization in an IOC system under an organization set up for that purpose.

Pooled interdependence, or a combination of interdependencies, implies more complex relationships between the members of the interorganizational set. These will require more institutionalized IOC structures: at the very least, an interorganizational group to plan or manage the organizations' interactions. Often, pooled or commensal interdependence, as in common resource pool networks, involves allocation or rationing of common resources among participating organizations. Another type of pooled interdependence involves allocations of costs among organizations involved in a common undertaking.

In both these situations, a less institutionalized IOC structure such as an interorganizational group may be enough to negotiate and adjudicate potential conflicts among members, if the network is small and has solidarity or associational links that provide the essential foundation of mutual respect and trust. If that is not the case, pooled interdependence will require more institutionalized IOC structures: coordinating units or organizations incorporating IOC systems, equipped with the authority to make and implement binding decisions.

Size

It is hard to see how the size of an interorganizational set, in itself, affects the fit of IOC structures, because size is related to so many other variables that clearly make a difference. All other things being equal, there is no intrinsic reason why one kind of IOC structure should fit small networks better than large ones, or another type should be more effective in large interorganizational sets than in small ones. In fact, we have seen almost every kind of IOC structure work in interorganizational networks of various sizes with varying success, and it would be easy to find an association between IOC structure, network size, and effectiveness, if there were any.

However, some of the components of size do make a difference. A relatively small interorganizational set, made up of several small organizations, is likely to be manageable with quite informal and uninstitutionalized IOC structures. An informal group of boundary spanners in the member organizations, or a coordinator for the network's common activities, or an interorganizational group of organizational representatives can be effective. Which of these IOC structures is the best fit depends on other factors, for example: the kind of interdependence linking the interorganizational set.

However, this may not work for an equally small interorganizational network, but one in which the components of size are different. For example, a set made up of fewer organizations, but very large ones, may need a much more institutionalized IOC structure: a formal interorganizational group endowed with delegated authority, a coordinating unit, or an organization.

There are several reasons for this. One is the difference in the member organizations themselves: large organizations are likely to be much more institutionalized than small ones, so the informal coordination that can work in a network of small organizations may not be feasible among large ones.[10] Another reason is the kind of link between the organizations in the set: small organizations are much more likely to be bonded by associative or solidarity links that engender mutual trust than large, institutionalized organizations are. This again makes a group of small organizations more manageable by informal IOC structures than a set of large organizations would be. Finally, the size of the members of the interorganizational set may be associated with more complex kinds of interdependencies, demanding more institutionalized IOC structures than simple sequential or reciprocal links.

But the relation between the scale of the interorganizational set, the size of its member organizations, and the appropriate IOC structures is not a simple one. For example, the moderately large organizations (the bus operators) in the Bay Area transit network were linked mainly be sequential interdependencies, were very homogenous (they all had the same function) and also had strong associational ties (the common professional background of their personnel). As a result, an informal IOC system, made up of dyadic links between informal boundary-spanners and a few interorganizational groups, worked quite well. This system would not fit at all in an interorganizational network of the same size, but one that is much more complex: in which member organizations were too diverse to share the functional orientation and professional links the Bay Area operators had in common.

The size of the interorganizational set, in terms of the number of its members, is associated with another factor that is important: complexity (which will be addressed below). The more organizations there are in a network, the more complex that network is likely to be. This is because both the components of complexity, heterogeneity and differentiation, are likely to grow as the number of organizations in the set increases. The larger the interorganizational set becomes, the less probable it will be that all its members will have the same domain of activity, and the larger the number of different sectors represented is likely to be. At the same time, as the number of organizations in the network increases, the likelihood that some of them will be more specialized and focused on one function grows.

Of course, this is not a deterministic law, and exceptions are obvious. The national trade association, for example, such as the National Association of Homebuilders, includes a large number of member firms, but only exhibits a moderate level of complexity. Its members are completely homogenous, but they are relatively specialized and focused on one task (construction). Here, however, it is not the network's complexity, but its size combined with its members' pooled interdependence that makes its institutionalized IOC structure (a mutual organization acting as a coordinating unit) necessary.

Structure

The structure of an interorganizational network is the result of a complex combination of factors that interact in the dynamic process of the interorganizational system's evolution. One of these is the IOC structure itself. This interdependence between network structuration and IOC structure turns the relationship between them into a "chicken and egg" question, as illustrated in many of the cases above.

Consequently, when we say, as we do, that more structured interorganizational networks will have more institutionalized IOC structures, we are describing an evolutionary association, rather than prescribing a norm for institutional design. This statement applies, however, differently to one dimension of structuration than to the other. Centeredness, more than connectedness, is directly linked to the emergence of more institutionalized IOC structures: formal interorganizational groups (such as governing boards or commissions), coordinating units, or organizations that form IOC systems with other IOC structures.

Connectedness, as we have seen, complements centrality in interorganizational networks. An interorganizational set with a ramified network of intensively used links, may be quite amenable to relatively informal coordination. In fact, the network's connectedness enhances its manageability and reduces its dependence on more institutionalized IOC structures. We have seen this illustrated in several cases of successful informal networks.

But this statement has to be qualified by another factor: the kind of interdependence linking member organizations. High connectivity in networks linked by sequential or limited reciprocal interdependence facilitates informal coordination, but its effect is more questionable when interdependence is more complex. In such situations, indeed, high connectivity may make more demands on network management, increasing the need for formal allocation or conflict adjudication, for example, and making more institutionalized IOC structures more rather than less necessary.

Complexity

Complexity is an important variable affecting the fit of IOC structures, but it is also associated with other characteristics of interorganizational networks in complex ways. We have already seen how it is related to the number of organizations in the action set. It is also associated with some kinds of interdependence: pooled commensal interdependence is likely to imply relatively low complexity, because their common interests (e.g., firms competing in one market, or agencies with a common funding source) make it likely that all the member organizations will have the same purpose, and will vary little in their relative specialization. Symbiotic interdependence, however, whether expressed in sequential or reciprocal links, implies higher complexity, in the form of either more heterogeneity among member organizations, or more differentiation between them, or both.

Both the dimensions of complexity, heterogeneity and differentiation, mitigate against informal coordination. The more homogenous the organizations in a network are, the more likely it is that they will have the kinds of associative bonds (common functional focus, professional background, organizational culture and values) that make informal links work.

The more differentiated member organizations are, the less likely it is that they can be coordinated through informal channels alone, and the more institutionalized the network's IOC structures will have to be. This is because each of the dimensions of differentiation enhances the differences between the organizations which inhibit mutual communication, respect, and trust. To the extent that an organization's functions span a wide array of services, sectors, or tasks, it is more likely that one or several of these will be the same as those of other organizations in the network, opening the possibility of effective informal links. But as member organizations are more narrowly focused, this potential for informal coordination fades. Similarly, when organizations are more specialized in a particular function, discipline, or technology, the likelihood that their domain will coincide or overlap with that of other organizations diminishes, and informal coordination becomes less feasible.

The difference between the Bay Area transit network and Milwaukee's network of organizations serving the frail elderly illustrates this beautifully. In the former, informal dyadic operational links were quite effective to link a simple network of very similar organizations. In the latter, member agencies and service providing organizations operated in very different sectors (from health, through social services, to transportation) and many were quite specialized in their own domains. Consequently, none of the kinds of links observed in the first network could develop, and coordination had to be effected at the administrative and policy levels, through more institutionalized interorganizational groups with representative membership. For each of these networks, at its own level of complexity, a different IOC structure was a good fit.

We can say with some confidence, then, that at the extremes of the range, complexity must be matched by the degree of institutionalization of IOC structures. The simplest interorganizational sets, in which both heterogeneity and differentiation are low, will be manageable by quite uninstitutionalized IOC structures. And the most complex networks, made up of widely differing organizations that are each highly focused and specialized, will need highly institutionalized IOC systems.

However, between these extremes, the components of complexity do not correlate in any simple way with IOC structures' fit. For example, one interorganizational network may be made up of organizations that are highly differentiated, but very homogenous. This will be a network of moderate complexity, but it may be quite amenable to relatively informal coordination. Some research consortia are this type of network, in which most of the interorganizational interactions are effectively managed by boundary-spanners and "gatekeepers".

On the other hand, a network of similar complexity, but made up of relatively undifferentiated organizations operating in very different sectors will raise very different demands. Some human services networks are this type. For example, the JOBS program implementation set, combining private sector firms (for on-the-job training and placement) with public educational institutions (for literacy training and basic skills) has none of the advantages the other network (like the research consortium) has, and needs a complex and institutionalized IOC system for it to run at all.

Autonomy

Two characteristics combine to determine a network's autonomy. The network's openness to its environment is one, which depends on the number and intensity of member organizations' mutual interactions, compared to their links to other organizations outside. This dimension is logically related to one aspect of network structuration, suggesting that more structured networks will be more autonomous as well. The reason is that high connectivity, which is positively associated with structure, means that a network would have to have much more intensive interaction with its environment to reach the same degree of relative openness that another, less connected network, would need.

This link between openness and structuration implies that more autonomous interorganizational sets will also have more institutionalized IOC structures. Again, as suggested above, this is an evolutionary association, not a normative prescription. But it is amply confirmed by experience, illustrated in many of the cases reviewed.

The other aspect of autonomy is dependence: the extent to which the interorganizational set depends on sources in its environment for essential resources. Obviously dependence and openness are related: a network's links with its environment will be more numerous and intensive when these links are a channel for the flow of resources which network organizations need.

An interorganizational set that is more dependent on its environment, therefore, will be less autonomous, directly due to its dependence, and indirectly because its dependence increases its openness. This aspect of autonomy, however, may seem to have opposite structuration effects than those described before. This is because dependence is frequently managed through formal and highly institutionalized IOC structures, in the context of frameworks mandated by legislation, regulations, or previously contracted obligations.

In such mandated frameworks there is an institutionalized IOC structure in the network's environment: a coordinating unit (such as the bureau managing a program in a federal agency, or the procuring organization's project office in contracting networks) or an organization: the lead organization in some program or subcontracting networks, or the organization that incorporates the partnership or joint venture. This IOC structure manages the network by making its interactions as predictable as possible, through formal rules, standard operating procedures, and bureaucratic monitoring and control. This may not be the most effective form of coordination from the perspective of the members of the implementation or action set, but frequently the legal and accountability demands of the mandated framework make it unavoidable.

This relation was also observed by Alter and Hage (1993: 234–240) between what they call vertical dependency and impersonal coordination. But this is also an artefact of how the network is delimited. For example, the subjects of Alter and Hage's analysis were all local human service networks, and their dependence on "outside" funding is the result of excluding the organizations providing and administering the resource flow from the relevant network.

When the network is defined to include these, it becomes much more autonomous (both because its dependence is reduced or eliminated, and because what were links to the environment are internalized) and more structured, with the IOC system or structures that were outside the network before, now an integral part of its own structure.[11] This resolves the apparent paradox raised above, of contradictory relationships between autonomy and structuration. If the relevant interorganizational set includes all its members' significant interactions and resource exchanges, more autonomous networks are likely to be more structured, and will have more institutionalized IOC structures.

Mission

The interorganizational network's mission is the function or purpose for which the organizations in the action set interact, or the mutual goal for which they have come together. This mission is distinct from the IOC structure's task, though in terms of defining them, the network mission and the IOC structure's task have many dimensions in common.

The scale of a network's mission could be associated with some of its other characteristics, such as size and complexity. But this is not a simple relationship, and is often mediated by other factors. For example, a relatively major mission could be undertaken by a large informal network if it involves simple sequential interdependencies (some production networks illustrate this), but if the mission demands more complex interaction between heterogenous organizations a smaller, but more structured network, might be the result.

Two factors combine to describe the mission's scale.[12] One is its scope: what is the intensity and duration of the interactions between the organizations that their mission demands, and what is the relative volume of the transactions between them. The other is the complexity of the mission: how uncertain, various and different are the tasks the member organizations contribute to the network's mission, and to what degree are specialized and differentiated subtasks involved.

Some of these factors are closely related to other network characteristics. Clearly, mission and network complexity are linked: the more complex the mission, the more complex the network is likely to be. The relationship between mission scope and network characteristics is more complicated. It is hard to imply or observe any association between mission scope and network size, even though, all other things being equal, a broader scope mission would suggest a larger network. But they are not equal, and so it is more likely that, rather than simply being larger to handle a broader mission, a network may be more structured or complex.[13]

The type of mission, too, that an interorganizational network may have, does not seem to be directly associated with any particular IOC structure. It is impossible to prescribe one type of IOC structure for people-processing networks, for example, another for production networks, and yet a third kind for promotional networks. We have found a wide variety of IOC structures, from informal boundary spanners to highly institutionalized coordinating units and special-purpose organizations, performing quite effectively in networks with different missions. The way mission type and scale affect the fit of IOC structures is indirectly, through the complex relation between these factors and the other network characteristics reviewed above.

10.4. The IOC Task

Research and experience combine to suggest that if the IOC structure is to be effective, the structure must fit its task. The IOC task is perhaps the most important of all the factors affecting the IOC structure's fit. The relationship between IOC structures and IOC tasks can be described in terms of two IOC structure attributes, and the different ways in which IOC tasks can be carried out.

We have referred to the IOC structure attributes already. One is its degree of institutionalization, which varies with the type of IOC structure, and can also vary considerably within each structure type. The other is its resource endowment: the authority, funds, or other assets with which the IOC structure is equipped, which of course differs in each particular case.

The different ways in which coordination can be effected also relate to these IOC structure attributes, and to the tasks the IOC structure is intended to perform. One way is coordination by authority: effecting other parties' decisions and actions by command and control. Another way is exchange: offering incentives (funds, information, votes, or other resources) in exchange for the desired action. The third way is trust: coordinating decisions and actions based on solidarity (shared values or goals), association (common traits such as ethnicity, culture, organizational function, and personnel's professional background), or reciprocity: the trust based on mutual interest, a history of positive experiences, and the expectation of reciprocal interaction.

We can identify four distinct types of IOC tasks, and relate them to IOC structures by looking at how each kind of task might be carried out. They are: information exchange, operational coordination, managerial or administrative coordination, and anticipatory coordination.

Information Exchange

Information exchange implies coordination by mutual adjustment. It is the main task many informal IOC structures have and perform best. All the IOC structures that supplement the market are premised on the value of information exchange between the actors. Interlocking corporate directorates, for example (when they are not reflecting equity participation) are designed to effect mutual adjustment among members of the network by exchanging relevant information between their representatives. Informal coordination among public agencies and service providers in a particular problem area is also effected by exchanging information between member organizations through interorganizational groups on which they are represented: commissions, advisory task forces, or boards.

In addition to any of their other tasks, all IOC structures also serve as arenas for information exchange among the members of the action set or interorganizational network. To the extent that an IOC structure's task is limited to information exchange, it can be quite effective without being very institutionalized, and does not require any resources other than the limited personnel and equipment that will enable the prescribed interactions to take place. Accordingly, IOC structures at the low end of the institutionalization scale will be a good fit: informal boundary-spanners or liaisons, coordinators, or interorganizational groups. Which of these is the best for a particular information-exchange task depends on many other factors in the interorganizational network and its environment.

Focusing the IOC structure's task on information exchange implies that network members' mutual adjustment, on the basis of the superior knowledge they acquire through the IOC structure, will be sufficient to elicit coordinated action, i.e., bring about the desired behavior of the organizational actors in the network. It also implies that coordination by mutual adjustment, in the absence of authority and resources, is here produced primarily by trust based on solidarity, association or reciprocity. There are many situations in which this is a plausible assumption, for example: reciprocal relations in informal entrepreneurial ventures, in many procurement or supply networks, in some scientific and technological research networks, in informal professional networks or political advocacy coalitions.

When these premises reflect reality, the principle of parsimony suggests informal IOC structures, avoiding the tangible and intangible costs of institutionalization. The institutional design problem, however, is to distinguish between this situation, and the illusion that coordination based on information exchange is enough. This illusion, the source of many of the coordination failures we have observed, can be wishful thinking born of the reluctance to accept the costs of more institutionalized coordination.

Operational Coordination

Operational coordination is essentially adaptive coordination between organizations involved in implementing preassigned tasks together. It may involve elaborating the division of labor between them in task fulfillment, deciding on subtask priorities and phasing, and determining on immediate or short-run mutual action in response to unforseen implementation problems.[14] Though it can be spontaneous at first, ongoing operational coordination implies the existence of an action set or an interorganizational network. Operational coordination, then, takes place in an existing context of informal interactions or a mandated framework of previous regulations, contracts or agreements between the involved organizations.

Information exchange to produce mutual adjustment is also part of operational coordination. But if the interorganizational network is not based on mutual reciprocity and trust alone, operational coordination will demand more than information exchange. At the task implementation level, coordinating action between organizations may also involve negotiation and bargaining about who does what, when, and how. This essentially invokes resource exchange, if in no broader sense than to agree that "if you do this for us today, we'll do that for you tomorrow". Resource exchange involving other assets may also come into play in negotiating and agreeing on action at the operational level, but these are likely to be limited, and the scope of action will be narrow and short-term (otherwise the object of discussion would be administrative or policy coordination, to be addressed below).

If it is in the context of a mandated framework, operational coordination can invoke interorganizational authority conferred by law, regulation, or previous mutual agreement between members of the network. In this type of context, operational coordination may be an adaptive supplement to impersonal monitoring and control. Here, interactions between member organizations' staff may involve interpreting regulations and agreements to translate them into concrete action in specific cases, and initiating action consistent with the mandated framework in unanticipated situations. IOC structures for operational coordination invoking command and control will need to be more institutionalized than those relying on information exchange and negotiation alone.

Any of the IOC micro-structures presented above, from the informal boundary-spanner to the institutionalized coordinating unit, can serve for operational coordination.[15] Operational coordination by negotiation and resource exchange can sometimes use relatively uninstitutionalized IOC structures. Which of these structures is the best fit, however, depends on many other factors, which were discussed above.

The kind of interdependence is one: coordination involving primarily sequential or limited reciprocal interdependence can be handled very well by informal or designated boundary-spanners for dyadic links, or a coordinator for multilateral ones. More complex multilateral reciprocal interdependence will require an interorganizational group: a team, a project group, a technical advisory committee.

But other factors may affect the fit of these IOC structures for operational coordination. One is network size: these informal IOC structures may fit relatively small, simple interorganizational networks quite well, while for a more numerous set of large organizations they may be inappropriate. In such a situation, for example, an interorganizational group might have to be more institutionalized and perhaps have some of the characteristics of a coordinating unit. The scale of the action set's mission can also affect the operational IOC structure's fit. The smaller and simpler the mission, the more likely it is that quite uninstitutionalized IOC structures will be a good fit; the larger and more complex the mission, the more institutionalized the IOC structure for its operational coordination will need to be.

The other relevant attribute of operational coordination structures that will affect their fit is their resource endowment. Here, the relationship between their expected coordination mode, the size of the interorganizational network and the scale of its mission, and the IOC structure's resources, is critical. IOC structures designed to effect operational coordination by negotiation and bargaining among the implementing organizations must have the resources that are appropriate incentives — what these are and how much of them the IOC structure needs is relative to each particular case. But the larger and more complex the interorganizational network, and the broader the scale of its mission, the greater the resource endowment the IOC structure will need to carry out its task of operational coordination effectively.

Similarly, IOC structures that depend on command and control for operational coordination must be equipped with the appropriate authority to carry out their tasks. This implies the formally delegated powers that accompany quite a high level of institutionalization. In the institutional design of operational IOC structures there can be a tradeoff, or substitution, between material resources and authority. Thus, for the same kind of interorganizational network with a similarly scaled mission, the IOC structure's appropriate resource endowment could be made up of authority, funds (or other material assets) or various mixtures of both. It is the mix and overall level of resource endowment (which of course can be much lower for operational coordination than for administrative or anticipatory coordination) which will be critical for the IOC structure's operational coordination performance.

Managerial or Administrative Coordination

Managerial or administrative coordination concerts actions among organizations at a higher level than operational coordination or task integration. Rather than involving the personnel who actually carry out the relevant tasks or operations, or their immediate supervisors, managerial/administrative coordination involves managers, administrators, and elite officials and decisionmakers. The scope of the coordination effort is also broader. Instead of focusing on the task or a narrow set of related operations, as operational coordination does, managerial/administrative coordination addresses the behavior, decisions, and interrelated actions of entire organizational units or organizations. The time-horizon of managerial/administrative coordination is correspondingly longer: it does not so much affect immediate action, as it sets the framework for operational decisions and program or project implementation.

Like operational coordination, managerial/administrative coordination among organizations can use information exchange, negotiation and resource exchange, and mandated command and control. The same relations between the factors characterizing the interorganizational network and mission, and IOC structures' attributes, that were discussed under operational coordination, apply to the fit of IOC structures for managerial/administrative coordination as well.

But there are some important differences. One is the environment in which managerial/administrative coordination is likely to take place. Often, operational coordination occurs in a framework that managerial/administrative coordination has set up, or under the umbrella of ongoing managerial/administrative coordination. In these situations (and assuming other appropriate interorganizational network characteristics), quite informal operational coordination can be very effective. But for managerial/administrative coordination this kind of framing is less probable. As a result, the higher-level coordination task is more likely to demand more institutionalized IOC structures than operational coordination would require in an otherwise identical context.

Another difference, however, can have a countervailing effect on the relation between the IOC structure's institutionalization and its fit. The fact is that the operational coordination situation described above may take the form of a mandated framework, which is more often absent at higher levels of coordination. This implies that negotiation and bargaining, and resource exchange, are more frequent than command and control at this level of coordination than they are at the operational level. To the extent that managerial/administrative coordination is expected to rely more on negotiation than on authority, less institutionalized IOC structures could be a better fit than more institutionalized ones.

Finally, the different dimensions of the coordination task at these two levels affects the respective fit of IOC structures. This applies both to their institutionalization and to their resource endowment. All other factors being equal, a managerial/administrative IOC structure will need to be more institutionalized, and have more authority or resources, than its counterpart engaged only in operational coordination. Given these differences, on balance there appear to be heavier resource demands on managerial/administrative IOC structures than on operational ones, and they are likely to have to be more institutionalized to be effective.

Anticipatory Coordination

To use March and Simon's (1958) distinction, we can identify operational coordination or task integration with adaptive coordination: concerting actions in real time through monitoring, feedback, and adaptive adjustment. Managerial/administrative coordination also has an element of adaptive coordination, but with a longer lead time. In this sense, it has an aspect of anticipatory coordination as well. This includes setting up mutually agreed on operating procedures, information processing formats, and schedules for member organizations' proposed actions, which become the framework within which operational coordination takes place.

Pure anticipatory coordination refers to coordination by plan: agreeing on mutual goals and objectives, developing common policies and plans for their realization, and designing or transforming institutions into the forms needed to turn projects into reality. Anticipatory coordination, then, occurs at the level of policy making, planning, and the institutional design of prospective lower-level IOC structures.

The respective importance of information exchange, bargaining, and control in anticipatory coordination, will differ from their relative roles in operational and managerial/administrative coordination. Depending, of course, on interorganizational network characteristics, information exchange and consequent mutual adjustment will be less salient.[16]

Negotiation between organizations in the action set or the emerging interorganizational network is much more likely to be used to arrive at common decisions, than it is in managerial/administrative or operational coordination. Such decisions may be formalized in agreements that set out the terms for resource exchange and the mutual obligations of member organizations in the interorganizational network. These agreements, resulting from the process of anticipatory coordination, are the framework for managerial/administrative and operational coordination and their IOC structures.

Interorganizational policy making and planning in the context of an externally mandated framework is much less likely than is mandated managerial/administrative or operational coordination. Authority, therefore, is less urgently needed in anticipatory coordination. In fact, anticipatory coordination is more likely to be a source of authority for lower-level coordination, than it is to be the arena to deploy authority conferred from above.

The mix of information exchange, negotiation, and control in anticipatory coordination has some implications for IOC structures' fit. It suggests that (again, depending on other factors too) IOC structures at intermediate levels of institutionalization will be more appropriate than totally informal ones, or highly institutionalized ones. Policy and planning coordination, then, may demand somewhat institutionalized interorganizational groups or coordinating units. Which of these is a better fit, and how institutionalized it should be, depend of course on the specific situation: the characteristics of the action set of organizations, and its actual or prospective mission.

Anticipatory coordination also differs from the other types of coordination in the resource endowment IOC structures need. This is because of the distance between planning and implementation, and their different demands in terms of commitment. Policies and plans are strategic frameworks for lower-level administrative and operational decisions, frameworks which pervasive uncertainty and the possibility of change makes less than binding.[17] Consequently, they demand less commitment from participating organizations than decisions with immediate operational consequences.

So effective coordination in the policymaking or planning stages of interorganizational interaction is less costly in terms of authority or incentives to arrive at agreed upon decisions, than managerial/administrative coordination would be. However, while anticipatory IOC structures may be quite effective without mandatory control and with little or no authority, it is likely that without some resources as incentives for purposeful negotiation, they will fail.

Reprise

In addressing interorganizational coordination, IOC meso- and micro-structures are the building-blocks of institutional design. But prescribing good institutional design is not simple. There is no universal algorithm that can present the IOC structure's critical attributes, identify the relevant factors in the IOC structure's setting, and describe their relationship in a way that offers a set of unequivocal design norms. There is so much variety and complexity in the interorganizational systems we are discussing, that it is unlikely that such a recipe will ever be found.

The cases show us, however, that organizations can be made to act together. If there is no formula for successful institutional design, it does seem that effective IOC depends on the fit between the coordination structures, and the action set of organizations they serve. Research and experience offer some suggestions for improving the fit of IOC structures and their effective performance. These relate the IOC structure's attributes to relevant characteristics of its setting.

Contextual factors describe the organizational environment, the interorganizational network and its mission. Interorganizational network attributes include the kinds of interdependencies between the organizations forming the action set, the network's size, structure, complexity, and autonomy, and the type and scale of its mission. IOC structures also have to fit their tasks: information exchange, operational coordination, managerial or administrative coordination, or anticipatory coordination in the development of policy or plans.

Institutional design for effective interorganizational coordination, then, is much more of an art than a science. In the exercise of her craft, the institutional designer has to use his judgement to assess the problem and its setting, and synthesize those prescriptions that are relevant, into a program for creating or transforming links between organizations into an appropriate IOC structure or system. This means selecting an IOC structure or structures, and adjusting its attributes: its institutionalization, and its resource endowment, to produce the best possible fit with the action set of organizations or the interorganizational network, with the network's purpose, and with the IOC structure's assigned task.

NOTES

1. A good deal of recent discussion has made this point, but more usually in terms of markets, networks and hierarchies (e.g., Thompson et al., 1991). I am using the term mandated framework rather than hierarchies, because hierarchy (i.e., coordination by command and control) is an attribute which is not limited to traditional organizational or political hierarchies.

2. This will be elaborated under meso- and micro-IOC structures later.

3. The relation between resources and task dimensions will be discussed in more detail later in reference to IOC micro-structures.

4. Paradoxically, this is true of markets within mandated frameworks as well. Such markets may be newly formed competitive markets established by legislative fiat (e.g., the market for airport landing slots created by U.S. deregulation of the airline industry), artificial markets within mandated frameworks (e.g., transferable development rights in the local land development regulation framework), or internal markets such as the "trading" of patients and funding between Health Authorities in the British National Health Service. The relevant resource in all these cases is the value assigned to the object of exchange.

5. The Appendix gives definitions of these characteristics. If each variable is assigned four or five states, we arrive at 10,000 possible combinations. Even allowing for a the "empty sets" of combinations that are logical or empirical impossibilities, the number of remaining possibilities is too large to provide a basis for systematic classification; see appendix.

6. This is Alter and Hage's (1993: 231) "Type 1" network.

7. Alter and Hage (1993: 231) cite the Japanese electronics supply network as an example of this type, which they call a "Type 2" systemic network.

8. This is Alter and Hage's (1993: 233) "Type 3" network; their Fulton County, Maryland Hospice Care network is a case.

9. This is an example of the interdependence between how an interorganizational network or system is delimited, and its characterization. Alter and Hage (1993: 233) cite the Japanese automotive supply network as a case of this type, noting that it is dependent on financing from the *keiretsu*. If the organizations (e.g., the banks and financial institutions) which are the source of capital were included in the network, it would become much more autonomous and would be better described under the previous type. The same is true of the local human services networks they describe, which externalize the (usually federal) regulating and funding agencies. Once these are included, the network would be the kind of mandated framework described under the last type.

10. This is illustrated by the ways in which different joint ventures are co-ordinated: the entrepreneurial partnership between a few small firms is relatively informal, while joint enterprises among large corporations (e.g., the Concorde, Airbus, and Switchco cases described above) have much more institutionalized IOC systems.

11. Redefining the relevant network in this way also gives a clue to possible solutions to the problems of dysfunctional bureaucratic coordination (such as the conflicts and "performance gap" observed by Alter and Hage (1993: 241–247) in vertically dependent networks. Solutions cannot be found by focusing on the "vertically dependent" network, but demand radical redesign of the IOC system in the more inclusive implementation or action set.

12. These combine several dimensions identified by many researchers. Alter and Hage (1993: 117–125) use a slightly different terminology: task scope to mean variability (here incorporated under complexity) and task scale to combine intensity, volume, and duration.

13. This association was also observed by Alter and Hage (1993: 166–167) in the human services networks they analyzed, and suggested by their four systemic network types (pp. 230–234) in which task scope and size are not related, but task scope and centrality are.

14. A more limited concept of operational coordination sees it as essentially regulating production, material-processing or people-processing flow (Thompson, 1967; Van de Ven, Delbecq and Koenig, 1976). Alter and Hage (1993) call this task integration, and focus on the flow of clients between the social service organizations in the networks they studied.

15. Applying the principle of parsimony, a complete organization just for operational coordination would be overkill.

16. Consequently, perfect markets which depend entirely on mutual adjustment need no planning at all (Alexander, 1992).

17. See Faludi (1987) and Alexander and Faludi (1989) for an elaboration of this view of planning and its consequences.

APPENDIX

Interorganizational Networks or Sets

Introduction

This systematic characterization of interorganizational networks or sets follows Alter and Hage's (1993: 149–162, 227–258) typology. They succeeded in describing four network types and using them for a theory of network evolution and coordination, because their focus was limited to networks of social service organizations and agencies (though their discussion is much more general). Their "Four Basic Forms of Systemic Networks" represent selected combinations of characteristics (Alter and Hage, 1993: 230–234). It is clear, however, that a much larger variety of combinations of network characteristics exists, as developed below.

Network Characteristics

Six variables represent the relevant characteristics of interorganizational networks. These have been developed by combining some characteristics that are related or positively associated. The variables and their respective component characteristics are as follows:

Interdependence: There are four possible states characterizing the type of interdependence between organizations in the relevant set or interorganizational network (see §2.2, pp. 21–36, above): 1) Sequential; 2) Reciprocal; 3) Pooled (symbiotic and/or commensal); 4) A combination of 2 and 3 or 1–3.

Size: The size of the interorganizational set or network is a combination of two characteristics: the number of member organizations, and the size of the member organizations. These combinations (a–i) can be reduced to five organizational sizes, ranging from 1 (largest) to 5 (smallest), as shown in Figure A1.

Size of organizations	No. of organizations		
	Many	Med.	Few
Large	a	b	c
Moderate	d	e	f
Small	g	h	i

a = 1 (largest); (b,d)= 2; (c,e,g)= 3; (f,h)= 4; i = 5 (smallest).

Figure A1. Size.

Structure: The degree of structuration of the interorganizational set or network reflects two interdependent characteristics. One is its centrality: the degree to which its member organizations are clustered around a central core. The other is the set's or network's connectedness: the number and intensity of links between the member organizations. The intensity of linkages represents the "volume" of flows through these channels; these include workflows (of clients, paperwork related to services, and goods or products in processing or production networks), communication flows (commands, monitoring, information) and resource flows (funding, personnel, expertise). These two characteristics are associated or complementary.

Alter and Hage (1993: 162) found a negative association in their sample of human services networks, but that is probably because their definition of centrality and connectivity was limited to workflows only. There is substitution, for example, between centrality and number of linkages: the most centralized form of network of (say) 6 organizations, the "wheel", needs only 5 links, while if the same six organizations were linked in the most random form of network they would need 15 links. An interorganizational set or network can range from highly structured to unstructured (1–5) depending on its combination of centrality and connectedness; see Figure A2.

Centrality	Connectedness		
	High	Med.	Low
Centralized	a	b	c
Diffused	d	e	f

a = 1 (highly structured); (b,d) = 2; (c,e) = 3; f = 4 (unstructured).

Figure A2. Structure.

Complexity: An interorganizational set or network's complexity also reflects two related characteristics. One is heterogeneity: the variety of sectors (in terms of their product, technology, or purpose) of its member organizations. The other is their differentiation: the depth to which member organizations are functionally specialized, and the degree to which they are limited to a narrow, specific function, or provide a broad array of different services or perform a variety of tasks.

While Alter and Hage (1993: 157–160) were at pains to distinguish between these two characteristics, their typical systemic networks (1993: 230–234) all show both in positive association. This is also to be expected: the more heterogeneous a network is, the more differentiated its members will be (e.g., symbiotic production joint ventures, or contracting networks). Organizations covering a broad domain of functions or tasks are more likely to be found in relatively homogenous networks (e.g., promotional networks such as trade associations). Levels of complexity (1–5), ranging from high heterogeneity and differentiation, to the lowest degree of both, can be developed by combining these characteristics as shown in Figure A3 below.

Autonomy: An interorganizational set's or network's autonomy means the degree to which it is separate and distinct from its organizational environment. This is reflected in two indicators. The first is the set's or network's openness: the number and intensity of network members' links with their organizational environment, compared with their links among themselves. This indicates the degree to which the network is open or closed, and how much it is a clearly differen-

Differen-	Heterogeneity		
tiation	High	Med.	Low
High	a	b	c
Med.	d	e	f
Low	g	h	i

a = 1 (complex); (b,d) = 2; (c,e,g) = 3; (f,h) = 4; i = 5 (simple).

Figure A3. Complexity.

tiated interorganizational system. The second is dependence: to what degree is the interorganizational set dependent on its environment for critical resources?

Exchange theory, which has been amply validated, suggests that these two characteristics are positively associated. Thus, the more autonomous network will be the set of organizations which is both less interconnected with its environment and less dependent on it, while the less autonomous set will be more interactive with its environment because it needs the resources that the environment provides. Combining high, moderate, and low levels of openness and dependence, as shown in Figure A4, produces five states of autonomy.

Dependency	Openess		
	High	Med.	Low
High	a	b	c
Med.	d	e	f
Low	g	h	i

a = 1 (most autonomy); (b,d)= 2; (c,e,g) = 3; (f,h) = 4; i = 5 (least autonomy).

Figure A4. Autonomy.

Mission: The purpose, mission, or task that is the reason why the organizations in the interorganizational set or network have come together, is another important distinguishing variable. Several related characteristics can be combined to describe a network's mission, from major: an important, long-range, broad-based, large-scale undertaking, to minor: a small-scale, short-term task with relatively narrowly focused impacts.

One dimension is task scale: this indicates the duration, intensity, and volume (or scale and diffusion of impacts) of what the interorganizational network has come into existence to produce, process, or do. The other is mission complexity, which is a combination of technological development and specialization, and the prevailing knowledge, as reflected in level of uncertainty, about the organization set's goals, mission, and environment. Figure A5 shows how these are combined.

Complexity	Task scope		
	High	Med.	Low
High	a	b	c
Med.	d	e	f
Low	g	h	i

a = 1; (b,d) = 2; (c,e,g) = 3; (f,h)= 4; i = 5.

Figure A5. Mission.

References

Adams, W.J. 1989. *Restructuring the French Economy: Government and the Rise of Market Competition Since World War II*. Washington, DC: The Brookings Institute.

Agranoff, R., and V.A. Lindsay. 1983. "Intergovernmental Management: Perspectives from Human Services Problem Solving at the Local Level", *Public Administration Review* 43(3):227–237.

Aldrich, H. 1979. *Organizations and Environments*. Englewood Cliffs, NJ: Prentice-Hall.

Aldrich, H. 1976. "Resource Dependence and Interorganizational Relations: Local Employment Service Offices and Social Services Sector Organizations", *Administration and Society* 7(4):419–454.

Aldrich, H., and D. Herker. 1977. "Boundary-Spanning Roles and Organization Structure", *Academy of Management Review* 2(3):217–230.

Aldrich, H., and D. Whetten. 1981. "Organization Sets, Action Sets and Networks: Making the Most of Simplicity", in: *Handbook of Organizational Design*, eds. P.C. Nystrom and W.H. Starbuck. Oxford: Oxford University Press.

Alexander, C. 1964. *Notes on the Synthesis of Form*. Cambridge: Harvard University Press.

Alexander, E.R. 1994. "To Plan or Not to Plan, That Is the Question: Transaction Cost Theory and Its Implications for Planning", *Environment and Planning B: Planning and Design* 21(3):341–352.

Alexander, E.R. 1992. "A Transaction Cost Theory of Planning", *Journal of the American Planning Association* 58(2):190–200.

335

Alexander, E.R. 1991a. "Improbable Implementation: The Pressman-Wildavsky Paradox Revisited", *Journal of Public Policy* 9(4):451–465.

Alexander, E.R. 1991b. "Sharing Power Among Organizations: Coordination Models to Link Theory and Practice", in: *Shared Power: What Is It? How Does It Work? How Can We Make It Work Better?* eds. J.M. Bryson and R.C. Einsweiler. Lanham, MD: University Press of America.

Alexander, E.R. 1990. "Interorganizational Coordination in Neighborhood Development: Four Cases", in: *Neighborhood Policy Can Work*, ed. Naomi Carmon. New York: Macmillan.

Alexander, E.R. 1987a. "Deductive Reasoning and Plan Review as an Analytic Tool: Development Policy and Plan Implementation in the Galilee", *Ir Ve'Ezor* 17:62–79 (Hebrew).

Alexander, E.R. 1987b. "Design in Planning and Decision Making: Theory and Its Implications for Practice", pp. 25–30 in: *Proceedings of the 1987 Conference on Planning and Design in Urban and Regional Planning*, ed. E.R. Alexander. Conference on Planning and Design Theory. Boston and New York: American Society of Mechanical Engineers.

Alexander, E.R. 1983. "Coordinating Care Services for the Frail and Incapacitated Elderly", pp. 86–89 in: *Advances in Health Care Research*, eds. S.M. Smith and M. Venkatesan, Provo, UT: Brigham Young University, Institute of Business Management.

Alexander, E.R. 1982. "Design in the Decision Making Process", *Policy Sciences* 14(3):279–292.

Alexander, E.R. 1981. *Effectiveness in Interorganizational Coordination: A Comparative Case Analysis*. Report R-81-4. Milwaukee, WI: Center for Architecture & Urban Planning Research, University of Wisconsin at Milwaukee.

Alexander, E.R. 1980. *Slum Rehabilitation in Israel: The Administrative-Institutional Context*. Working Papers #1-9. Haifa: The S. Neaman Institute for Advanced Studies in Science and Technology, Technion (Israel Institute for Technology).

Alexander, E.R. 1978. "Theory, Plan and Reality: The Lakhish Regional Plan as Applied Location Theory", *Growth and Change* 9(3):44–52.

Alexander, E.R., R. Alterman and H. Law-Yone. 1983. *Evaluating Plan Implementation: The National Statutory Planning System in Israel*. Oxford: Pergamon.

Alexander, E.R., and A. Faludi. 1989. "Planning and Plan Implementation: Notes on Evaluation Criteria", *Environment and Planning B: Planning and Design* 16(1):127-140.

Allison, G.T. 1971. *Essence of Decision: Explaining the Cuban Missile Crisis*. Boston: Little Brown.

Alter, C., and J. Hage. 1993. *Organizations Working Together*. Newbury Park, CA: Sage.

Alterman, R. 1988. "Implementing Decentralization for Neighborhood Regeneration: Factors Promoting or Inhibiting Success", *Journal of the American Planning Association* 54(4):454–469.

Alterman, R. 1987. "Opening up the 'Black Box' in Neighborhood Programs: The Implementation Process in Israel's Project Renewal", *Policy Studies Journal* 16(2):347–361.

Alterman, R., N. Carmon and M. Hill. 1985. *Comprehensive Evaluation of Israel's Project Renewal*. Haifa: S. Neaman Institute for Advanced Studies in Science & Technology, Technion (Israel Institute for Technology) (Hebrew).

Anderson, M. 1964. *The Federal Bulldozer: A Critical Analysis of Urban Renewal, 1949–62*. Cambridge: MIT Press.

Appleyard, D. 1976. *Planning a Pluralist City: Conflicting Realities in Ciudad Guyana*. Cambridge: MIT Press.

Ardagh, J. 1982. *France in the 1980s*. London: Secker & Warburg.

Argyris, C. 1964. *Integrating the Individual and the Organization*. New York: Wiley.

Arnold, J.L. 1971. *The New Deal in the Suburbs: A History of the Greenbelt Town Program 1935–54*. Columbus: Ohio State University Press.

Arnold, P. 1991. "The Invisible Hand in Healthcare: The Rise of Financial Markets in the U.S. Hospital Industry," pp. 293–316 in: *Governance of the American Economy*, eds. J.L. Campbell, J.R. Hollingsworth and L.N. Lindberg. Cambridge: Cambridge University Press.

Barrett, S., and C. Fudge, Eds. 1981. *Policy and Action: Essays in the Implementation of Public Policy*. London: Methuen.

Bars, B.A., K.B. Baum and J. Fiedler. 1976. *Politik und Koordinierung*. Göttingen: Verlag Otto Schwartz & Co.

Beder, H. 1987. "Collaboration as a Competitive Strategy", pp. 85–95 in: *Competitive Strategies for Continuing Education*, ed. C. Baden. San Francisco: Jossey-Bass.

Bennis, W.G. 1966. *Changing Organizations*. New York: McGraw-Hill.

Ben Porat, Y. 1980. "The F-Connection: Families, Friends and Firms in the Organization of Exchange", *Population and Development Review* 6(1):1–30.

Benson, J.K. 1982. "A Framework for Policy Analysis", in: *Interorganizational Coordination: Theory, Research and Implementation*, eds. D.L. Rogers, D.A. Whetten and Associates. Ames, IO: Iowa State University Press.

Benson, J.K. 1975. "The Interorganizational Network as a Political Economy", *Administrative Science Quarterly* 20(2):229–249.

Bolan, R. 1991. "Planning and Institutional Design". *Planning Theory* 5/6: 7–34.

Bosselman, F., D. Callies and J. Banta. 1973. *The Taking Issue: An Analysis of the Constitutional Limits of Land Use Control*. Washington, DC: USGPO.

Bowen, E.R. 1982. "The Pressman-Wildavsky Paradox: Four Addenda", *Journal of Public Policy* 2(1):1–22.

Bowman, J.R. 1989. *Capitalist Collective Action*. New York: Cambridge University Press.

Bradach, J.L., and R.G. Eccles. 1989. "Price, Authority and Trust: From Ideal Types to Plural Forms", *Annual Review of Sociology* 15:97–118.

Brager, G., and S. Holloway. 1978. *Changing Human Service Organizations: Politics and Practice*. New York: Free Press.

Branco, R.J. 1984. *The U.S. and Brazil: Opening a New Dialogue*. Washington, DC: National Defense University Press.

Brandl, J. 1988. "On Politics and Policy Analysis as the Design and Assessment of Institutions". *Journal of Policy Analysis and Management* 7(3):419–424.

Braybrooke, D., and C.E. Lindblom. 1963. *A Strategy of Decision: Policy Evaluation as a Social Process*. Glencoe, IL: Free Press.

Brickman, R. 1979. "Comparative Approaches to R&D Policy Coordination", *Policy Sciences* 11(1):73–91.

Brooks, C.G., J.M. Grimwood and L.S. Swenson Jr. 1979. *Chariots for Apollo: A History of Manned Lunar Spacecraft*. Washington, DC: National Aeronautics and Space Agency.

Bryson, J.M., and P.S. Ring. 1990. "A Transaction-Based Approach to Policy Intervention", *Policy Sciences* 23(2):205–229.

Buchanan, J.M., and G. Tullock. 1967. *The Calculus of Consent: Logical Foundations of Constitutional Democracy*. Ann Arbor: University of Michigan Press.

Bulmer, S., and W. Wessels. 1987. *The European Council: The European Council: Decision Making in European Politics*. Middlestoke: Macmillan.

Burby, R.J., E.J. Kaiser, and D.H. Moreau. 1988. "Coordination of Water and Sewer Extension Policy with Land Use Planning: Key Factors Influencing the State of Practice", *Journal of Urban Affairs* 10(2):119–139.

Burns, M., and A. Manet. 1984. "Administrative Freedom for Interorganizational Action", *Administration and Society*, 16(3):289–305.

Burns, T., and G.M. Stalker. 1961. *The Management of Innovation*. London: Tavistock.

Burt, R.S. 1982. *Corporate Profits and Cooptation: Networks of Market Constraints and Directorate Ties in the American Economy*. New York: Academic Press.

Camagni, R., Ed., 1991. *Innovation Networks: Spatial Perspectives*. London: Belhaven Press.

Cameron, K.S., and D.A. Whetten. 1983. "Organizational Effectiveness: One Approach or Several", pp. 1–24 in: *Organizational Effectiveness: A Comparison of Multiple Models*, eds. K.S. Cameron and D.A. Whetten. New York: Academic Press.

Campbell, J.L., and L.N. Lindberg. 1991. "The Evolution of Governance Regimes", pp. 319–355 in: *Governance of the American Economy*, eds. J.R. Campbell, J.R.Hollingsworth and L.N.Lindberg. New York: Cambridge University Press.

Carmon, N. 1987. "A Neighborhood Program that Works: Israel's Project Renewal", *Policy Studies Journal* 16(2):362–376.

Carney, M.G. 1987. "The Strategy and Structure of Collective Action", *Organization Studies* 8(4):341–362.

Chase, G. 1979. "Implementing a Human Services Program: How Hard Will It Be?" *Public Policy* 27(4):385–436.

Chisholm, D. 1989. *Coordination Without Hierarchy: Informal Structures in Multiorganizational Systems*. Berkeley: University of California Press.

Chivers, H. 1956. *The Story of De Beers*. London: Cassell.

Congressional Research Service. 1973. *The Central City Problem and Urban Renewal Policy: A Study Prepared for the Subcommittee on Housing and Urban Affairs*. U.S. Senate Committee on Banking, Housing and Urban Affairs. Washington, DC: USGPO.

Corbett, T.J. 1993. "Strategies for Coordination at the Local Level", pp. 161–174 in: *Welfare System Reform: Coordinating Federal, State and Local Public Assistance Programs*, eds. E.T. Jennings and N.S. Zank. Westport, CT: Greenwood Press.

Corden, C. 1977. *Planned Cities: New Towns in Britain and America*. Beverly Hills: Sage.

Crevoisier, O. 1993. "Spatial Shifts and the Emergence of Innovative Milieux: The Case of the Jura Region Between 1960 and 1990", *Environment & Planning C: Government and Policy* 11(4):419–430.

Cross, N. 1987. *Developments in Design Methodology*. Chichester, Sussex: Wiley.

Crozier, M. 1964. *The Bureaucratic Phenomenon*. Chicago: University of Chicago Press.

Danielson, A.L. 1982. *The Evolution of OPEC*. New York: Harcourt, Brace Jovanovitch.

DeHoog, R.H. 1990. "Competition, Negotiation and Cooperation: Three Models for Service Contracting", *Administration and Society* 22(3):317–340.

Derthick, M. 1974. *Between State and Nation: Regional Organizations of the U.S.* Washington, DC: The Brookings Institute.

Donahue, J.D. 1989. *The Privatization Decision: Public Ends, Private Means*. New York: Basic Books.

Duncan, R.B. 1972. "Characteristics of Organizational Environments and Perceived Environmental Uncertainty", *Administrative Science Quarterly* 17(4):313–321.

Dunkerly, D., T. Spybey and M. Thrasher. 1981. "Interorganizational Networks: A Case Study of Industrial Location", *Organization Studies* 2(3): 229–247.

Dunshire, A. 1978. *The Execution Process*. Vol. 2: *Control in a Bureaucracy*. London: Martin Robertson.

Durant, R.F. 1992. "Beyond Markets, Hierarchies or Clans: Lessons from Natural Resource Management in the Reagan Era", *Administration and Society* 24(3):346–374.

Elmore, R.F. 1987. "Instruments and Strategy in Public Policy", *Policy Studies Review* 7(1):174–186.

Erdstrøm, A., B.Hågberg and L.E.Norbøck. 1984. "Alternative Explanations of Interorganisational Cooperation: The Case of Joint Programmes and Joint Ventures in Sweden", *Organisation Studies* 5(2):147–168.

Evan, W.M. 1966. "The Organization Set: Toward a Theory of Interorganizational Relations", pp. 175–190 in: *Approaches to Organizational Design*, ed. J.D. Thompson. Pittsburgh, PA: University of Pittsburgh Press.

Evan, W.M., and R.C. Klemm. 1980. "Interorganizational Relations Among Hospitals: A Strategy, Structure and Performance Model", *Human Relations* 33(5):315–337.

Faludi, A. 1987. *A Decision Centred View of Environmental Planning*. Oxford: Pergamon.

Faludi, A., and A. v.d. Valk. 1994. *Rule and Order: Dutch Planning Doctrine in the Twentieth Century*. Dordrecht: Kluwer.

Farley, D., and B.K. Misechok. 1993. "JOBS and JTPA: Single Point of Contact in Pennsylvania", pp. 175–184 in: *Welfare System Reform: Coordinating Federal, State and Local Public Assistance Programs*, eds. E.T. Jennings and N.S. Zank. Westport, CT: Greenwood Press.

Fennell, M.L. 1980. "The Effects of Environmental Characteristics on the Structure of Hospital Clusters", *Administrative Science Quarterly* 25(3):485–510.

Fennell, M.L., and J.A. Alexander. 1993. "Perspectives on Organizational Change in the U.S. Medical Care Sector", *Annual Review of Sociology* 19: 485–510.

Franz, H.J. 1986. "Interorganizational Arrangements and Coordination at the Policy Level," pp. 479–510 in: *Guidance, Control and Evaluation in the Public Sector: The Bielefeld Interdisciplinary Project*, eds. F.-X. Kaufmann, G. Majone and V. Ostrom, Berlin: De Gruyter.

Franz, H.J., B. Rosewitz and H. Wolf. 1986. "Association and Coordination", pp. 531–555 in: *Guidance, Control and Evaluation in the Public Sector: The Bielefeld Interdisciplinary Project*, eds. F.-X. Kaufmann, G. Majone and V. Ostrom, Berlin: De Gruyter.

Franz, H.J. 1985. "Interorganizational Arrangements and Coordination at the Policy Level", pp. 479–510 in: *Guidance, Control and Evaluation in the Public Sector: The Bielefeld Interdisciplinary Project*, eds. F.-X. Kaufmann, G. Majone and V. Ostrom, Berlin: De Gruyter.

Freeman, R.E. 1984. *Strategic Management: A Stakeholder Approach*. London: Pitman.

Freidson, E. 1986. *Professional Powers: A Study of the Institutionalization of Formal Knowledge*. Chicago: University of Chicago Press.

Frieden, B.J., and L.B.M. Kaplan. 1975. *The Politics of Neglect: Urban Aid from Model Cities to Revenue Sharing*. Cambridge: MIT Press.

Frieden, B.J., and L.B. Sagalynn. 1989. *Downtown Inc.: How America Rebuilds Cities*. Cambridge: MIT Press.

Friend, J. 1980. "Planning in a Multi-Organizational Context", *Town Planning Review* 51(3):261–269.

Frisken, F. 1991. "The Contributions of Metropolitan Government to the Success of Toronto's Public Transit System: An Empirical Dissent from the Public Choice Paradigm", *Urban Affairs Quarterly* 27(2):268–292.

Gage, R.W. 1984. "Federal Regional Councils: Networking Organizations for Policy Management in the Intergovernmental System", *Public Administration Review* 44(2):134–144.

Galbraith, J.R. 1977. *Organization Design*. Reading, PA: Addison-Wesley.

Galbraith, J.R., and R.K. Kazanjian. 1986. *Strategy Implementation: Structure, Systems and Processes*, 2nd ed. St. Paul, MN: West.

Gans, H.J. 1968. *People and Plans: Essays on Urban Problems and Solutions*. New York: Basic Books.

Gansler, J.S. 1980. *The Defense Industry*. Cambridge: MIT Press.

Gargan, J.A. 1993. "Specifying Elements of Professionalism and the Process of Professionalization", *International Journal of Public Administration* 16(12): 1861–1884.

Garlichs, D., and C. Hull. 1978. "Central Control and Information Dependence: Highway Planning in the Federal Republic of Germany", pp. 143–165 in: *Interorganizational Policy Making: Limits to Coordination and Central Control*, eds. K. Hanf and F.W. Scharpf, Beverly Hills: Sage.

Gerlach, M.L. 1992. "The Japanese Corporate Network: A Blockmodel Analysis", *Administrative Science Quarterly* 37(1):105–139.

Giddens, A. 1984. *The Constitution of Society: An Introduction into the Theory of Structuration*. Cambridge: Polity Press.

Giddens, A. 1979. *Central Problems in Social Theory*. Berkeley: University of California Press.

Gillespie, D.F., and D.S. Mileti. 1979. *Technostructures and Interorganizational Relations*. Lexington, MA: Heath.

Goggin, M.L., A.O'M. Bowman, J.P. Lester and L.J. O'Toole Jr. 1990. *Implementation Theory and Practice: Toward a Third Generation*. Glenview, IL: Scott Foresman.

Gomez-Ibanez, J.A., and J.R. Meyer. 1990. "Privatizing and Deregulating Local Public Services: Lessons from Britain's Buses", *Journal of the American Planning Association* 56(1):9–21.

Gottfredson, L.S., and P.E. White. 1981. "Interorganizational Agreements", pp. 471–486 in: *Handbook of Organizational Design*, eds. P.C. Nystrom and W.H. Starbuck. New York: Oxford University Press.

Grandori, A. 1987. *Perspectives on Organization Theory*. Cambridge, MA: Ballinger.

Gray, B. 1989. *Collaborating: Finding Common Ground for Multiparty Problems*. San Francisco: Jossey-Bass.

Gray, B. 1985. "Conditions Facilitating Interorganizational Collaboration", *Human Relations* 38(10):911–936.

Haar, C.M. 1975. *Between the Idea and the Reality: A Study in the Origin, Fate and Legacy of the Model Cities Program*. Boston: Little-Brown.

Hage, J. 1975. "A Strategy for Creating Interdependent Delivery Systems to Meet Complex Needs", in: *Interorganizational Theory*, ed. A. Negandhi. Kent, OH: Kent State University Press.

Hage, J. 1974. *Coordination and Organizational Control: Cybernetics in Health and Welfare Settings*. New York: Wiley.

Hage, J., and M. Aiken. 1970. *Social Change in Complex Organizations*. New York: Random House.

Hage, J., M. Aiken and C.B. Marrett. 1971. "Organization Strategy and Communications", *American Sociological Review* 36(2):158–169.

Hall, R.A., J.C. Clark, P.C. Giordano, P.V. Johnson and M.V. Rockel. 1976. "Patterns of Interorganizational Relationships", *Administrative Science Quarterly* 22(3):457–474.

Halpert, B.P. 1982. "Antecedents", in: *Interorganizational Coordination: Theory, Research and Implementation*, eds. D.L. Rogers, D.A. Whetten and Associates. Ames: Iowa State University Press.

Hannan, M., and J.Freeman. 1989. *Organizational Ecology*. Cambridge: Harvard University Press.

Hansen, N.M. 1970. Rural Poverty and the Urban Crisis. Bloomington: Indiana University Press.

Harbin, G., J.J. Gallagher, T. Lillie and J. Eckland. 1992. "Factors Influencing State Progress in the Implementation of PL99-457 Part H", *Policy Sciences* 25(2):103–115.

Hardin, G. 1968. "The Tragedy of the Commons", *Science* 162:1243–1268.

Harris, L.A. 1993. "Lafayette Court Family Development Center: Bringing Social Services and Housing Programs Together", pp. 185–198 in: *Welfare*

System Reform: Coordinating Federal, State and Local Public Assistance Programs, eds. E.T. Jennings and N.S. Zank. Westport, CT: Greenwood Press.

Harrison, B. 1994. "The Italian Industrial Districts and the Crisis of the Cooperative Form: Part I", *European Planning Studies* 2(1):3–22.

Heclo, H., and A. Wildavsky. 1974. *The Private Government of Public Money*. Berkeley: University of California Press.

Hegner, F. 1986. "Solidarity and Hierarchy: Institutional Arrangements for the Coordination of Actions", pp. 408–429 in: *Guidance, Control and Evaluation in the Public Sector: The Bielefeld Interdisciplinary Project*, eds. F.-X. Kaufmann, G. Majone and V. Ostrom, Berlin: De Gruyter.

Herbert, M. 1980. "The British New Towns: A Review Article", *Town Planning Review* 51(4):414–420.

Hjern, B., and D.O. Porter. 1981. "Implementation Structures: A New Unit of Administrative Analysis", *Organization Studies* 2(3):211–227.

Hoffman, C. 1986. *Project Renewal: Community and Change in Israel* (Renewal Dept., Jewish Agency for Israel). Jerusalem: Halberstad Communications.

Honadle, G., and L. Cooper. 1989. "Beyond Coordination and Control: An Interorganizational Approach to Structural Adjustment, Service Delivery and Natural Resource Management", *World Development* 17(10):1531–1541.

Hopkins, K.R. 1993. "The Presidency and the Coordination of Public Assistance", pp. 25–32 in: *Welfare System Reform: Coordinating Federal, State and Local Public Assistance Programs*, eds. E.T. Jennings and N.S. Zank. Westport, CT: Greenwood Press.

Howe, E. 1981. "Code Enforcement in Three Cities: An Organizational Analysis", *The Urban Lawyer* 13(1):65–88.

Hult, K.M. 1987. *Agency Merger and Bureaucratic Redesign*. Pittsburgh, PA: University of Pittsburgh Press.

Hult, K.M., and C. Walcott. 1990. *Governing Public Organizations: Politics, Structures and Institutional Design*. Pacific Grove, CA: Brooks-Cole.

Huntingdon, S. 1968. *Political Order in Changing Societies*. New Haven: Yale University Press.

Ilchman, W.F., and N.T. Uphoff. 1969. *The Political Economy of Change*. Berkeley: University of California Press.

International Committee for the Evaluation of Project Renewal. 1985. *Summary of Findings and Recommendations*. Jerusalem: Van Leer Institute.

Jansen, D. 1992. "Policy Networks and Change: The Case of High T_c Superconductors", pp. 137–168 in: *Policy Networks*, eds. B. Marin and R. Mayntz. Frankfurt am Main: Campus Verlag.

Jennings, E.T. 1994. "Building Bridges in the Intergovernmental Arena: Coordinating Employment and Training Programs in the American States", *Public Administration Review* 54(1):52–60.

Jennings, E.T., and D. Krane. 1993. "Community Level Coordination of the JOBS Program", pp. 211–227 in: *Welfare System Reform: Coordinating Federal, State and Local Public Assistance Programs*, eds. E.T. Jennings and N.S. Zank. Westport, CT: Greenwood Press.

Jennings, E.T., and N.S. Zank. 1993. "The Coordination Challenge", pp. 3–19 in: *Welfare System Reform: Coordinating Federal, State and Local Public Assistance Programs*, eds. E.T. Jennings and N.S. Zank. Westport, CT: Greenwood Press.

Jepperson, R.L. 1991. "Institutions, Institutional Effects and Institutionalism", pp. 143–163 in: *The New Institutionalism in Organizational Analysis*, eds. W.W. Powell and P.J. Dimaggio. Chicago: University of Chicago Press.

Johnson, C. 1982. *MITI and the Japanese Miracle: The Growth of Industrial Policy 1925–1975*. Stanford, CA: Stanford University Press.

Kamerman, S.B., and A.J. Kahn, Eds. 1989. *Privatization and the Welfare State*. Princeton: Princeton University Press.

Kaplan, M. 1971. "Model Cities and National Urban Policy", pp. 28–35 in: *ASPO Proceedings*. Chicago: American Society of Planning Officials.

Katz, D., and R.L. Kahn. 1966. *The Social Psychology of Organizations*. New York: Wiley.

Kaufmann, F.-X. 1986. "The Relationship Between Guidance, Control and Evaluation", in: *Guidance, Control and Evaluation in the Public Sector: The Bielefeld Interdisciplinary Project*, eds. F.-X. Kaufmann, G. Majone and V. Ostrom. Berlin: De Gruyter.

Kaufmann, F.-X., G. Majone and V. Ostrom. 1986. "Experience, Theory and Design", in: *Guidance, Control and Evaluation in the Public Sector: The Bielefeld Interdisciplinary Project*, eds. F.-X. Kaufmann, G. Majone and V. Ostrom, Berlin: De Gruyter.

Keller, L.F. 1984. "The Political Economy of Public Management: An Interorganizational Network Perspective", *Administration and Society* 15(4):455–474.

Kenis, P., and V. Schneider. 1992. "Policy Networks and Policy Analysis: Scrutinizing a New Analytical Toolbox", pp. 25–59 in: *Policy Networks*, eds. B. Marin and R. Mayntz. Frankfurt am Main: Campus Verlag.

Kessler, M. 1987. "Interorganizational Environments, Attitudes and the Policy Outputs of Public Agencies: A Comparative Case Study", *Administration and Society* 19(1):48–73.

Kirst, M.W., G. Meister and S.R. Rowley. 1984. "Policy Issue Networks: Their Influence on State Policymaking", *Policy Studies Journal* 13(3):247–264.

Knight, D., F. Murray and H. Wilmott. 1993. "Networking as Knowledge Work: A Study of Strategic Interorganizational Development in the Financial Services Industry", *Journal of Management Studies* 30(6):976–995.

Kochen, M., and C.W. Deutsch. 1980. *Decentralization: Sketches toward a Rational Theory*. Cambridge, MA: Oelgeschlager, Gunn and Hain.

Koenig, C., and R.-A. Thietart. 1988. "Technology and Organization: The Mutual Organization in the European Aerospace Industry", *International Studies of Management and Organization* 17(4):6–30.

Kramer, K.L., and J.L. King. 1979. "A Requiem for USAC", *Policy Analysis* 5(3):313–349.

Larson, A. 1992. "Network Dyads in Entrepreneurial Settings: A Study of the Governance of Exchange Relationships", *Administrative Science Quarterly* 37(1):76–104.

Laumann, E.O., and D. Knoke. 1987. *The Organizational State: Social Choice in National Policy Domains*. Madison: University of Wisconsin Press.

Lawrence, P.R., and J.W. Lorsch. 1967. *Organization and Environment*. Cambridge: Harvard University Press.

Lehman, E.W. 1975. *Coordinating Health Care: Explorations in Interorganizational Relations*. Beverly Hills: Sage.

Levin, P.H. 1976. *Government and the Planning Process*. London: Allen & Unwin.

Levine, R.A. 1972. *Public Planning: Failure and Redirection*. New York: Basic Books.

Lewis, R.S. 1974. *The Voyages of Apollo: The Exploration of the Moon*. New York: Quadrangle/NYT Book Co.

Lindblom, C.E. 1988. *Democracy and Market Systems*. Oslo: Norwegian University Press.

Lindblom, C.E. 1965. *The Intelligence of Democracy*. New York: Free Press.

Linder, S.H., and G. Peters. 1987. "A Design Perspective on Policy Implementation: The Fallacies of Misplaced Prescription", *Policy Studies Review* 6(3): 459–475.

Logsden, J.M. 1991. "Interests and Interdependence in the Formation of Social Problem Solving Collaborations", *Journal of Applied Behavioral Science* 27(1):23–37.

Longford, E. 1969. *Wellington: The Years of the Sword*. London: Weidenfeld & Nicholson.

Lowry, K. 1985. "Assessing the Implementation of Federal Coastal Policy", *Journal of the American Planning Association* 51(3):288–298.

Lowry, K., and T. Eichenberg. 1986. "Assessing Intergovernmental Coordination in Coastal Zone Management", *Policy Studies Review* 6(2):321–329.

Luke, J.S. 1991. "Managing Interconnectedness", pp. 25–50 in: *Shared Power*, eds. J.M. Bryson and R.C. Einsweiler, Lanham, MD: University Press of America.

Lukes, S. 1974. *Power: A Radical View*. London: Macmillan.

Lustick, I. 1980. "Explaining the Variable Utility of Disjointed Incrementalism: Four Propositions", *American Political Science Review* 74(2):342–353.

MacDonald, H.I. 1992. "Special Interest Politics and the Crisis of Financial Institutions in the USA", *Environment and Planning C: Government and Policy* 10(2):123–146.

Macdonald, J.S. 1980. "Planning Implementation and Social Policy: An Evaluation of Ciudad Guyana: 1965 and 1975", pp. 111–211 in: *Progress in Planning*, Vol. 11, eds. D.R. Diamond and J.B. McLoughlin. Oxford: Pergamon.

Majone, G. 1986. "Mutual Adjustment by Debate and Persuasion", pp. 446–458 in: *Guidance, Control and Evaluation in the Public Sector: The Bielefeld Interdisciplinary Project*, eds. F.-X. Kaufmann, G. Majone and V. Ostrom, Berlin: De Gruyter.

Mandell, M. 1984. "Application of Network Analysis to Implementation of a Complex Project", *Human Relations* 37(8):659–679.

March, J.C., and H.A. Simon with H. Guetzow. 1958. *Organizations*. New York: Wiley.

Marin, B., and R. Mayntz. 1992. "Introduction: Studying Policy Networks", pp. 11–23 in: *Policy Networks*, eds. B. Marin and R. Mayntz. Frankfurt am Main: Campus Verlag.

Mastop, H. 1983. "Coordination in Dutch Planning: A Case Study", pp. 173–192 in: *Evaluating Urban Planning Efforts*, ed. I. Masser. Aldershot: Gower.

Mathiesen, T. 1971. *Across the Boundaries of Organizations*. Berkeley, CA: Glendessary Press.

May, P.J., and J.W. Handmer. 1992. "Regulatory Policy Design: Cooperative vs. Deterrent Mandates", *Australian Journal of Public Administration* 51(1): 43–53.

McCann, J.E. 1983. "Design Guidelines for Social Problem-Solving Interventions", *Journal of the American Behavioral Scientist* 19(2):177–182.

Medefind, H. 1975. *Organization Europa*. Bonn: Europa Union.

Melman, S. 1970. *Pentagon Capitalism: The Political Economy of War*. New York: McGraw-Hill.

Metcalfe, J. 1976. "Organizational Strategies and Interorganizational Networks", *Human Relations* 29(4):327–343.

Mills, C.W. 1956. *The Power Elite*. New York: Oxford University Press.

Milner, M. Jr. 1980. *Unequal Care: A Case Study of Interorganizational Relations in Health Care*. New York: Columbia University Press.

Milward, H.B. 1991. "Current Institutional Arrangements that Create or Require Shared Power", pp. 51–75 in: *Shared Power: What Is It? How Does It Work? How Can We Make It Work Better?* eds. J.M. Bryson and R.C. Einsweiler. Lanham, MD: University Press of America.

Milward, H.B. 1982. "Interorganizational Policy Systems and Research on Public Organizations", *Administration and Society* 13(4):457–478.

Milward, H.B., and G.L. Wamsley. 1985. "Policy Subsystems, Networks and the Tools of Public Management", pp. 105–130 in: *Policy Implementation in Federal and Unitary Systems*, eds. K. Hanf and T.A.J. Toonen. Dordrecht: M. Nijhoff.

Mintzberg, H.J. 1989. *Mintzberg on Management: Inside our Strange World of Organizations*. New York: Free Press.

Mintzberg, H.J. 1979. *The Structuring of Organizations: A Synthesis of the Research*. Englewood Cliffs, NJ: Prentice-Hall.

Mintzberg, H.J., and J.B. Quinn. 1991. *The Strategy Process: Concepts, Contexts, Cases*, 2nd ed. Englewood Cliffs, NJ: Prentice-Hall.

Mitroff, I.A. 1974. *The Subjective Side of Science: A Philosophical Enquiry into the Psychology of the Apollo Moon Scientists*. New York: Elsevier.

Mizruchi, M.S., and L.B. Stearns. 1988. "A Longitudinal Study of the Formation of Interlocking Directorates", *Administrative Science Quarterly* 33(2): 194–210.

Mulford, C.L. 1984. *Interorganizational Relations: Implications for Community Development*. New York: Human Sciences Press.

Mulford, C.L., and D.L. Rogers. 1982. "Definitions and Models", in: *Interorganizational Coordination: Theory, Research and Implementation*, eds. D.L. Rogers, D.A. Whetten and Associates. Ames, IO: Iowa State University Press.

Mullen, P.M. 1991. "Which Internal Market: The NHS White Paper and Internal Markets", pp. 96–104 in: *Markets, Hierarchies and Networks: The Coordination of Social Life*, eds. G. Thompson, J. Frances, R. Levacic and J. Mitchell. London: Sage.

Murakami, Y. 1982. "Toward a Socioinstitutional Explanation of Japan's Economic Performance", pp. 39–40 in: *Policy and Trade Issues of the Japanese Economy: American and Japanese Perspectives*, ed. Y. Yamamura. Seattle: University of Washington Press.

Murray, C., and C.B. Cox. 1989. *Apollo: The Race to the Moon*. New York: Simon & Schuster.

Nuehring, E.M. 1978. "The Characteristics of Interorganizational Task Environments: Community Mental Health Centers and their Linkages", *Administration and Society* 9(4):425–446.

Okimoto, D.I. 1990. *Between MITI and the Market: Japanese Industrial Policy for High Technology*. Stanford, CA: Stanford University Press.

Ostrom, E. 1990. *Governing the Commons: The Evolution of Institutions for Collective Action*. New York: Cambridge University Press.

O'Toole, L.J., and R.S. Mountjoy. 1984. "Interorganizational Policy Implements: A Theoretical Perspective", *Public Administration Review* 44(6):491–503.

Ouchi, W.D. 1980. "Markets, Bureaucracies and Clans", *Administrative Science Quarterly* 25(1):129–141.

Oxford English Dictionary. 1971. New York: Oxford University Press.

Palumbo, D. 1987. "Implementation: What Have We Learned and Still Need to Know?" *Policy Studies Review* 7(1):91–102.

Patricios, N.N., Ed. 1986. *International Handbook on Land Use Planning*. Boulder, CO: Greenwood Press.

Paulson, S.K. 1977. "Interorganizational Strategies for Solving Organizational Problems: A Synthesis of Theory and Research on Health and Welfare Organizations", *Organization and Administrative Sciences* 8(1):63–76.

Paulson, S.K. 1974. "Causal Analysis of Interorganizational Relations: An Axiomatic Theory Revised", *Administrative Science Quarterly* 19(3):319–337.

Peres, S. 1970. *David's Sling*. London: Weidenfeld & Nicholson.

Pfeffer, J. 1982. *Organizations and Organization Theory*. Boston: Pitman.

Pfeffer, J. 1972. "Merger as a Response to Organizational Interdependence", *Administrative Science Quarterly* 17(3):383–394.

Pfeffer, J., and G.R. Salancik. 1978. *The External Control of Organizations: A Resource Dependence Perspective*. New York: Harper & Row.

Platt, R.H. 1991. *Land Use Control: Geography, Law and Public Policy*. Englewood Cliffs, NJ: Prentice-Hall.

Polivka, L., A.W. Imershein, J.W. White and L.S. Stivers. 1981. "Human Services Reorganization and Its Effects: A Preliminary Assessment of Florida's Services Integration Experiment", *Public Administration Review* 41(3):359–365.

Porter, D.O., and E.A. Olsen. 1976. "Some Critical Issues in Government Centralization and Decentralization", *Public Administration Review* 36(1):76–84.

Powell, W.W. 1990. "Neither Market Nor Hierarchy: Network Forms of Organization", pp. 295–336 in: *Research in Organizational Behavior*, Vol. 12, eds. B.M. Staw and L.L. Cummings.

Pressman, N., and A. Wildavsky. 1973. *Implementation*. Berkeley: University of California Press.

Provan, K.G., J.M. Beyer and C. Kruytbosch. 1980. "Environmental Linkages and Power in Resource-Dependence Relations Between Organizations", *Administrative Science Quarterly* 25(2):200–225.

Rabe, B.G. 1986. *Fragmentation and Integration in State Environmental Management*. Washington, DC: The Conservation Foundation.

Rabinowitz, F., J. Pressman and M. Rein. 1976. "Guidelines: A Plethora of Forms, Authors and Functions", *Policy Sciences* 7(4):399–416.

Raelin, J.A. 1982. "A Policy Output Model of Interorganizational Relations", *Organizational Studies* 3(3):243–267.

Raelin, J.A. 1980. "A Mandated Basis of Interorganizational Relations", *Human Relations* 33(1):23–39.

Rafter, D.O. 1992. "Hennepin County Light Rail Transit Plan", Planners' Casebook 4. Washington, DC: American Institute of Certified Planners.

Rapkin, C. 1979. "An Evaluation of the Urban Renewal Experience in the U.S.," pp. B.1–B.19 in: Appendix to *Research Report on Slum Rehabilitation and the Prevention of Neighborhood Deterioration in Israel*, eds. N. Carmon and M. Hill. Haifa: S. Neaman Institute for Advanced Studies in Science & Technology, Technion (Israel Institute for Technology).

Roberts, J.T. 1976. *General Improvement Areas*. Farnborough: Saxon House.

Roberts, N.C. 1991. "Towards a Synergistic Model of Power", pp. 105–121 in: *Shared Power: What Is It? How Does It Work? How Can We Make It Work Better?* eds. J.M. Bryson and R.C. Einsweiler. Lanham, MD: University Press of America.

Robins, J.A. 1987. "Organizational Economics: Notes on the Use of Transaction-Cost Theory in the Study of Organizations", *Administrative Science Quarterly* 32(1):68–86.

Roddewig, R.J., and C.A. Ingraham. 1987. TDRs and the Real Estate Marketplace: Planning Advisory Service Report #401. Chicago: American Planning Association.

Rodwin, L., and Associates. 1969. *Planning Urban Growth and Regional Development: The Experience of the Guyana Program of Venezuela*. Cambridge: MIT Press.

Rogers, D.L., and C.L. Mulford. 1982. "Consequences", pp. 73–94 in: *Interorganizational Coordination: Theory, Research and Implementation*, eds. D.L. Rogers, D.A. Whetten and Associates. Ames, IO: Iowa State University Press.

Rogers, D.L., D.A. Whetten and Associates. 1982. *Interorganizational Coordination: Theory, Research, and Implementation*. Ames, IA: Iowa University Press.

Rosenthal, S.R. 1984. "New Directions for Evaluating Intergovernmental Programs", *Public Administration Review* 44(6):469–476.

Ross, A.G. 1979. "The Emergence of Organization Sets in Three Ecumenical Disaster Recovery Organizations: An Empirical and Theoretical Exploration", *Human Relations* 33(1):23–39.

Rothblatt, D.N. 1971. *Regional Planning: The Appalachian Experience*. Lexington, MA: D.C. Heath.

Rubenstein, J. 1978. "French New Towns Policy", pp. 75–104 in: *International Urban Policies: New Town Contributions*, ed. G. Golany, New York: Wiley.

Rubin, H.J. 1984. "The Meshing Organization: A Catalyst for Municipal Coordination", *Administration and Society* 16(2):215–238.

Rubin, C.B., and D.G. Brabee. 1985. "Disaster Recovery Hazard Mitigation: The Intergovernmental Gap", *Public Administration Review* 45:57–63 (Special Issue).

Rummler, G.A. 1990. *Improving Performance*. San Francisco: Jossey-Bass.

Rustow, D.A., and J.F. Mugno. 1976. *OPEC: Success and Prospects*. London: Martin Robertson & Co.

Sabatier, P.A. 1988. "An Advocacy-Coalition Framework of Policy Change and the Role of Policy-Oriented Learning Therein", *Policy Sciences* 21(2–3):129–168.

Sachar, H.M. 1987. *A History of Israel*, Vol 2. Oxford: Oxford University Press.

Salerno, R., and J.S. Tompkins. 1969. *The Crime Confederation: Cosa Nostra and Allied Operations in Organized Crime*. Garden City, NY: Doubleday.

Sampson, M.W. III. 1983. *International Policy Coordination: Issues in OPEC and EACM*. Denver: Graduate School of International Studies, University of Denver.

Savas, E.S. 1982. *Privatizing the Public Sector: How to Shrink Government*. Chatham, NJ: Chatham House.

Scharpf, F.W. 1978. "Interorganizational Policy Studies: Issues, Concepts and Perspectives", pp. 345–370 in: *Interorganizational Policy Making: Limits to Coordination and Central Control*, eds. K. Hanf and F.W. Scharpf, Beverly Hills: Sage.

Scharpf, F.W., B. Reissert and F. Schnabel. 1978. "Policy Effectiveness and Conflict Avoidance in Intergovernmental Policy Formation", pp. 57–112 in: *Interorganizational Policy Making: Limits to Coordination and Central Control*, eds. K. Hanf and F.W. Scharpf, Beverly Hills: Sage.

Schleicher, H. 1986. "Building Coordination Structures", pp. 511–530 in: *Guidance, Control and Evaluation in the Public Sector: The Bielefeld Interdisciplinary Project*, eds. F.-X. Kaufmann, G. Majone and V. Ostrom, Berlin: De Gruyter.

Seidman, H. 1980. *Politics, Position and Power: The Dynamics of Federal Organization*, 3rd ed. New York: Oxford University Press.

Seymour, I. 1980. *OPEC: Instrument of Change*. London: Macmillan.

Sharpe, L.J. 1985. "Intergovernmental Policy-Making: The Limits of Subnational Autonomy", pp. 159–181 in: *Guidance, Control and Evaluation in the Public Sector: The Bielefeld Interdisciplinary Project*, eds. F.-X. Kaufmann, G. Majone and V. Ostrom, Berlin: De Gruyter.

Sink, D. 1985. "An Interorganizational Perspective on Local Emergency Management", *Policy Studies Review* 4(4):698–708.

Skelcher, C., B. Hinings, S. Leach and S. Ranson. 1983. "Centre-Local Linkages: The Impact of Policy Planning Systems", *Journal of Public Policy* 3(4):419–434.

Sofer, C. 1972. *Organizations in Theory and Practice*. New York: Basic Books.

Spekman, R.E. 1979. "Influence and Information: An Exploratory Investigation of the Boundary Role Person's Basis of Power", *Academy of Management Journal* 22(1):104–117.

Stern, R.N. 1979. "The Development of an Interorganizational Control Network: The Case of Intercollegiate Athletics", *Administrative Science Quarterly* 24(2):242–266.

Terreberry, S. 1968. "The Evolution of Organizational Environments", *Administrative Science Quarterly* 12(4):560–613.

Thompson, G., J. Frances, R. Levacic and J. Mitchell, Eds. 1991. *Markets, Hierarchies and Networks: The Coordination of Social Life*. London: Sage.

Thompson, J.D. 1967. *Organizations in Action*. New York: McGraw-Hill.

Thorelli, H.B. 1986. "Networks: Between Markets and Hierarchies", *Strategic Management Journal* 7(1):37–51.

Trist, E. 1983. "Referent Organizations and the Development of Interorganizational Domains", *Human Relations* 36(3):269–284.

Tucker, D.J. 1980. "Coordination and Citizen Participation", *Social Service Review* 54(1):13–30.

Tuite, M. F. 1972. "Toward a Theory of Joint Decision Making", pp. 1–8 in: *Interorganizational Decision Making*, eds. M. Tuite, R. Chisholm and M. Radnor. Chicago: Aldine.

Turner, A. 1978. "New Towns in the Developing World: Three Case Studies", pp. 249–276 in: *International Urban Policies: New Town Contributions*, ed. G. Golany, New York: Wiley.

Tushman, M. 1977. "Special Boundary Roles in the Innovation Process", *Administrative Science Quarterly* 22(4):587–605.

Van de Ven, A.L. Delbecq and R. Koenig Jr. 1976. "Determinants of Coordination Modes within Organizations", *American Sociological Review* 41:332–338.

Van de Ven, D.C. Emmett and R. Koenig, Jr. 1975. "Frameworks for Interorganizational Analysis", in: *Interorganizational Theory*, ed. A. Negandhi. Kent, OH: Kent State University Press.

Van de Ven, A.H., and G. Walker. 1984. "The Dynamics of Interorganizational Coordination", *Administrative Science Quarterly* 29(4):598–621.

Van de Ven, G. Walker and J. Liston. 1979. "Coordination Patterns within an Interorganizational Network", *Human Relations* 32(1):19–36.

Walton, R.E. 1972. "Interorganizational Decision Making and Identity Conflict", pp. 94–111 in: *Interorganizational Decision Making*, eds. M. Tuite, R. Chisholm and M. Radnor. Chicago: Aldine.

Wamsley, G.L. 1985. "Policy Subsystems as a Unit of Analysis in Implementation Studies: A Struggle for Theoretical Synthesis", pp. 71–96 in: *Policy Implementation in Federal and Unitary Systems*, eds. K. Hanf and T.A.J. Toonen. Dordrecht: M. Nijhoff.

Warren, R., S. Rose and A.F. Bergunder. 1974. *The Structure of Urban Reform*. Lexington, MA: D.C. Heath.

Weimer, D.L. 1992. "Claiming Races, Broiler Contracts, Heresthetics and Habits: Ten Concepts for Policy Analysis", *Policy Sciences* 25(2):135–159.

Weiss, J.A. 1989. "Pathways to Cooperation Among Public Agencies", *Journal of Policy Analysis and Management* 7(1):94–117.

Weiss, J.A. 1981. "Substance vs. Symbol in Administrative Reform: The Case of Human Services Coordination", *Policy Analysis* 7(1):21–45.

Whetten, D.A., and B. Bozeman. 1991. "Policy Coordination and Interorganizational Relations", pp. 77–104 in: *Shared Power: What Is It? How Does It Work? How Can We Make It Work Better?* eds. J.M. Bryson and R.C. Einsweiler. Lanham, MD: University Press of America.

White, P.E., S. Levine and G.J. Vlasak. 1975. "Exchange as a Conceptual Framework for Understanding Interorganizational Relationships", in: *Interorganizational Theory*, ed. A. Negandhi. Kent, OH: Kent State University Press.

Wildavsky, A. 1979. *Speaking Truth to Power: The Art and Craft of Policy Analysis.* Berkeley: University of California Press.

Williams, W.W. 1975. "Implementation Analysis and Assessment", *Policy Analysis* 1(3):531–566.

Williams, W.W. with B.J. Narver. 1980. *Government by Agency: Lessons from the Social Program Grants-In-Aid Experience.* New York: Academic Press.

Williamson, O.A. 1991. "Comparative Economic Organization: The Analysis of Discrete Structural Alternatives", *Administrative Science Quarterly* 36(2): 269–296.

Williamson, O.A. 1985. *The Economic Institutions of Capitalism.* New York: Free Press.

Williamson, O.A. 1981. "The Modern Corporation: Origins, Evolution, Attributes", *Journal of Economic Literature* 19(4):1537–1568.

Williamson, O.A. 1975. *Markets and Hierarchies.* New York: Free Press.

Williamson, O.A. 1971. "The Vertical Integration of Production: Market Failure Considerations", *American Economic Review* 61(2):112–123.

Wistrich, E. 1990. *After 1992: The United States of Europe.* London: Routledge.

Wren, D.A. 1967. "Interface and Interorganizational Coordination", *Academy of Management Journal* 10(1):69–82.

Wright, M., and S. Young. 1975. "Regional Planning in Britain", pp. 237–268 in: *Planning, Politics and Public Policy*, eds. J. Hayward and M. Watson. London: Cambridge University Press.

Wrong, D.H. 1979. *Power, Its Forms, Bases and Uses.* New York: Harper & Row.

Yandle, B. 1989. *The Political Limits of Environmental Regulation: Tracking the Unicorn.* New York: Quorum Books.

Yukl, G.A. 1989. *Leadership in Organizations*, 2nd ed. Englewood Cliffs, NJ: Prentice-Hall.

Zammuto, R.F. 1982. *Assessing Organizational Effectiveness: Systems Change, Adaptation and Strategy.* Albany, NY: SUNY Press.

Zank, N.S., and E.T. Jennings Jr. 1993. "Coordinating Public Assistance Programs in the U.S.", pp. 231–242 in: *Welfare System Reform: Coordinating Federal, State and Local Public Assistance Programs*, eds. E.T. Jennings and N.S. Zank. Westport, CT: Greenwood Press.

Zeitz, G. 1989. "Interorganizational Dialectics", *Administrative Science Quarterly* 25(1):72–88.

INDEX

A

AC Electronics (corporation) 181
Action set 27, 36, 43, 52, 53, 60, 61, 67–69, 274, 278, 289, 298, 306, 313, 316, 317, 324, 325, n.327
Adams, W.J. 230, 335
Adjustment 6, 21, n.22, n.23
mutual — *see* mutual adjustment
partisan mutual — *see* mutual adjustment
Administration for Children and Families (U.S.) 245
Adoption network n.77
Advanced Factories Program (U.K.) 130
Advocacy coalition 27, 43, 58, 60, 86, 90, 224, 319
Aemilia Romagna (Italy) 91, 214
Aerospace industry xvii, 63, 65, 66, 82, 154, 165, 179, 181, 206, 214, 217–220
AFL–CIO 108, 165, 214
Agency for Aging (U.S.) 103
Agreement/s xii, 18, 29, 37, 38, 39, 42, 53, 54, 59, 70, 96, 98, 102, 150, 165, 173, 191, 192, n.197, 200, 206, 207, 209, 210, 216, 218, 224, 225, 229, 247, 248, 259, 263, 286, 297, 320, 324
Agronoff, R. 138, 139, 176, 335
Aid to Families with Dependent Children (AFDC) (U.S.) 10, 178, 179
Aiken, M 42, 58, 89, 342
Airbus Industrie 14, n.76, 217–220
Air Force, U.S. 180

Air pollution 27, 138, 233–234, 236
Alabama (U.S.) 166, n.196
Alameda–Contra Costa County Transit District (AC) 95, 96, 97, 98
Aldrich, H. xix, 11, 20, 26, 27, 28, 61, 64, 119, 199, 285, 335
Alexander, C. n.294, 335
Alexander, E.R. xv, n.23, 37, 38, 40, 41, n.45, 51, 62, 63, 65, 66, n.78, 85, 104, n.112, 129, 130, n.151, n.152, 177, 183, 184, n.196, n.197, 244, 250, n.265, 287, n.294, n.295, n.327, 335, 336
Alexander, J.A. 154, 340
Algeria 210
Alliance/s xii, xiii, 30, 43, 58, 81, 86, 88, 106, 107, 108, 228, 277
Allied Chemicals 108
Allison, G.T. n.76, 336
Alter, C. 5, 6, 17, 18, n.23, 40, n.45, 62, n.77, 85, 86, 91, 92, n.111, n.113, 165, 199, 200, 201, 206, 217, 220, n.225, n.226, 253, n.294, 307, 308, 316, n.326, n.327, 329–331, 336
Alterman, R. 127, 129, n.151, n.152, n.196, 336, 337
Amateur Athletic Union (AAU) 159
American Federation of Labor–Congress of Industrial Organizations — *see* AFL–CIO
American Hospital Supply 206
American Telephone & Telegraph — *see* AT&T
Ames Research Center 180

Amouzegar, Jamshid xii

Anderson, M. n.112, 337

Apollo 13 mission xi

Apollo program x–xi, xii, n.xxii, 179, 180–183

Appalachian/s 166, 169
  Regional Commission (ARC) 154, 166–170, 176
  Regional Development Act (ARDA) 167

Appleyard, D. n.197, 337

Arab 144, 211

Area Redevelopment Administration (U.S.) 239

ARCO (Atlantic Richfield Corporation) 108

Ardagh, J. 230, 337

Argyris, C. 288, 337

Armstrong, Neil x, n.xxii, 183

Arnold, J.L. 51, 184, 337

Arnold, P. 88, 184, 337

Assistant Secretaries Working Group (U.S.) 259

Assistant Secretary for Community Development (U.S.) 261

Association/s 17, 29, 43, 54, 56, 62, 69, 84, 86, 87, 89, 107, 108, 171, 172, 200, 205, 213, 214, 224, 272, 277, 286, 298
  common resource pool — see common resource pool association
  kinship 41, 92
  mutual — see mutual association
  trade — see trade association
  voluntary — see voluntary association

Athletic/s 29, 159–164, 225, 253

Atomic Energy Commission (U.S.) 290

Australia n.196, 238–239

Authority/tative 5, n.22, 36, 38, 44, 54, 56, 57, 59, 60, 65, 66–68, 72, 75, n.76, 85, 86, 121, 124, 131, 133, 142, 144, 145, 147, 149–151, 155, 158, 167, 168, 170, 174, 176, 186, n.196, 224, 249, 253, 259, 262, 263, 277, 282, 284, 285, 288, 289, 292, 297, 303, 305, 310, 318–321, 323–325

Automobile
  industry 73, 74
  manufacturing xvii, 179, 206, 214, 220

Autonomy 159, 162, 251, 263, 297, 300
  organizational autonomy 65, 66, 149, n.151, n.152, 153, 174, n.196, n.197, n.265, 286
  network autonomy 306–308, 315–316, 325, n.326, 331

AVCO (corporation) 181

B

Baden–Württemberg (Germany) 214

Baghdad (Iraq) xii, 209

Baltimore, Maryland 138, 190–195
  City Health Department 194
  Department of Social Services 194
  Health Commissioner 191
  Housing and Community Development Commissioner 190
  Housing Authority 191
  Office of Employment Development 192
  Office of Manpower Resources 192
  Private Industry Council (PIC) 191
  Social Services Director 191

Bank/s 221–222, n.326

Banta, J. n.264, 337

Barclays Bank 205
Bargaining 5, n.22, 35, 37, 38, 39, 44, 57, 204, 229, 277, 320, 323
industry-wide 13, 32, 60
Bar Lev, Chaim (Israel Minister for Commerce & Industry) 144, 145
Barrett, S. 82, 337
Bars, B.A. 20, 128, 135, 137, 337
BART (San Francisco Bay Area Rapid Transit System) 95, 96, 97, 98, 99, 101
Baum, K.B. 20, 128, 135, 337
Beder, H. 37, 337
Begin, Israeli Prime Minister Menachem 122
Bennis, W. 288, 337
Ben Porat, Y. 87, 337
Benson, J.K. 7, 8, 337
Bergunder, A.F. 28, 62, 351
Berlin (Germany) 135, 136
"Big Ten" 229
Betancourt, Venezuelan President Romulo 185
administration 186
Blücher, Marshall ix
Board 41, 53, 64, 67, n.77, 104, 107, 121, 142, 155, 156, 159–161, 171, 173, 174, 192, 210, 218, 225, 259, 260, 262, 272, 279, 286, 319
advisory 67
membership, overlapping: 29, 37, 40, 41, n.45, 61, 64, 101–102, n.113, n.114, 278
Boeing Corporation xvii, 108, 206
Bolan, R. 51, n.264, 337
Bosselman, F. n.264, 337
Boundary-spanning/er 16, 29, 53, 64, 95, 117–121, 142, 150, 225, 228, 254, 273, 287–289, 298, 309, 311, 312, 315, 317, 319, 320
Bowen, E.R. xiii, xiv, 338
Bowman, J.R. n.226, 338

Bozeman, B. 48, 176, 351
Brabee, D.G. 349
Bradach, J.L. 54, 224, 338
Brager, G. 37, 38, 338
Branco, R.J. 230, 338
Brandl, J. 51, 338
Braybrooke, D. 57, 338
Brazil 230
Breyer, J.M. 9, 31, 156
Brickman, R. 47, 49, 338
Britain/ish x, xii, xviii, n.xxii, 9, 14, 27, 39, 65, 122, 130–133, 147–149, n.152, 183–185, 201, 205, 206, 217, 218, 230–232, 233, 254, 289–291, 300
British Aircraft Company (BAC) 217
British Petroleum (BP) 205, n.226
British Telecommunications (BT) 205
Broker/s 91, 225, 253, 300
Brooks, C.G. x, 182, 338
Bryson, J.M. 14, 338
Buchanan, J.M. 4, 227, 338
Budget/s/ing 65, 66, 70, 82, 122, 123, 124, 126, 128, 131, 153, n.196, 204, 237, 258, 275, 286
allocation 42, 44
displacement 126
joint 29, 42, 43
signoff 41, 48, 127, 278
Bulmer, S. n.226, 338
Bülow, General von ix
Burby, R.J. 239, 338
Bureau of Inland Revenue (U.K.) 60
Bureau of Land Management (U.S.) 55
Bureau/cracy/tic 17, 32, 41, 42, 50, 62, 65, 72, n.77, 82, 84, 89, 122, 128, 129, 135, 137, 142, 147, n.151, 174, n.196, 213, 224, 249, 258, 259, 261, 263, 288, 316, n.327

Burns, M. 11, 288, 338
Burt, R.S. 41, 62, 101, 338
Bush (U.S. President George)
　administration 135
Business/es 16, 20, 54, 57, 87, 93,
　n.112, 214, 233

C

Cable & Wireless (company) 205
Cairo (Egypt) 209
California 20, 28, 97, 140, 177, 233,
　234, n.265
　Coastal Development
　　Commission 166, n.196
　Department of Housing and
　　Community Development
　　((HCD) 177, 257
　Department of Transportation —
　　see Caltrans
　Housing and Development
　　Commission 177
　water resource associations 5, 59,
　　233
Callies, D. n.264, 337
Caltrans 257
Camagni, R. 74, 338
Cameron, K.S. 83, 338
Campbell, J.L. 73, 74, 85, 272, 339
Canada/ian 369
Cape Canaveral, Florida x, 182
Carmon, N. 127, n.151, 337, 339
Carney, M.G. 19, 33, 34, 201, 205,
　339
Caroni (Venezuela)
　Dam 185
　district 186
Cartel xii, xiii, 62, 63, 68, 70, 74,
　81, n.115, 195, 206, 207–213,
　225, n.226, 272
Carter, U.S. President Jimmy 108
　administration 107–109

Case/s 20, 22, 48, 49, 82–83, 91–92,
　93–95, 95–101, 102–106, n.112,
　120–121, 122–129, 130–133,
　133–135, 135–139, 140–141,
　142–144, 144–147, 147–149,
　n.151, n.152, 155–157, 157–158,
　159–164, 166–170, 170–174, 175,
　177, 178–179, 180–183, 185–190,
　190–194, n.196, n.197, 201–204,
　205, 207–213, 215–217, 217–220,
　221–224, 230–232, 233–235,
　237–239, 240–244, 245–248, 249,
　250–252, 255–256, 257, 258–263,
　273, 282, 283, 287, 288, n.294,
　n.295, 325, n.326, n.327
　management 48, 65, 105, 178,
　　192, 194, 246, 248, 264
　manager/s 143, 150, 192, 194;
　　general 143–144, 150
　work/er/s 21, n.76, 86, 91, 200,
　　246, 253
Categorical grant program/s 9,
　19, 38, 60, 138, 249, 259–260,
　261, 286
Cellular Radio Ltd. 205
Census Bureau (U.S.) 173
Center for Law in the Public
　Interest (CFLPI) 257
Century Freeway (Los Angeles,
　California) 177, 257
CETA 173, 177, 250
Chase, G. 19, 339
Chicago, Illinois 120–121, 159, 162,
　228
Child/children xvi, xvii, 9, 86,
　190, 249
　child-care programs 5, 192, 247
　handicapped children education
　　programs 263–264
　protection caseworkers n.76, 86,
　　91–92, n.113, 200, 224
　welfare organizations xvi, 91–92
Chisholm, D. 41, n.76, 95, 99, 101,
　105, 111, n.114, 339
Chivers, H. 207, 339

Chrysler Corporation 108, 179

City/ies 48, 50, 68–70, 81, 133, 135, 136, 172, 186, 189, 240, 242, 251, 257, 258, 260–262
central cities 21, n.112, 242, 258
city hall 258, 260, 262
inner cities n.51, 63, 241

Ciudad Guyana (Venezuela) 186, 188–189

Civil defense 64
agency 157–158

Clan/s 55, 56, 58, 81, 84, 86–87, 90

Clean Air Act of 1970 (U.S.) 233, 236
1977 Amendments 234

Cleveland, Ohio 180

Clinton (U.S. President) administration 52

Coalition/s 37, 38, 58, 86, 106, 107, 163, 172, 260, 272
see advocacy coalitions

Coastal Zone Management program (U.S.) n.196

Collaboration 6, n.23, 29, 37, 176, 204, 278

Collegium 58, 89

Collins Radio (corporation) 181

Colocation 20, 42, 43, 178, 179, 182, 247, 248, 280

Columbus, Ohio 138

Comisión de Estudios para la Electrificación del Caroni (CEEC) 185

Command 54, 84, 86, 277, 279, 297, 320–323

Commensal/ity 11, 19, 33–34

Commission/s 41, n.46, 64, 102, 104, 107, 121, 142, n.152, 171, 186, 225, 254, 286, 298, 313, 319
on Aging (Milwaukee, WI) 103, 104, n.114
see planning

Commitment 19, 86, 94, 129, 131, 195, 244, 259, 261, 286, 289–293, n.295, 303, 305, 324

Committee/s xvi, 4, 38, 43, 53, 64, 68, 89, 90, 109, 121, 129, 135–137, 139, 145, 159, 161, 163, 168, 180, 204, 209, 217, 220, 224, 225, 238, 240, 288
advisory 104, 241–242, 256, 257, 259, 262, 263
see congressional
see steering committee's

Common Market n.226

Common resource pool association/s 5–6, 59, 232–233, n.264

Communication/s 9, 29, 40, 41, 42, 44, 71, 94, 95, 107, n.151, 204, 247, 248, 256, 292, 314, 330

Community/ies 30, 56, 86, 88, 125, 183, 215, 216, 232, 247, 258
action agency/ies 126, 258, 259
center/s 21, 139
organizations 28, 47, 245, 246
see European Community

Community Development Block Grants (U.S.) 138, 172, 173, 190, 191, 249–250, 261

Community Education and Employment Act (U.S.) 138

Compagnie Francoise des Petroles n.226

Competition 11, 12, 14, 17, 33, 38, n.45, 51, 52, 73, 155, 159, 161, 163, 180, 217, 218, 220, 221, 229, 231, 232, 234, 235, 273

Complex/ity xv, xvi, 20, 22, 52, n.113, 117, 127, 150, 161, 179, 182, 183, 188, 190, n.196, 200, 201, 250–254, 257, 261, 271, 274, 283, 306–308, 310–312, 313–315, 317, 321, n.327, 331, 333

Comprehensive Employment and Training Act (U.S.) — see CETA

Concord, California 206

Concorde 14, 217–220

Conference of Appalachian
  Governors (CAG) 166

Conflict/s 6, 20, 37, 58, 122, 136,
  137, 139, 212, 260, n.327
  domain 20, 22, 125

Conglomerate 12, 30, 50, 53, 91,
  206, 207, 220, 233, 275, 298

Congress/ional (U.S.) x, 68, 109,
  167, 168, 180, 234, 258, 260
  committees xviii, 50, 62, 107, 109,
    224
  hearings 62, 107
  Research Service n.265, 339

Consensus 16, 29, 37, 55, 58, 59,
  83, 89, 99, 136, 139, 165, 213,
  243, 244
  see domain

Consortium/ia xx, 11, 12, 30, 34,
  43, 51, 62, 63, n.76, 90, 181, 185,
  201, 204–206, 225, n.226, 277,
  279, 315

Consultation 42, 278

Consultants xvii, xviii, 13, 104,
  134, 149, 181, n.196, n.197

Contingency 300
  theory 7, 10–12, 14, 21, n.23, 270,
    272

Contract/s/ing xviii, 12, 13, n.23,
  31, 32, 36, 38, 40, 41, 42, 44, 48,
  70, 73, n.77, 103, 105, 120, 150,
  163, 165, 172, 179, 181, n.196,
  200, 211, 225, 228, 229, 247, 248,
  275, 277–279, 287, 297, 298, 316,
  331
  cooperative 229–230
  municipal services 14, 39,
    228–229
  relational 13, 32, 39, 60, 229

Contractor/s xvii, 13, 54, 177, 229
  defense xviii, 13, 230
  main xvii, 63
  prime- and sub- x, 150, 165, 181,
    214, 307

Control 4, 6, 7, 9, 10, 12, 18, 21, 32,
  42, 44, 50, 54, 59, 60, 61, 72, 73,
  84, 86, 91, 94, 155, 163, 164, 172,
  176, 177, n.197, 213, n.226, 230,
  271, 275, 277–279, 285, 288,
  n.294, 316, 320, 322–324
  central/ized 39, 41, 52, 191
  fiscal 44, 153
  flight 181, 182
  Mission 181–183
  strategies 36, 39

Cooper, L. 42, 43, 343

Cooperation 6, 11, 14, 17, 22, 36,
  39, 44, n.45, 54, 62, 63, 68,
  n.113, 165, 200, 217, 247, 275,
  298
  intergovernmental 188, 189,
    238–239

Cooperative/s 5, 18, 74, 94, 206,
  221, 233
  see strategy

Cooptation 37, 44, n.45, 277

Coordinating unit 32, 53, 63,
  65–66, 72, n.77, 117, 127, 128,
  138, n.152, 153–177, 190, 195,
  n.195, n.196, n.197, 213, 220,
  225, 228, 236, 240, 243, 245, 248,
  252, 254, 255, 257, 262–264,
  n.265, 282–288, 298, 301, 305,
  306, 310–313, 316, 317, 320, 321,
  324
  area 165–174
  functional–sectoral 157–165

Coordination
  adaptive 44, 323
  administrative 40, n.226, 322–323
  anticipatory 36, 42, 44, 323–325
  central 54, 262
  central–local 125, 129
  costs 13, 16, 18
  failure xi, n.196
  horizontal 38, 125, 129, 133,
    250–252, 262, 263
  informal 41, 44, 101, 110–111
  local-level 38, 247

market/-like 14, 57, 60
mechanisms xvii, 31, 33, 40, 41,
    44, 47, 49, 54
nightmare xi, 32
non-hierarchical 110–111
operational 248, 263, 319–322,
    n.327
preconditions 15–21
see definitions
see hierarchy
see strategies
see structures
see tools
systems — see IOC
task coordination — see IOC
vertical 125, 133, 250, 262
voluntary 8, 12, 21, 29
Coordinator 31, 49, 53, 64, 65–66,
    91, 95, 117, 123, 127, 142–151,
    175, 225, 248, 252, 253, 255, 258,
    263, 264, 277, 279, 284, 287–289
Coordinator of Government
    Activities in the Galillee (Israel)
    65, 144–147
Corbett, T.J. 179, 339
Corden, C. 291, 339
CORDIPLAN 189
Corning Glass (Corporation)
    n.111, n.112
Corporate/ion/s xvi, xvii–xix, xx,
    7, 10, 13, n.23, 30, 32, 33, 50, 51,
    53, 62, 63, 67, 68, 69, 73, 82, 88,
    90, 107, 108, 121, 140, 154, 155,
    156, 165, 184, 187, 204, 214,
    220–223, 225, 233, 234
    holding companies 50, 154, 220,
        221, 230
    law 13, 32, 60, 85
    oil 207–212
    see mergers
    structure 33, 37
    system 30, 43, 62
Corporación Venezolana de Fomento
    (CVF) 185

Corporación Venezolana de Guyana
    (CVG) 185–190, 195
Cost/s xvi, 11, 12, 18, n.78, 123,
    128, 169, 191, 218, 219, 229,
    231–233, 243, 244, 251, n.264,
    288, 310
    containment/control 12, 106
    coordination costs 13, 16, 18, 22
    organizational/political costs 38,
        127, 288–290
    transaction — see transaction
        cost/s
Council/s 150, 159, 160, 254, 259,
    263
    Group Presidents' Council, 222
    of Governments 138, 225
    of Presidents 225
County/ies 170–173
Cox, C.B. xi, n.xxii, 180, 182, 347
Crevoisier, O. 74, 91, 339
Crisis xix, xx, 20, n.76, 82, 110, 111,
    122, 157, 182, 194. 211, 289, 303,
    305
Cross, N. 294, 339
Crozier, M. 288, 339
Culture/al 28, 88, 200, n.294
    American 17, 74
    Japanese 17, 74
    norms 16, 87
    organizational 16, 22, 28, 213
    shared 54, 90, 111, 166, 314, 318

D

Dai-Ichi Kangyo (corporation) 221
Danielson, A.L. 209, 212, n.226, 339
Data 18, 64, 171, 172, 201, 221,
    n.226, 248, 282
Day care program, Title XX (U.S.)
    191, 192
Dayton, Ohio 138
De Beers (corporation) 206

Decentralized/ation 125, 128, 170, n.265, 289

Decision/s xiii–xv, 3, 6, 8, 12, 21, n.23, 29, 30, 35, 37, 42, 48, 56, 58, 60, 64, 70, 83, 89, 93, 121, 125, 127, 128, 147, 149, 163, 180, 213, n.226, 249, 270, 297, 299
  center/s 49, 53, 117
  concerted 6, 56, 62, 64, 67, 82
  coordinated 3, 4, 5, 21, 57, 59, 153, 272
  location xv, 9
  makers/ing 19, 41, 71, 120, 168, 169, 261, 273, n.295
  organizations' 21, 44, 59
  rules 3, 4, 57, 59

Defense xvii, 160, 230
  contractors xviii, 13
  see civil defense
  see Defense Department

Definition/s n.22, 41, n.75
  of collaboration 6, n.23
  of coordination/IOC 3–7, 12, 14, 21, n.23, 67, 269–271

DeHoog, R.H. 14, 38, 39, 229, 339

Delbecq, A.L. n.327, 351

Demonstration Cities and Metropolitan Development Act (U.S.) 258

Demonstration City Agency/ies (DCA) 259–263

Den Bosch (Netherlands) 133

Department
  of Defense (U.S.) 86
  of Economic Affairs (U.K.) 130
  of Employment (U.K.) 131
  of Energy (U.S.) 108
  of Health and Human Services (U.S.) — see DHHS
  of Health, Education and Welfare (HEW) (U.S.) 185, 259
  of Housing and Urban Development (U.S.) — see DHUD

  of Justice (U.S.) 259
  of Labor (U.S.) 154, 177, 245, 258
  of Trade and Industry (U.K.) 131
  of Trade, Industry and Regional Development (U.K.) 130, 131
  of Transportation (U.S.) 257, n.265
  of the Environment (U.K.) 131, 148, 254
  of the Interior (U.S.) 108

Deputy Prime Minister (Israel) 123, 126, 145

Derthick, M. 61, 65, 121, 170, 184, n.196, 339

Design 49, 283, n.294, 299
  see institutional design

Deutsch, C.W. 6, 344

Deutsche Airbus 307

Deutscher Gewerkschaftenbund 214

DHHS (U.S.Dept.of Health and Human Services) 26, 103, 245

DHUD (U.S.Dept. of Housing and Urban Development) 108, 129, 172, 176, 184, n.196, 250, 258–263, 290

Director/ate/s n.46, 63, 73, 102, 121, 138, 155, 168, 173, 221, 225, 259, n.265, 272
  interlocking 103, 221, 228

District Commissioner (Israel) 211

District Committee for Planning and Building (Israel) 65, 146, 147, n.152, n.196

District Planning Bureau (Israel) 146, n.152

Domain 62, 63, 118, 135, 136, 138, 158, 165, 273, 278, 279, 312, 314, 331
  consensus 8, 20, 22, 139
  organizations' 38, 42, 274
  see policy domain

Dommeldal (Netherlands) 133–135

Donahue, J.D. xix, 228, 339

Douglas (corporation) 181

Duncan, R.B. 82, 339
Dunkerly, D. 9, 340
Dunshire, A. 271, 340
Durant, R.F. 55, 340

E

Eastern Kentucky Regional
  Planning Commission 238
Eccles, R.G. 54, 224, 338
Ecology/ical 11, 58, 88, n.196
  concepts 19, 33
  niche xx, 10, 11
  see organizational
Economic Empowerment Task
  Force (U.S.) 257–258
Economy/ic/s xx, 7, 12, 21, 28, 33,
  89, 94, n.115, 210, 227, 240, 258,
  260, n.264
  environment 4, 290
  market/s 4, 13, 57, 84, 297, 299
  objectives 200, 206
  sector/s 33, 51, 73, 272
Education/al xix, 14, 17, 48, 58,
  82, 88, 135, 138, 164–165, 188,
  189, 225, 239, 240, 245–248, 249,
  260, 264, n.264
  adult education 192, 246
  background 17, 54, 89, 111
  Educational Service Agencies
    (ESAs) 164–165
  vocational education 244, 245,
    248
Edwards High Speed Flight
  Station 180
Effectiveness xix, xx, 19, 27, 40, 83,
  92, 95, 131, 133, 146, 149, 158,
  164, 168, n.196, n.197, 243, 244,
  256, 260, 264, n.265, 269,
  280–284, n.295, 304, 305, 311,
  317, 322, 323, 325
Eichenberg, T. 244, 345
Eindhoven (Netherlands) 133

Eisenhower, General Dwight D.
  n.xxii
Eisenstadt, S. 285
Elderly 38, 103–105
Elmore, R.F. 40, 340
Emergency management 226
Emmett, D.C. xvi, 30, 351
Emmission/s rights, tradeable 26
Employment 26, 234, 244, 245, 248
  and training xiii, 138, 154, 177,
    194, 215, 245–247, 260
  and Training Administration
    (U.S.) 153, 250
  Employment Service (State) 246,
    247
Energy 211
  policy 106, 107–109, 200
England 130
Entrepreneur/s/ial 93–95, 111, 225
Environment/al xvii, 3, 4, 9, 11,
  21, 26, 28, 30, 40, 51, 57, 58, 62,
  67, 71, 88, 90, 119, 141, 148, 194,
  257
  management 82, 255–256
  organizational environment 4, 6,
    7, 10–12, 16, 19, 22, n.22, 26,
    34, 51, 57, 82, 83, 94, 108, 110,
    118, 119, 158, 175, 184, 200,
    205, 260, 270, 271, 273, 274,
    278, 284, 288, 300, 303,
    304–309, 315, 316, 325, 331–333
  protection xvi, 135
  regulation/s 51, 59, 60, 66,
    233–235, 236, 255–256
  turbulent xiv, 47, 82, 92, 101, 110,
    189, 274, 281
  uncertain/ty 47, 74, 82, 101, 110,
    189, 274, 288
Environmental Control Procedures Act (Washington State)
  256
Environmental Policy Institute 108
Environmental Protection Agency
  (EPA) (U.S.) 62, 234–235, 236,
  255

Environmental Quality Protection
   Act (New York State) 256
Equador 210
Erdström, A. 34, 40, 340
Établissement Public d'Amenagement
   184
Europe/an 58, n.76, 109, n.112,
   244, 254
European Community (EC) xix,
   88, n.226
European Union (EU) n.226
Evaluation xx, 27, 42, 44, n.76,
   82–83, 104, n.112, 121, 127, 139,
   149, n.152, 168, 175, 194, 229,
   280–282, n.295
Evan, W.M. xix, 26, 30, 62, 340
Exchange 4, 5, 13, n.23, 31, 35, 37,
   38, 42, 44, 54, 55, 58, 60, 67, 72,
   73, n.76, 155, 236, 271, 297–299,
   303, 315, n.326
   market/-like 13, 30, 43, 54, 57,
   59, 70, 84, 227–228
   see resource exchange
   Exchange Theory 7–10, 12, 14,
   21, n.23, 35, 71, n.76, 164, 270,
   272, 332
Expectations xviii, 6, 36, 216, 231,
   261, 291, 292, 305, 318
Expert/ise xvii, xix, 8, 13, 17, 29,
   58, 89, 172, 176, 205, 229, 254,
   256, 330
Exxon (oil corporation) n.226

F

Factors xx, 4, 7, 11, 22, 33, 48, 49,
   58, n.294, 312, 325
   affecting governance regime
   73–75
   contextual xx, 15, 16, 21, 304, 325
   enabling IOC 15–21, 273–274
   interpretive 15, 16
   limiting IOC 15–21

Falk, v.d., A. 340
Faludi, A. 129, n.152, 244, n.265,
   n.327, 336, 340
Family 27, 50, 54, 56, 58, 69, 84, 85,
   86–87, 90, 135, 194
   business/es 54, 90, 221
   development center 190–195
   Family Services Unit 194
   Family Social Services 85, 253
   Family Support Act (U.S.) 341
   planning services 194, 244
Farley, D. 143, 340
Farnham Co., Maryland 85,
   215–217
   Alliance for the Mentally Ill
   (AMI) 215–216
   Community Mental Health
   Center 215–216
Federal 38, 65, 66, 86, 129, 141,
   142, 166, 167, 236, 245, 249, 255,
   257–263
   agencies xiv, 67, 68, 158, 167–169
   Federal Communications
   Commission (FCC) 235
   federal department/s — *see*
   specific names
   Federal Emergency Management
   Agency (FEMA) 157
   Federal Highway Agency
   (FHWA) 257
   Federal Housing Authority
   (FHA) 184
   Federal Interagency Regional
   Councils 121, 129
   Federal Land Development
   Authority (Malaysia) 184
   Federal Ministry for Research
   and Technology (BMFT)
   (Germany) 203, 204
   Federal Regional Councils 129
   National Mortgage Agency
   (FNMA) 184
   programs xiii, 60, 290–291
   see Veterans Administration

Federation/s 11, 29, 30, 43, 53, 70, n.76, 81, 200, 201, 206, 209, 253, 277, 279
  "peak" federations 213
  trades union 30, 165
Federation of Homebuilders 137
Fennell, M.L. 11, 154, 214, 227, 340
Fiat (corporation) 206
Fiedler J. 20, 128, 135, 337
Financial Basin Agencies (France) 254
First Arab Petroleum Congress 294–295
Fit xxi, 10, 11, 175, 176, n.226, 282–284, 287, 294, n.294, 304, 309, 311, 314, 315, 317, 319–325
Florida 142, 263
Food Stamps (U.S. program) 340
Ford (U.S. President Gerald) administration 365
Ford Foundation 254
Ford Motors (corporation) 206
Framework/s
  conceptual 71, 275
  consensual 59, 85
  market-like 5, 38, 39, n.45, 53, 59
  see mandated framework
  solidarity 56, 57–58
France/French xviii, n.xxii, 14, 184, 217, 218, 254
Frankfurt 393
Franz, H.J. 37, 214, 340
Freeman, J. 11, n.76, 341, 342
Freeway — see highway
Freidson, E. 89, 341
Frieden, B.J. xix, 39, 129, 158, 185, n.265, 341
Friend, J. 141, 341
Frisken, F. 244, 341
Fudge, C. 82, 337
Fuji (corporation) 206, 221
Fulton Co., Maryland 85

Fund/s/ing xviii, 5, 8, 9, 10, 17, 19, 32, 38, 42, 69, 87, 89, 90, 92, 96, 103, 104, 158, 120, 123–125, 153–156, 161, 164, 167, 169, 173, 174, 191, 194, 203, 204, 216, 229, 237, 239, 244–251, 257–259, 261–263, 303, 316, 318, 321, 330
  agency/ies 67, 68, n.326

G

Gabon 210
Gage, R.W. 122, 341
Galbraith, J.R. xvii, 10, 50, 51, 60, 341
Galillee (Israel) 65, 144–147, n.152
Galveston, Texas 234
Gans, H.J. n.112, 341
Gansler, J.S. 230, 341
Gargan, J.A. 89, 341
Garlichs, B. 41, 244, 341
Garrett Corporation 181
Gerlach, M.L. 221, 223, 341
Gemini program n.xxii
General Accounting Office (U.S.) n.45
General Dynamics (corporation) 181
General Electric (corporation) 181
General Improvement Area/s program (U.K.) 27, 65, 147–149, n.152
General Motors 108, 206
General Revenue Sharing (U.S.) 35, 138
Geological Survey (U.S.) 237
Georgia (U.S.) n.196
German/y 20, 35, 37, 41, n.78, 204, 206, 218, 224, 244, 250–252, 254, n.265
  German Manufacturers' Association 214
Giddens, A. n.45, 69, 71, n.77, 341

Gillespie, D.F. 20, 341
Glenn, John (astronaut) 180
Gneisenau, General August
 Wilhelm v, n.xxii
Goal/s 5, 6, n.23, 29, 36, 48, 49, 59,
 68, n.77, 101, 131, 136, 141, 168,
 176, 200, 217, 239, 252, 258, 292,
 293, n.295, 303, 333
 acheivement 83, 194, n.197, 252
 common/mutual/shared 19, 27,
  54, 57, 87, 111, 157, 219, 244,
  272, 274, 289, 292, 317, 318,
  323
 program 10, 261
Goggin, M.L. 236, 244, 342
Golden Gate (transit system) 95,
 97, 98
Gomez-Ibanez, J.A. 232, 342
Gottfredson, L.S. 42, 342
Governance 13, 58, 104, 150, 161,
 163, n.195, 200, 282
 bilateral 13, 32, 60
 regimes 73–74, 272
Governor/s n.151, 166, 168, 263
Government/s xiii, xvi, 13, 17, 21,
 35, 50, 57, 66, 69, 72, 89, 90,
 102, 106, 107, 109, 121–123, 126,
 130, 131, 134, 144, 145, 147, 149,
 157, 158, 166, 177, 184, 205,
 208–210, 212, 213, 225, n.226,
 227, 228, 230, 231, 237, 255,
 290, 300
 bureaus 8, 164
 central 35, 38, 121, 122, 124, 125,
  129, 132, 148, 157, 298
 Labour (party, U.K.) 189
 see federal government
 see local government
 see state government
Grandori, A. 7, 10, n.23, 28, n.45,
 47, 54, n.76, 342
Grant/s 35, 42, 97, 120, 130, 167,
 169, 216, 249, 251, 258, 260, 262,
 290
 see categorical grant programs

Gray, B. 6, n.23, 342
Great Britain — see Britain
Greenbelt Towns Program (U.S.)
 184, 290–291
Grimwood, J.M. x, 182, 338
Grumman Aircraft (corporation)
 181
Group/s n.23, 29, 39, 40, 88,
 137, 271
 interagency 135
 intergovernmental 195
 see interorganizational
 steering 130, 133, 134
 work/ing 58, 131, 135, 141, 259
Gulf Oil (Corporation) 108, n.226
Guri Dam (Venezuela) 267
Gurupu 310
Guyana (region, Venezuela)
 185–190

H

Haar, C.M. n.265, 342
Hage, J. xvi, 5, 6, 17, 18, n.23, 38,
 40, 42, n.45, 58, 62, n.77, 85, 86,
 89, 91, 92, n.111, n.113, 165, 199,
 200, 201, 204, 227, 220, n.225,
 n.226, 253, n.294, 307, 308, 316,
 n.326, n.327, 329–331, 336, 342
Hall, R.A. 6, 8, n.23, 62, 102, 271,
 n.294, 342
Halpert, B.P. n.23, 342
Handmer, J.W. 239, 346
Hannan, M. 11, 342
Hansen, N.M. n.196, 342
Harbin, G. 263, 342
Hardin, G. n.264, 342
Harris, L.A. 194, 342
Harrison, B. 91, 343
Head Start program (U.S.) 191, 249

Health 48, 60, 65, 103, 106, 194, 229, 240
  care system (U.S.) 17, 38, 52, 58
  Health Management Organization (HMO) 154, 214
  policy 106, 109, 200
  see mental health
  services xx, 9, 11, 19, 21, 28, 29, 154, 206, 214, 227, n.264
  U.S. Department of Health and Human Services — *see* DHHS
Heclo, H. 65, 122, 343
Hegner, F. 30, 55, 56, 58, 343
Hennepin County, Minnesota 240–244, 253
  Downtown Advisory Committee 242
  Intergovernmental Advisory Committee (IAC) 241, 243
  Regional Railroad Authority (HCRRA) 240, 241, 243
Herbert, M. 183, 343
Herker, D. 119, 335
Hierarchy/ical n.23, 30, 35, 36, 43, n.45, 49, 53, 54, 55, 56, 57, 58, 60, 62, 65, 72, 74, n.76, 88, n.113, n.114, 131, 135, 137, n.151, n.152, 161, 165, 184, 195, 199, 200, 206, 224, 225, n.225, 228, 235, 243, 275, 277, 284, 285, 297, 298, 301, 302, n.326
  control 52, 91, 288
  coordination 32, 81, 106, 110, 216, 270
  coordination/IOC structures 22, 33, 64, 72, 84, 85, 92, 117, 222, n.225
  linkages 62, n.77, 84, 85, n.113, 150, 235
  organization 12, 13, 14, 22, n.23, 29, 30, 43, 50, 72, 73, 90, 94
  see network
Highway planning and construction 41, 64, 167, 244

Hill, M. 127, n.151, 337
Hjern, B. xix, 27, 61, 214, 244, 343
Hoechst (corporation) 204
Hoffman, C. n.151, 343
Högberg, B. 34, 40, 340
Holding company 50
Holloway, S. 37, 38, 338
Honadle, G. 42, 43, 343
Honeywell Corporation 181
Hopkins, K.R. 129, 343
Hospice care 85, 253
Hospital/s xx, 11, 12, 19, 28, 29, 48, 51, 57, 85, 103, 104, 135, 154, 184, 206, 214–216, 228, 249, 275
House of Commons Expenditures Committee n.152
Household/s xv, 4, 10, 57, 59, 84, 109, 127, 232, 237
Housing xvi, xx, 64, 90, 124, 126, 135, 189, 190, 191, 250, 260, 289–291
  -home finance coalition 86
  policy 86, 189
  public housing 148, 190
Housing Act of 1969 (U.K.) 148
Housing and Community Development Act of 1974 (U.S.) 261
Houston, Texas ix, n.xxii, 181, 183
Howe, E. 19, 20, 343
HTS Committee (German) 204
Hughes Aircraft (corporation) 181
Hull, C. 41, 244, 341
Hult, K.M. 39, 61, 185, n.195, 343
Human Resources Council (Pueblo, NM) 138
Human services 38, 39, 40, 49, 58, 64, 65, 66, 82, 89, 102–106, 138, 214, 225, 29, 240
Huntingdon, S. 285, 343
Huntsville, Alabama 182
  Marshall Space Flight Center, NASA 3
Hyde, Floyd 259, 261

I

IBM xix, 26

ICC 122, 123–129
  Budget Committee 180

Ideology/ical 30, 43, 122, 290, 305
  common/shared 37, 54, 58, 87,
    88, 91, 157

Ilchman, W.F. 5, 57, 227, 343

Illinois (U.S.) 170, 255–256
  Illinois Department of
    Transportation 172
  Illinois Environmental Protection
    Agency (IEPA) 255, 256
  Illinois Pollution Control Board
    (IPCB) 255

Implementation xiii, xiv, xv, xix,
    17, 44, 48, 49, 52, 55, 61, 62, 82,
    99, n.112, 123–128, 132–134,
    136, 142, 147, 149, 170, 171, 173,
    176, 179, 186, 188, 191, 229, 230,
    234, 238, 239, 244, 252, 256, 259,
    261, 263, n.265, 289, 320–322,
    324
  program 9, 60, 256, 258, 263
  set xix, 27, 43, 52, 53, 61, 68, 214,
    225, 236, 244, 278, 298, 304,
    306–308, 315, 316

Incentive/s 9, 10, 19, 32, 35, 37, 38,
    42, 44, 59, 60, 89, 93, 94, 132,
    147, 155, 159, 187, 207, 218, 219,
    236–239, 249–253, 262, 274, 277,
    278, 280, 290, 324, 325

Income tax (U.S.) — see tax

Individual/ism xx, 5, 17, 29, 49,
    52, 57, 65, 70, 86, 99, 110, 111,
    221, 235, 248, 254, 287, 292

Indonesia 210

Industry/ial xvi, xx, 5, 9, 11, 13,
    28, 31–34, 55, 65, 74, 130, 140,
    185, 187–189, 201, 204, 206, 214,
    219, 221, 223, 272
  computer 26, 33, 93
  garment 93, 301

petrochemical refining industry
    32, 184
  see aerospace industry
  see automobile industry
  see oil industry
  -wide bargaining 37, 61

Industrial Development
    Certificates (U.K.) 130

Industrial Telecommunications
    Supply Association (U.K.) 201

Informal linkages n.45, 53, 62, 64,
    n.77, 86, 89, 90, 91–115, n.113,
    n.114, 117, 121, 220, 224, n.225,
    275, 277, 278, 287, 298, 305, 314

Information 4, 5, 12, 17, 18, 29, 33,
    41, 60, 70, 72, 83, 84, 92, 94,
    102, n.112, 119, 120, 121, 122,
    127, 134, 135, 136, 156 172, 176,
    178, 200, 210, 213, 229, 235, 248,
    250, 270, 272, 299, 300
  -based strategies 36, 37
  exchange 17, 25, 63, 85, 89, 92,
    94, 141, 149, 150, 201, 204,
    227, 254, 278, 282, 284, 301,
    302, 318–320, 322–325
  sharing 42, 44, 64

Infrastructure xiii, xvii, xviii, 9, 10,
    124, 126, 132, 134, 148, 165, 170,
    187, 211, 244, 260
  planning and construction 64,
    82, 186, 240

Ingraham, C.J. 5, 349

Innovation/s xix, xx, 16, 26, 90,
    91, 94, 136, 181, 182, 291

Institute of Environmental Quality
    256

Institution/s xiv, xvi, 10, 30, 51,
    119, n.226, 247, 250, 262, 285,
    293, 323
  financial 86, 118, 221–222

Institutional/ization 12, 13, 14, 16,
    35, 49, 55, 91, 117, n.152, 195,
    205, 275, 277, 285–293, n.294,
    n.295

institutional design xxi, 51–52,
57, 59, 64, 75, 85, 86, 125, 175,
228, 230, 232, 235, 253, 283,
293, 301, 303, 305, 309, 313,
321, 323, 325
Integration n.45, 135, 205
hierarchical 94, 165, 228
horizontal and/or vertical 13,
32, 39, 43, 73, 74, 184
operational 94–95
see task
strategic 94–95
Interaction/s xiii, xxi, 7, 16, 21,
n.23, 30, 31, 32, 40, n.45, 52, 54,
60, 62, 69, 90, 94, 95, 106, 107,
108, 119, 120, 134, 149, n.151,
170, 224, 235, 236, 256, 263,
272, 273
dyadic 100, 170, 174
informal n.22, 31, 88, 216
interorganizational 8, 11, 19–21,
29, 35, 49, 56, 57, 64, 68, 72,
n.76, 82, 121, 225, 244, 274,
278, 279, 285
market 60, 70, 109
potential, organizations' 16,
19–21
reciprocal 58, 71, 318
voluntary 37, 44
Interagency Federal Regional
Councils (U.S.) 65
Interdependence/ies/nt xvi, xx, 6,
7, 8, 11, 13, 19, 22, 25, 27, 28,
29, 31–36, 42, 43, n.45, 52, 56,
61, 62, 64, 68, 69, 70, 71, 72, 75,
82, 93, 95–97, 99, 105, 106, 170,
175, 140, 141, 163, 165, 190,
n.264, 271–274, 278, 301–302,
306, 309–310, 311, 313, 321,
325, n.326, 329–330
behavior 35, 44
commensal 19, 33–35, 44, 69, 184,
232, 274, 313
competitive 33–34, 44, 184

formative 34, 44
mutual 21, 35, 69, 111, 149, 170,
171, 213
operating 35, 44, 95, 96, 98
outcome xvi, 34, 43
pooled 33–35, 44, 69, 302, 308,
310, 313
reciprocal 32–35, 44, 69, 105, 111,
149, 302, 307, 309–310, 321
sequential 31–35, 44, 69, 111, 302,
307, 309, 312, 317, 321
serial 31–32
symbiotic 19, 33–34, 44, 69, 184,
214, 217, 220, 221, 274, 313
Interest/s n.xxii, 35, 36, 38, 72,
n.78, 89, 106, 111, 134, 137,
n.152, 162, 168, 170, n.196, 207,
211, 213, 237, 244, 262, 291, 301
groups 39, 57, 162, 165, 227, 254
mutual/shared xiv, 29, 59, 62, 63,
68, 135, 140, 170, 200, 201,
243, 259, 318
organizations xvi, 88, 156, 308
vested 18, 22, 38
Interministerial Committee for the
Development of the Galillee
(Israel) 144
Interministerial Coordinating
Committee (Israel) — see ICC
International Aero Engines 206
International City Management
Association 137
International Committee for the
Evaluation of Project Renewal
n.151, 343
Interorganizational
coordination — see IOC
field/s xx, 25, 28–30, 31, 35, 43,
47, 48, 105, 170, 275, 277–279
group/s — see
interorganizational group
see agreements
see interactions

see linkages
see network/s
set 329–333
structures — *see* IOC
system/s 5, 13, 14, n.23, 27, 28,
    40, 49, 50–53, 54, 58, 65, 66,
    67, 68, 72, 74, 75, 82–86, 88,
    92, 93, 96, 110, 111, 117, 121,
    142, 150, 153, 183–184, 275,
    n.326
Interorganizational group 53,
    64–65, 66, 70, n.77, 85, 95, 99,
    103, 117, 121–142, 149, n.151,
    n.152, 153, 171, 175, 180, 194,
    n.195, n.196, 204, 213, 225, 228,
    240, 245, 248, 252–254, 256–258,
    262–264, n.265, 277–279, 283,
    285–287, 289, 290
International Aero Engines
    (corporation) 290
International Business Machines
    — *see* IBM
Interstate Regional Commission/s
    (U.S.) 106, 142
IOC — Interorganizational
    coordination
costs 18, 22
preconditions 15–22, n.23
see definitions
see mandated frameworks
see strategy/ies
see theory/ies
see tools
structures xiv, xxi, 3, 5, 10, 12,
    14, 20, 21, n.23, 30, 34–36,
    n.45, 49, 50–67, 70–72, 75,
    n.75, n.76, 81–264, 271–275,
    277–279, 280–295, 297–327;
    see hierarchical; *see* mandated
task/s 318–325
systems 253–264, n.327
Investment/s xix, 7, 120, 131, 132,
    169, 187, 188, 194, 211, 229, 250,
    252, 258, 290
transaction-specific 13, 31, 32, 73

Iran xii, n.xxii, 209, 210–212
Iraq n.xxii, 209, 210
Israel 65, 122–129, 142, 144–147,
    n.152, 177, 184, n.196, 230, 254,
    n.265
Issue/s xvi, 20, 22, 26, 29, 30, 37,
    41, 64, 65, n.76, 82, 106, 109,
    122, 129, 133, 135, 136, 139, 166,
    254, 272, 286, 298
Isuzu (corporation) 206
Italy/ian 74, 91, 206

J

Jansen, D. 204, 343
Japan/ese 5, 63, 84, 201, 206,
    220–224
culture 17, 54, 221, 224
industry 74, 221–224
Ministry of Trade and Industry
    — *see* MITI
Japan Aero Engines (corporation)
    206
Japan Aircraft Corporation 206
Japan Aircraft Development
    Corporation 206
Jennings, E.T. 5, 6, 40, 42, n.114,
    177, 215, 244, 246, 248, 258, 264,
    343, 344, 352
Jepperson, R.L. 285, n.294, 344
Jew/ish
    Agency 122, 123, 126, 145, n.152
    community/ies 81, 122, 123
    settlement/s 208
Jezreel Valley (Israel) 208
Jimenez, Pedro (Venezuelan
    President) 185
    regime 186
Job/s 178, 250
    Jobs Service (Wisconsin) 178
    training and placement 191, 194,
        216, 245–248

Job Opportunities and Basic Skills Program (U.S.) — *see* JOBS 177, 178, 191, 244–248
Job Training Partnership Act (U.S.) — *see* JTPA
Johns Hopkins Institute for Policy Studies 194
Johnson, C. 74, n.226, 344
Johnson (U.S. President Lyndon B.) administration 290
Johnson Manned Spacecraft Center 181
Joint venture/s xvii, 18, 30, 34, 43, 53, 62, 63, 67, 68, 69, 70, 72, n.76, 81, 85, n.112, n.113, 185, 205–206, 217–220, 225, 228, 277, 279, 288, 331
JTPA 143, 177, 191, 245–247, 257, n.265

K

Kahn, A.J. xix, 228, 344
Kahn, R.L. 62, 344
Kaiser, E.J. 239, 338
Kamerman, S.B. xix, 228, 344
Kansas (U.S.) 9
Kaplan, M. 129, n.265, 341, 344
Katz, D. 62, 344
Kaufmann, F.-X. xv, 6, 14, 344
Kawasaki (corporation) 206
Kazanjian, R.K. xvii, 10, 61, 341
Keiretsu 63, 220, 221–224, 225
Keller, L.F. 9, 344
Kenis, P. 62, 109, 224, 344
Kenosha County, Wisconsin 177, 178–179
Kennedy, U.S. President John F. x, 180
  administration 166
Kennedy Space Flight Center 3, 182

Kentucky (U.S.) 166, n.196
Kessler, M. 244, 344
King, J.L. 177, 345
Kinship 17, 54, 90
Kirst, M.W. xvi, 27, 61, 85, 253, 254, 344
Klemm, R.C. 30, 62, 340
Knight, D. 185, 344
Knoke, D. 106, 109, 345
Kochen, M. 6, 344
Koenig, R. Jr. xvi, 14, 30, 62, 199, 219, n.327, 345, 351
Kramer, K.L. 177, 345
Krane, D. n.114, 215, 248, 344
Kruitbosch, C. 9, 156, 347
Kuwait n.xxii, 209, 210

L

Lakhish region (Israel) 184, 400
Lafayette Court Family Center 190–194, 195, n.197
Lafayette Homes (Baltimore, Maryland) 190–194
  Residents' Advisory Council 191
  Tenants' Council 191
Land (Germany) 135, 250–252
  Minister/y of the Interior 251, 252
Lands Authority (Israel) 145, n.152
Langley, Virginia x, 180
Language 19, 22, 71, 89, 229
Larson, A. 93, 95, 111, 345
Laumann, E.O. 106, 109, 345
Lawrence, P.R. 10, 288, 345
Laws — *see* legislation
Law-Yone, H. 129, n.152, n.196, 336
Lead agency 103, 177, n.196, 255, 257, 263
Lead organization xii, xiii, 53, 63, 64, 66, 72, n.76, 150, 153,

177–183, 191, 195, n.196, n.197, 214, 216, 223, 225, 230, 252, 262, 264, 277, 279, 286, n.294, 298, 307

Leadership xx, n.xxii, 16, 258

Learning 135, 293
  collaborative 18, 137
  institutional 128, 129

Lebanon/ese 144

Legal aid services 244

Legislated/ion xvi, n.xxiii, 9, 38, 42, 44, 51, 59, 62, 74, n.77, 162, 163, 184, n.226, 236, 240, 245, 249, 258, 262, 272, 278, 297

Legislator/s xvi, 4, 42, 57

Legislature 135, 240, 243

Lehman, E.W. xx, 28, 29, 30, 62, 65, 66, 176, 303, 345

Levin, P.H. n.295, 345

Levine, S. 8, 60, 249, 345, 352

Lewis, R.S. 182, 183, 345

Lewis Research Center 180

Liaison xii, 43, 49, 53, 64, n.112, n.113, 117–121, 142, 147, 150, 175, 228, 248, 252, 277, 279, 287, 289, 298, 309, 319

Libya 210

Licencing 42

Likud (party) administration 145

Lindberg, L.N. 73, 74, 85, 272, 339

Lindblom, C.E. 4, 6, n.22, n.23, 53, 57, 338, 345

Linder, G. 49, 345

Lindsay, V.A. 138, 176, 335

Linkage/es xiv, 9, 25, 35, 40, 41, 42, 43, 44, 56, 62, 63, 73, 84, 85, 90, 120, 121, 164, 176, 200, 206, 214–216, 220, 221, 224, 225, n.226, 271, 277, 278, 286, 289, 301, 309, 315, 330
  associative 85, 86–87, 88, 89, 90, 91, 111
  devices 40–43, 53

dyadic 92–95, 96, 99, 101, 228, 301, 312
  formal 57, n.77, 117
  interpersonal 54, 90
  non-hierarchical 84, 87, 89, n.113
  professional 90–91
  promotional 63, 176
  see hierarchical
  see informal

Liston, J. 29, 215, 351

Litton Industries 104

Litwak, E. 47

Lloyds 393

Local Employment and Finance Acts of 1963 (U.K.) 130

Local government/Authority/s (U.K.) xviii, 35, 39, 62, 66, 120–122, 125, 131, 133, 140, 147–149, 150, n.152, 157, 158, 177, 186, n.197, 231, 233, 237, 239, 249–252, 258, 260, 289, 298, 300

Local Steering Committee (Israel) — see LSC

Lockheed Corporation 181

Logsden, J.M. 140, 345

London (England) 131, 132

Longford, E. ix, n.xxii, 345

Lorsch, P.W. 10, 288, 345

Los Angeles, California 177, 257
  Housing Advisory Committee (HAC) 257

Low Income Opportunity Board (U.S.) 257

Low Income Opportunity Working Group (U.S.) 129

Lowry, K. n.196, 244, 345

LSC (Israel — Project Renewal) 123, 125, 126, 128, 142

Luke, J.S. xvi, 345

Lukes, S. 285, 345

Lustick, I. xv, 345

M

Macdonald, H.I. 86, 346

Macdonald, J.S. n.197, 346

Mafia n.115

Majone, G. 6, 14, 58, 74, 89, 344, 346

Malaysia 184

Manage/r/s/ment 18, 48, 49, 51, 55, 60, 65, 80, 82, 99, 155, 156, 218, 322

  coastal zone management n.196, 244

  environmental management 255–256

  flood plain development management 237–240

  see case management

  see city management

Manchester (U.K.) 148

Mandate/d/s 9, 19, 20, 42, 44, 67, 142, 150, 272

  coordination/IOC structures xiv, 21, 73, 75, n.77

  frameworks 10, n.23, 32, 36, 38, 53, 57, 59–61, 63, n.76, n.77, 85, 165, 166, 170, 175, 176, 177, 183, 225, 228, 232, 233, 235–253, 263, 264, n.265, 277, 279, 284, 286, 289, n.295, 297–300, 302–303, 308, 316, 320, 323, 324, n.326

Mandell, M. 257, 346

Manet, A. 34, 338

Manufacture/er/ing xvii, xviii, xix, 8, 13, 33, 63, 66, 67, 73, 82, 91, 93, 101, 120, 140, 165, 181

March, J.C. 28, 36, 323, 346

Marin, B. 62, 346

Marin County (California) 95

Market/s xx, 4, 5, 10, 12, 13, 21, n.23, 26, 28, 30–32, 38, 39, 43, n.45, 52, 53–62, 67, 68, 72, 73, n.77, 82, 120, 187, 190, 199, 200, 205–212, 217–219, 224, n.226, 270–272, 275, 277, 286, 297, 299–300, 302, 303, 307, 313, 318, n.326

  artificial 51, 74, 85, 227–235, 277, 299

  economic 4, 57, 61, 84, 277, 297, 299

  managed 70, 228–232, 235, 249, 277, 300

  "perfect" 57, 60, 67, 70, n.76, 84, 120, 227, 228, n.327

  quasi 5, 59, 70, 72, 81, 227–228

  see political

Marketing xvii, xviii, 8, 10, 32, 33, 63, 68, 70, n.112, 120, 206, 208, 224

Marrett, C.B. 42, 342

Marshall Space Flight Center x, 181–182

Martin–McDonnell Corporation 181

Maryland (U.S.) 166, n.196

  State Public Aid Office 216

  State Vocational Rehabilitation Office 216

Mastop, H. 133, 346

Mathiesen, T. 118, 119, n.151, 346

May, P.J. 239, 346

Maynz, R. 62, 346

Mayor/s 135, 259

Mazda (corporation) 206

McCann, J.E. 49, 346

McDonnell (corporation) 258

Medefind, H. n.226, 346

Medicaid (U.S.) 184

Melman, S. 230, 346

Meister, G. xvi, 27, 61, 86, 253, 254, 344

Mental/ly

  ill, chronically (CMI) 215

  health 103; services 215–216, 224

Mental Health Planning Council
(Milwaukee, Wisconsin) 103,
104

Mercury Program (NASA) 180, 182

Merger 32, 34, 39, 43, n.45, 51, 61,
73, 74, 184–185, 194

Metcalfe, J. 36, n.45, 346

Meuse (river) 133

Mexico 206

Meyer, H. 47

Meyer, J.R. 232

Milan 214

Mileti, D.S. 20, 341

Mills, C.W. n.115, 346

Milner, M. Jr. 19, 37, 228, 346

Milward, H.B. 42, 61, 66, 244, 346,
347

Milwaukee, Wisconsin 102–106

Milwaukee County (Wisconsin)
Community Relations–Social
Development Commission
103, 104
Department of Social Services
103, 104

Minister for Commerce and
Industry (Israel) 144

Minister of Finance (Israel) 146

Minister of the Interior, *Land*
(Germany) 349

Ministry for Commerce and
Industry (Israel) 145, n.152

Ministry for Local Government
and Regional Planning
(U.K.) 189

Ministry of Education
(Venezuela) 188

Ministry of Housing and Building
(Israel) 122–124, 126, 145,
n.152, 177

Ministry of Justice (Sweden) 118

Ministry of Labor and Welfare
(Israel) 122

Ministry of Local Government
and Regional Planning (U.K.)
131

Ministry of Technology (U.K.) 131

Ministry of the Interior (Israel)
145, 146, 254

Ministry of the Interior (*Land*,
Germany) 251, 252

Ministry of Tourism (Israel) 145,
n.152

Ministry of Trade and Industry
(Japan) — *see* MITI

Ministry of Trade and Industry
(U.K.) 131, 190

Ministry of Transportation (Israel)
145, n.152

Minneapolis, Minnesota 184, 242,
243
Community Development
Agency 184
Housing and Redevelopment
Authority 184
Industrial Development
Commission 185
Transportation and Public Works
Committee 242

Minneapolis–St.Paul Metropolitan
Area (Twin Cities) 240–244,
256–257
Council ("Metro" Council) 240,
243
Regional Transit Facilities Plan
243
Regional Transportation Board
(RTB) 240, 243

Minnesota (U.S.) 14, 49, 240, 257
Department of Energy, Planning
and Development 185
legislature 240, 244

Mintzberg, H.J. xx, 49, 51, 54, 65,
n.76, 147, 347

Misechok, B.K. 143, 340

Mission 42, 150, 151, 180, 181
Mission Control n.xxii, 182

organizational mission 17, 18, 20, 119, 292, 294, 306–308, 317–318, 321, 322, 325, 333

Mississippi (U.S.) n.196

MITI 74

MIT Instrumentation Laboratories 181

Mitroff, I. n.115, 347

Mitsubishi (corporation) 206, 221

Mitsui (corporation) 221

Mizruchi, M.S. 41, 62, 101, 347

Mobil Oil (corportation) n.226

Model Cities
  Administration n.196, 258–260, 262
  program 33, 35, n.45, 64, n.76, 129, n.151, 177, n.196, 258–263, n.265

Monitoring 29, 36, 40, 42, 60, 72, 73, n.78, 179, 183, 234, 237, 238, 245, 248, 249, 277, 316, 320, 330

Moreau, D.H. 239, 338

Morgan State University (Baltimore, Maryland) 191

Motoren-und-Türbinen Union (corporation) 206

Mountjoy, R.S. 19, 31, 33, 34, 35, 347

MTC (San Francisco Bay Area Metro-transportation Commission) 99

Mugno, J.F. xi, n.xxii, 349

Mulford, C.L. 3, 4, 8, 36, 39, 40, 48, 83, 270, 347, 349

Mullen, P.M. 233, 347

MUNI (San Francisco Municipal Railway) 95, 99

Municipal/ity/ies 133, 170, 171, 173 174, 186, 244, 250–252
  services xix, 14, 38, 39, 48

Murakami, Y. 84, n.226, 347

Murray, C. xi, n.xxii, 180, 182, 347

Murray, F. 185, 344

Mutual adjustment n.xxii, 4, 5, 6, 8, 12, 14, 21, n.22, 28, 29, 30, 31, 35, 52, 53, 56, 57, 58, 61, 67, 84, 102, n.226, 227, 228, 232, 270, 271, 275, 319, 320, n.327

Mutual associations/organizations 30, 42, 53, 56, 62, 70, n.76, 154, 159, n.195, 199–206, 225, 228, 298

N

Napoleon, Bonaparte ix, xii, n.xxii

NAFTA 88

NASA x–xi, xii, n.xxii, 179, 180–183

National Advisory Committee for Aeronautics (NACA) 180

National Aeronautics and Space Administration — see NASA

National Association of Homebuilders 86

National Association of Manufacturers 214

National Association of Realtors 86

National Bus Company (NBC) (U.K.) 230

National Cancer Society 85

National Collegiate Athletics Association (NCAA) 159–164, 176, n.195, 200, 253

National Commission on Employment Policy n.294

National Council of Savings Institutions 86

National Health Service (U.K.) 233

National Planning Council (Israel) 65

National Resources Council 108

National Welfare Association (Sweden) 118, 119

Negotiation/s 14, n.22, 36, 39, 163, 191, 218, 227, 229, 248, 259, 282, 284, 320, 324, 325

Netherlands 65, 129, 133–135, 254
Network/s
  associational 30, 253
  caseworkers' 76, 86
  competitive 285
  cooperative 201–213
  dyadic 310, 312
  informal 61–62, 64, 74, 89,
    91–115, n.113, 117, 254, 301,
    304, 305, 313, 317
  obligational 63, 74, 175, 200, 201,
    206
  of organizations/interor-
    ganizational xviii, xix, 8, 9,
    18, 19, 25, 28, 29, 31, 40, 42,
    43, n.45, 48, 53, 54, 61, 62, 65,
    73, n.76, 77, 85, 86, 87, 88, 90,
    91, 95, 105, n.111, 118, 119,
    120, 135, 137, 140, 141, 149,
    154, 155, 156, 159, 164, 165,
    170, 174–177, 179, 181, 183,
    185, n.195, n.196, 199–226,
    232, 233, 236, 240, 244, 248,
    249, 253, 264, n.265, 277, 279,
    281, 286, 289, 292, 297, 298,
    300–302, 304, 306–325, n.326,
    n.327, 329–333
  people-processing 214,
    215–217, n.327
  production 91, 183, 214,
    217–224, 330
  promotional 89, 90, 200, 213,
    228, 331
  see policy issue network
  see procurement
  see purchasing
  subcontractors 4, 91, 214,
    228, 230, 287, 298
  symbiotic 63, 200, 214
New Communities Development
  program (U.S.) n.78, 183, 250,
  290–291
New Deal xx, 183
New Jersey (U.S.) 234
"New Society" 290

New South Wales (Australia)
  238, 240
New Town Corporation (U.K.)
  n.152, 183, n.196, 289, 291
New Towns program (U.K.)
  289–290
New York (U.S.) n.196, 214
  Department of Environmental
    Conservation 255
Nigeria 209
Nissan (corporation) 206
Nixon (U.S. President Richard M.)
  administration 121, 259
Non-administered program n.45,
  53, 60, n.77, 249–252, 262, 277,
  286, 290, n.294
Nordbäck, L.E. 34, 40, 340
Norm/s 14, 16, 21, 36, 39, 54, 59,
  60, 71, 74, 87, 89, 228, 230, 236,
  270, 286, 313, 325
North Africa 210
North American Free Trade
  Association — see NAFTA
North American Rockwell
  (corporation) 181
North Brabant (Netherlands) 133
North Carolina (U.S.) 166, n.196
North East Energy Corporation
  66, 165, 175
North Rhine–Westphalia
  (Germany) 349
Nuclear power industry 119
Nuehring, E.M. 20, 347

O

Oakland, California xiii, 28, 98
Objectives 9, 63, 65, 67, 68, 75, 87,
  111, 195, 200, 244, 249, 250, 252,
  262, 282, 292
Occidental Petroleum
  (corporation) 210

Office of Economic Opportunity (OEO) (U.S.) 259

Office of Management & Budget (OMB) (U.S.) 66, 107, 108, 121, 172, 175

Office of Vocational Rehabilitation (Pennsylvania State) 143

Ohio (U.S.) n.196, 206

Ohio River 254

Oil 26
corporations xi, 107, 108, 109, 207–212
exporting countries — see OPEC
price/s xii, xiii, 6, n.xxii, n.77, 208–213; increase/s 210, 211
production 207, 208, 212, 213
supply n.xxii, 208, 212

Okimoto, D.I. 74, n.226, 347

Olsen, B. 28, n.265, 348

OPEC xi–xii, xiii, n.xxii, 67, 68, 69, 70, n.77, 195, 207–213

Organization/s/al
adaptation 10–11, 26, 51, 175–176, 288
charitable 118, 155
coordination between — see IOC
ecology 7, 10–12, 14, 21, 272
focal xix, 26, 27, 28, 36, 37
matrix 10, 50, 61, 147
"meshing" organization 170–174, 176
population/s 11–12
see "action set"
see culture
see environment
see hierarchical
see implementation set
see mutual
see structure/s
see theory
set xix, xx, 26, 27, 28, 36, 43, 157
single xx, 10, 11, 13, 29, 32–34, 43, n.45, 53, 61, 66, 153, 183–195, 287, 291

unitary 53–56
volunteer 155, 253

Organization of Petroleum Exporting Countries — see OPEC

Orinoco
delta 188
steel mill 187

Ostrom, E. 5, 59, 232, 233, 299, 347

Ostrom, V. 6, 14, 344

O'Toole, L.J. 19, 31, 33, 34, 35, 347

Ouchi, W.D. 58, 84, 347

Outcome/s xiv, xvi, n.xxii, 3–6, 21, 34, 39, 106, 109, 261, 280–282
interdependence 34, 43
types 20, 39

Outstationing 75, 278

Oxford English Dictionnary (OED) n.113, n.295, 347

P

Palumbo, D. xvi, 348

Paris, France xii

Partisan mutual adjustment — see mutual adjustment

Partners/hip/s 70, 72, 85, 93, 111, 185, 207, 218, n.226, 260, 277, 279, 285, 288, 308
public–private xviii, xix, n.23, 39, 68, 69, 147, 158, 185

Passenger Transport Executive (PTE) (U.K.) 321

Patricios, N.N. 236, 348

Paulson, S.K. 20, n.294, 348

Pennsylvania (U.S.) 166, n.196, 234

Peres, S. 229, 348

Persian Gulf 210

Peters, G. 49, 345

Petroleum — see oil
Petroleum Consulting Committee 209

Pfeffer, J. 8, 33, 34, 37, 38, 39, 61, 62, 184, 348

Phillipines 97

PIC 178, 245–247, 258, 264, n.265

Pittsburgh, Pennsylvania 143–144, 150

Local Management Committee 143, 144

Pittsburgh Partnership 143

Plan/s 36, 43, 44, 51, 52, 57, 133–135, 146, n.152, 172, 233, 245, 293, 323

floodplain management plans 237–238

local development plans 250–251

see transportation

Planning 31, 36, n.45, 48, 52, 60, 65, 66, 81, 95, 96, 103, 104, 105, n.112, n.114, 123–125, 127–129, 135–137, 139, 142, 146, 147, 149, n.152, 168, 169, 180, 181, 190, 191, n.196, 236, 238, 239, 246–248, 250, 254, 260, 263, n.265, 289–291, 323, 324, n.327

committee/s 136, 254

commission/s: local 65, 70, 124, 254; national 129, n.196, 254; regional 65, 146, 166, 254, 171

coordinative 36, 256

frameworks 240–244, 277

freeway/highway 41, 64, 257

joint 29, 40, 41, 42, 43, 44, 85, 179, 278, 280

local development (Germany) 250–252

physical 65, 133

Planning Administration (Israel) 254

regional 82, 130, 131, 133, 169, 240

strategic 26, 133

transportation 172, 240–244

water quality 246–247

Planungsausschuss 135, 136

Platt, R.H. 233, n.264, 348

Policy/ies xiv, xvi, xix, 8, 14, 17, 19, 20, 26, 27, 47, 48, 51, 52, 57, 64, 74, n.75, 83, 86, 127, 129, 134, 135, 162, 187, 210, 220, 234, 236, 239, 244, 272

coordination 48, 320

domain 62, 106–110

implementation xiv, 13, 51, 55, 61

instruments 40, 44

issue network xvi, 27, 43, 61, 62, 86, 90, n.114, 224, 253–254, 298, 308

-making/ers 127, 138, 323, 324

public policy xvi, xx, 61, 228, 239

see advocacy coalition

see regional development

Politics/al n.xxii, 8, 20, 38, 57, 63, 88, 137, 165, 200, 236, 249, 250, 252, 258, 260, 290, 291, 293, 298, 305

alliances 58, 86

decentralization 258, n.265

dynasties 54, 87, 90

markets 4, 5, 38, 57, 61, 84, 227

parties 57, 87

see commitment

see power

Polivka, L. 65, 143, 348

Porter, D.O. xix, 27, 61, 214, 244, n.265, 343, 348

Powell, W.W. 85, 199, 206, 214, 348

Power/s 5, 7, 37, 38, 63, 74, 131, 132, 147, 156, 235, 249, 252, 257, 271, 285, 289, n.294, 301

elite 28, n.115

political xx, 200, 274, 288

regulatory 9, 255

Pratt & Whitney (corporation) 206

President's Appalachian Regional Commission (PARC) 167

Pressman, N. xiii, 60, 249, 348

Price/s 4, 54, 56, 68, 70, 81, 206, 207, 224, n.226, 227, 272, 277

see oil

Prison Bureau (Sweden) 118

Private sector xvi, xvii, xviii, 7, 8, 13, 37, 39, 51, 61–62, 63, 64, 65, 66, n.77, 102, 135, 140, 179, 225, 228, 250

Private Industry Council (U.S.) — see PIC

Privatization xix, 17, n.23, 228, 230–232, 299, 300

Problem/s 5, n.23, 32, 37, 39, 64, 73, n.75, 82, 83, 85, 92, 128, 135–137, 139, 140, 141, 165, 166, 170, 182, 183, 186 187, 189, 207, 234, 256, 260, 270, 286, 289–291, 293, n.295, 305, 325
  characteristics 20, 22, 38, 39
  maintenance problems 37, 38
  mutual n.23, 42, 171
  structural 37, 38

Procedure/s 17, 31, 39, 42, n.78, 250, 252, 255
  standard operating procedures 40, 42, 288, 316, 323

Procurement xviii, 42, 120, 179, 229, 230
  network/s 63, 206, 225, 307, 319

Producer/s xviii, 4, 8, 57, 59, 68, 74, 207, 209
  cartels 81, 207

Product/s/ion xvii, xviii, 7, 10, 13, 17, 32, 63, 64, 68, 70, 73, 91, 179, 183, 208, 212, 308, 330

Profession/s/al/ism 17, 48, 54, 58, 74, 82, 87–89, 91, 99, 101, 111, n.152, 164, 165, n.226, 255, 260, 314, 318

Professionalization 17, 36, 89

Program/s xiv, xvii, xix, 5, 18, 19, 20, 27, 31–34, 38, 47, 49, 51, 52, 61, 64, 65, 68, 70, n.77, n.78, 83, 90, 103, 104, 105, 106, 107, 120, 122, 123, 124, 125, 126, 127, 128, 129, 142, 143, 166–169, 170, 177–183, 185, 188, 190–194, 214–216, 236, 237, 239, 244, 245–248, 258–263, 277, 279, 289–293, 325
  categorical grant — see categorical grant program/s
  development programs: regional 130–132, 166, 188–189; national 186
  effectiveness 42, 44
  evaluation n.23, 27, 263
  goal/s 10, 32
  implementation set 27, 225
  management devices/tools 42, 44
  see employment and training
  see Model Cities
  see New Communities Development
  see non-administered
  see STOP

Project/s xv, xvii, xix, xx, 19, 27, 42, 52, 61, 64, 65, 84, 91, 94, 95, 124–128, 147, 148, 150, 154, 170, 174, 176, 183, 186, 187, 189, 214, 217–219, 225, 236, 244, 251, 257, 260, 277, 279, 321
  director 123, 125, 142
  implementation 11; set 55
  manager/ment 65, 123, 150, 219, 225
  office 66, 154
  see team/s

Project Mercury (U.K.) 288

Project Mercury (U.S.) n.xxii

Project Renewal (Israel) 122–129, 142, n.151, n.265

Provan, K.G. 9, 156, 348

Prussia/n ix, xii, n.xxii

Public
  –private partnerships — see partnerships
  sector xvi, xviii, 7, 13, 33, 37, 38, 62, 63, 64, 66, 102, 120, 135, 158, 179, 225, 228, 250

Public Expenditure Survey Committee (U.K.) 65, 122, 129

Public Housing Authority (U.S.)
    184
Pueblo, New Mexico 138
Purchasing 120, 206, 228, 307
    agent 120–121, 225, 228

Q

Qatar 210
Quinn, J.B. 51, 347

R

Rabe, B.G. 256, 348
Rabin (Israel Prime Minister
    Itzhak) government 144
Rabinowitz, F. 60, 249, 348
Raelin, J.A. 8, 9, n.76, 235,
    n.265, 348
Rafter, D.O. 243, 348
Railroads 13, 32, 73
Rapkin, C. n.265, 349
Ravard, General Rafael Alonzo
    185, 186
Reagan (U.S. President Ronald)
    administration 121
Region/al 39, 51, 65, 66, 129, 131,
    140, 157, 172, 185, n.196
    coordination 61, 131
    councils 105
    development xvii
    policy 130–134, 242
    program/s 131, 186–18
    see planning
    small-industry networks 74, 91
Regional Development Division
    (U.K.) 130
Regional Economic Policy Boards
    (U.K.) 130–133
Regional Economic Policy
    Commissions (U.K.) 130–133

Regional Planning Commission/s
    (U.S.) 65
Rein, M. 60, 249, 348
Reissert, B. 350
Reorganization 38, 39, 41, 44, 48,
    59, 123, 127, 131, 132, 181, 194,
    251, 255, 277, 288, 289
Research xx, 3, 20, n.23, 26, 28, 39,
    51, 63, 66, 81, 87, 89, 118, 201,
    203, 204, n.226, 270, 294, 304,
    315, 318
    and development (R&D) xvii,
        xviii, 26, 31, 33, 47, 58, 62–63,
        82, 90, n.112, 119, 120, 201, 230
    institute/s 26, 32, 204
    laboratory/ies xviii, 53
    see superconductivity
Resettlement Administration
    (U.S.) 184, 291
Resource/s 4, 5, 11, 17, 18, 19, 31,
    34, 35, 37, 38, 55, 57, 60, 65, 66,
    68, 69, n.78, 83, 92, 95, 96, 121,
    125, 127, 130, 142, 145, 147, 150,
    151, n.152, 158, 163, 164, 171,
    174, 175, 176, 183, 185, 200, 207,
    216–218, 229, 249, 252, 253, 258,
    263, n.264, 274, 282–285, 288,
    292, 293, 298, 301, 303–306, 308,
    310, 316, 319, n.326, 330, 332
    allocations 20, 38, 59, 60, 280,
        288, 292, 297
    dependence 9, 11, 21, 22, n.23,
        29, 34, 65, 70, 71, 72, 74, n.76,
        156, 201, 272, 315
    endowment 318, 321–322, 324,
        325
    exchange 4, 6, 7–10, 17, n.23, 37,
        42, 44, 57, 60, 62, 73, 89, 277,
        278, 282, 316, 320, 322–324
    human resources 36, 61
Rijksplanologiesedienst
    (Netherlands) 254
Ring, P.S. 14, 338
Risk/s xx, 18, 68, 237, 288

River Valley Planning
  Commission/s (U.S.) 129
Roberts, J.T. 148, 149, 349
Roberts, N.C. n.294, 349
Robins, J.A. n.23, 349
Roddewig, R.J. 5, 349
Rodwin, L. n.197, 349
Rogers, D.L. 3, 8, 36, 39, 40, 48,
  270, 347, 349
Role/s 17, 41, 42, n.46, 49, 52, 65,
  70, 71, 74, 91, 95, 104, n.113,
  118, 120, 121, 136, 137, 264, 278,
  283. 284, 292
  see boundary-spanning
Rolls-Royce (company) 206, 218
Roosevelt (U.S. President Franklin
  D.) administration 183
Rome n.226
Rose, S. 28, 62, 102, 351
Rosenthal, S.R. 40, 42, 43, 349
Rosewitz, B. 214, 340
Ross, A.G. 285, 349
Rothblatt, D.N. n.196, 349
Routine/s/ization 17, 36, 39, 42,
  64, n.77
Rowley, S.R. xvi, 27, 61, 85, 253,
  255
RTA (San Francisco Bay Area
  Regional Transit Association) 99
Rubenstein, J. 184, 349
Rubin, C.B. 349
Rubin, H.J. 170, 174, 176, 349
Ruhr Valley 254
Ruhrgenossenschaften 254
Rule/s 3, 5, 14, 21, 34, 40, 57, 59,
  60, 69, 70, 71, 74, n.77, n.78,
  159, 160–164, 174, 236, 270,
  n.294, 316
  enforcement 160–163
  market structuring rules 299–300
Rummler, G.A. 51
Russia x, 180
Rustow, D.A. xi, n.xxii, 349

S

Sabatier, P.A. 27, 61, 86, 350
Sachar, H.M. 230, 350
Sagalynn, L.B. xix, 39, 158, 185, 341
Salancik, G.R. 8, 33, 34, 37, 38, 62,
  184, 348
Salerno, R. n.115, 350
Sampson, M.W. III, n.226, 350
Samtrans 95
San Francisco, California 98
  Bay Area 41, n.114
  county 95
  Metropolitan Transportation
    Commission 96
  Municipal Railway System
    — *see* MUNI
  Northwest Corridor Study 99
  public transit system 41, n.76,
    95–101, 111, 224
  Rapid Transit — *see* BART
  Regional Transit Association
    — *see* RTA
San Mateo (California) County
  95, 140
Santa Clara (California) County 95
Sanwa (corporation) 221
Saturn (lunar launch vehicle) 259
Saudi Arabia n.xxii, 208, 210–212
Savas, E.S. xix, 228, 350
Scharpf, F.W. 35, 37, 38, 42, 48, 350
Schleicher, H. 49, 66, n.75, 244,
  254, 350
Schnabel, F. 350
Schneider, V. 62, 109, 224, 344
School/s xvi, 14, n.23, 246, 254
  district/s 48, 164–165, 246
  financing 353
Scottish Bus Company (SBC) 230
Seattle, Washington 138
Secretary of Commerce (U.S.) 167
Seidman, H. 139, 176, 350

Senate (U.S.) 86

Settlement Department (Jewish Agency) n.152

Seymour, I. n.226, 350

Sharpe, L.J. 37, 39, 350

Shell (Oil Corporation) 108, n.226

Siedlungsverband Ruhrkohlenbezirk (Germany) 238

Silicon Valley, California 84, 90, 140

Simon, H.A. 36, 323, 346

"Single Point of Contact" (SPOC) program 143–144, 150

Sink, D. 158, 350

Skelcher, C. 8, 350

Socal (corporation) n.226

Socialist International 134

Social Policy Team (Israel) 123

Social Security (program, U.S.) 304

Society/ies/al xv, xx, 5, 12, 58, 64, 69, 71, n.77, 81, 86, 88, 93, 124, 125, 157, 260, 290
  context 28, 54, 72, 75, n.77, 291
  modern xv, 57, 86
  service/s 8, 9, 21, n.45, 47, 62, 63, 66, 67, 135, n.226
  structure 69–72, n.77, 271
  see structuration theory
  traditional 30, 57, 86
  work/ers 48, 118

Sofer, C. 288, 350

SOHIO (Corporation) 234

Solidarity 42, 54–56, 84, 200, 225, 305, 318, 319
  fields, interorganizational 30
  framework/s 56, 57–58
  links 84–88, 310, 311

Sonoma County (California) 95

South Carolina (U.S.) n.196

Southern Intercollegiate Athletic Conference 229

Soviet Russia — *see* Russia

Special Revenue Sharing (U.S.) 260

Special Service District/s 16

Spekman, R.E. 120, 121, 350

Sputnik x, 180

Spybey, T. 9, 340

Stalker, G.M. 288, 338

Standordtsprogramme (Germany) — *see* STOP

State/s 10, 74, 141, 166–169, n.226, 234, 235, 238, 240, 244, 245, 258
  agencies 177, 245–247, 255–256, 257
  Department of Health and Human Relations 255
  education agency 245, 246
  employment service 245, 246
  Job Service (Pennsylvania) 143
  National Guard 226
  Office for Children 263
  public health department 255
  State Job Training Coordination Council (SJTCC) 245, 258, n.265

Steering committee/s 64, 123, 125, 257

Stearns, L.B. 41, 62, 101, 347

Stern, R.N. 29, 163, 164, n.195, 350

STOP n.78, 250–252, 253

St. Paul, Minnesota 335, 339

Strategy/ies/ic ix, 14, 19, 20, 29, 34, 37, n.45, 49, 139, 272
  competition 14, 38, 41, 44
  control 36–38, 44
  cooperative 14, 37–38, 41, 44, n.45
  coordination — *see* IOC below
  cultural 36–37
  informational 37, 44
  IOC 4, 14, 26, 30, 35–40, 41, 44, n.45, 47–49, 275–277
  organizational 10, 35–40
  structural 38, 39, 41, 44

Structuration 312, 313, 315, 316, 330–331
  theory n.45, 69–72, n.77, 165; of IOC 66–75, 271

Structure/s
  coordination — *see* IOC
  see hierarchical
  see interorganizational/IOC
  meso- 53, 61–64, n.76, 85, n.112,
    117, 177, 195, n.195, 252, 253,
    277, 284, 286, 287, n.294, 298
  meta- 52, 56–61, 64, 117, 235, 277,
    284, 286, 287, 297–303
  micro- 53, 64–66, 85, n.112, n.113,
    117–152, 225, 253, 263, 277,
    284, 287, 298
  non-hierarchical 84–85, 86
  organizational xvii, 10–11, 17, 19,
    22, 47
Subcontractors/ing x, xi, xii, xvii,
    xix, 54, 63, 74, 91, 120, 179, 181,
    214, 228, 230, 232, 298
Sud Aviation (corporation) 217
Sumitomo (corporation) 221
Superconductivity research
    201–204
Supervisor/ision 77, 91, 120, 249
Suzuki (corporation) 206
Sweden/Swedish 28, 34, 118, 230
Swenson, L.S. Jr. x, 182, 338
Switzerland/Swiss 74, 91
System X (U.K.) 288

T

Task/s xiv–xvi, 17, 19, 36, 63,
    65–67, n.75, 111, 139, 140, 141,
    150, 153, 154, 158, 175, 176, 177,
    181, 185, 200, 225, n.226, 278,
    279, 282–284, 291, 292, 294, 304,
    306, 314, 317, 331
  characteristics (complexity, scale,
    scope) 17, 19, 201, 281, 303,
    n.327, 333
  coordinating 29, 289
  force/s 29, 43, 53, 64, 65, 70,
    n.113, 129, 135, 138, 141, 225,
    248, 258, 284, 285, 288, 319

integration 40, 216, 323, n.327
joint/shared xiv, 58
see IOC
standardization 17, 42, 44
Tax/es xv, 60, 68, 109, 131, 208,
    215, 216, 243, 244
  incentives 42, 278
  income 60; U.S. system n.78, 249
  windfall profits 108, 109
TDR — *see* Transferable
    Development Rights
Team/s 40, 85, 128, 131, 138, 256,
    263, 278, 279, 280, 310, 321
  interagency teams 85, 135–137
Teamsters' Union 161
Technical — *see* technological
Technology/ical 18, 19, 33, 60, 63,
    67, 68, 70, 73, 74, 82, 90, 93, 96,
    119, 139, 156, 186, 188, 189, 190,
    200, 201, 208, 229, 230, 234, 274,
    278, 321, 331
  assistance 42, 93, 239, 258
  complementary 22, 63
  innovations x, xx, 201, 205,
    206, 278
  linkages 13, 19, 32, 274
Teheran xii, 210
Tennessee (U.S.) n.196
Tennessee Valley Authority
    184, 237
Terreberry, S. 82, 350
Texaco (corporation) n.226
Texas/n 9, 214
Theory/ies 39, 40, 81, 274, 275, 329
  IOC xxi, 28
  organization 7, 10, 11, 13, 47, 48,
    49, 54
  see contingency
  see exchange
  see structuration
  theoretical premises 7–14, 21
  see transaction cost
Thietart, R.-A. 14, 30, 62, 219, 345

Thompson, G. n.326, 351

Thompson, J.D. 31, 32, 33,
n.327, 351

Thorelli, H.B. 206, 351

Thrasher, M. 9, 340

Time 20, 22, 36, 69, 71, 140,
229, 323
lead/startup-time 129, 260, 323

Tompkins, J.S. n.115, 350

Tool/s 13, 20, 130, 139, 293
coordination/IOC 25, 26, 30, 36,
37, 38, 40–43, 44, n.45, 48, 49,
248, 275, 278–280

Toronto, Ontario 244

Town and Country Planning Act
of 1947 (U.K.) 130, 131

Toxics Advisory Committee
(Illinois, U.S.) 256

Toxics Project Team (Illinois,
U.S.) 256

Trade association/s xx, 11, 34, 51,
62, 63, 67, 68, 69, 86. 107, 108,
165, 201, 206, 213–214, 228,
308, 312

Tradeable Emission Rights 5,
233–235

Trades Union Council (U.K.) 412

Trade/s union/s 108
federation 30, 165, 213

Training 16, 17, 42, 43, 51, 178,
191, 244–248, 278
see employment and training
programs

Transaction/s 4, n.22, 30, 31, 32,
33, 34, 54, 56, 60, 224,
227–229, 233, 300–303, 317
idiosyncratic 32, 33, 94
see cost/s
voluntary 10, 270

Transaction cost/s 12–14, 21, n.23,
37, 60, 72, 73, 165, 229
theory 7, 12–14, 18, 19, 21, n.23,
31, 53, 54, 61, 72, 184, 273

Transbay Terminal 96
Advisory Committee 99

Transferable Development Rights
(TDRs) 5, 59, 233

Transit xix, 74, n.76, 95–101, 111
light rail 240–244
local bus (U.K.) 230–232

Transport Act of 1985 (U.K.) 230,
232

Transportation xiii, xvi, 54, 107,
170, 187, 208, 250
plan/ning 172, 173, 240–244,
256, 257

Treasury Department (U.K.) 122

Treaty of Rome n.226

Tribe/al 56, 69, 86, 87

Tripoli 210

Trist, E. 165, 175, n.196, 351

Trust 16, 54, 55, 56, 66, 74, 87, 88,
93–94, 95, 96, 224, 277, 298,
305, 314, 319

TRW (Corporation) 108

Tucker, D.J. 42, 351

Tulloch, G. 4, 227, 338

Tuite, M. 6, 351

Turner, A. 184, 351

Tushman, M. 119, 351

U

Union Carbon 108

United Airways 172

United Arab Emirates 210

United States of America
— see U.S.

United Way 104, 155–157, 175

University/ies 52, 90, 159–164,
203, 204
of Minnesota 242
Swedish universities 55–56

Urban Renewal Administration
(U.S.) 260

Urban Information Systems
    Interagency Committees (U.S.)
    177
Uphoff, N.T. 5, 57, 227, 343
U.S. xvi, xviii, xx, n.xxii, 5, 26, 35,
    38, 39, 51, 63–66, 73, 74, n.75,
    n.77, n.78, 86, 107–109, n.112,
    129, 138–139, 142, n.151, 154,
    155, 175, 177, 180, 184, 200,
    206, 207, 209, 214, 230,
    233–235, 236, 237–238, 239,
    244, 245–248, 250, 254–256,
    257, 258–263, 289, 290–292
U.S. League of Savings
    Institutions 86
U.S.S.R. — see Russia
U.S. Steel 108

V

Value/s xx, 18, 20, 36, 43, 58, 83,
    110, 111, 273, n.326
  common/shared xiv, 19, 37, 54,
    56, 57, 58, 87, 88, 274, 276,
    314, 318
Ven, van de, A.H. xvi, 9, 29, 30,
    215, n.294, n.327, 351
Venezuela n.xxii, 184, 185–190,
    209, 210, 212
Veterans
  Veterans Affairs Committee
    (Senate) 86
  Veterans Administration 86
  Veterans of Foreign Wars
    (organization) 86
Vienna 210
Virginia (U.S.) 166, n.196
Visiting Nurses Association 85, 103
Vlasak, G.J. 8, 352
Volkswagen (corporation) 234
Voluntary Action Center 85
Voluntary associations 16, 103, 233

Voluntary Hospitals of America
    206
Vostok 180
Votes/ers 5, 8, 57, 227

W

Walcott, C. n.195, 343
Walker, G. 9, 29, 215, n.294, 352
Walton, R.E. 19, 351
Wamsley, G.L. 27, 42, 347, 351
Warren, R. 28, 62, 102, 351
Washington, D.C. 86, 259, 261
Washington (State) Department
    of Ecology 255
Waterloo, Battle of ix, n.xxii
Weimer, D.L. 85, 351
Weiss, J.A. 17, 18, 49, 164, n.295,
    351
Welfare department, County 53,
    178–179
Wellington, Arthur Wellesley
    Duke of ix, n.xxii
Wessels, W. n.226, 338
West Virginia (U.S.) 166, n.196
Whetten, D. xix, 3, 26, 27, 28, 48,
    83, 335, 338, 351
White, P.E. 8, 42, 342, 352
White House (U.S.) 107, 108, 259
White Paper (U.K.) 219
Whitehall (U.K.) 131, 132
Wildavsky, A. viii, xx, 3, 4, n.23,
    61, 65, 122, 227, 343, 352
Williams, W. 60, 177, 249, 250, 352
Williamson, O.A. 19, 32, 39, 60,
    184, 352
Wilmott, H. 185, 344
Wisconsin (U.S.) n.xxiii, 55,
    177–179
  WIN program 287
Wistrich, E. n.226, 352

World Bank 393
Wolf, H. 214, 340
World War II n.xxii, 289
Work Experience and Job Training
    (WEJT) program (U.S.) 177
Wren, D.A. 66, 352
Wright, M. 133, 352
Wrong, D.H.. 285, 352

Y

Yandle, B. 5, 235, 352
Yom-Kippur War 211

Young, S. 133, 352
Yukl, G.A. n.xxiii, 352

Z

Zaibatsu 63, 221
Zammuto, R.F. 83, 352
Zank, N.S. 5, 177, 244, 248, 258,
    264, 344, 352
Zeitz, G. 8, 352
Zoning 59, 173, 233, 236–238,
    254, n.265